THE JUSTIFICATION OF GOD

An Exegetical and Theological Study
of Romans 9:1-23

John Piper

BAKER BOOK HOUSE

Grand Rapids, Michigan 49506

To

Daniel Payton Fuller,

priceless friend

TABLE OF CONTENTS

PREFACE

As soon as my doctoral studies were completed in
1974 I devoted myself to write a book on Romans 9. The
God of Romans 9 took me captive while I was yet in
seminary. No other picture of God ever commended itself
to me as more true to what the Creator must be. If
there is a God, he must be the God of Romans 9. After
seven years of effort to understand this chapter it
still seems to me that its essence is this: God's
righteousness consists in his being an all-glorious
God, and refusing to be anything less than all-glorious.
It has been the delight of my life in these years to
behold this God and to ponder his awesome sovereignty.
If this book had never been published it would still be
a treasure to me. No one asked me to write it. Few
people knew it was emerging. The Grand Subject drew me
on. And to him I owe all "the willing and running."

Under his providence I was granted a sabbatical by
Bethel College in 1979, during which many loose ends
were drawn together. I feel a special debt to George
Brushaber for his constant support of my scholarly
labor while at Bethel. Sara Kreps did a beautiful job
preparing the final typescript, while Gwen Knight
endured the tedium of typing the indexes. Tom Steller,
my friend and colleague, prepared the author and text
indexes. I owe thanks also to three journals in which
material from the book has been previously published:
Journal of the Evangelical Theological Society ("Prole-
gomena to Understanding Romans 9:14,15: An Interpretation of Exodus 33:19," JETS 22, 1979, pp 203-216),
Journal for the Study of the New Testament ("The Demonstration of the Righteousness of God in Romans 3:25,26,"
JSNT 7, 1980, pp 2-32) and Theologische Zeitschrift
("The Righteousness of God in Romans 3:1-8," ThZ 36,
1980, pp 3-16).

My wife Noël not only created the shalom at home
so the work could be done; she was also ready anytime
to share the proofreading. Our lives are so happily
and thoroughly meshed that it is hopeless to identify
all her peculiar influences on the work. Under God she
holds first place in my affection.

But this time the book had to be dedicated to
Daniel Fuller, Professor of Hermeneutics at Fuller
Theological Seminary. The feelings of joyful indebted-
ness which I have toward the man and his hermeneutic
are too deep for words. Suffice it to say, I love him.

ABBREVIATIONS

ATD	Altes Testament Deutsch
ATR	Anglican Theological Review
BDB	Hebrew and English Lexicon of the Old Testament (Brown, Driver, Briggs)
BJRL	Bulletin of the John Rylands Library
CJT	Canadian Journal of Theology
EHAT	Exegetisches Handbuch zum Alten Testament
EQ	Evangelical Quarterly
ET	English translation
ET	Expository Times
EvTh	Evangelische Theologie
FRLANT	Forschungen zur Religion und Literatur des Alten und Neuen Testaments
HAT	Handbuch zum Alten Testament
HNT	Handbuch zum Neuen Testament
HNTC	Harper's New Testament Commentary
HThK	Herders theologischer Kommentar
HTR	Harvard Theological Review
ICC	International Critical Commentary
IDB	Interpreter's Dictionary of the Bible
Interp	Interpretation
JBL	Journal of Biblical Literature
JTS	Journal of Theological Studies
MK	Meyers Kommentar
MNTC	Moffatt New Testament Commentary
MT	Masoretic text
NASB	New American Standard Bible
NIC	New International Commentary
NIGTC	New International Greek Testament Commentary
NT	New Testament
NTD	Neues Testament Deutsch
NTS	New Testament Studies
OT	Old Testament
RB	Revue Biblique
RevExp	Review and Expositor
RGG³	Die Religion in Geschichte und Gegenwart, 3rd ed
SBT	Studia Biblica et Theologica
SJT	Scottish Journal of Theology
SNTS	Society for New Testament Studies
StTh	Studia Theologica
TDNT	Theological Dictionary of the New Testament
THAT	Theologisches Handwoerterbuch zum Alten Testament
TheolBeit	Theologische Beitraege
ThQ	Theologische Quartalschrift
ThW	Theologisches Woerterbuch zum Neuen Testament
ThZ	Theologische Zeitschrift

TLZ	Theologische Literaturzeitung
TOTC	Tyndale Old Testament Commentary
WJT	Westminster Journal of Theology
WUNT	Wissenschaftliche Untersuchungen zum Neuen Testament
ZNW	Zeitschrift fuer die neutestamentliche Wissenschaft
ZST	Zeitschrift fuer Systematische Theologie
ZThK	Zeitschrift fuer Theologie und Kirche

CHAPTER ONE

INTRODUCTION

This study was conceived as an attempt to understand how Paul defends the righteousness of God in Rom 9:14-23. It has thus involved a broader effort to grasp what Paul means by the righteousness of God, and has necessarily raised the subordinate question of election and predestination. On this latter issue I have tried to answer with as much exegetical integrity as I can two crucial questions: Does election in Rom 9:1-23 concern nations or individuals? And does it concern historical roles or eternal destinies?

I do not consider my conclusions novel from a historical viewpoint. Nevertheless, with regard to both the righteousness of God and the election of men, the conclusions are not in vogue today, and so exegetical explanation and defense are needed.

It has become evident to me over the years that one of the devices used to take the sting out of Rom 9 is the fostering of a certain stereotype. The stereotype is that if a work focuses on Rom 9 and deals with predestination, then it may be discounted as too limited in its scope and blinded by its dogmatic concerns to the larger redemptive-historical issues. When a work is thus branded, it may be safely set aside. In this way the troublesome chapter is usually spared the penetrating analysis that other less troublesome texts enjoy among scholarly monographs.

But this book bears witness to my conviction that one can, with care, deal with Rom 9:1-23 without losing sight of its larger textual and historical context and without forcing it to answer dogmatic questions for which it was never intended. In following Paul's argument here I have tried to employ the care and precision which is the mark of critical exegesis on other texts, but which often is replaced by imprecise and unsupported generalizations on this theologically explosive section of Scripture.

One may legitimately question the wisdom of limiting the monograph to Rom 9:1-23 (especially since verse 23 ends in the middle of a sentence), but I have tried to show in Chapter Ten (Section 1) the rationale for this limitation and how it does conform to the structure of Paul's argument. And would it not mean an end to all careful

1

scholarship if it were not possible to focus on one tree
without losing sight of the forest?

With regard to secondary literature, I have tried
at every crucial point to make the alternative interpretations clear by interacting with competent exegetes and
theologians who see things differently than I do.   I
hope that I have not misrepresented anyone's view, for
that would not only be discourteous, but would also
weaken my own case.   I do not offer a systematic history
of the interpretation of Rom 9, but for this commend the
works of K.H. Schelkle, V. Weber, E. Weber, W. Beyschlag,
and J. Morison listed in the bibliography.

To understand the structure of the book's argument
the following observations may be helpful.   The starting
point of my reflections was the question how (and if)
Rom 9:15ff was intended by Paul to demonstrate the
righteousness of God.   Rom 9:14 asserts that there is no
unrighteousness with God, and verse 15 seems to give the
basis for this assertion: "For to Moses [God] says: I
will have mercy on whomever I have mercy and I will have
compassion on whomever I have compassion" (Ex 33:19).
In order to answer the question how (and if) Paul was
defending God's righteousness, I had to find out what it
was in Rom 9:1-13 that seemed to call God's righteousness
into question (Chapters Two and Three) and what the
supporting quote from Ex 33:19 meant in its OT context
(Chapter Four).   With those questions answered, my
analysis of Rom 9:14-18 could begin (Chapter Five).
But to test my emerging hypothesis about Paul's argument
it became necessary to ask more precisely what Paul
actually meant by God's righteousness.   To answer this
question I devoted a chapter to the righteousness of
God in the OT (Chapter Six) and two chapters to Paul's
understanding of divine righteousness in Rom 3:1-8
(Chapter Seven) and Rom 3:25,26 (Chapter Eight).   On the
basis of these analyses I returned to complete the
analysis of Rom 9:14-18 (Chapter Nine).   Then (in
Chapter Ten) I tried to follow Paul's justification of
God through to its climax in Rom 9:23.   The final
chapter is a concluding summary of the argument and some
of its implications.

The reader who desires to know my exegetical and
theological conclusions before reading the supporting
arguments may consult Chapter Eleven.

CHAPTER TWO

MY KINSMEN ARE ACCURSED!

ROMANS 9:1-5

1. The place of Romans 9:1-5 in the argument

If the main aim of this book is to understand the defense of God's righteousness in Rom 9:14-23, why devote a whole chapter to Rom 9:1-5? The reason is that Paul's argument in the chapter is so tightly woven that understanding one stage depends on understanding the others. The justification of God in 9:14-23 can be properly understood only in light of the assertions of 9:6b-13 which have seemed to call God's righteousness into question. Then again 9:6b-13 is Paul's effort to show that the word of God has not fallen (9:6a), and this effort can be understood only when we see why and in what sense the word of God has been called into question. This is what Rom 9:1-5 tells us and that is why we must include a chapter on this unit.

Excursus - The place of Romans 9-11 in the epistle

Of course, the whole epistle is woven together so that each part is illuminated somewhat by the others. But every study has its limits. Therefore I will content myself with a brief excursus concerning the recent discussion of the relationship between Rom 1-8 and Rom 9-11, and simply align myself with the view that seems to me to accord best with Paul's intention.[1] C.H. Dodd is often cited, but less often followed, as a representative of those who stress the independence of Rom 9-11 from Rom 1-8 (Romans, 161). For example, A.M. Hunter, in explicit dependence on Dodd, writes, "Paul may have written this section earlier as a separate discussion of a vexed question. It forms a continuous whole and may be read without reference to the rest of the letter" (Introducing the N.T., 96).

W.G. Kuemmel has demonstrated the inadequacy of the efforts to account for the presence of Rom 9-11 in the letter on the basis of the personal situation of Paul (e.g. preparing for his defense in Jerusalem[2]) or the concrete problems of the church in Rome (e.g. the presumptuousness of the Jewish Christians[3]). "Why these chapters are found

3

in Romans can only be answered when the theological
meaning of the chapters both in connection with the
rest of Romans and Pauline theology is explained"
(Kuemmel, "Probleme von Roemer 9-11," 26). Thus
the purpose of Rom 9-11 must be explained in relation to the purpose of the whole letter. Kuemmel
is right, I think, that no suggested purpose for
the letter is more probable than the one implied in
1:10ff and 15:20ff: "Paul writes to this community
because in spite of the existence of a Christian
community there he feels obligated to preach the
gospel there too (1:15), and because he desires the
material help of the Romans for his mission plans
in Spain and the spiritual help of the Romans for
his perseverance in Jerusalem (15:24)" (Kuemmel,
27). Paul aims to lay before this church the
Christian gospel which he preaches so that they can
see "the grace given to me by God to be a minister
of Christ Jesus to the Gentiles in the priestly
service of the gospel of God" (15:15f). Since the
gospel that he proclaims in Rom 1-8 is the power of
God unto salvation "to the Jews first" (1:16) and
since the Christ is "descended from David according
to the flesh" (1:3) and "there is great value in
circumcision" (3:2) and "the faithlessness of the
Jews does not nullify the faithfulness of God"
(3:3) and a saving promise was made "to Abraham and
his descendants" (4:13), the question of Israel's
destiny becomes acute. It grows necessarily out of
the exposition of Rom 1-8.

Leenhardt argues that between Rom 1-8 and 9-11
"there is a very close connection; furthermore a
real logical necessity compels the apostle to deal
with the subject which he now broaches [in Rom
9-11]."[4] A little differently than Leenhardt, but
following Goppelt,[5] I see the necessity for Rom
9-11 in this: the hope of the Christian, with
which Rom 1-8 came to a climax, is wholly dependent
on God's faithfulness to his word, his call
(8:28,30). But, as Gutbrod asks, "Can the new
community trust God's Word when it seems to have
failed the Jews?" (TDNT, III, 386). The unbelief
of Israel, the chosen people, and their consequent
separation from Christ (Rom 9:3) seem to call
God's word into question and thus to jeopardize not
only the privileged place of Israel, but also the
Christian hope as well.[6] Therefore, in Paul's
view, the theme of Rom 9-11 is not optional; it is
essential for the securing of Rom 1-8. This view
of Rom 9-11 assumes that Rom 9:6a (God's word has

4

not fallen) is the main point which Rom 9-11 was
written to prove, in view of Israel's unbelief and
rejection.[7] What is at stake ultimately in these
chapters is not the fate of Israel; that is penultimate. Ultimately God's own trustworthiness is
at stake.[8] And if God's word of promise cannot be
trusted to stand forever, then all our faith is in
vain. Therefore our goal in analyzing Rom 9:1-5
is to see precisely how Paul conceives of the
tension between God's word and the fate of Israel.
What is it precisely that makes God's word appear
to have fallen, but, in fact, does not impugn God's
faithfulness at all?

2. Exegesis of Romans 9:1-5

The following division of verse parts aims to
highlight the text's structure and to facilitate precision of reference in the exegesis.

1a   I speak the truth in Christ.
 b   I do not lie,
 c   my conscience bearing witness with me in the
    Holy Spirit
2   that I have great grief and unceasing pain in
    my heart.
3a   For I myself could wish to be anathema,
    separated from Christ
 b   on behalf of my brothers, my kinsmen according
    to the flesh,
4a   who are Israelites;
 b   whose are the sonship (ἡ υἱοθεσία)
        and the glory (ἡ δόξα)
            and the covenants (αἱ διαθῆκαι)[9]
        and the giving of the law (ἡ νομοθεσία)
          and the service of worship (ἡ λατρεία)
            and the promises (αἱ ἐπαγγελίαι);
5a   whose are the fathers
 b   and from whom is the Messiah according to the
    flesh,
 c   who is God over all, blessed for ever. Amen.

In Rom 9:1-3 Paul avers his pain over the plight of
his people. In 9:4,5 he describes the privileges of
"his kinsmen according to the flesh." The glorious
privileges of 9:4,5 stand in vivid contrast to the
sorrow of 9:3 and account for its intensity.[10] It is
precisely this contrast between the privileges of Paul's
kinsmen in 9:4,5 and their plight in 9:3 which seems to
imply that God's word has fallen. What are these privileges (2.1) and this plight (2.2)?

5

2.1 The privileges of Paul's kinsmen, Romans 9:4,5

The structure of Rom 9:4,5 is tantalizing. It allures us to see intentional patterns, but in places eludes our desire for complete symmetry. The first characteristic of Paul's kinsmen is that "they are Israelites" (9:4a). This designation is probably intended to resonate with a richness that sums up all the other privileges in 9:4,5. Not only does it stand at the head of the list of privileges, but also grammatically the rest are subordinate to it. Its significance for Paul is unfolded through three relative clauses (ὧν . . . ὧν . . . ἐξ ὧν) whose antecedent in each case is Ἰσραηλῖται.[11] Within the first relative clause (9:4b) six feminine nouns, each connected simply with καί, describe the privileges belonging to the "Israelites." The formal pattern of these six nouns is visibly (and was audibly) obvious:

ἡ υἱο<u>θεσία</u> καὶ ἡ   δό<u>ξα</u> καὶ αἱ   δια<u>θῆκαι</u>
καὶ ἡ νομο<u>θεσία</u> καὶ ἡ λατρε<u>ία</u> καὶ αἱ ἐπαγγελ<u>ίαι</u>

The list falls into two groups of three with endings corresponding between the first and fourth, second and fifth, third and sixth.[12] This observation alone may be enough to account for the <u>hapax legomenon</u> νομοθεσία (instead of Paul's usual νόμος which would have matched υἱός but not υἱοθεσία) and for the unusual use of the plural αἱ διαθῆκαι to produce the assonance with αἱ ἐπαγγελίαι.

Two other implications of this structure emerge for interpretation. First, the willingness to choose some words on the basis of rhyme or assonance implies that the meaning may lie more in the total, unified impact of the six-fold group than in the separate, distinct meanings of each member. We will have to test this implication as we analyze the individual members below. Second, since such a symmetrical structure tends to resist alteration and facilitate memory, it suggests that the unit is perhaps traditional rather than created <u>ad hoc</u> for this occasion. The occurrence of the unusual νομοθεσία and the plural διαθῆκαι could also suggest that Paul is here using a traditional Jewish list of privileges. Otto Michel and Lucien Cerfaux have argued for this view.[13]

But since Paul was one of the most creative and seminal theologians of the early church, we should consider seriously whether Rom 9:4 reflects his own selectivity, artistry and theology. This would not have to mean that Paul composed this list of privileges just for this letter. The letter clearly reflects Paul's give-and-take with Jewish and Greek listeners during his missionary efforts.[14] It would be likely then that if Rom 9:4 is Paul's own composition, it originated as early as his reflection on the problem of Israel's rejection (Rom 11:14,15). If this were the case, the intervening years of repeatedly handing on this teaching to various groups would justify calling Rom 9:4 both genuinely Pauline as well as "traditional."

In fact the arguments that Paul used a Hellenistic-Jewish tradition here are not persuasive. We have already shown that the poetic structure could have easily originated in Paul's preaching and that therefore the appearance of words not common in Paul need not contradict his authorship since the demands of assonance in the parallel structure can adequately account for the unusual words. Moreover it remains to be proved that the other words, e.g. υἱοθεσία, are used here in a different sense from Paul's usual usage (Michel). On the contrary, especially υἱοθεσία points to a Pauline origin since the word is used only by him in the NT (Rom 8:15,23; 9:4; Gal 4:5; Eph 1:5), does not occur in the LXX, and has virtually no history with a religious meaning prior to Paul.[15] But most important of all is the observation of Ulrich Luz, which has been borne out in my own study, that there simply are no parallels in the Jewish literature of a list of the prerogatives of Israel in anything approximating this form or selection.[16] Therefore, it is more probable that Rom 9:4 reflects Paul's own art and theology. This will have a significant bearing on the exegesis.

The second relative clause attached to "Israelites" is "whose are the fathers" (ὧν οἱ πατέρες, 9:5a). Structurally the main question here is why πατέρες is introduced with its own relative pronoun (ὧν) rather than simply being added to the list of prerogatives in 9:4b. The answer is probably that as a seventh member of the list it would have destroyed the symmetry of three rhyming pairs, especially since πατέρες is masculine while the other members of the list are all feminine. Moreover, it refers to persons while the other members are all concepts. However, it is not as easy to say something positive about why πατέρες receives its own separate clause. There may be no other significance than what was just said, together with Paul's desire not to put the patriarchs and the Messiah together in one clause (9:5ab) and thus imply that they are privileges on the same level. But two possible implications of the

structure may be suggested. Michel (Roemer, 227 note 2)
points out how the trio, Israelites (9:4a) and fathers
(9:5a) and Messiah (9:5b), may reveal an intention to
move from the many through the few to the one. Another
possibility is that after listing the benefits of being
Israelites in 9:4b, Paul closes with a kind of structure
that brackets Israel's history: the patriarchs inaugu-
rate Israel and the Messiah brings its history to a
climax (see below p 27). Or it may simply be that, in
view of the theological significance Paul ascribes to
the fathers (11:16,28), he felt the need to include them
among Israel's benefits, and here in 9:5a is where they
fit best.

One final observation of form is that the third
relative clause (9:5b) differs from the first two (ἐξ ὧν
instead of ὧν). The reason for this is so closely
related to the meaning of the verse that we will post-
pone our discussion until the exegesis below (see pp
26-28).

2.11 "Who are Israelites"

It is of utmost importance to notice that the
antecedent of οἵτινες is Paul's kinsmen according to the
flesh who are anathema, separated from Christ (9:3); and
that this group of unbelievers is even now called
Israelites (present tense: 9:4a). The tense of the
verb[17] in 9:4a as well as the relationship[18] between
9:1-5 and 9:6a resists every effort (e.g. of Johannes
Munck and Lucien Cerfaux) to relegate the prerogatives
of Israel to the past.[19] Furthermore, Paul's bold
assertion that the glorious privileges of Israel belong
to unbelieving Israel (the antecedent of οἵτινες, 9:4a)
resists the effort of Erich Dinkler ("Praedestination,"
88) to argue from 9:6b ("Not all those from Israel are
Israel") that "the promises refer not to the empirical-
historical Israel, but to the eschatological Israel"
(by which he means the Church, without regard to ethnic
origins). Whether the second "Israel" in 9:6b is the
Church or the believing portion of empirical-historical
Israel, the point there is this: the privileges given
to Israel can never be construed to guarantee the salvation of any individual Jew or synagogue of Jews, and
therefore the unbelief of Paul's kinsmen cannot immediately be construed to mean that God's word of promise
has fallen. But in no way does 9:6b exclude the possibility that God's intention may someday be to save "all
Israel" (11:26). And therefore 9:6b does not give us a
warrant to construe the privileges of 9:4,5 (against the
wording of the text) as the privileges of eschatological

Israel (= the Church) to the exclusion of empirical-
historical Israel. Why should Dinkler prefer to see a
contradiction between Rom 9:1-13 and 11:1-32 than to
allow God's intention for Israel's future in 11:1-32 to
help him see that Rom 9:6b should not be construed to
rule out a future for ethnic Israel?

Excursus - The theological unity of Romans 9 and 11

W.G. Kuemmel ("Probleme von Roemer 9-11," 30f)
thinks that "the central problem in the interpretation of Rom. 9-11" is whether Paul "destroys or
employs conceptions of redemptive history." He
cites Dinkler ("Praedestination," 97), Luz
(Geschichtsverstaendnis, 295, 299) and Guettgemanns
("Heilsgeschichte," 40. 47. 54. 58) as representatives of the exegetes who tend to emphasize the
existential dimension of Paul's meaning here to the
exclusion of the historical. Over against this
group Kuemmel finds an "excellent assumption for
the interpretation of Rom 9-11" in the emphasis of
Kaesemann ("Rechtfertigung und Heilsgeschichte,"
134), Mueller (Gottes Gerechtigkeit, 105) and
Stuhlmacher ("Zur Interpretation von Roemer
11, 25-32," 560) on the indispensably historical,
linear dimension of the doctrine of justification.
It seems to me also, especially in view of Rom
9-11, that the latter view is more faithful to
Paul's intention. But rather than address the
issue of existence vs history in general, I aim
in this excursus to treat an offshoot of it,
namely, the theological unity of Rom 9 and 11. The
question of unity is related to the larger hermeneutical question because Rom 9 seems to support
the first view mentioned above, while Rom 11 seems
to support the second.

Dinkler ("Praedestination," 90) argues that
there is an unresolvable contradiction between
Rom 9:6-13 and 11:1-32. His position is akin to
Bultmann's ("Geschichte und Eschatologie," 101),
though he does not say, as Bultmann does, that
Paul's effort to preserve a future for historical
Israel springs from his "speculative fantasy"
(Bultmann, Theology, II, 132). In Dinkler's words:
"The analysis of the three chapters shows that
there is a decisive contradiction between 9:6-13
and 11:1-32. In chapter 9 the theological problem
of the rejection of the elect people is resolved
by means of a reinterpretation of the term 'Israel',
namely by introducing an eschatological

9

understanding of the term. This is different from chapter 11 where the historical role of ethnic Israel continues as an enduring entity of redemptive history. According to chapter 9 the promises belong not to the historical people of Israel but to the eschatological ἐκλογή. According to chapter 11 the promises are still the inalienable possession of the historical people of Israel" (my emphasis). He grants that the contradiction is somewhat meliorated by the fact that Paul does not claim every individual Israelite has a share in the promise and that the end-time generation will be saved "only on the basis of the electing call of God." Nevertheless "there remains a theological contradiction," because it is "precisely because of the promise, because of the past election of the people Israel, that the historical people must be saved" (91).

I agree with Dinkler that in Rom 11:1-32 the Israel that will be saved (11:26) is historical Israel and not merely the Church as "the Israel of God" (Gal 6:16). But why this must contradict Rom 9:6ff I cannot see. His argument proceeds at two levels. First he argues that the second Israel in Rom 9:6b ("Not all those from Israel are Israel") refers not to a remnant of Jewish Christians but to eschatological Israel, the Church consisting of Jew and Gentile. His support (88 note 19) is fourfold: "1) The following verses 7 and 8 say explicitly that the promise of God, not natural descent, is decisive for sonship. 2) Already in 2:28 the term 'Jew' was interpreted dialectically, and in chapter 4 Abraham was shown to be the father of all believers. 3) Gal 6:16 refers Ἰσραὴλ τοῦ θεοῦ to the church in general. 4) The dialectical use of Ἰουδαῖος and Ἰσραὴλ is only the logical consequence of Rom 1:18-3:2 and corresponds to the thesis expressed in Gal 3:28." This is an entirely feasible view of the second "Israel" in 9:6b even though 9:7-13 does seem to restrict its focus to election within historical Israel.

So let us suppose for now that Dinkler is right about 9:6b. Then Paul would be saying that even though historical Israel for the most part is accursed (see below, Section 2.2), God's word of promise has not fallen (9:6a) because the people to whom the promises belong are not all the Israelites but only the people whom God elects freely, both

10

Jew and Greek (9:6b). Those who have the faith of Abraham are children of Abraham (Gal 3:7) and thus heirs according to promise (Gal 3:29). But I ask, why does this contradict the divine intention sovereignly to bring the end-time generation of historical Israel to faith and to membership in the "eschatological Israel," the Church (Rom 11:25-27)? Dinkler recognizes that this is not readily obvious and thus moves to another level of argument.

His second level of argument (which is really implicit in the first) is not based on an exegesis of Rom 9:1-13 but on the theological insight that "there is no partiality with God" (οὐ γάρ ἐστιν προσωπολημψία παρὰ τῷ θεῷ, Rom 2:11). But if the end-time generation of ethnic Israel is to be saved "because of the promise, because of the past election of the people Israel" (91), then it appears that this past election of Israel forces God into being partial to the future historical Israel and thus contradicting his free bestowal of righteousness on whomever he wills. This argument is indeed the heart of the problem and must be answered if we are to maintain both the prerogatives of historical Israel as well as coherence in Paul's thought. Does the salvation of the end-time generation of empirical-historical Israel in fulfillment of promises to the fathers (11:25-28) contradict God's freedom to elect whom he wills without being determined by human distinctives outside himself (9:10-13)?

The nature of a free and sovereignly bestowed promise is such that it defines and limits the activity in which God can righteously exercise his freedom; but this limitation does not originate from outside God's knowledge and ultimate intentions, and, therefore, does not jeopardize the freedom of Rom 9:11,12 by which God retains complete sway in election. Promises always limit and define part of our future behavior, but for God, who foresees all future eventualities, the decision to make a promise involves him only in those restrictions which he foresees and thus freely chooses. Therefore the fulfillment of a divine promise cannot properly be described as God's being unable to do otherwise because he is controlled by human circumstances; but rather the fulfillment of a divine promise is simply a climactic exercise of the same freedom in which God chose to make the promise in the first place. When all

11

eventualities are seen ahead of time the inscrutable decision to make a free promise implies that
all the acts performed in the fulfillment of that
promise are just as free and just as inscrutable
as the initial choice.

Therefore, since God's free and unconstrained
election of Israel from all the nations of the
earth (Deut 7:6) embraced from the outset his
intention to bless Israel for centuries in unique
ways among the nations and in the last days to
purify and save the whole people, his fulfillment
of this intention is just as free from human
constraints as the initial election of Abraham.
We may infer from Rom 9:6ff that God has employed
four thousand years of redemptive history to teach
that he is free and not bound to save anyone
because of his Jewishness nor to condemn anyone
because of his non-Jewishness. Can he not at the
end of the age, having demonstrated his freedom
beyond the shadow of a doubt, bring his free and
sovereign election of Israel to a climax by
banishing ungodliness from Jacob and saving the
whole people?

But, someone may say, if he saves the whole
end-time generation, an Israelite will be able to
boast legitimately: I was saved because I am a
descendant of Abraham and so had a sufficient
merit in God's eyes! There are two responses to
this objection: 1) the banishing of ungodliness
from Israel (Rom 11:26) will mean the elimination
of precisely that attitude; 2) if anyone does
manifest that attitude he will not be saved, since
salvation is always on the same basis for Jew and
Gentile (Rom 2:6-10; 3:21-26). This loss would
not jeopardize the fulfillment of the promise,
because "all Israel" need not be taken with mathe-
matical rigidity (cf 1 Kgs 12:1; 2 Chr 12:1;
Sanhedrin 10:1).

Some have also thought that the ostensible
contradiction between 9:6-13 and 11:1-32 can also
be seen in the tension that appears between Rom
1:16; 2:9,10; 3:1,2 on the one hand, and Rom 2:11;
3:9,22; 10:12 on the other. On the one hand, "the
gospel is the power of God to everyone who
believes, both to the Jew first and to the Greek"
(1:16); and in the judgment both punishment and
glory belong to "both the Jew first and to the
Greek" (2:9,10). On the other hand, "there is no

12

partiality with God" (2:11) and "there is no
difference between Jew and Greek" (10:12; οὐ γάρ
ἐστιν διαστολὴ Ἰουδαίου τε καὶ Ἕλληνος, cf
3:22).

Both Rom 3:22 and 10:12 define and limit the
sense in which "there is no difference between Jew
and Greek." In 3:22 there is no difference in the
sense that "all have sinned and lack the glory of
God" (3:23). In 10:12 there is no difference in
the sense that "the same Lord is over all, rich to
all who call upon him" (10:12; cf 3:29f). Therefore, Michel (Roemer, 105) on 3:22 and Kuss
(Roemerbrief, III, 767) on 10:12 go beyond what the
text implies when they claim these verses abolish the
privileged place of Israel. Sanday and Headlam
(Romans, 84) are more careful. On 3:22 they say,
"The Jew has (in this respect) no real advantage
over the Gentile; both alike need a righteousness
which is not their own; and to both it is offered
on the same terms." Also Heinrich Schlier
(Roemerbrief, 314) on 10:12 says, "Between Jew and
Gentile there is no difference in reference to
salvation through faith and confession" (my emphasis). Therefore Rom 3:22 and 10:12 cannot be
played off against the privilege of Israel. They
limit and help define it, but do not exclude it.

Concerning 3:9, Cranfield's (Romans, I, 187-191)
careful exegesis is wholly commendable. He argues
from Paul's passage (1 Cor 16:12; 5:10) that the
answer to the question, "Have we (Jews) any
advantage over them (sc. the Gentiles)?" is "Not
altogether" (οὐ πάντως) rather than "Not at all"
(against Gifford, Romans, 85; Alford, III, 340;
Murray, Romans, II, 102). Cranfield explains how this
answer suits the context: "Paul has said in 3:2
that the Jew has an advantage which is great and
important in every respect. He now indicates that,
while the Jews have this altogether great advantage, they are not at an advantage in every
respect. (These two statements are not contradictory.) There is at least one respect in which
they are at no advantage--the matter of sinfulness,
of having no claim on God in virtue of their merit"
(190, similarly Schlier, Roemerbrief, 98;
Kaesemann, Romans, 84; Lagrange, Romains, 69).
Therefore, neither may Rom 3:9 be used to exclude
a prerogative for Israel in Paul's theology.

13

Now what about the assertion that "there is no partiality with God" (Rom 2:11, οὐ γάρ ἐστιν προσωπολημψία παρὰ τῷ θεῷ; cf. Eph 6:9; Col 3:25; Jam 2:1; Gal 2:6; Jude 16; 1 Pt 1:17; Mt 22:16 par; Acts 10:34)? Does this contradict the phrase "to the Jew first and also to the Greek" (Rom 1:16; 2:9,10)? For a good survey of the scholarly discussion see Dieter Zeller, Juden und Heiden, 141-45, 149-51. To see the question in its proper light we must realize that, on the one hand, the impartiality of God is an essential feature of Jewish as well as Pauline theology (TDNT, VI, 779; Deut 10:17; 2 Chr 19:7), and on the other hand it was never seen (by the Jews or Paul) to contradict the election of Israel ("The Lord your God has chosen you to be a people for his own possession, out of all the peoples that are on the face of the earth," Deut 7:6; "You only have I known of all the families of the earth," Amos 3:2). Holding the question in this light helps us see that impartiality must be defined with great precision lest it become a kind of twentieth-century egalitarian slogan that ends up forcing God to bless equal percentages of every class and race with identical blessings.

It is crucial to notice that in the NT the impartiality of God is never a description of his election. In Paul it is, with one possible exception, a description of how God performs the final judgment (Rom 2:11; Eph 6:9; Col 3:25; Gal 2:6 is only a partial exception: Paul does not care about the rank of the pillar apostles because πρόσωπον θεὸς ἀνθρώπου οὐ λαμβάνει: God does not make his judgments on the basis of rank either). A judge's impartiality in the OT sense (Deut 10:17; 16:19; 2 Chr 19:7) depends on the existence of an objective standard of judgment from which the judge will not deviate even for a bribe. This is the sense of Rom 2:11 also. Rom 2:6 lays down the standard: "He will render to each according to his works." Both Jew and Greek will be saved or condemned by the same standard (2:9,10). Lest anyone think that this impartiality (2:11) is contradicted by the greater revelation that the Jews had in the law, Paul affirms that "as many as sinned without the law, will perish without the law, and as many as sinned with the law will be judged through the law" (2:12).

14

Therefore, we may say that for Paul, God's impartiality assures only that in the last judgment salvation and condemnation will not be determined by race or class or wealth or intellect but only by the "obedience of faith." This does not rule out that the Judge may deal with Jews first (in climactic fulfillment of his free election of Abraham and his seed) nor does it say anything with regard to the criteria of divine election. In fact the decisive difference between God's impartiality in judgment and his freedom in election can be clearly seen by contrasting Rom 2:6-11 and 9:11-13: he judges each man according to a lifetime of good or evil works (2:6); he elects "before they have done anything good or evil" (9:11). In the one case he impartially applies the standard he has set, in the other case he chooses in inscrutable freedom ἵνα ἡ κατ' ἐκλογὴν πρόθεσις τοῦ θεοῦ μένῃ οὐκ ἐξ ἔργων ἀλλ' ἐκ τοῦ καλοῦντος (Rom 9:11,12). Therefore, I conclude that the evidence does not require us to follow Dinkler and others who insist that Paul contradicts himself in maintaining the freedom of God in election and the hope that God will in the end save "all Israel."[20]

In view of Paul's argument in chapter 11 that "all Israel" will someday be saved (precisely because of the "fathers"; compare 11:28 and 9:5a) we should allow the privileges of 9:4,5 to apply, as their wording suggests, to Paul's (now) unbelieving "kinsmen according to the flesh"--not, of course, to every individual Jew, but as 9:6b says, to the elect among them and, as 11:25f suggests, to "that part of the historical people in existence at the end of the age" (Dinkler, "Praedestination," 90--but admittedly we are here reaching forward to Paul's solution of a paradox which in Rom 9:1-5 is only presented and not yet resolved). A similar line of argument has been developed also by Walter Gutbrod,[21] Martin Rese[22] and Ulrich Luz.[23]

The first privilege of Paul's kinsmen is that they are "Israelites."[24] The word is redolent with a blessed antiquity and a glorious future (Is 49:3; 56:8; 66:20; Joel 2:27; 4:16 MT; Ob 20; Ps 25:22; 53:6; 130:7f). It sums up all the other privileges in its richness (see p 6). Its promissory import is evident from Paul's use of it in Rom 11:1f: "I say therefore, has God rejected his people? No indeed! For I myself am an Israelite, from the seed of Abraham, of the tribe of Benjamin. God has not rejected his people whom he foreknew." To be an "Israelite" is to be

15

among the people of God, and God does not reject his people. What could be more auspicious than to be called an "Israelite"!

2.12 "To whom belongs the sonship"

Most commentators relate this privilege of sonship to Ex 4:22f, which was also viewed by the rabbis as the "classic Scripture text to ground Israel's sonship":[25] "And you shall say to Pharaoh, 'Thus says the Lord, Israel is my first-born son, and I say to you, Let my son go that he may serve me; if you refuse to let him go, behold, I will slay your first-born son.'" Under appeal to this and other OT texts Charles Hodge and John Murray argue that the sonship of Rom 9:4b is very different from the sonship of Christians described in Rom 8:15,23; Gal 4:5; Eph 1:5.

Hodge (Romans, 298f): "As Paul is speaking here of the external or national Israel, the adoption or sonship which pertained to them, as such, must be external also, and is very different from that which he had spoken of in the preceding chapter. . . . So the sonship of the Israelites was an adumbration of the sonship of believers. That of the former was in itself, and as common to all the Jews, only the peculiar relation which they sustained to God as partakers of the blessings of the theocracy." Murray (Romans, II, 5): "'Adoption' is the filial relation to God constituted by God's grace (cf Ex 4:22f; Deut 14:1,2; Is 63:16; 64:8; Hos 11:1; Mal 1:6; 2:10). This adoption of Israel is to be distinguished from that spoken of as the apex of NT privilege (8:15; Gal 4:5; Eph 1:5; cf John 1:12; 1 John 3:1). This is apparent from Gal 4:5, for here the adoption is contrasted with the tutelary discipline of the Mosaic economy. Israel under the OT were indeed children of God but they were as children underage (cf Gal 3:23; 4:1-3)."

The assumption at work in both of these arguments is the same one we saw earlier in Munck, Kuss and Cerfaux (see note 19); namely, that the privileges of Rom 9:4f are "theocratic" and thus oriented to the past rather than the future. That the sonship of 9:4b must be external and natural because the Israel of 9:3 is the historical-empirical Israel of Paul's day, is a valid argument only if one denies that the ethnic and religious continuity of corporate Israel enables Paul to assign to Israel now what may be experienced corporately only in the future. To be sure Murray is right that Christian sonship is contrasted with "the tutelary

16

discipline of the Mosaic economy," but has he disproved that it is precisely the underaged children to whom belong the full sonship? I do not think that Hodge or Murray has been able to show that the sonship of Rom 9:4b is any other than the sonship of Gal 4:5 and Rom 8:15,23, or that this sonship is not uniquely the prerogative of corporate Israel, whether they experience it now or only in the future.

To support this position we make the following observations. 1) As noted earlier (p 7) υἱοθεσία is an unusual word: only Paul uses it in the NT (Rom 8:15,23; 9:4; Gal 4:5; Eph 1:5), it does not occur in the LXX and it has virtually no history with a religious meaning before Paul. So the only pertinent evidence we have for υἱοθεσία used of sonship in relation to God is the evidence in Paul. Therefore only if the context absolutely demands it should we assign a different meaning to υἱοθεσία in Rom 9:4b than we find in all Paul's other uses. Lexical considerations are all in favor of construing the sonship of Rom 9:4b with the fullest saving significance of Rom 8:15,23.[26]

2) What Murray seems to overlook is that the olive tree analogy in Rom 11:17 implies that whatever blessings the Church enjoys it does so because it has been grafted into the cultivated tree to share in its rich root (11:17). It is the Jews who are the "natural branches" (11:21) which, though now broken off (by a temporary hardening, 11:7,25), will be grafted in again (11:24): "all Israel will be saved" (11:26). If the Church enjoys divine sonship, it must remember that it does so by participating in the people of God which is historical Israel "by nature" (i.e. by a special act of sovereign election). It is not surprising, then, for Paul in Rom 9:4b to ascribe to Israel the very privilege of sonship which Christians now enjoy.[27]

3) Already in the OT (Is 43:6; 45:11; 63:16,17; 64:8-12; Hos 2:1 MT; Mal 3:17) the sonship of Israel had come to imply a glorious future for Israel beyond the old theocratic blessings. The future implications of Israel's sonship were expressed also in the intertestamental literature (e.g. Jubilees 1:24f; Ps of Sol 17:26f); and the rabbis discussed frequently the relationship between Israel's sonship and future salvation, with the view frequently expressed that Israel's salvation (sometimes every individual) is secured by its sonship.[28] Therefore there is no reason in Paul's milieu to cause us to construe the sonship of Israel in

17

Rom 9:4b as a merely past or temporary blessing (contra Cerfaux, "Privilège," 360).

I conclude, therefore, with Martin Rese (note 26), Heinrich Schlier[29] and Ulrich Luz[30] that the effort to distinguish the sonship of Rom 9:4b from that of 8:15,23 does not have the preponderance of evidence on its side. It is precisely because the prerogative of υἱοθεσία is so rich with saving implications that the problem of Israel's unbelief is so intense.

2.13 "And the glory"

The usual interpretation is that the "glory" which belongs especially to the Israelites refers here to the theophanies of God in the OT, especially God's manifestation of his presence (the rabbinic "shekinah") in the early wilderness experience (Ex 16:10; 24:16; 29:43; 33:18; 40:34; Lev 9:23).[31] Paul uses the term δόξα some seventy times, and only in one place (2 Cor 3:7-11) does it refer to an OT theophany. This alone should give us pause in the facile assignment of this meaning to δόξα in Rom 9:4b.

The absolute use of δόξα without any modifier (as in Rom 9:4b) refers regularly in Paul not to a past but to a future, eschatological glory (Rom 2:7,10; 8:18; 9:23; Col 1:27; 3:4; 2 Tim 2:10; 2 Cor 4:17).[32] Especially noteworthy is Rom 2:10 where it says that God will render "glory, honor and peace to everyone who does good, to the Jew first and also to the Greek." This implies that for Paul the glory of the age to come was in a special sense the prerogative of Israel. The same thing is implicit in Rom 9:23f where Paul says that God "makes known the wealth of his glory on the vessels of mercy which he prepared beforehand for glory, whom also he called: us, not only from the Jews but also from the Gentiles." The phrase "not only Jews but also Gentiles" reveals that Paul expects the reader to infer naturally that vessels prepared for glory include Jews. Why? Probably because "to Israelites belong the (eschatological) glory!" (Rom 9:4b). Furthermore in Rom 8:18 δόξα is used absolutely (as in 9:4b) with reference to the future age; but in 8:21 it is called "the glory of the children (τέκνων) of God" which links it in an essential way with eschatological υἱοθεσία of 8:23. It seems to me therefore that we have no good grounds from the Pauline context to give δόξα a different historical orientation than we gave υἱοθεσία just before it. They both look to the future with roots in the past.

18

The OT and Paul's Jewish milieu give good reason
to think that Paul would view Israel's glory in this
way. Is 43:7 stands out for special consideration as
an expression of post-exilic hope: "Bring my sons from
afar . . . whom I created for my glory." That the
glory of the Lord is the special portion of Israel is
expressed again and again (Is 40:5; 42:8; 46:13; 48:11;
58:8; 60:1,2,7; 62:2,3; 66:11,18; Jer 13:11; Hag 2:7,9;
Zech 2:5). "To an extraordinary degree . . . the δόξα
of God is . . . a theme of religious hope and an established part of eschatological expectation."[33]

Naturally the end-time manifestation of God's
glory to and for Israel became an expectation of later
Jewish apocalyptic writings (e.g., 4 Ezra 7:91-98;
2 Bar 21:23-26; 51:1-10; cf Ps of Sol 17:32-35). In the
NT, Lk 2:32 probably gives us a glimpse of popular
messianic expectation: Simeon, having seen the Messiah,
blesses God and says, "My eyes have seen your salvation
which you prepared before all the peoples, a light for
revelation to the Gentiles, and for the glory of your
people Israel." We may conclude, therefore, that in
Paul's Jewish milieu there is more than adequate
stimulus to direct his thought toward an eschatological
δόξα as one of Israel's privileges. And, as we saw,
his own particular usage makes this interpretation of
Rom 9:4b most probable. It is precisely this destiny
of Israel that makes the problem of Israel's unbelief
so intense!

2.14 "And the covenants"[34]

There is no consensus among the commentators concerning which covenants are referred to. Murray
(Romans, II, 5) suggests the covenants with Abraham,
Moses and David. Munck (Christ and Israel, 31), Alford
(II, 404), Schlatter (Gerechtigkeit, 294), and Sanday
and Headlam (Romans, 230) refer to the covenants "from
Abraham to Moses." Schlier (Roemerbrief, 287) includes
the covenant with Noah. Barrett (Romans, 177f) follows
a rare rabbinic reference (Strack-Billerbeck, III, 262)
to "three covenants within the great covenant of the
Exodus--a covenant at Horeb, a second in the plains of
Moab, and a third at Mounts Gerizim and Ebal." What we
may learn from this assortment of guesses is that Paul's
term "covenants" in Rom 9:4b is open-ended. It does not
limit itself to any group of covenants. Hence the
contradictions among the commentators.

Here we should recall the observations made earlier
(pp 5,6) concerning the structure of Rom 9:4b. I

suggested there that the unusual plural αἱ διαθῆκαι may well have been used to create the assonance with the structurally corresponding αἱ ἐπαγγελίαι, and that this willingness to let form influence the particular words of the text probably means that the meaning lies more in the total general impact of the list than in unique, particular meanings of each word. This is another warning against trying to specify a limited number of covenants to which Paul is referring here. In fact the parallel with ἐπαγγελίαι inclined Lietzmann (Roemer, 89) to settle for the simple observation that the "covenants" are simply "synonymous with the promises."

In view of the parallel structure and the open-endedness of the term, this is probably very nearly the case. In other words Paul probably means that Israel-ites are the people whose destiny has been, and will be, determined by the fact that God has made covenants/promises with them. The one other place where Paul uses the plural διαθῆκαι is in the phrase ξένοι τῶν διαθηκῶν τῆς ἐπαγγελίας (Eph 2:12). The phrase "covenants of promise" confirms the view that covenants and promises are probably indistinguishable in Rom 9:4b.

The upshot of this open-ended view of "covenants" in Rom 9:4b is that it would be wholly arbitrary to exclude from Paul's meaning the only other covenant mentioned in Romans, namely, Rom 11:26f: "And thus all Israel will be saved just as it is written: The deliverer will come from Zion, he will turn ungodliness from Jacob; and this will be for them a covenant with me when I take away their sins." This appears to be a loose, composite paraphrase of Is 59:20,21; 27:9, and certainly refers to the "new covenant" which Paul construes as a promise of the salvation of all Israel.[35] If we have properly determined the scope of the διαθῆκαι of Rom 9:4b it is not surprising that it should align itself with the other eschatologically promising prerog-atives of Israel: sonship and glory.

2.15 "And the giving of the law"

The term νομοθεσία is taken by Gutbrod (TDNT, IV, 1089) and Hodge (Romans, 299) to refer to the content and possession of the OT law rather than the stupendous events of its promulgation at Sinai, "because the possession of the law was the grand distinction of the Jews, and one on which they peculiarly relied" (Hodge). Most commentators, however, whether because that would simply be redundant with "covenants" or because the pecular word νομοθεσία (instead of νόμος) calls for a

peculiar meaning, prefer to interpret νομοθεσία as the
divine act of giving the law.[36] H.A.W. Meyer (Romans,
II, 116) also rejects the meaning, νόμος, and asks, "Why
should Paul not have written this?"

Here again I must appeal to my structural analysis
on p 6 and answer: Paul probably did not use νόμος
because νομοθεσία provided the rhyming balance with the
word υἱοθεσία, just as the unusual plural αἱ διαθῆκαι
provided the rhyming counterpart to αἱ ἐπαγγελίαι.
Moreover in Hellenistic-Jewish literature νομοθεσία is
often virtually a synonym with νόμος (2 Macc 6:23;
4 Macc 5:35; 17:16; Aristeas, 15, 176 in reference to
OT; Philo, Abr 5; Cher 87; Josephus, Ant 6, 93). In
view of these linguistic and structural observations it
does not seem possible to argue persuasively that Paul
intended to stress the event at Sinai rather than the
possession and content of the law.

This does not mean we can say nothing about Paul's
meaning. When one reflects for a moment, the rigid
distinction between the law and its promulgation becomes
artificial.[37] The very character of the law is that it
is divine revelation and was, therefore, given. And the
giving would be empty and without effect if there were
no valuable gift. Nevertheless Martin Rese ("Vorzuege,"
216) insists that "the giving of the law at Sinai
expressed God's saving purpose for Israel, while the
law itself, according to Paul, did not become the salvation of Israel." It is true that the law had not
resulted de facto in the salvation of Israel, but
neither have the promises! It is not legitimate to play
off the actual (and temporary!) effect of the law
against the divine intention of its content. J.W. Doeve
("Notes") has shown that "the λόγια τοῦ θεοῦ mentioned
as a great privilege for Israel in Rom 3:2 refers to
God's revelation in Holy Scripture" (121) including the
Torah, and that the possession (cf ἐπιστεύθησαν, 3:2),
not just the receiving, of this revelation is considered
by Paul to be a great blessing.

The objection that the law in itself cannot be
received as a blessing is generally based on the assertions that "the law is not from faith" (Gal 3:12) and
that the law "increases the trespass" (Rom 5:20) and
"arouses sinful passions" (Rom 7:5), and that "Christ
is the end of the law" (Rom 10:4). But this objection
rests, I think, on a misunderstanding of these crucial
texts. Daniel P. Fuller[38] and Charles Cosgrove[39] have
shown that, in spite of the widespread notion that the
law and faith are contrary terms in Paul, in fact Christ

21

is not the end of the law but its goal, and both Christ
and the law teach faith not legalism. For this reason
Paul can say, "through faith we establish the law" (Rom
3:31), and "those who walk according to the Spirit [i.e.
by faith] fulfill the just requirement of the law" (Rom
8:4), and "the doers of the law will be justified" (Rom
2:13; cf Cranfield, I, Romans, 155; see also Rom 2:26).
And for this reason too Paul can argue in Rom 9:31f that
the reason Israel did not attain to the righteousness which
the law commends is that they pursued it οὐκ ἐκ πίστεως
ἀλλ᾽ ὡς ἐξ ἔργων--"not from faith but as though it were
from works"--when in fact it is not from works, and the
law never taught that it is.

Therefore, I conclude that, since in the law itself
God expressed his saving purpose for Israel (Ex 19:6;
29:45f; 31:16f; 32:13; 33:19; 34:6f) and taught the way
to life through faith (Rom 9:32), both the giving of the
law and the possession of its message were a great privilege for Israel, full of grace and a window of hope
toward the future.

2.16 "And the service of worship"

Paul uses the word λατρεία one other time: Rom
12:1, "I urge you therefore, brothers, through the
mercies of God to present your bodies a living sacrifice, holy, acceptable to God, which is your reasonable
service of worship." Elsewhere in the NT it is used
once in John (16:2--they will think that killing you is
offering service to God) and twice in Hebrews (9:1,6--
with reference to the priestly activities in the OT
sanctuary). In the LXX the term refers three times to
the performance of the Passover or feast of unleavened
bread (Ex 12:25,26; 13:5), once to the sacrifices at the
altar built by the Reubenites, Gadites and half-tribe
of Manasseh (Josh 22:27), once to the total priestly
ministry in the temple of Solomon (1 Chr 28:13) and four
times in the Maccabean context with reference to sacrifices to pagan deities (1 Macc 1:43; 3 Macc 4:14) as
over against the true worship of the fathers (1 Macc
2:19,22). Strathmann is probably right that against
the background of the LXX "the concrete idea of sacrifice seems [in the NT] always to cling to the noun no less
than the verb" (TDNT, IV, 65). In the context of law
and covenants[40] (Rom 9:4), λατρεία would naturally be
construed to refer to the various sacrificial provisions
in the OT.

The benefit of these provisions is seen first in
the fact that through the priestly ministry "atonement"

was made for the sins of Israel (Ex 29:35-37; Lev 1:4) so that they could be "forgiven" (Lev 4:20,26,31,35; 5:10,16,18; 6:7) and enjoy "acceptance" with Yahweh (Ex 28:38). The promise that God would be Israel's God and dwell with them was secured through the establishment of the sacrificial system:

> There I will meet with the people of Israel, and it shall be sanctified by my glory; I will consecrate the tent of meeting and the altar; Aaron also and his sons I will consecrate, to serve me as priests. And I will dwell among the people of Israel, and will be their God... who brought them forth out of the land of Egypt that I might dwell among them; I am the Lord their God (Ex 29:43-46).

This observation alone would justify Paul's including λατρεία among the privileges of Israel so rich with promise ("I will be their God!").

But there is reason to see even more portent in this privilege. The Passover celebration was the inaugural λατρεία (Ex 12:25-27) at the beginning of Israel's history as a nation. Paul's view is that Israel's Messiah has come and offered himself as the decisive Passover lamb (1 Cor 5:7) for the sake of his people. This sacrifice is at the heart of the gospel (1 Cor 15:3) which is "the power of God to everyone who believes, to the Jew first and also to the Greek" (Rom 1:16; cf Acts 13:46). We will probably not go beyond the implications of Paul's list in Rom 9:4b in saying that since the OT λατρεία was the prerogative of Israel, therefore the fulfillment of that prerogative through the death and resurrection of the Messiah (who came "only to the lost sheep of the house of Israel," Mt 15:24) is also the prerogative of Israel; and for this reason the good news of that fulfillment is preached "to the Jew first."

2.17 "And the promises"

The word ἐπαγγελία "has no preliminary history in the OT" (TDNT, II, 579). Of the six uses in the LXX none refers to divine promises, the use in Amos 9:6 and Ps 55 (56):9 being probable misunderstandings of the Hebrew. But the term already came to refer to divine promises before the NT (Test Jos, 20; Ps of Sol 12:6; Prayer of Man 6; Josephus, Ant 2,219; 3,77) and the rabbis developed a corresponding Hebrew term.[41] Within

23

the Pauline corpus the word is used twenty-five times,
five of which are plural (Rom 9:4; 15:8; 2 Cor 1:20;
7:1; Gal 3:16).

As with διαθῆκαι so with ἐπαγγελίαι we do best not
to specify which divine promises are meant and which are
not.[42] They no doubt embrace the "promises to the
patriarchs" (Rom 15:8; Gal 3:16), but the use of the
plural in 2 Cor 7:1 with reference to a collage of
prophetic promises (2 Cor 6:16-18) and the absolute use
in 2 Cor 1:20 ("all the promises of God are Yes in him")
forbid that we limit its meaning in Rom 9:4b.

With regard to the content of the promises, Paul
does not limit himself to looking for precise one-to-one
fulfillments. In Rom 4:13 he says that the promise to
Abraham and his seed was that he is to be "heir of the
world."[43] The OT does not make this promise in just
these words, though Gen 18:18 and 22:17 ("possess the
gates of their enemies") point in this direction.
Cranfield (Romans, I, 239f) is probably right that Paul's
meaning is best expressed in 1 Cor 3:21-23, "All things
are yours, whether Paul or Apollos or Cephas or the
world or life or death or the present or the future, all
are yours; and you are Christ's; and Christ is God's."
Possessing or being heir of all things surely means that
all things will work for the benefit of Abraham and his
seed (cf Rom 8:28,32). But is this not implied in a
promise like "I will be their God and they shall be my
people" (2 Cor 6:16; 7:1)? If all that God is in his
sovereign majesty over the world belongs to Israel for
her benefit, then the hope of "inheriting the world"
(Rom 4:13; cf Mt 5:5) is not arbitrary. So we can see
that for Paul the promises of God flow together into a
summation of all the good that God can possibly offer
his people.[44] "The content of the promises ... is
always Messianic salvation" (TDNT, II, 583).

Today it is Christians--Jew and Gentile--who enjoy
the "blessing of Abraham" (Gal 3:14): "If you are
Christ's then you are Abraham's seed, heirs according
to the promise" (Gal 3:29). The enjoyment of this
blessing and this promise is the enjoyment of salvation.
But Paul's word to the Gentiles is: Do not become
proud; remember "you do not support the root, but the
root supports you" (Rom 11:18). Eph 3:6 reminds us of
the "mystery" that Gentiles may become συμμέτοχα τῆς
ἐπαγγελίας ἐν χριστῷ 'Ιησοῦ. They become fellow beneficiaries of promises which already belong to the
"saints," the "household of God" (Eph 2:19). Only by
being grafted into the cultivated olive tree do the

24

Gentiles become heirs of the promise (Rom 11:17). Therefore the salvation which Gentile believers enjoy as
beneficiaries of the promises of God is a salvation
which belongs to Israel because "theirs are the
promises" (Rom 9:4b).

Let us make some summary remarks now about the six-
member list of Israel's privileges in Rom 9:4b. The
analysis has shown that Paul's intention is missed if
these privileges are described as mere antiquarian,
theocratic distinctives or as simply passing over from
Israel to the Church. Rather, the privileges are in
some sense still the prerogative of historical Israel.
And each one, more or less clearly, is laden with saving
implications and eschatological promise.[45] "The gifts
and call of God are irrevocable" (Rom 11:29). To miss
this combined impact of the unit is to fail to see the
intensity of the tension between Rom 9:3 and 9:4,5 which
Paul devoted three chapters (9-11) to resolving.

2.18 "To whom belong the fathers" (Romans 9:5a)

This now is the second of three relative clauses
which unfold the significance of the designation
"Israelites" in Rom 9:4a. For the grammatical and
structural considerations see pp 5-7. Paul uses the
term "father" often in reference to God and occasionally
in normal reference to a child's parent (Col 3:21; Eph
6:2,4). In the singular it can also refer to Abraham
(Rom 4:11,12,16,17,18) and Isaac (Rom 9:10) and in the
plural it can refer to all the early Israelites (1 Cor
10:1) or to the earliest patriarchs (probably Rom 11:28;
15:8; cf Ex 3:13,15; 13:5). The reference in Rom 9:5a
is probably to Abraham, Isaac and Jacob since the
privilege would lose its point if "fathers" meant all
the ancestors, and since these three patriarchs are
alluded to in 9:6-13.[46]

The decisive text for clarifying how Paul conceives
of the fathers being a benefit to Israel is Rom 11:28f.
Just after announcing that all Israel will be saved when
the deliverer comes to banish ungodliness and forgive
sins, Paul says, "According to the gospel they are
enemies for your [i.e. the Gentiles] sake; according to
election they are loved for the sake of the fathers; for
the gifts and call of God are irrevocable."

We may dismiss the suggestion that Paul shares the
conception of some rabbis[47] and probably many common
folk[48] that the merits of the patriarchs were so great
that they are transferred to the descendants,

25

guaranteeing their salvation. This is excluded, first,
by the logic of 9:1-13: belonging to historical Israel
is no guarantee of salvation because God elects freely
(9:11) from among the "seed of Abraham" who will be the
"children of God" (9:7,8). But it is also excluded by
the logic of Rom 11:28f: Paul grounds his claim that
Israel is "loved for the sake of the fathers" with the
argument that "the gifts and call of God are irrevocable." In other words the fathers are significant not
as those who merited such great blessing but as those
to whom the free and irrevocable promises were made.
This is the point of the words κατὰ δὲ τὴν ἐκλογήν in
11:28. The saving intention of God for "all Israel"
accords with God's election of Abraham and his seed,
which according to 9:11,12 is based on no merit of the
fathers at all.

Therefore when Paul mentions the fathers as one of
Israel's privileges in Rom 9:5a he is not referring to
the distinction that is associated with being the
descendants of notable men highly favored by God.[49] He
is referring to a theological fact which guaranteed the
salvation of "all Israel"--albeit in a "mysterious"
(Rom 11:25) way unexpected by any of Paul's contemporaries.[50] The privilege of having "the fathers" is,
therefore, almost synonymous with the privilege of the
"covenants" and the "promises" in 9:4b. This confirms
our suggestion that Paul is not assembling in Rom 9:4,5
a set of precisely distinct prerogatives of Israel but
rather is piling up overlapping privileges all of which
point to the surety of Israel's salvation and together
create a total impact which puts the condemnation of
Paul's kinsmen (9:3) into a very paradoxical
perspective.

2.19 "And from whom is the Messiah according to the
flesh, who is God over all, blessed forever.
Amen."

This is the third and final relative clause
describing what it means to be "Israelites" (9:4a, see
note 11). Grammatically it differs from the first two
(9:4b and 9:5a) in that the relative pronoun (ὧν) is
preceded by the preposition ἐξ. Paul does not say
explicitly that the Messiah belongs to the Israelites,
but that he is "from" them. The analogies[51] to this
construction with ἐξ show that what Paul means is that
the Messiah is an Israelite, he was born of Jewish
stock.

Why does Paul change the grammar to say "from whom is the Messiah" instead of "whose is the Messiah"? It is not because the latter is theologically demeaning to the Christ, for then Paul would surely not have been able to say that the δόξα of God belongs to Israel either (9:4b). He would simply have meant that the Christ belongs to Israel in the sense that he comes from Israel and for the sake of Israel (cf Rom 15:8). In fact, Paul probably does not want us to repudiate this meaning but to see more. But what more? It seems banal for him to switch from a grammatical construction which would stress significantly that the Christ belonged to Israel for her benefit, to a bland construction which merely denotes the Christ as an Israelite. The most likely explanation of Paul's intention is that Paul saw "the fathers" standing at the beginning of Israel's history and "the Christ" standing at the culmination of that history.[52] Since he did not want merely to coordinate "the fathers" and "the Christ" ("<u>whose</u> are the fathers and <u>whose</u> is the Christ") but rather wanted to highlight the climactic character of Christ's coming, he employed a grammatical construction which indeed does have a climactic ring to it ("and <u>from</u> whom"). The fathers, at the beginning, give rise to the people of Israel; the Christ, at the end, comes <u>from</u> the people. Therefore Paul is saying far more than that the Messiah is a Jew. He is stressing that, with the coming of Christ, the privileges of Israel have reached their decisive climax. And this is true not only temporally, but also as we shall see, in a theologically qualitative sense.

The final and decisive emergence of the Christ from Israel is qualified by the phrase τὸ κατὰ σάρκα (Rom 9:5b).[53] Nowhere else in the NT does this phrase occur with τό. The effect of the τό, according to Blass/ Debrunner (section 266), is to strongly emphasize the limiting effect of the phrase.[54] Another effect of the τό is to prevent us from making κατὰ σάρκα an adjectival modifier of the masculine χριστός. The phrase is adverbial and has "the same import as the similar expression in Rom 1:3" (Murray, <u>Romans</u>, II, 6; I, 9). The Christ has sprung from Israel only in a physical, earthly sense.

It is important to detect the different accent that κατὰ σάρκα carries here than it did in Rom 9:3b ("my brothers, my kinsmen <u>according to the flesh</u>"). In 9:3b the phrase means that Paul's fellow Jews are physically his kinsmen but spiritually they are alienated from him through their unbelief. But between 9:3 and 9:4,5 a shift takes place from viewing Paul's kinsmen as

27

unbelievers under God's curse to viewing them as the privileged "Israelites" under God's blessing. The antecedent of ὧν in 9:5b "from whom" the Christ has sprung is not Paul's unbelieving contemporaries in 9:3b, but "Israelites" (9:4a), described in the most positive terms in 9:4,5a. Therefore, unlike the κατὰ σάρκα in 9:3b the τὸ κατὰ σάρκα in 9:5b does not aim to say that the Christ is akin to Israel physically but spiritually alien (due to Israel's sin). The Israel from which the Christ originated is not being viewed as sinful and unbelieving, but as the privileged and blessed people of God. There is no theological necessity for Paul to qualify Christ's descent from Israel viewed in this way. Therefore a very different line of thought must have prompted the use of κατὰ σάρκα in 9:5b.

Why then does Paul add τὸ κατὰ σάρκα? Surely the best clue to his line of thought is found in Rom 9:5c ("who is God over all, blessed forever. Amen"). The climactic privilege of the Israelites is that their Messiah is vastly greater than they had ever dreamed. Paul knows him now from the standpoint of Christian revelation as the universal Lord. He may have his human origin in Israel (τὸ κατὰ σάρκα), but he is God over all and his blessed life is eternally indestructible.55 The privileges of Israel could not come to a higher climax: the long-awaited deliverer (11:26), the savior (Lk 1:68-79) of Israel has come and he can be resisted by no one, for he is God over all. His saving purpose for his people cannot be frustrated. This is the ultimate meaning of the promise, "I will be their God and they will be my people" (cf Gen 17:7; Lev 26:12; Jer 31:33; 32:38; Ezek 37:27). The sovereign God himself (cf "Emmanuel," Mt 1:23) comes for his own. Can Israel then be lost? Rom 9:1-3 gives the answer.

2.2 The plight of Paul's kinsmen, Romans 9:1-3

Among the various problems in Rom 9:1-3 the only one we are concerned with here is the plight of Paul's kinsmen alluded to in 9:3a. It is only expressed indirectly, but it is the main point of verses 1-3. "I could wish that I myself were anathema, separated from Christ." In the LXX ἀνάθεμα (or ἀνάθημα, a classical, earlier form with no difference in meaning, TDNT, I, 354) almost always translates חֵרֶם. It can mean positively "a thing devoted to the Lord as holy" (Lev 27:28; Judith 16:19; 2 Macc 9:16; 3 Macc 3:17; cf Lk 21:5), or negatively "a thing devoted to destruction" (Num 21:3; Deut 7:26; 13:16,18; 20:17; Josh 6:17,18; 7:1,11,12; Zech 14:11). Deut 13:18 is especially helpful for showing how the meaning of ἀνάθεμα shifts from "votive offering" to "accursed thing doomed to destruction." Paul always uses the term in its negative sense of "accursed" (1 Cor 12:3; 16:22; Gal 1:8,9).

The gravity of ἀνάθεμα in Rom 9:3a is specified with the words ἀπὸ τοῦ χριστοῦ. In the NT, ἀπό can at times have an instrumental meaning (Lk 7:35; 22:45; 6:18; Acts 15:4; 20:9) in which case Paul would here be expressing his willingness to be "accursed by Christ." But three observations stand in the way of this interpretation and point to another. 1) Ἀνάθεμα is not a verbal noun and so does not explicitly contain action which must be performed by anyone. 2) The closest parallel in Paul to ἀνάθεμα εἶναι . . . ἀπὸ τοῦ χριστοῦ is 2 Thess 1:9 where those who do not know God and do not obey the gospel will pay the penalty of ὄλεθρον αἰώνιον ἀπὸ προσώπου τοῦ κυρίου.[56] The Semitic προσώπου shows that the "destruction" (which corresponds to ἀνάθεμα in Rom 9:3a) involves separation from the Lord (not excluding, of course, that the Lord himself is the avenger). 3) Our artificial chapter and verse divisions obscure the fact that, when Romans was read in the churches, 9:3 would have been heard only seconds after 8:35 which asks, "Who will separate us <u>from the love of Christ</u>?" Therefore, Paul's statement in 9:3 must be taken to mean that he "could wish"[57] to experience what 8:35-39 said the Christian never would experience: to be separated from the love of God in Christ and left under his eternal (2 Thess 1:9) wrath (Rom 5:9).

All agree that Rom 9:3 is an intense expression of Paul's love for his kinsmen according to the flesh--a love which forms the repeated backdrop of Rom 9-11 (cf 10:1; 11:14). But Paul's emotion is not the main point of Rom 9:1-5.[58] Paul's response in 9:6a to 9:1-5 is, "But it is not such that the word of God has fallen." Therefore, the point of 9:1-5 must appear to call God's word into question. But Paul's affection for Israel and Israel's privileged status do not appear to jeopardize God's word at all. Rom 9:6a demands, therefore, that we construe Paul's expressions of love in 9:1-3 as vehicles which are carrying some tremendously heavy theological and historical freight, namely, the ominous assertion: my brothers, my kinsmen according to the flesh are anathema, cut off from Christ! Paul's willingness to be cut off from Christ ὑπὲρ τῶν ἀδελφῶν μου makes sense only if Paul believes his brothers are in a plight as serious as the one he is willing to enter for their sake. Thus the words Paul chooses with which to express his love are chosen also because they express

29

(albeit indirectly and thus sensitively) the precise condition of his unbelieving kinsmen: they are anathema, separated from Christ.[59]

2.3 Summary

Rom 9:1-5 falls into two units: 9:1-3 and 9:4,5. The first describes the plight of Paul's unbelieving Jewish kinsmen, the second describes their divinely given privileges. The analysis of 9:4,5 showed that the privileges have not simply been transferred to the Church but apply in a real sense[60] to the Israel of Paul's own day, most of whom are unbelieving. The analysis also showed that the privileges taken as a whole are redemptive and eschatological, not merely theocratic and historical. They appear to guarantee the salvation of Israel. But how?

The plight of Paul's kinsmen is as dark as their privileges are bright. They are accursed, separated from Christ and thus doomed to eternal destruction (2 Thess 1:9) under the wrath of God.

Now it is clear what is at stake in Rom 9-11. Rom 9:1-5 states the problem: it appears that what God has guaranteed is in fact not happening--the end-time salvation of Israel. Has then the word--the reliability-- of God fallen, and with it the Christian hope as well?

CHAPTER THREE

THE PURPOSE THAT ACCORDS WITH ELECTION

ROMANS 9:6-13

1. Orientation

In the preceding chapter we clarified the question
Paul is trying to answer in Rom 9-11: Since Israel is
the real heir of God's promises which include personal,
eternal salvation (9:4,5), how is it that most of the
Israelites of Paul's day are accursed and cut off from
Christ (9:3)? Why are only "some" being saved (11:14)?
Has God's word fallen? We must stress very heavily that
the problem Paul is grappling with is the condemnation
of many within Israel. Most of his kinsmen are incurring "the punishment of eternal destruction and exclusion from the presence of the Lord" (2 Thess 1:9; see
Chapter Two, pp 28,29), while only "some," the remnant of
11:5, have the hope of sharing the eternal blessings of
Christ. The reason this must be stressed is that
correctly understanding Paul's question in Rom 9:1-5
will guard us from impertinent and imaginary reconstructions of the first part of his answer in 9:6-13. Many
commentators give little evidence that they are holding
Paul's precise question in view as they interpret the
first part of his answer in 9:6-13. One common result
is that Paul is made to prove things that are of no use
in answering his precise question. Consequently the
discussion of God's righteousness (9:14ff) which springs
out of 9:6-13 gets skewed in the wrong direction and the
whole theodicy[1] (9:14-23) is enveloped in a fog.

The goal of this chapter, therefore, is to keep the
problem of Rom 9:1-5 (as well as other contextual considerations) clearly in view as we try to construe
Paul's response in 9:6-13. I hope in this way to discover as precisely as possible what Paul said or implied
in 9:6-13 which brought on the accusation that he makes
God out to be unrighteous (9:14). By this means our
subsequent discussion of God's righteousness will avoid
an inappropriate dogmatic orientation and will be rooted
in the historical situation and biblical context.

Following is the division of verses I will use in
referring to the different parts of Rom 9:6-13.

6a But it is not such that the word of God has
    fallen.

b   For all the ones from Israel, these are not
Israel;
7a neither, because they are seed of Abraham, are
all children;
b   but in Isaac shall your seed be called (Gen
21:12).
8a That is, the children of the flesh, these are
not children of God;
b   but the children of promise are counted as seed.
9a For the word of promise is this: at this time I
will come
b   and Sarah will have a son (Gen 18:10,14).
10a And not only (does Sarah illustrate the point)
b   but also Rebecca,
c   who became pregnant by one man, our father Isaac.
11a For, although (Jacob and Esau) had not yet been
born
b   and had not done anything good or evil,
c   in order that the purpose of God according to
election might remain,
12a not from works
b   but from the one who calls,
c   it was said to her: the elder will serve the
younger (Gen 25:23);
13a just as it is written: Jacob I loved
b   but Esau I hated.

2. Romans 9:6a

An unacceptable "solution" to the paradox of 9:1-5
would be: God's word has fallen. Paul denies this
"solution" without stating it explicitly:[2] "It is not
such that the word of God has fallen!" (Rom 9:6a). The
"word of God" has been variously construed as God's
promises to Israel[3] (cf ἐπαγγελίας ὁ λόγος, Rom 9:9a), or
more broadly as all God's words of revelation (cf τὰ
λόγια τοῦ θεοῦ, Rom 3:2; Schlier, Roemerbrief, 290), or
more narrowly as "the proclamation of the gospel" in
Paul's ministry,[4] or as "an expression of the intention
and will of God."[5]

If we were on the right track in our interpretation
of Rom 9:1-5, each of the benefits listed in 9:4,5 has
saving, eschatological implications for Israel. Therefore, it is not just one of these things that seems to
have fallen but all of them, including the work of the
Messiah. Therefore, Paul does not assert that one of
them (e.g. the promises, or the covenants) has not
fallen but rather he chooses a broader term, namely,
"the word of God has not fallen." This is the reality
which establishes or is embodied in each of the

preceding privileges or benefits. The intention of
God, the plan of God, the revelation of God, we might
say, which found expression in all these benefits--this
has not fallen.[6]

This interpretation of "the word of God" finds
support in the probability that Rom 9:11c says positively what 9:6a says negatively. In Rom 9:11c Paul
says that God elected Jacob and not Esau "in order that
the purpose of God according to election might remain."
The remaining of God's electing purpose is the opposite
of the falling of God's word.[7] If this is so then the
λόγος of God is parallel to the πρόθεσις of God and
should be understood as an expression of God's intention
or will. In the Greek OT both the will and word of God
are said "to remain" forever: Prov 19:21, πολλοὶ
λογισμοὶ ἐν καρδίᾳ ἀνδρός, ἡ δὲ βουλὴ τοῦ κυρίου εἰς τὸν
αἰῶνα μένει. Is 40:8, τὸ δὲ ῥῆμα τοῦ θεοῦ ἡμῶν μένει
εἰς τὸν αἰῶνα (cf Is 14:24). This use of μένειν is
substantially, if not explicitly, the opposite of the
"falling" of God's word or will (cf the use of ἐκπίπτειν
of God's word with Josh 23:14; 1 Kgs 8:56; 1 Sam 3:19).
Also in the NT, the opposite of ἡ ἀγάπη οὐδέποτε πίπτει
is νυνὶ δὲ μένει . . . ἀγάπη (1 Cor 13:8,13).[8] Therefore, what has "not fallen" but has "remained" active
and effectual is God's purpose which has come to
expression throughout redemptive history in manifold
communications which may be summed up as "the word of
God."

Rom 9:6b-13 is written to support this assertion.
The support consists therefore in showing what in fact
the purpose of God has always been in his communications
with Israel. If Paul can show that God's ultimate
"purpose according to election" never included the
salvation of every individual Israelite, then the situation described in Rom 9:1-5 would not so easily[9] jeopardize God's reliability (though, of course, it might open
him to other serious charges which Paul deals with in
Rom 9:14ff).

3. The purpose of God which remains

Our aim now, therefore, is not to discuss all the
exegetical problems of Rom 9:6b-13 but to answer the
question: How does Paul conceive of this "purpose"
(9:11c) or "word" (9:6a) of God which, in spite of the
damnation (ἀνάθεμα 9:3; Cranfield, Romans, II, 457) of
many in Israel, has not fallen? Not only is this the key
exegetical question forcing itself on us from the
context; it is also of tremendous doctrinal

33

significance. The issue of how Paul understood divine
election and predestination is inescapable, and it
surfaces precisely in the interpretation of ἡ κατ'
ἐκλογὴν πρόθεσις (Rom 9:11c). What exactly is this
purpose which "remains" and has not "fallen"?

It would be fitting in one sense to give a brief
sketch of the argument in Rom 9:6b-13 at this point, so
that our discussion of 9:11c could be oriented within
the near context from the outset. But I opt not to do
this because such a brief sketch would have to assume
the results of numerous smaller exegetical decisions
and would thus prejudice the reader too quickly for or
against the conclusions of the following discussions.
I will assume instead that the text has been carefully
read and that the gist of the argument relating to
Isaac/Ishmael and Jacob/Esau is in mind.

3.1 God's means of maintaining his purpose:
predestination

Rom 9:11-13 is one sentence.[10] The clauses in
11ab are genitive absolutes which stand in an adversative relation to the main clause of 12c: "although
they had not yet been born, nor had done anything good
or evil . . . it was said to [Rebecca]: The elder [Esau]
will serve the younger [Jacob]." The clause in 9:11c,
on the other hand, gives the aim or purpose of God in
making this prediction before the birth of Esau and
Jacob, namely, "in order that the purpose of God
according to election might remain." The divine words
"The elder will serve the younger" (from Gen 25:23),
must, therefore, be more than a wish or even a statement of foreknowledge. If these words have as their
aim (ἵνα) to secure and establish God's purpose, then
they must express a decision on God's part to intervene
in the lives of Jacob and Esau in such a way that those
words come true. The word pre-destine is an apt
description of the divine act expressed in the words
"The elder shall serve the younger." It is an act of
predestination because it happened "before Esau and
Jacob had been born or had done anything good or evil"
(9:11ab). It is an act of predestination (rather than
pre-recognition) because by means of it (ἵνα) the
purpose of God according to election remains rather
than falls (9:11c). No matter how one conceives of the
distinction God will actually make between Esau and
Jacob, it is clear that he has pre-determined what that
distinction will be; that is, he has decided and
promised so to act that the distinction will definitely
come about.

That the destinies of Esau and Jacob were pre-determined was sufficiently proven by the words μήπω γὰρ γεννηθέντων (Rom 9:11a). But Paul wants to say more about this determination than that it took place before the birth of Esau and Jacob. Hence he adds μηδὲ πραξάντων τι ἀγαθὸν ἢ φαῦλον (9:11b). With this additional clause Paul is not stressing that God's determination of Esau's and Jacob's future is prior to their behavior (that was already said in 9:11a), but rather that it is not based on their behavior.

That this is the point of 9:11b is confirmed by the phrase οὐκ ἐξ ἔργων ἀλλ' ἐκ τοῦ καλοῦντος in 9:12ab. G. Stoeckhardt[11] argues that this twofold phrase modifies the following clause: "it was said to her not from works but from the one who calls." H.A.W. Meyer,[12] on the other hand, argues that the twofold phrase must modify the preceding μένῃ: "that the purpose of God according to election might remain not from works but from the one who calls." Alford (II, 407) and Sanday and Headlam (Romans, 245) reject the dilemma and make the phrase "a general characteristic of the whole transaction." The differences among the three views are not substantial. The sentence, "The elder will serve the younger" (Rom 9:12c), is a historical expression of the purpose of God according to election (9:11c). Therefore, if one (9:12c) is οὐκ ἐξ ἔργων, the other (9:11c) must be also. What we have then in the phrase "not from works but from the one who calls" (9:12ab) is an enlargement of the point made in 9:11b "though they had not done anything good or evil."

It enlarges on this point in two ways. First, with the use of the preposition ἐξ Paul makes explicit that God's decision to treat Esau and Jacob differently is not merely prior to their good or evil deeds but is also completely independent of them. God's electing purpose (Rom 9:11c) and his concrete prediction (9:12c) are in no way based on the distinctives Esau and Jacob have by birth or by action. This rules out the notion of the early Greek and Latin commentators that election is based on God's foreknowledge of men's good works.[13] Second, Rom 9:12b enlarges on 9:11b by going beyond the negation of human distinctives as the ground for God's predestining of Esau and Jacob. It makes the positive affirmation that the true ground of this election is God himself, "the one who calls." The intended force of the phrase "not from works but from the one who calls" is felt most strongly when one contrasts it with the similar Pauline phrase "not from works but from faith."[14] In Paul's thinking the latter phrase

35

describes the event of __justification__ (Rom 9:32; Gal
2:16), never the event of election or predestination.
Paul never grounds the "electing purpose of God" in
man's faith. The counterpart to works in conjunction
with election (as opposed to justification) is always
God's own call (Rom 9:12b) or his own grace (Rom 11:6).
The predestination and call of God precede justification
(Rom 8:29f) and have no ground in any human act, not
even faith. This is why Paul explicitly says in Rom
9:16 that God's bestowal of mercy on whomever he wills
is based neither on human __willing__ (which would include
faith) nor on human __running__ (which would include all
activity).

So far then we may say that the prediction of Rom
9:12c ("the elder will serve the younger") is an
expression of God's predetermination of (at least some
aspect of) the destinies of Jacob and Esau. Moreover
this predetermination is not __based on__ any actual or
foreknown distinctives of the brothers. It is based
solely on __God__ who calls. This act of predestination
is an instance of the means (ἵνα, 9:11c) God uses to
maintain (μένῃ, 9:11c) his purpose in history--a purpose
which we can now see is very aptly defined as κατ'
ἐκλογήν (9:11c). The phrase κατ' ἐκλογήν is in the
attributive position in relation to πρόθεσις and therefore functions like the κατὰ φύσιν in Rom 11:21
(Kaesemann, __Romans__, 264): it defines God's purpose as
an electing purpose, a purpose to be one who selects[15]
on the basis described in 9:11ab and 9:12ab, namely,
freely, with no constraint from or ground in human
distinctives. In short God's purpose is to be free
from all human influences in the election he performs.[16]

Excursus - The time of God's choice

Johannes Munck (__Christ and Israel__, 424)
represents those exegetes who are so eager to
protect Paul from a doctrine of predestination "as
commonly understood" that they come within a hair
of explicitly contradicting Rom 9:11,12. Munck
argues as follows, "God's choice of a founder for
his people is made in the midst of history and not
before the creation. In the example of Isaac's
sons it is in fact emphasized that the word of
promise was spoken before the two children were
born in order that God's selective purpose might
stand, based not upon deeds but upon him who
called. This election does not presuppose predestination as commonly understood, a choice by
God prior to creation. If that were the case, the

time at which knowledge of the choice was made
known would be of no significance. The announcement of the choice must be made immediately after
the decision; God's choice is determined in the
midst of history. God acts in history, decides,
and--as we shall see--makes new decisions, because,
while his intention of salvation stands, it is
achieved by constant interventions into the
changing circumstances of history."

Munck's single argument here is that if God's
choice of Jacob over Esau was made before creation
"the time at which knowledge of the choice was made
known would be of no significance." Therefore,
since Paul does ascribe significance to the time of
the announcement, the choice must have been made
"immediately" before this announcement and not
before creation. My answer to this argument is
that even if God's choice was made before creation,
the time of its announcement is significant in
Paul's context because he does not assume that his
opponents agree that God's decision to bless Jacob
over Esau was prior to their birth and their deeds.
Whether or not Paul thought God's choice was made
before creation he must make clear to his Jewish
opponents that the decision was before the birth
of Jacob and Esau and therefore independent of
their works. To do this he pointed out that the
announcement of God's decision happened before
they were born. Therefore, even if Paul conceived
of God's predestining choice as taking place before
creation, the timing of its announcement is
significant in the present context.

But we can say more about Munck's position.
There is no reason to agree with him that "the
announcement must be made immediately after the
decision." In fact on close inspection Munck's
view implies a relationship between God and history
which at least implicitly (if not explicitly)
contradicts Paul's meaning in Rom 9:11,12. Munck
admits that the choice of Jacob over Esau (to be
founder of Israel) was prior to their birth and
therefore undetermined by their own character and
deeds. But for some reason he will not allow that
God's choice of Jacob for this role was made before
creation: "God's choice is determined in the midst
of history" (my emphasis; this seems also to be the
position of H.H. Rowley in The Biblical Doctrine of
Election, 130). This must mean that, while the
"willing and running" (Rom 9:16) of Jacob and Esau

did not determine God's choice, the "willing and running" of some other person or persons did. The "good or evil deeds," i.e. the works, of some persons or societies must have maneuvered history into the condition which resulted in God's choice being determined in favor of Jacob. I can see no other way to construe Munck's words without forcing him ultimately to put God's choice prior to creation, which he is loath to do.

But does this conception of God's relationship to history accord with Paul's meaning in Rom 9:11,12? Surely Paul does not intend to say that God's electing purpose will remain so long as God's choices are based not on the works of the persons chosen but on the works (the willing and running) of their predecessors in human history! For the opposite of "not from works" (Rom 9:12a) is not "but from the ebb and flow of historical circumstance" (which is nothing but the complex sum of men's willing and running); but rather the opposite of "not from works" is "but from the one who calls," namely God alone. This seems to me to be a clear antithesis to Munck's view implied in the sentence, "God's choice is determined in the midst of history."

To be sure Paul is not trying to prove that God's decision was made before creation.[17] He wants to prove that it is free from and not determined by the will and acts of men. The time of God's choice is significant only as it affects the ground of his choice. Paul established the latter (God's free, self-determination) and left the former, so far as it is necessary to discuss, for his readers to infer. I would probably not quarrel with a theologian who found a way to put the time of God's electing decision within history while keeping it wholly free from human determination.

3.2 Predestination of whom to what? Individuals versus nations, eternal destinies versus historical tasks

We may now take the next step in clarifying how Paul conceives of the "purpose" (Rom 9:11c) or "word" (9:6a) of God which has not "fallen" but "remains" in spite of the fact that many of Paul's kinsmen according to the flesh are accursed and cut off from Christ (9:3). The clarifying question that must now be posed is this: If, as we have seen (p 36), God's purpose is to perform his act of election freely without being determined by

38

any human distinctives, what act of election is intended
in Rom 9:11-13--an election which determines the eternal
destiny of individuals, or an election which merely
assigns to individuals and nations the roles they are to
play in history? The question is contextually appropriate and theologically explosive.[18] On one side,
those who find in Rom 9:6-13 individual and eternal
predestination are accused of importing a "modern
problem" (of determinism and indeterminism) into the
text, and of failing to grasp the corporateness of the
election discussed.[19] On the other side, one sees in
the text a clear statement of "double predestination" of
individuals to salvation or condemnation and claims that
"the history of the exegesis of Rom 9 could be described
as the history of attempts to escape this clear observation" (Maier, Mensch und freier Wille, 356). The
exegetical and theological controversy on how to interpret the election of Rom 9:11 is as early as the art of
NT exegesis. K.H. Schelkle has gathered relevant material
from the early church fathers.[20] We will not rehearse that
discussion here. Erasmus[21] on one side, Luther[22] and
Calvin[23] on the other, represent the reformation controversy.[24] Among modern scholars the list of those who
see no individual predestination to eternal life or
death is impressive.[25] Sanday and Headlam (Romans,
245), for example, take the position that "the absolute
election of Jacob . . . has reference simply to the
election of one to higher privileges, as head of the
chosen race, than the other. It has nothing to do with
their eternal salvation. In the original to which St.
Paul is referring, Esau is simply a synonym for Edom."
Similarly G. Schrenk (TDNT, IV, 179) says on Rom 9:12,
"The reference here is not to salvation, but to position
and historical task, cf the quotation from Gen 25:23 in
v 12: 'The elder shall serve the younger.'" And
finally J. Munck (Christ and Israel, 42) argues that
"Romans 9:6-13 is therefore speaking neither of individuals and their selection for salvation, nor of the
spiritual Israel, the Christian church. It speaks
rather of the patriarchs, who without exception became
founders of peoples."

The list of modern scholars on the other side is
just as impressive.[26] For example, John Murray (Romans,
II, 19) argues that "the interpretation which regards
the election as the collective, theocratic election of
Israel as a people must be rejected and the 'purpose of
God according to election' will have to be understood
as the electing purpose that is determinative of and
unto salvation and equivalent to that which we find
elsewhere (Rom 8:28-33; Eph 1:4; 1 Thess 1:4 et al)."

On the larger context (including Rom 9:16) Henry Alford (II, 408f) writes, "I must protest against all endeavors to make it appear that no inference lies from this passage as to the salvation of individuals. It is most true that the immediate subject is the national rejection of the Jews: but we must consent to hold our reason in abeyance if we do not recognize the inference that the sovereign power and free election here proved to belong to God extend to every exercise of his mercy-- whether temporal or spiritual . . . whether national or individual."

It is a remarkable and telling phenomenon that those who find no individual predestination to eternal life in Rom 9:6-13 cannot successfully explain the thread of Paul's argument as it begins in Rom 9:1-5 and continues through the chapter. One looks in vain, for example, among these commentators for a cogent statement of how the corporate election of two peoples (Israel and Edom) in Rom 9:12,13 fits together in Paul's argument with the statement, "Not all those from Israel are Israel" (9:6b). One also looks in vain for an explanation of how the pressing problem of eternally condemned Israelites in Rom 9:3 is ameliorated by Rom 9:6-13 if these verses refer "not to salvation but to position and historical task." I have found the impression unavoidable that doctrinal inclinations have severely limited exegetical effort and insight--not so much because the answers of these exegetes are not my own, but because of the crucial exegetical questions that simply are not posed by them. In what follows, therefore, I will try to keep before me the crucial contextual questions of how Rom 9:6-13 hangs together both in itself and with what precedes (9:1-5) and follows (9:14-23).

3.21 Restating the argument for corporate election to historical tasks

The basic argument against seeing individual, eternal predestination in Rom 9:6-13 is that the two OT references on which Paul builds his case do not in their OT contexts refer to individuals or to eternal destiny, but rather to nations and historical tasks. The argument carries a good deal of force, especially when treated (as it usually is) without reference to the logical development of Paul's argument in Rom 9:1-13. In describing this interpretation of Rom 9:6-13 we will keep the OT contexts before us.

40

In Rom 9:6b-9 Paul cites two OT texts: 6b) "For all the ones from Israel, these are not Israel; 7a) neither, because they are seed of Abraham, are all children; 7b) but in Isaac shall your seed be called (Gen 21:12). 8a) That is, the children of the flesh, these are not children of God; 8b) but the children of promise are reckoned for seed. 9a) For the word of promise is this: At this time I will come 9b) and Sarah will have a son (Gen 18:10,14)." The quotation of Gen 21:12 is identical to the LXX which renders the Hebrew literally (cf also Heb 11:18). The quotation in verse 9 is a combination of Gen 18:10 and 14.

The two texts come from the story of Isaac's relationship to Ishmael as Abraham's seed. In Gen 12:1-3 and 13:15f, God promised Abraham that he would have innumerable descendants who would be a "great nation." In Gen 15:4 God told Abraham that Eliezer his slave would not be his heir but "your own son shall be your heir" and "Abraham believed the Lord" (15:6). But in Gen 16 Abraham undertakes to solve the problem of his wife's barrenness by having a son by Hagar, her Egyptian handmaid. When Hagar was pregnant with Ishmael the Lord promised her, "I will so greatly multiply your descendants that they cannot be numbered for multitude . . . Behold you are with child, and shall bear a son; you shall call his name Ishmael; because the Lord has given heed to your affliction. He shall be a wild ass of a man, his hand against every man and every man's hand against him, and he shall dwell over against all his kinsmen" (Gen 16:10-12).

Then in Gen 17 God makes a covenant with Abraham, the essence of which is, "I will establish my covenant between me and you and your descendants [seed] after you throughout their generations for an everlasting covenant, to be God to you and to your descendants [seed] after you . . . and I will be their God" (Gen 17:7,8). Then, to Abraham's dismay, God says that Sarah will have a son to inherit this covenant promise. Abraham pleads, "O that Ishmael might live in thy sight!" (17:18). But God answers, "No, but Sarah your wife shall bear you a son and you shall call his name Isaac. I will establish my covenant with him as an everlasting covenant for his descendants [seed] after him. As for Ishmael, I have heard you; behold, I will bless him and make him fruitful and multiply him exceedingly; he shall be the father of twelve princes, and I will make him a great nation. But I will establish my covenant with Isaac, whom Sarah shall bear you at this season next year" (Gen 17:19-21).

41

This promise concerning Isaac is reaffirmed in Gen
18:10,14 in spite of Sarah's skepticism about her own
and Abraham's age: "Is anything too hard for the Lord?
At the appointed time I will return to you, in the spring,
and Sarah shall have a son" (= Rom 9:9). Later, after
the birth of Isaac, Abraham is distraught at Sarah's
intention to banish Hagar and Ishmael. But God reas-
sures him with the words, "Whatever Sarah says to you,
do as she tells you, for in Isaac shall your seed be
called" (Gen 21:12 = Rom 9:7b).

Concerning Ishmael God promises again in 21:13,18
to make him a great nation. In Gen 21:20 we read that
"God was with the lad, and he grew up; he lived in the
wilderness, and became an expert with the bow." Finally,
in Gen 25:12-18 Ishmael's descendants are listed to
show that the promises concerning him were fulfilled:
twelve princes had come from him (Gen 25:16 = 17:20)
and "he dwelt over against all his people" (25:18 =
16:12).

In general the commentators who find no predestination to eternal life in Rom 9:6-13 interpret Paul's
use of Gen 21:12 and 18:10,14 as follows. Gen 21:12,
introduced in Rom 9:7b with ἀλλά, gives the OT alternative to the view denied by Paul in Rom 9:7a, namely,
that because a person is a physical descendant of
Abraham he is by virtue of that descent a "child" who
will benefit from the covenant promises. It is evident,
Paul says, from the patriarchal narrative[27] that even
though Ishmael was just as much a physical descendant
of Abraham as Isaac, nevertheless God chose Isaac (even
before he was born) and not Ishmael to be the beneficiary of the covenant promises (Gen 17:21). God did
promise to make Ishmael a great nation (Gen 16:10;
21:13,18), but never said to him, "I will be your God"
(Gen 17:7,8), or "I will give you the land of your
sojournings" (Gen 17:8). By this election of Isaac
instead of Ishmael God shows that physical descent from
Abraham does not guarantee that one will be a beneficiary of the covenant made with Abraham and his seed.
Something more must be true about a physical descendant
if he is to be an heir of the covenant.

What that something more is is described in Rom
9:8,9. One must be a "child of promise" (9:8b) not
just a "child of the flesh" (9:8a). A child of promise
is a descendant of Abraham whom God freely designates
by his own sovereign design to be a beneficiary of the
covenant promises. The miraculous birth of Isaac by
the Lord's free exercise of power ("Is anything too hard

for the Lord! . . . I will come!" Gen 18:14 = Rom 9:9)[28]
illustrates that God is free in designating the beneficiaries of his promises; he is never trapped into making
any particular physical descendant (like Ishmael) the
heir of his covenant.

But, the interpretation continues, the covenant
blessings for which Isaac is freely chosen (before his
birth) and from which Ishmael is excluded (in spite of
descendancy from Abraham) do not include individual,
eternal salvation. One cannot legitimately infer from
Rom 9:7-9 that Ishmael and his descendants are eternally
lost[29] nor that Isaac and his descendants are eternally
saved. What God has freely and sovereignly determined
is the particular descendant (Isaac) whose line will
inherit the blessings of the covenant: multiplying
exceedingly, fathering many nations, inhabiting the
promised land and having God as their God (Gen 17:2-8).
This benefit, not eternal salvation, is what is not
based on physical descent from Abraham, but on God's
unconditional election.

Before criticizing this interpretation we will
follow it on through Rom 9:10-13. Rom 9:10-13 are
necessary to buttress the argument for God's freedom in
9:7-9 because of a possible loophole in that argument.
It is possible that Paul's opponents (who apparently
think physical Jewishness is the basis for being blessed
by God)[30] would say: Of course Ishmael was excluded
from the covenant; for one thing his mother was an
Egyptian (Gen 21:9) and for another the promises made
about Isaac in Gen 17:21; 18:10,14; 21:12 were all made
after the birth of Ishmael so that God could see what
sort of person he was.[31] So since he was a "wild ass
of a man" (Gen 16:12) and had an Egyptian mother, God
rejected him and chose Isaac. Now we are all legitimate, full-blooded heirs of Isaac and so may count on
God's covenant blessing.

Therefore, to demonstrate that they have not yet
grasped the significance of God's free and sovereign
election, Paul presents his opponents with another OT
illustration to close the loophole in the first one.
The birth to Isaac and Rebecca of their twin sons,
Jacob and Esau, was announced to Rebecca in Gen 25:23,
"Two nations are in your womb, and two peoples, born of
you, shall be divided; the one shall be stronger than
the other, the elder shall serve the younger."[32] How
it became possible for Jacob and his descendants to
gain the ascendancy over Esau and his descendants, even
though the right of primogeniture belonged naturally to

43

Esau, is described in Gen 25:29-34 and Gen 27:18-29.
In the first passage Esau "despised his birthright"
(v 34) and sold it to Jacob for a bowl of pottage. In
the second passage Jacob tricks Isaac into giving him
the blessing of the first-born--a blessing which
included the words, "Be lord over your brothers and may
your mother's sons bow down to you" (27:29). Thus in
the lives of Jacob and Esau the conditions were met for
the fulfillment of the promise concerning their descendants, the nations Israel and Edom.

Paul's purpose in referring to God's choice of
Jacob over Esau is to show that there is no way to evade
the implications of God's unconditional election here.
Unlike Isaac and Ishmael, Jacob and Esau had the same
parents who were both Jews ("From one man Rebecca became
pregnant," Rom 9:10c). Also unlike Isaac and Ishmael,
when the determining promise was made concerning Jacob
and Esau (Rom 9:12c = Gen 25:23), both were yet unborn
and had done nothing good or evil (Rom 9:11ab). Moreover they were twins in the same womb at the same time
and by all human standards the elder Esau should have
received the blessing of headship over his brother.
Here there are no loopholes. God's choice of Jacob over
Esau cannot be due to any human distinctives possessed
by birth (like Jewishness) or action (like righteousness). It is based solely on God's own free and
sovereign choice.

But again, as with the election of Isaac, it is
argued that "the absolute election of Jacob . . . has
reference simply to the election of one to higher
privileges as head of the chosen race, than the other.
It has nothing to do with their eternal salvation"
(Sanday and Headlam, Romans, 245).[33] In fact "the story
of the reconciliation of Esau with Jacob [Gen 33] makes
the strong impression that Esau had now taken the right
attitude toward God" (Stoeckhardt, Roemer, 430).[34] The
stress in this interpretation falls very heavily on the
fact that in Gen 25:23, which Paul cites in Rom 9:12c,
peoples not individuals are chosen. One cannot therefore, it is argued, infer anything about the election
of individuals from God's unconditional election of
Israel over Edom to be his covenant people.

The quote from Mal 1:2 ("Jacob I loved but Esau I
hated," Rom 9:13) is taken to confirm this view, since
the hate of Esau is illustrated in Mal 1 by God's
historical judgments upon Edom the people, not by God's
eternal condemnation of Esau the individual. The
context of Mal 1:1-4 is important:

1) The burden of the word of Yahweh to <u>Israel</u> in the hand of Malachi. 2) "I loved you," says Yahweh. Yet you say, "Wherein did you love us?" "Was not <u>Esau Jacob's</u> brother?" says Yahweh, "but I <u>loved Jacob</u>, 3) and <u>Esau</u> I hated. And I made his mountains a desolation and appointed his inheritance to the jackals of the wilderness. 4) For <u>Edom</u> says, 'We are beaten down but we shall return and rebuild the waste places.'" Thus says the Lord of hosts, "They shall build but I will throw down, and they shall be called the border of wickedness and the people with whom the Lord is angry forever."

The prophet's logic is very similar to Paul's. God's love for Jacob/Israel is not grounded in Jacob's or Israel's superiority over Esau/Edom. Rather Yahweh asks rhetorically: "Was not Esau Jacob's brother?" The implication of this question is that there was no basis in human distinctives for Yahweh to love Jacob and hate Esau. His choice was made solely on the basis of free grace.[35] This is what makes the quotation of Mal 1:2 so apt in Rom 9:13. Some take the term hate in a softened sense of "loved less" or "did not prefer."[36] Others argue from Mal 1:4 that it must involve real animosity and opposition.[37] But what is crucial for this interpretation is not the meaning of hate but the meaning of Esau as Edom and the fact that the different destinies for Jacob/Israel and Esau/Edom are historical and not necessarily eternal. Therefore, Paul teaches the sovereign freedom of God in determining which of Isaac's sons will be the beneficiary of the covenant promises and procreate the nation which will enjoy so many of God's earthly privileges. But Paul does not teach here that God exercises that same unconditional election toward individuals and eternal life.

3.22 Critique of the foregoing position and argument for an alternative

A plausible case can be made for the position that "Paul is no longer concerned with two peoples and their fate but rather in a permanent way with the election and rejection of two persons [Jacob and Esau] who have been raised to the level of types" (Kaesemann, <u>Romans</u>, 264). I think this is probably true and that there is warrant in the patriarchal narratives themselves for drawing conclusions about the individual salvation of Isaac and Jacob. But I will not try to prove this because the decisive flaw in the collectivist/historical

45

position is not its failure to agree with Kaesemann's
contention. Its decisive flaw is its failure to ask how
the flow of Paul's argument from 9:1-5 on through the
chapter affects the application of the principle Paul
has established in Rom 9:6b-13. The principle established is that God's promised blessings are never
enjoyed on the basis of what a person is by birth or by
works, but only on the basis of God's sovereign, free
predestination (Rom 9:11,12). The ultimate decision of
who will experience God's grace or mercy is never based
on a person's "willing or running" (Rom 9:16). We may
grant, for the sake of the argument, that in the demonstration of this principle of God's freedom in election
Paul uses OT texts that do not relate explicitly to
eternal salvation.[38] What cannot be granted without
further argumentation is that Paul intends for this
principle of God's predestining freedom to be limited
to God's choice of persons or nations for historical
roles. Paul establishes from OT texts that God chooses
the beneficiaries of his promised blessing apart from
all human distinctives. But it is an unwarranted leap
to infer against the context of Rom 9 that this principle applies when the promised blessing at stake is
"theocratic blessing" or a "historical role" but does
not apply when the promised blessing is personal,
eternal salvation (as Paul views it in Rom 4:13; Gal
3:14,16). To show that in fact this inference is
against the context of Rom 9 is the goal of what
follows.

3.221 The significance of Romans 9:1-5

As we said at the beginning of the chapter, to
understand Paul's precise intention in Rom 9:6-13 we
must keep in view that these verses are an initial
attempt to solve the problem raised in 9:1-5, namely
that many within the elect nation of Israel are accursed
and cut off from Christ. Many individual Israelites
within the chosen people are not saved (cf Rom 11:14).
Paul is not moved to constant grief (9:2) because
corporate Israel has forfeited her non-salvific "theocratic privileges" while another people (the Church or
the remnant) has taken over this "historical role." He
is grieved because all the privileges of Israel listed
in Rom 9:4,5 imply the eschatological, eternal salvation
of this people (see Chapter Two) but many individual
Israelites--his kinsmen according to the flesh--are
damned in their unbelief (see Chapter Two, note 59).
Therefore the solution which Rom 9:6-13 develops in response to this problem must address the issue of individual,
eternal salvation. John Murray and E. Weber[39] see this most

clearly of all the commentators I have read. Murray
argues as follows:

> The thesis that Paul is dealing merely with
> the election of Israel collectively and apply-
> ing the clause in question ["the elder shall
> serve the younger"] only to this feature of
> redemptive history would not meet the precise
> situation. The question posed for the
> apostle is: how can the covenant promise of
> God be regarded as inviolate when the mass of
> those who belong to Israel, who are comprised
> in the elect nation in terms of the Old Tes-
> tament passages cited above [Deut 4:37; 7:7,8;
> 10:15; 14:2; 1 Kgs 3:8; Ps 33:12; 105:6,43;
> 135:4; Is 41:8,9; 43:20-22; 44:1,2; 45:4;
> Amos 3:2], have remained in unbelief and come
> short of the covenant promises? His answer
> would fail if it were simply an appeal to the
> collective, inclusive theocratic election of
> Israel. Such a reply would be no more than
> an appeal to the fact that his kinsmen were
> Israelites and thus no more than a statement
> of the fact which, in view of their unbelief,
> created the problem. Paul's answer is not
> the collective election of Israel but rather
> "they are not all Israel, who are of Israel."
> And this means, in terms of the stage of
> discussion at which we have now arrived,
> "they are not all elect, who are of elect
> Israel" (Romans, II, 18).

3.222 The significance of Romans 9:6b

The force of this argument is increased when we
turn our focus from Rom 9:1-5 to the assertion in 9:6b,
οὐ γὰρ πάντες οἱ ἐξ Ἰσραήλ, οὗτοι Ἰσραήλ, which I translate, "For all those from Israel, these are not Israel."
For two reasons I have construed the οὐ to modify the
clause οὗτοι Ἰσραήλ rather than πάντες.[40] In the first
place the demonstrative οὗτοι refers to a definite
group of people, but the negation οὐ πάντες is very
indefinite. It does not work to say, "Not all the ones
from Israel, these are Israel." In the second place
Rom 7:15, a very close parallel to the grammatical
structure of Rom 9:6b, has οὐ in the same anterior
position as here but there it definitely modifies the second
clause: οὐ γὰρ ὃ θέλω τοῦτο πράσσω, ἀλλ' ὃ μισῶ τοῦτο
ποιῶ. The οὐ in Rom 7:15 cannot modify θέλω because
that would make Paul say: "I practice what I do not
will." But this is tantamount to what Paul says in the

47

next clause ("what I hate this I do") which is intended
to be a contrast (ἀλλ') not a repetition. Therefore
the only feasible construction of Rom 7:15 is, "What I
want, this I do not do, but what I hate this I do."
Therefore, the similarly positioned οὐ in Rom 9:6b very
probably negates the clause "these are Israel."

Also the demonstrative pronoun οὗτοι has its parallel in the τοῦτο of Rom 7:15. The force of this redundant pronoun is to put heavy emphasis on what is being
negated. Hence: "What I want, this very thing I fail
to do." And in Rom 9:6b the stress can be shown by the
translation, "For all those from Israel, these are
certainly not Israel." The impression created is that
πάντες οἱ ἐξ Ἰσραήλ was a popular catch-phrase designating those who would be the beneficiaries of the
Messianic salvation, namely, all Israelites. If this
were true then the word of God has fallen, since many
Israelites are accursed and cut off from the Messiah.
So Paul asserts emphatically these are not Israel, that
is, πάντες οἱ ἐξ Ἰσραήλ are not the group to whom salvation was assured by God's word.

This confirms Murray's argument that Paul's main
goal in Rom 9:6b-13 was not to prove that God freely
elected the nation of Israel, but rather his goal was to
establish a principle by which he could explain how
individual Israelites were accursed and yet the word of
God had not fallen. What Rom 9:6b proves is that in
Paul's mind the election of Isaac over Ishmael and Jacob
over Esau established an ongoing principle[41] whereby God
elects unconditionally the beneficiaries of his blessing
not only in the establishment of the nation Israel by
Jacob and his sons, but also within that very nation so
that "all those from Israel, these are not Israel."
Since the unconditional election of Israelites from
within (physical) Israel to be (true, spiritual) Israel
cannot be construed as an election to "theocratic
privileges" (for all physical Israel has those), and
since the immediately preceding distinction made between
some Israelites and others (Rom 9:3-5) was that some are
accursed and cut off from Christ, therefore we must
conclude that Paul views "the purpose of God according
to election" (9:11c) as a purpose to be free from human
influence not only in the determination of historical
roles but also in the determination of who within Israel
are saved and who are not.

3.223 The vocabulary and structure of Romans 9:6b-8

Further contextual evidence that Paul is thinking

48

in terms of election unto eternal salvation is found in
the vocabulary and structure of Rom 9:6b-8. The corresponding elements in the structure become clear when
printed as follows:

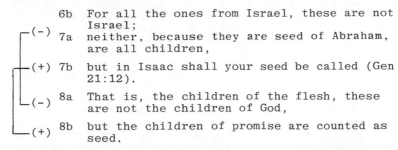

       6b For all the ones from Israel, these are not
           Israel;
(-) 7a neither, because they are seed of Abraham,
           are all children,

(+) 7b but in Isaac shall your seed be called (Gen
           21:12).

(-) 8a That is, the children of the flesh, these
           are not the children of God,

(+) 8b but the children of promise are counted as
           seed.

The "that is" of 8a introduces Paul's clarification of
what he argued in 6b-7. Verse 8 is not simply an interpretation of the OT reference in 7b (as in Rom 10:6-8),
but is a restatement and interpretation of all of 6b-7.
The evidence for this is the way 8b corresponds to 7b
and 8a corresponds to 6b and 7a. The reason we know 8a
corresponds not only to 7a but also to 6b is that the
distinctive grammatical structure of 8a is identical to
the structure of 6b (note the anterior negative particle
and the redundant demonstrative pronoun):

| 6b | οὐ | γὰρ | οἱ ἐξ Ἰσραήλ | οὗτοι Ἰσραήλ |
| 8a | οὐ | | τὰ τέκνα τῆς σαρκὸς | ταῦτα τέκνα τοῦ θεοῦ |

The intended paralleling of "all those from Israel"
with "the children of the flesh," and "these are not
Israel" with "these are not children of God" is unmistakable. The implication of this interpretative paralleling is that Paul is not abandoning his initial
concern expressed in 6b, namely, a concern with distinctions within Israel. Therefore it goes against
Paul's intention to construe "children of God" in 9:8a
to refer to persons who are "bound to God by all those
ties which have been the privilege and characteristic
of the chosen race" (Sanday and Headlam, Romans, 242).
This view not only contradicts the parallelism that
exists between "children of God" in 9:8a and a limited
group within the chosen race in 9:6b; it also contradicts Paul's uniform usage of τέκνα τοῦ θεοῦ. Every-
where else the term occurs in Paul (Rom 8:16,17,21; Eph
5:1; Phil 2:15) it refers to believers. The same is
true for the synonymous[42] phrase υἱοὶ τοῦ θεοῦ (Rom
8:14,19; 9:26; 2 Cor 6:18; Gal 3:26; 4:5).[43] Therefore,

whether Paul sees the election of Isaac (Rom 9:7b) as
the election of an individual[44] to salvation or as the
election of his posterity[45] for a historical task, the
principle[46] of unconditional election is immediately
applied by Paul to the present concern, namely, who in
reality does constitute true, spiritual "Israel" (9:6b),
whose salvation is guaranteed by God's word? If not all
physical descendants of Abraham, who are the "children
of God"?

The answer Paul gives in Rom 9:8b is "the children
of the promise are reckoned as seed." Besides the
immediate context, three other texts in Paul (Gal
3:26-29; 4:21-31; Rom 2:25-29) offer valuable evidence
for interpreting this sentence. It is clear from the
parallelism of "children of God" and "seed" in 9:8 that
"seed" here (unlike 9:7a)[47] refers to the same spiritual
group within Israel as "children of God" in 9:8a and the
second "Israel" of 9:6b. The sequence of thought in Gal
3:26-29 confirms this identification of "children of
God" and "seed of Abraham." In Gal 3:26 Paul argues
that "in Christ Jesus you are all sons of God through
faith" and concludes in 3:29, "And if you are Christ's,
then you are Abraham's seed, heirs according to
promise." This text confirms, therefore, not only the
identity of "children of God" and "seed of Abraham"
but also confirms our contention earlier that Paul's
reference in 9:8 is not to a group with theocratic or
merely historical privileges (i.e. physical Israel) but
rather to persons who are heirs of eternal salvation.

Such persons are called "children of promise"
(9:8b) as opposed to "children of flesh" (9:8a). The
term "children of promise" occurs only one other place
in Paul, Gal 4:28. Since the subject matter of the
Gal context, like the Rom context, is the implication
of the births of Isaac and Ishmael for Paul's contemporaries, it would be very unlikely that the rare term
"children of promise" would carry significantly different meanings in these two contexts.[48] In Gal 4 Paul
sees an allegorical (4:24) lesson for his contemporary
situation in the ancient fact that Ishmael "the son of
the slave [Hagar] was born according to the flesh, but
[Isaac] the son of the free woman [Sarah] was born through
promise" (4:23). Paul's application goes as follows:
"Now we, brothers, like Isaac are children of promise
(κατὰ Ἰσαὰκ ἐπαγγελίας τέκνα ἐστέ). But just as the
one born according to the flesh persecuted the one born
according to the Spirit, so it is also now" (4:28f).

The meaning of the term "children of promise" becomes clear when we compare Gal 4:23 and 4:29. In 4:23 the contrast is between the child born "according to the flesh" (κατὰ σάρκα) and the child born "through promise" (δι' ἐπαγγελίας). In 4:29 the contrast is between the child born "according to the flesh" (κατὰ σάρκα) and the one born "according to the Spirit" (κατὰ πνεῦμα). Note that "according to the Spirit" stands in the place of "through promise." Two inferences may be drawn: first, the term "children of promise" does not mean "promised children" or "children who are heirs of the promise," but rather "children born by or through promise." A "child of promise" is a child whose existence is owing to "the creative power of the divine promise."[49] Second, the term κατὰ πνεῦμα in Gal 4:29 signifies that the power of the promise is the power of the Spirit. To be born "through promise" involves being born "according to the Spirit." Thus, as Luz argues, Paul understands God's promise as a word which effects its own purpose[50] (see note 28).

Note that in Gal 4:28 Christians are "children of promise" κατὰ Ἰσαάκ. That is, the correspondence is not exact. The birth spoken of concerning Isaac was his actual physical (though miraculous) birth; the birth spoken of concerning Christians (Gal 4:29) is their conversion (their adoption through the Spirit to be sons of God, Rom 8:14). In a similar way the "children of promise" in Rom 9:8b need not correspond exactly to Isaac (9:7b).[51] But there is a real and decisive correspondence: just as Isaac was a child of promise in that God willed in advance for him to be the heir of the covenant promises and then worked sovereignly ("I will come!" 9:9) to fulfill his will, so also God wills in advance for particular individuals within Israel to be his "children" and then by his Spirit sovereignly begets them anew. Thus the principle of unconditional election, evident in God's choice of Isaac to be heir of the covenant, is applied now to Paul's contemporaries to explain how it can be that only "some" (Rom 11:14) Israelites are saved and yet the promissory word (9:6a) or purpose (9:11c) of God has not fallen. God's promissory word has not fallen precisely because it is an "electing purpose" which does not depend at all on human "willing" or "running" and which therefore irresistibly accomplishes its goal by itself alone.

Besides the immediate context and the analogous texts in Gal 3:26-29 and 4:21-29, we will look at one other text to confirm our interpretation of Rom 9:8. Rom 2:25-29 is linked to Rom 9:8 in three ways: subject

matter, vocabulary and grammatical structure. Each text
refers in its own terms to the fact that not all Israel
is Israel (9:6b) or not every Jew is a Jew (2:28). The
vocabulary link is the word λογίζομαι.[52] Rom 9:8b says
that "children of promise are counted as seed." Rom
2:26 says, "If the uncircumcised man keeps the just
requirements of the law, will not his uncircumcision be
counted as circumcision?" It is the same paradox in
both texts: being (truly) circumcised does not depend
on being circumcised; being a (true) seed does not
depend on being a seed. The saving spiritual reality
depends on a "counting" or "reckoning" which God performs, not man.[53] One final confirmation that Paul is
in fact thinking along the same lines in Rom 2:25-29
and in Rom 9:6-8 is found in the similar distinctive
grammatical constructions:[54]

Rom 2:28a	οὐ	γὰρ	ὁ ἐν τῷ φανερῷ (Ἰουδαῖος)	Ἰουδαῖός ἐστιν
28b	οὐδὲ		ἡ ἐν τῷ φανερῷ ἐν σαρκὶ (περιτομή)	περιτομή (ἐστιν)
9:6b	οὐ	γὰρ	οἱ ἐξ Ἰσραήλ	οὗτοι Ἰσραήλ
7a	οὐδ'		ὅτι εἰσὶν σπέρμα Ἀβραάμ	πάντες τέκνα
8	οὐ		τὰ τέκνα τῆς σαρκὸς	ταῦτα τέκνα τοῦ θεοῦ

We may conclude, therefore, from the logical structure of Rom 9:6b-8, its vocabulary and other analogous
texts in Paul, that Paul is by no means concerned only
with nations or merely with the historical destinies
of persons and peoples. The evidence is overwhelmingly
in favor of the view that Paul's concern is for the
eternal destinies of those within the nation Israel who
are saved and who are accursed.[55]

3.224 The significance of Romans 9:14-23

Erich Dinkler ("Praedestination," 88) is right when
he says, "In the following section, Rom 9:14-23, Paul
defends the divine election and makes clear that its
real meaning is to be seen not in the election of an
empirical people as a whole, but in the election of
individuals." Similarly Ernst Kaesemann says concerning
the view that only peoples and not individuals are in
view, "The example of Pharaoh [9:14-18] will absolutely
not allow such an understanding" (my translation of

Roemer, p 253). The detailed verification of these contentions will be presented in Chapters Nine and Ten.

3.225 Jewish antecedents of Paul's teaching

Gerhard Maier has provided a very helpful analysis of the issue of predestination and free will in a key segment of Paul's Jewish milieu. His book is entitled Mensch und freier Wille nach den juedischen Religionsparteien zwischen Ben Sira und Paulus (1971). On pages 351-81 he argues successfully for the position 1) that Paul stands within a tradition of predestination rooted in OT teachings[56] which developed through Sirach (33:7-15)[57] to its most radical form embracing individuals and salvation in Qumran (1 QS 3:15-4:26; 11:10f)[58] which offers the closest analogies to Paul's own statements; and 2) that Paul formulates his own position in Rom 9 in conscious opposition to the pharisaic insistence (expressed, e.g., in Ps Sol 9:4,5[59] but going back also to Sirach 15:11ff) that free will is a prerequisite of accountability if God is to be righteous (see note 16).

Another brief and helpful overview of the teaching on predestination and human accountability in Paul's environment is an excursus on pp 98-101 of. Erich Dinkler's essay, "Praedestination bei Paulus." Like Maier, Dinkler is impressed with the similarity between Rom 9 and Qumran on the issue of predestination. (He cites 1 QS 3:15-21; 11:7f,10f,15-22.) But Dinkler also raises the question whether perhaps the teachings of Jesus may also have given direction to Paul on this issue: "The thought of election and predestination together with an assumption of individual responsibility is found also in the proclamation of Jesus. To be sure Jesus speaks in pictures and parables and not in abstract concepts and so does not present the paradox as sharply as Paul does. Yet, as K. Stendahl ['The Called and the Chosen'] has impressively demonstrated, it can be found in sayings like Mt 22:14, 'Many are called, but few are chosen'" (101).

What is important to stress at this stage of our study is that Dinkler's survey and Maier's very plausible historical orientation of Paul's view within his own religious setting show that the interpretation of Rom 9:6-13 which I have argued for in this chapter should not be faulted as a modernizing distortion or as the result of a dogmatically tendentious exegesis which ignores the original contextual and historical realities.

53

4. Conclusion

In answer to the question how it can be that many individuals within Israel are accursed, cut off from Christ (Rom 9:1-5), Paul answers: it is not because the word of God has fallen (9:6a); on the contrary, God's expressed purpose remains firm (9:11c). The reason this situation does not mean the failure of God's word is that his purpose expressed in that word never has been to guarantee the salvation of every Israelite. It is an "electing purpose" by which God aims to preserve his complete freedom in determining who will be the beneficiaries of his <u>saving</u> promises, who will be the "Israel" within Israel (9:6b). It is therefore a purpose maintained by means of the predestination of individuals to their respective eternal destinies.

The interpretation which tries to restrict this predestination or unconditional election to nations rather than individuals or to historical tasks rather than eternal destinies must ignore or distort the problem posed in Rom 9:1-5, the individualism of 9:6b, the vocabulary and logical structure of 9:6b-8, the closely analogous texts elsewhere in Paul, and the implications of 9:14-23. The position is exegetically untenable.

Paul's solution to the problem of 9:1-5 is that "all those from Israel are not Israel" (9:6b). Within the context of Rom 9 this means that God maintains his sovereign purpose of election by determining before they are born who will belong to the "saved" among Israel. And this determination is not based on what any man is or wills or does (9:11,12,16), but solely on God whose word or call effects what he purposes (9:12b). For this reason Paul is confident that God's word has not fallen but is in fact working out God's sovereign purpose even in the unbelief of Paul's kinsmen.

CHAPTER FOUR

EXODUS 33:19 IN ITS OLD TESTAMENT CONTEXT

1. The problem

Before analyzing in detail the structure of Rom
9:14-18 (see Chapters Five and Nine) it is necessary to
make a foray into OT exegesis. In Rom 9:14 Paul denies
that anything he has said implies unrighteousness in
God. Then in 9:15 he writes, "For to Moses [God] says,
'I will have mercy on whomever I have mercy and I will
have compassion on whomever I have compassion.'" There
is a lot of disagreement about how Paul understands
this quotation from Ex 33:19.

M. Lagrange (Romains, 233) argues that Paul construes the quotation as a particular act of mercy
toward Moses rather than a general principle about God's
activity: "The authentic reading, τῷ Μωϋσεῖ γὰρ λέγει,
puts the person of Moses in stronger relief than if
Paul had said, τῷ γὰρ Μωϋσεῖ λέγει, which could have
passed for a simple citation. According to Juelicher
and Kuehl Moses is viewed as the legislator to whom God
revealed his plan. But the contrast with Pharaoh [Rom
9:17] shows rather that Moses is of interest here for
his own person. If anyone would be able, by his admirable virtues, to weigh heavily in the divine balances,
it would be Moses. But it is precisely to him that God
says: ἐλεήσω ὃν ἂν ἐλεῶ..."[1] On the other side
Heinrich Schlier (Roemerbrief, 295) contends that "Paul
ignores the [OT] context and...raises the sentence to a
general self-expression of God concerning the fact and
right of his own decision." Others, of course (e.g.
Calvin, Romans, 204), agree that the quotation is a
general principle but deny that this ignores the OT
context. Finally some argue that the point of the
quotation for Paul is that in it he found "the proclamation of Yahweh's name"[2]--a fact which takes on
special importance when one notices that the word to
Pharaoh in Rom 9:17 also aims at proclaiming God's
"name." In deciding which, if any, of these interpretations is how Paul understands Ex 33:19, a necessary
first step is to try to understand the OT text on its
own terms. This, together with a subsequent analysis
of Paul's own context, will, we hope, enable us to
decide how Paul used this OT quotation in Rom 9:15 and
whether that use accords with the OT meaning itself.

55

Since I want to interpret the same text Paul did,
my focus will not be on the history of the traditions
behind the canonical text,[3] but rather on the final
form of the text in its present context. But I also
want to avoid, as far as I can, reading Paul's theology
into Ex 33:19. Thus I agree with August Dillmann
(Exodus, 385) when he says, "The use of the expression
['I will have mercy on whom I have mercy and I will have
compassion on whom I have compassion'] in Rom 9:15
cannot determine its meaning in its original [OT] context." Accordingly my primary goal in this chapter is
to discover the meaning of Ex 33:19 in its present OT
context.

2. The text

The context of Ex 33:12-34:9 is crucial for understanding Ex 33:19 and therefore merits a careful
reading at the outset. Following is my own translation
of the Hebrew with the most significant renderings of
the LXX in parentheses.

33:12a And Moses said to Yahweh, "Behold, you say to
        me, 'Cause this people to go up' [from Sinai
        to the promised land, cf 33:1],
   12b but you do not make known to me whom you will
        send with me [cf 32:34; 33:2; 23:20].
   12c And you said to me, 'I know you by name (MT:
        בְשֵׁם; LXX: παρὰ πάντας, cf 17c)
   12d and also you have found favor in my sight.'
   13a Now, please, if I have found favor in your
        sight,
   13b then cause me to know, please, your way (MT:
        דְּרָכֶךָ; LXX: σεαυτόν)
   13c so that I will know you,
   13d in order that I might go on finding favor in
        your sight.
   13e And behold that this nation is your people"
        (LXX: ἵνα γνῶ ὅτι λαός σου τὸ ἔθνος τὸ μέγα
        τοῦτο).
   14a And he [Yahweh] said, "My presence (MT: פָּנַי ;
        LXX: αὐτός = I myself) will go,
   14b and I will give you [singular] rest."
   15a And [Moses] said to him, "If your presence
        (LXX: αὐτὸς σύ) does not go,
   15b then do not cause us (LXX: με) to go up from
        this place.
   16a For how shall it then be known (LXX: adds
        ἀληθῶς) that I have found favor in your
        sight, I and your people?
   16b Is it not in your going with us that we, I

56

and your people, are distinguished (MT:
וְנִפְלֵינוּ ; LXX: ἐνδοξασθήσομαι) from every
people which is on the face of the earth?"
[cf 34:10].

17a And Yahweh said to Moses, "Even this word
     which you spoke I will do,
17b because you found favor in my sight
17c and I know you by name" [cf verse 12c].
18   And he [Moses] said, "Cause me to see your
     glory."
19a And he [Yahweh] said, "I will cause to pass
     before your face all my goodness. (MT: טוּבִי ;
     LXX: δόξῃ μου)
19b And I will proclaim the name Yahweh before
     you [cf 34:5f].
19c And I will be gracious to whom I will be
     gracious (MT: וְהַנֹּתִי אֶת־אֲשֶׁר אָחֹן ; LXX: καὶ
     ἐλεήσω ὃν ἂν ἐλεῶ);
19d and I will be merciful to whom I will be
     merciful" (MT: וְרִחַמְתִּי אֶת־אֲשֶׁר אֲרַחֵם ; LXX: καὶ
     οἰκτιρήσω ὃν ἂν οἰκτίρω).
20a And he [Yahweh] said, "You will not be able to
     see my face
20b because a man will not see me (LXX: πρόσωπόν
     μου) and live."
21   But Yahweh said, "Behold there is a place by
     me and you shall stand on the rock.
22   And it shall be that as my glory passes by I
     will put you in the cleft of the rock and
     will cover you with my hand until I have
     passed by;
23   and I will remove my hand, and you will see
     my back, but my face shall not be seen."
34:1-4 (omitted: Moses ascends Mount Sinai with
        newly cut tablets to meet Yahweh)
5a   And Yahweh descended in a cloud and he stood
     with him there,
5b   and he proclaimed the name of Yahweh (MT: =
     33:19b וַיִּקְרָא בְשֵׁם יְהוָה ; LXX: ἐκάλεσεν τῷ
     ὀνόματι κυρίου).
6a   And Yahweh passed before his face [cf
     33:19a,22]
6b   and proclaimed, "Yahweh, Yahweh (LXX: only
     one κύριος), a God merciful and gracious [cf
     33:19cd], slow to anger and abounding in
     steadfast love and faithfulness (MT: וְרַב־חֶסֶד
     וֶאֱמֶת ; LXX: πολυέλεος καὶ ἀληθινὸς),
7a   keeping steadfast love (MT: חֶסֶד ; LXX:
     δικαιοσύνην) unto thousands,
7b   forgiving iniquity, rebellion and sin.
7c   But he shall not leave completely unpunished

(MT: וְנַקֵּה לֹא יְנַקֶּה; LXX: οὐ καθαριεῖ τὸν
ἔνοχον),

7d visiting the iniquity of the fathers upon the
sons and upon the sons' sons, upon the third
and upon the fourth" (LXX: adds γενεάν).

8   And Moses hastened and bowed his head to the
ground and worshipped.

9a And he said, "If now I have found favor in
your sight, O Lord,

9b then may the Lord go in our midst.

9c For (MT: כִּי ; LXX: γάρ) it is a stiff-necked
people [cf 33:5] ,

9d but you shall forgive our iniquities and our
sins,

9e and you shall take us for an inheritance"
(MT: וּנְחַלְתָּנוּ ; LXX: ἐσόμεθα σοι).

It is probably pointless to try to decide whether
Paul was familiar with this passage in the Hebrew or
the Greek, for he no doubt "knew both the Massora and
the Greek translation."[4] To be sure Rom 9:15 is
identical to the Greek version of Ex 33:19cd, but as
S.R. Driver (Exodus, 363) says, "The quotation (from
the LXX) in Rom 9:15 expresses the sense [of the Hebrew]
exactly." What this sense is I will examine more
closely below, but first let us orient ourselves in the
wider context.

3. The context of Exodus 32-34

Brevard Childs (Exodus, 557f) provides a concise
description of the larger literary unit in which our
text is found. Concerning Ex 32-34 he writes,

First of all, the chapters have been placed
within an obvious theological framework of sin
and forgiveness. Chapter 32 recounts the
breaking of the covenant [the golden calf
incident] ; ch 34 relates its restoration.
Moreover, these chapters are held together
by a series of motifs which are skillfully
woven into a unifying pattern. The tablets
[of the ten commandments] are received, smashed
in ch 32, recut, and restored in ch 34.
Moses' intercession for Israel begins in ch
32, continues in ch 33, and comes to a climax
in ch 34 [verses 9,10] . The theme of the
presence of God which is the central theme of
ch 33 joins, on the one hand, to the prior
theme of disobedience in ch 32, and, on the

58

other hand, to the assurance of forgiveness in ch 34 [verses 6,9] .

In Ex 32:9f God accused Israel of being a stiff-necked people and told Moses, "Let me alone that my wrath may burn hot against them and I may consume them." Moses pleads with God not to destroy the people because, on the one hand, the Egyptians would then gloat over their demise and ascribe evil intent to Yahweh (32:12, cf Num 14:15f) and, on the other hand, God swore by his own self to Abraham, Isaac, and Israel that their descendants should inherit the promised land (32:13). So God relents from the intention to fully destroy Israel (32:14) and chastises them with slaughter by the sons of Levi (32:25-29).

Then again Moses pleads with God to forgive the sin of Israel: ". . . and if not, blot me, I pray thee, out of thy book which thou hast written" (32:32). God responds that each man will bear his own sin (32:33) and that Moses should go ahead and lead the people to the promised land (32:34; 33:1). But Moses still did not have from God the promise he wanted, for God said, "I will not go up with you, lest I consume you on the way, for you are a stiff-necked people. . .if for a single moment I would go up with you, I would consume you" (33:3,5). Instead of his own presence in their midst God promises that his angel will go before them (32:34; 33:2). Moses is still not satisfied with Yahweh's concession. After the reference to Moses' communion with Yahweh in the tent of meeting outside the camp (33:7-11),[5] Moses takes up his intercession for the people again in 33:12, where our text begins.

4. The context of Exodus 33:12-34:9

Ex 33:12-34:9 has a twofold theme. On the one hand there is Moses' prayer that God himself go up to the promised land in the midst of Israel his people (33:12b,13e,15-16; 34:9). On the other hand there is Moses' prayer to know God and to see his glory (33:13a-c,18)--a prayer which is answered in 34:5-7 with the theophany atop Mt. Sinai. The relationship between these two themes in 33:12-34:9 is the key to understanding this literary unit.

Moses had pursued God relentlessly on behalf of idolatrous Israel ever since the incident of the golden calf. Now in 33:16 we see what he is truly seeking. His aim is that God himself go up with the people, but not only that. He desires that the people be restored

to God's full favor (16a) and that God distinguish
Israel as his own unique people from all the peoples on
the face of the earth (16b). In the end God does
restore the covenant and he promises to do just what
Moses asked (34:10; 33:17).

Moses was aware of what a positive response to his
request would involve. He was asking that a stiff-
necked and idolatrous nation be distinguished above all
the nations as God's own people! It was, in a sense,
an unthinkable request in view of what God had said in
33:5--"You are a stiff-necked people; if for a single
moment I should go among you, I would consume you." It
is precisely the apparent presumption of Moses' prayer
which demanded the second theme of 33:12-34:9, namely
Moses' desire to know God's way and his glory
(33:13,18). In other words, the magnitude of his
request drives Moses to probe into the very heart of
God, as it were, to assure himself that God is in his
deepest nature the kind of God who could "pardon our
iniquity and our sin, and take us for [his] inheritance"
(34:9de). Moses is not yet content with God's promise
in 33:17a, "Even the word which you spoke I will
do."[6] He responds with the plea, "Cause me to see your
glory." In view of 1) the following verse, which
relates the revelation of this glory to God's goodness
and his mercy, and 2) its fulfillment in 34:5-7 in
terms of God's moral character, and 3) the inference
which Moses draws in 34:9, it is impossible to construe Moses' request in 33:18 as an expression of a
desire mystically to enjoy God's essence. Rather the
request to see God's glory should be understood in this
context as a desire to have God confirm his astonishing
willingness to show his favor to a stiff-necked, idolatrous people (33:16f).[7] The confirmation is to consist
in a revelation of that glory which is the ground or
source of such great mercy (cf Section 6.3).

It is clear then that the theme of God's accompanying Israel and distinguishing her above all the nations
and the theme of God's personal revelation to Moses are
intimately related. The final proof of this is in 34:9
where, after having received the revelation of God's
name (34:5-7), Moses repeats his earlier request that
God would go up in their midst. Then, as if to stake
everything on the mercy that had just been revealed, he
grounds this request with the words "for[8] it is a stiff-
necked people." In view of the mercy, grace, love,
faithfulness and forgiveness declared in 34:6, Moses is
emboldened to call on God to demonstrate his great mercy
on Israel precisely because she is in need of mercy as

a stiff-necked people. Moses exploits the grace of God
to the full and lets it shine in all its freedom in
that he appeals to no merit in the people or in himself[9]
and to no extenuating circumstances; but rather he
expresses his certainty[10] that on the basis of God's
promise (33:17) and his revealed nature (34:6-7) the
sins of Israel will be forgiven and God will make
Israel his own personal inheritance (34:9de). Moses'
anxiety, therefore, about the future of Israel is
resolved through a personal revelation of God as a God
who is merciful and gracious. Who God is grounds the
assurance of how he will act.[11] With this general
picture of the OT context before us we may now attempt
to determine the specific meaning of Ex 33:19cd.

5. The grammar and vocabulary of Exodus 33:19cd

J.P. Lange (Exodus, 141) translates Ex 33:19c "I
have been gracious (or) am gracious to whom I will be
gracious" and comments on the sentence thus: "It
distinguishes two periods of time . . . Accordingly the
Hebrew expression affirms: 'My grace is in such a
sense consistent and persistent that wherever I show
it, it is based on profound reasons belonging to the
past.'" Lange's translator quite rightly calls this
translation and comment "singularly infelicitous," for
"the two verbs [וְחַנֹּתִי and אָחֹן] in the Hebrew are both
future [i.e. imperfect] (the first made such by the Vav
Consecutive[12]), so that Lange's statement, that the
text 'distinguishes two periods of time'. . . conveys a
misrepresentation." It is not necessary that there be
any particular reference to time in the imperfect and
converted perfect tenses of 33:19cd. This "tense" in
Hebrew can refer to past, present or future action; the
emphasis falls not on the time but on the incomplete-
ness of the action.[13] Whether we construe the verbs
to refer on the one hand to a specific act of grace in
the future--say, to Moses in the theophany of 34:5-7--
or on the other hand to the general principle by which
God always dispenses grace, will depend on how we
relate verse 19cd to 19b. (See Section 6.)

Brevard Childs (Exodus, 596), J.P. Hyatt (Exodus,
317) and S.R. Driver (Exodus, 362) among others have
pointed out that to understand the intention of Ex
33:19cd one must recognize that it is an example of the
Hebrew formula called idem per idem. Other examples of
the idiom are Ex 4:13 ("I pray, Lord, send now by the
hand you will send"); Ex 16:23 ("Bake what you will
bake, boil what you will boil"); 1 Sam 23:13 ("They
went about where they went about"); 2 Sam 15:20 ("Shall

I make you go with us while I go where I go"); 2 Kgs
8:1 ("Sojourn where you sojourn"). By leaving the
action unspecified the force of this idiom is to preserve the freedom of the subject to perform the action
in whatever way he pleases. By simply repeating the
action without adding any stipulations the idem per
idem formula makes clear that the way the action is
executed is determined by the will of the subject within
the limits of prevailing circumstances. Therefore when
God says, "I will be gracious to whom I will be gracious
and I will be merciful to whom I will be merciful," he
is stressing that there are no stipulations outside his
own counsel or will which determine the disposal of his
mercy and grace. As Childs (Exodus, 596) says, "The
circular idem per idem formula of the name--I will be
gracious to whom I will be gracious--is closely akin to
the name in Ex 3:14--I am who I am--and testifies by
its tautology to the freedom of God in making known his
self-contained being."

This understanding of the grammatical construction
of 33:19cd coheres with the vocabulary of the propositions, namely the basic meaning of grace and mercy.
Against K.W. Neubauer, Walther Zimmerli argues that
God's graciousness (חנן) is always a free gift rather
than a kind of social obligation between lord and
servant.[14] H.J. Stoebe (THAT, I, 595) confirms this
view of God's freedom in being gracious by pointing
out that while grace is often a response to man's
plight and plea (cf Ps 4:2; 6:3; 9:14; 27:7; 30:11;
41:5 etc) nevertheless (as the "perhaps" of Amos 5:15
and 2 Sam 12:22 shows) God remains sovereignly free in
his decision to bestow grace or not.

Given the nature of Hebrew parallelism and the
stereotyped character of the pair, "be gracious (חנן)
and show mercy (רחם)" (Ex 34:6; Joel 2:13; Jon 4:2;
Ps 86:15; 103:8; 111:4; 145:8; 2 Chron 30:9; 2 Kgs
13:23; Is 27:11; 30:18 etc), we should not demand a
major distinction in meaning between the two halves of
Ex 33:19cd.

Nevertheless, by way of confirmation one could
note the following use of רחם ("show mercy").
In Is 54:8,10 and Lam 3:32 "the proclivity of
God to show חֶסֶד ('loving kindness') is
apparently the precondition of his actual
bestowal of mercy (רחם)" (THAT, II, 766). Now
this might seem to diminish the freedom of
God in the bestowal of his mercy since the
concept of חֶסֶד is often construed to grow out

of the covenant between God and Israel and
thus express mutual obligations of both partners. For example, Bultmann (TDNT, II, 479)
says, "In the OT חֶסֶד denotes an attitude of
man or God which arises out of a mutual relationship . . . The reciprocity of the חֶסֶד
obligation is the content of the covenant
(1 Sam 20:8)."[15] But in his article on חֶסֶד
in THAT, I, 615, H.J. Stoebe argues from Deut
7:7-9 as follows: "The observation that
hesed is behavior that results from the
covenant is formally correct, but too narrow.
Precisely in the older parts of Deuteronomy
bᵉrīt is subordinated to God's oath to the
fathers and is thus anchored in a free decision of Yahweh and has a promissory character. Even here in Deut 7:8 the love of God
is given precedence and in general 'hb, 'love,'
has become equivalent to hesed . . ." Therefore God's חֶסֶד (and the "mercy," רחם, which
flows from it), understood in its most fundamental sense, precedes and grounds the
covenant rather than vice versa. It is that
which moved God in his sovereign freedom to
graciously initiate a relationship with
Israel. If this חֶסֶד is the only precondition of God's "bestowing mercy" (רחם) then
it too, along with the bestowal of grace
(חנן), is owing solely to the sovereignty
of God.

Therefore both the grammar (idem per idem) and the
vocabulary (grace and mercy) of Ex 33:19cd cohere to
stress that in dispensing mercy and grace God is
dependent on nothing but his own free and sovereign
choice.

6. The glory, goodness and name of Yahweh in relation
   to Exodus 33:19cd

6.1 We turn now to the relationship between Ex 33:19cd
and the preceding clauses of verses 18 and 19: "And
[Moses] said, 'Cause me to see your glory.' And [Yahweh]
said, 'I will cause to pass before your face all my
goodness (טוּבִי ; LXX: δόξα), and I will proclaim the
name of Yahweh before you, and I will be gracious to
whom I will be gracious and I will be merciful to whom
I will be merciful.'" The commentators are divided on
how to construe the relationship between the revelation
of God's name (19b) and the declaration that he will be
gracious to whom he will be gracious (19c). Keil and

Delitzsch (Pentateuch, II, 237) represent one group when they assert, "The words . . . וְחַנֹּתִי [19cd], although only connected with the previous clause by the copulative waw, are to be understood in a causative sense, as expressing the reason why Moses' request was granted, viz that it was an act of unconditional grace and compassion on the part of God, to which no man, not even Moses, could lay any just claim" (so Noth, Exodus, 258, and Beer, Exodus, 159). Brevard Childs and George Bush argue persuasively against this interpretation, replacing it with the view that 19cd does not ground the revelation of God's name to Moses but rather interprets the essence of the name. There are basically two arguments. First, Childs (Exodus, 596, 563) points out the parallel between the idem per idem formula here and the same formula in Ex 3:14 where it interprets the name of Yahweh. Second, and this seems to me decisive, Bush points out that the very same pair of words ("be gracious" and "show mercy") used in 19cd is used in 34:6 as an explication of the name of Yahweh: "And Yahweh passed before his face and proclaimed: 'Yahweh, Yahweh, a God merciful and gracious . . .'" Bush (Notes, I, 239) is therefore correct in concluding that "the meaning [of 33:19b-d] is: 'I will proclaim myself in passing by thee as the Lord whose prerogative it is to be gracious to whom I will be gracious and to have mercy upon whom I will have mercy. This shall be the substance of what I will proclaim respecting the import of that great and fearful name.' The clause [verse 19cd] thus understood is therefore a mere brief compend of the more expanded declaration in ch 34:6,7."[16]

The parallels between the promise of theophany in 33:19ff and its fulfillment in 34:5-7 can be taken a step farther.[17] Not only does the pair, grace and mercy, define Yahweh's name in 33:19 and 34:6, but even the indefiniteness of the idem per idem formula of 33:19 is preserved in the peculiar content of the formulation[18] of God's character in 34:6,7. Its peculiarity and indefiniteness are seen when we contrast it with its close parallel in Ex 20:5,6.

Ex 20:5,6	Ex 34:6,7
I the Lord your God am a jealous God, visiting the iniquity of the fathers on the children, on the third and the fourth generations of those who hate me, but showing steadfast love to	Yahweh, Yahweh, a God merciful and gracious, slow to anger and abounding in loving kindness and faithfulness, keeping steadfast love to thousands, forgiving iniquity and rebellion

thousands, <u>to those who love me and keep my commandments</u>.

and sin, but he shall not leave completely unpunished,[19] visiting the iniquity of the fathers upon the sons and upon the sons' sons, upon the third and upon the fourth generation.

The two basic differences between these two versions are ones that link 34:6,7 very closely to 33:19cd. First the order: unlike Ex 20:5,6, in Ex 34:6,7 the declaration of grace <u>precedes</u> that of judgment and is expanded sixfold. Thus the stress is put on grace. This recalls 33:19cd where <u>only</u> grace and mercy are mentioned (it does not say "I will visit iniquity upon whom I will visit iniquity"). Second, 34:6,7 omits all reference to the character of those who are shown mercy and those who are punished.[20] Ex 20:5,6 specifies these as "those who love me" and "those who hate me," but 34:6,7 remains indefinite (cf Ps 99:8). This indefiniteness corresponds perfectly to the indefiniteness of the <u>idem per idem</u> formula of 33:19cd. These parallels thus provide further confirmation of Bush's comment above that Ex 33:19cd "is a mere brief compend of the more expanded declaration in ch 34:6,7." Accordingly there is good ground for construing 33:19cd as an explication of the name of Yahweh (verse 19b), that is, of "his self, his real person."[21]

6.2 Continuing our effort to understand the relationships between the propositions in Ex 33:18,19 we now pose the question how the name of Yahweh (19b), which has been defined as his sovereign freedom in dispensing grace (33:19cd; 34:6f), relates to the "goodness" of Yahweh in 19a and the "glory" of Yahweh which Moses asked to see (18) and which Yahweh promises will pass by (22a). The texts we must keep before us are the following:

Ex 33:18,19

And [Moses] said, "Cause me please to see your glory." And [Yahweh] said, "I will cause to pass before your face all my goodness, and I will proclaim the name of Yahweh before you, and I will be gracious to

Ex 34:5,6

And Yahweh descended in a cloud and stood with him there and he[22] proclaimed the name of Yahweh. And Yahweh passed before his face and proclaimed: "Yahweh, Yahweh, a God merciful and gracious, whom I will be gracious, and I will be merciful to whom I will be merciful." slow to anger and abounding in steadfast love and faithfulness, keeping steadfast love unto thousands, forgiving iniquity, rebellion and sins . . ."

At least two facts suggest that the "goodness" of Yahweh in 33:19a is a moral rather than an aesthetic[23] ("goodliness") term and that as such it is virtually tantamount to Yahweh's name in this context. First, the immediate sequence between "I will show my goodness" and "I will proclaim my name" leads us to think that God's "goodness" is part of this "proclamation" and thus not a visible manifestation. Second, there is a very close parallel between the promise of 33:19 and the fulfilment of 34:6:

Ex 33:19ab   Ex 34:6ab

I will cause to <u>pass</u> <u>before</u> your <u>face</u> all my goodness— and I will <u>proclaim</u> the name of <u>Yahweh</u> . . .

Yahweh <u>passed before</u> his <u>face</u>

and <u>proclaimed</u> <u>Yahweh</u>, <u>Yahweh</u> . . .

In this parallel Yahweh himself has taken the place of the promised goodness, but nothing is said here of a visible appearance of Yahweh.[24] Instead he "passes by" in the sense that his character or essential nature is made known to Moses in a personal encounter (34:5) and in the proclamation of his name. Herein then consists the "passing by" of God's goodness, namely in the revelation of his person or his name in terms of mercy, grace, steadfast love and forgiveness (34:6). This is confirmed by numerous texts where God's "goodness" consists in his steadfast love (חסד) and mercy (רחם): Ps 86:5; 145:9; Is 63:7 and many others cited in THAT, I, 663.

6.3 How then, we may ask next, does the name of God, revealed in the "passing by" of his goodness and the revelation of his free grace, relate to his glory which Moses asked to see in 33:18? I have argued earlier (pp 60,61) that Moses' request in 33:18 was prompted by the amazing willingness of God, expressed in 33:17, to take a stiff-necked, idolatrous people and distinguish them as those on whom his favor rests (33:16). Therefore, while Moses' plea to see God's glory probably included a hope for some visible manifestation (cf

33:20-23)[25] nevertheless what was clearly at the heart
of Moses' request was a longing to know the glory of
God's character from which flowed the mercy which he
had just been promised. As the succeeding verses show
it is precisely this moral aspect of God's glory which
is revealed to Moses (33:19; 34:6,7) while the visible
aspect is minimized (33:20-23). Therefore, when we
consider carefully the larger context of Ex 33:12-34:9
we are inclined to construe the manifestation of God's
glory as embracing the "passing by" of his goodness and
the proclamation of his name.

A broad lexical study of the name (שֵׁם) and glory
(כָּבוֹד) of God in the OT supports this conclusion.
Jonathan Edwards in his Dissertation Concerning the End
for Which God Created the World (first published in
1765) demonstrated clearly that "God's name and his
glory, at least very often, signify the same thing in
Scripture."[26] A.S. van der Woude in his article on שֵׁם
(name) in THAT, II, 958, comes to the same conclusion.[27]

7. Conclusion

Ex 33:19cd ("I will have mercy on whom I have
mercy, and I will have compassion on whom I have compassion"), as a brief, preliminary declaration of the
verbal theophany which follows in 34:6,7, constitutes
a manifestation of God's glory (33:18), a "passing by"
of his goodness (33:19a) and a proclamation of his
name (33:19b). These three realities overlap in the
present context so that we can say God's glory and his
name consist fundamentally in his propensity to show
mercy and his sovereign freedom in its distribution.[28]
Or to put it more precisely, it is the glory of God and
his essential nature mainly to dispense mercy (but also
wrath, Ex 34:7) on whomever he pleases apart from any
constraint originating outside his own will. This is
the essence of what it means to be God. This is his
name.

Therefore, with regard to the varying views
referred to in Section One of this chapter we may say
the following. In its OT context, Ex 33:19 is not
merely a description of how God acted in any particular
instance toward Moses in granting him a theophany or
toward Israel in renewing the covenant. Rather it is a
solemn declaration of the nature of God, or (which is
the same thing) a proclamation of his name and glory.
So the view of Luz, Mueller and Maier (see note 2) that
Paul saw in Ex 33:19 a paraphrase of God's "name" is
surely most in accord with the OT context. Does the

67

<u>Pauline</u> context bear this out? And if so, how does Rom 9:15 argue for the righteousness of God?

CHAPTER FIVE

THE JUSTIFICATION OF GOD: ROMANS 9:14-18
PART I

1. The text and the problem

9:14a   What then shall we say?
    b   There is no unrighteousness with God, is there?
    c   By no means!
  15a   For to Moses he says, I will have mercy on
              whomever I have mercy,
    b   and I will have compassion on whomever I
              have compassion.
  16a   Therefore, it is not of the one who wills nor
          of the one who runs
    b   but it is of God who has mercy.
  17a   For the Scripture says to Pharaoh: "For
              this very thing I raised you up:
    b   that I might demonstrate by you my power
    c   and that my name might be proclaimed in all
              the earth."
  18a   Therefore, on whom he wills he has mercy
    b   and whom he wills he hardens.

        The surface structure of Rom 9:14-18 is fairly
simple.   In his customary manner Paul raises a possible
objection to what he has just said, denies the objection
and gives reasons for the denial.[1] The reasons for his
denial of the conclusion that God is unrighteous are given
in two OT quotations, each introduced by γάρ (15,17). After
each of these quotations an inference is drawn (ἄρα οὖν,
16,18) about the way God acts in his righteousness.
But as soon as a reader probes beneath this surface
structure to the inner logic of Paul's thought, things
are not so readily clear.   The main problem is <u>how</u> the
quotations of Ex 33:19 (Rom 9:15) and Ex 9:16 (Rom 9:17)
help Paul answer the objection that God is unrighteous.
As we shall see, numerous commentators think that in
fact these quotations do not provide any argument for
9:14 and that, therefore, Paul was not even trying to
answer the objection.   But before we can address this
chief issue, we must clarify for ourselves just what
objection is raised in Rom 9:14.   What had Paul said
that for his opponent implied that God is unrighteous?   And what view of righteousness lay behind the
opponent's objection?   Does Paul share this view of
God's righteousness?

2. "There is no unrighteousness with God, is there?"
   (Romans 9:14b)

The grammatical form of this question creates a
difficulty and yet signals a solution for understanding
the word "unrighteousness." The question is expressed
in a form which expects a negative answer (μή instead
of οὐκ). Therefore, the difficulty is created that, on
the one hand, the question is supposed to reflect an
opponent's objection (why else even raise the problem?)
but, on the other hand, Paul's opinion rather than the
objector's comes to expression in the question. Paul,
not the opponent, expects the negative answer. In the
closest analogy to Rom 9:14 Paul does the very same
thing: Rom 3:5, "If our unrighteousness confirms the
righteousness of God, τί ἐροῦμεν; μὴ ἄδικος ὁ θεός ...;
... μὴ γένοιτο." Here again the ostensible objection
to Paul's theology is phrased in words which reflect
his own attitude rather than the opponent's. In fact
every place in Paul where μὴ γένοιτο answers a question
stated in a negative form, the negative used in the
question is μή (Rom 3:3f,5f; 9:14f; 11:1,11). We may
conclude, therefore, that a typical rhetorical device
of Paul is to introduce his opponent's objections in a
form which already contains Paul's denial. Perhaps by
this means Paul aims to keep his lips free from words
which he considers blasphemous and thus avoids having
to always insert κατὰ ἄνθρωπον λέγω after stating an
opponent's view.[2]

The recognition of this formal device helps us now
to understand the meaning of ἀδικία (9:14b). It alerts
us to the possibility that ἀδικία is carrying two
meanings: the opponent's and Paul's. In other words,
since Paul has not recorded the opponent's objection
with stenographic fidelity but has expressed it in a
form revealing his own position, we would not be sur-
prised if the ἀδικία which Paul denounces in 9:14
involves aspects of his own concept of divine righteousness which may be different from his opponent's.

The safest way to decide what in Rom 9:6-13 had
appeared unrighteous to Paul's opponent is to determine
the link between 9:6-13 and Paul's response to the
opponent in 9:14-18. That is, if Paul is responding to
an objection to something he said in 9:6-13, we would
expect that in his response he would refer to whatever
it was that caused the offense. In fact this is just
what he does. In 9:16 Paul draws the conclusion from
Ex 33:19 that when a person receives mercy he owes it
neither to his willing nor his running but wholly to

God who has mercy. This virtually restates the assertion of 9:11,12, that the divine choice of Jacob over
Esau was before they were born or had done any good or
evil so that God's electing purpose might remain not
from works but wholly from God who calls. Nor is this
the only link; also 9:18 ("he has mercy on whomever he
wills and he hardens whomever he wills") unmistakably
recalls, "Jacob I loved and Esau I hated" (9:13). We
will not be far off, therefore, if we infer that the
offense in 9:6-13 which evoked the charge of divine unrighteousness is Paul's assertion that God, in determining the beneficiaries of his mercy, does not base
his decisions on any human distinctives that a person
may claim by birth or effort. Therefore, the view of
divine righteousness which the objection presupposes is
that a righteous God must elect persons on the basis of
their real and valuable distinctives, whether racial
(Jewishness) or moral (keepers of the law).[3] On this
assumption God would indeed be unrighteous to elect
Jacob over Esau "before they were born or had done anything good or evil."

If Paul shares his opponent's conception of divine
righteousness, then no defense is possible. He can
protest as he wills, but by definition the radical
freedom Paul ascribes to God in election is in fact
unrighteous. But on the face of it, at least, Paul
does seem to try to defend the righteousness of God (cf
γάρ in 9:15,17). Thus we recall an earlier point,
namely, that in framing the question, "there is no unrighteousness with God, is there?" Paul may well
ascribe to ἀδικία a meaning different from his opponent's.[4] If so the peculiar references to Ex 33:19
(= Rom 9:15) and Ex 9:16 (= Rom 9:17) might have more
integrity as <u>arguments</u> than is often thought. Can we
find help here by analyzing the wider use of ἀδικία in
Paul?

Excursus - Ἀδικία in Paul

The word occurs in Rom 1:18,29; 2:8; 3:5;
6:13; 9:14; 1 Cor 13:6; 2 Cor 12:13; 2 Thess
2:10,12; 2 Tim 2:19. What appears from these
texts is that ἀδικία is not merely the opposite of
δικαιοσύνη (Rom 3:5) but is also the opposite of
"truth" (ἀλήθεια). Ἀδικία, therefore, is a
disposition and conduct which contradicts truth,
particularly the truth about God, namely, that he
is glorious above all creation and worthy of all
honor, thanks, and trust. The person whose life

71

does not conform to this truth is in the grip of ἀδικία.[5]

The term appears twice in 2 Thess 2:9-12 where the final appearance of the "Lawless One" and of Christ is described. The Lawless One will come "in all deception of unrighteousness (ἐν πάσῃ ἀπάτῃ ἀδικίας) to those who are perishing, because they did not receive a love of the truth that they might be saved. On account of this God sends to them a working of deceit that they might believe a lie in order that all who do not believe the truth but delight in unrighteousness (εὐδοκήσαντες τῇ ἀδικίᾳ) might be judged." Here the opposite of "believing the truth" is "taking pleasure in unrighteousness." And the "deceit" of the Lawless One which draws men away from a love of the truth is called "deceit of unrighteousness." We may infer, therefore, that ἀδικία necessarily includes deception and thus contradicts truth (about God in the gospel, cf 2:13).

According to Rom 1:18 "the wrath of God is revealed from heaven against all ungodliness and ἀδικίαν of men who hold down the truth in ἀδικίᾳ." Unrighteousness is a disposition to reject and conceal the truth that God is worthy to be glorified and thanked above all creation (1:21). It is the power that inclines a person "to exchange the truth of God for a lie and worship and serve the creature above the creator" (1:25).

In Rom 2:6-8 the last judgment is described: "God will render to each according to his works: to those who in the patience of good work seek glory and honor and immortality (he will give) eternal life; but to those who from vain ambition disobey the truth but obey ἀδικίᾳ he will give wrath and fury." Here again ἀδικία is the opposite of truth--the truth that selfish ambition is folly and that a happy future can be found only in the glory and honor of the creator. In the grip of ἀδικία a person "holds down" this truth, and exalts himself, thus dishonoring his maker. His conduct contradicts the truth about God.

In 1 Cor 13:6 Paul says that love "does not rejoice in ἀδικίᾳ but rejoices together in the truth." Love is humble and is not driven by the "selfish ambition" (Rom 2:8) which distorts and "holds down the truth" (Rom 1:18). Therefore,

72

love is a friend to truth and delights to bring
its own actions into accord with reality. But
this means it can take no pleasure in "unrighteousness" because unrighteousness, as we now see, is a
disposition and conduct which contradicts reality--
the reality of God.

Finally, the parallel sentences of Rom 3:4-7
confirm this understanding of ἀδικία and provide
us with a bridge to move from the human to the
divine righteousness. Verses 5 and 7 are parallel.
Verse 5 begins, "If our ἀδικία confirms the
δικαιοσύνην of God. . ." while verse 7 begins, "If
the truth of God abounds to his glory in my falsehood . . ." Therefore, the person who is guilty
of ἀδικία is living a lie (ψεύσματι, 3:4,7). And
the righteousness of God is his truth, his unswerving commitment always to bring his actions
into accord with the reality of his infinitely
worthy glory (see Chapters Six-Eight). Precisely
in this context the closest NT parallel to Rom
9:14b is found, namely Rom 3:5b: μὴ ἄδικος ὁ
θεός. This is virtually synonymous with μὴ ἀδικία
παρὰ τῷ θεῷ (9:14b).

I conclude, therefore, that the particular
usage of ἀδικία seen in 2 Thess 2:10,12; Rom 1:18;
2:8; 3:5; 1 Cor 13:6 is very probably the one Paul
has in view in Rom 9:14. If so, his assertion would be that God cannot be faulted with a
disposition or conduct that contradicts the truth
of who he is.[6] This truth is that he is infinitely
glorious and worthy of all honor and thanks (Rom
1:21). God is totally devoted to uphold and
display this truth in all his actions.[7] If he
failed to act in this way he would be unrighteous.
This, I suggest, is what Paul asserts when he says,
"There is no unrighteousness with God."

3. The defense of God's righteousness in predestination

We concluded in Chapter Three that in Rom 9:6-13
Paul teaches that God predestines individuals to their
respective eternal destinies. The unconditionality of
this election is judged by Paul's opponent to be
unrighteous because when a righteous God makes his
choices he must take into account the things that distinguish one person from another. As we have just
seen, Paul does not share the opponent's narrow view of
God's righteousness. If he did, he would indeed have
to acknowledge that there is unrighteousness with God.

73

But instead it appears that Paul undertakes in 9:14-18 to exonerate God from the charge of unrighteousness. But is this in fact his intention?

It may be more a symptom of our own anti-rational age than the result of sound exegesis that an outcry against "Theodicy" echoes through the contemporary treatments of Rom 9. The titles of the books by Beyschlag, Kuehl, and Weber are virtually unthinkable today.[8] One of the most forceful spokesmen against construing Rom 9:14ff as a theodicy is Anders Nygren (Romans, 365):

> The whole matter under discussion is how the righteousness of God . . . is manifested; and in such there is no place for unrighteousness. But in Paul's "By no means!" there is a more fundamental fact. Paul does not merely answer the question with a negative. He denies the propriety of the framing of the question.
>
> The question asked comes quite close to the traditional issue in theodicy. It is of interest to see how Paul by his answer completely rejects the issue. Otherwise we should have expected that, when the question was raised, he would have presented an array of arguments to defend the righteousness of God. But there is not a trace of that in Paul. We get the impression that the problem of theodicy does not even exist for him--and that for good reasons. For there is a basic fault in all that concerns theodicy: it measures God by human standards. But when man sets out to judge God's dealings by man's own standards, the results cannot be other than the conclusion that God's goodness is faulty.
>
> Paul proceeds in a wholly different manner. When he is faced with the question of the justice or injustice of God's dealings, he does not enter at all on any argument on the level of that issue. He simply disallows the question.

For Nygren, then, the γάρ introducing Rom 9:15 merely connects Paul's "rejection of the issue" (9:14) with an OT text which shows that the unconditional election of

9:11-13 "is in entire harmony with the way God has always acted" (366).

Following in his train are Althaus,[9] Plag,[10] Kaesemann,[11] Kuss,[12] Kuemmel,[13] and others. Among this group Johannes Munck (Christ and Israel, 44) makes the most sweeping statement:

> Paul answers by pointing out that God's pro-
> cedure here is witnessed to in Scripture
> which says that God has mercy on whomever he
> wills. Therefore, it cannot be said that
> Paul gives a negative answer to the question
> in v 14 [!]. Both here and later Paul rejects
> the objections made by his opponents. It is
> therefore incorrect to designate the fol-
> lowing passages as Paul's theodicy. A
> defence of God cannot be drawn up within
> early Christian theology, not even in answer
> to Jewish opponents.

In all these protests against theodicy two factors seem to be at work: 1) the exegetical difficulty of con-struing Rom 9:15-18 as a compelling ground for 9:14, and 2) the theological conviction that all attempts by men to justify God are wrong because, as the Reforma-tion stressed (RGG[3] VI, 742), it is man, not God, who is in the dock, and God should not be measured by human standards.

First some brief comments on the second factor: yes and no. Yes, man is in the dock as a guilty sinner before God. But a guilty man does not and should not cease to exercise his judgment concerning the various advocates who offer him their help. To be sure he is in no position to be arrogant or presumptuous, but if he is to act as a man (and as the Scripture expects him to act) he must think about the reliability of the different lawyers and make a judgment as to who is most trustworthy. Therefore, the propriety of raising the question of God's righteousness is not excluded by man's dire condition as a sinner.

Also yes, God should not be measured by human standards, if by "human standards" is meant standards distorted by sin or standards which derive their appropriateness from man's creatureliness. To be sure some of the guiding values which men have are evil through the deceitfulness of sin, and some attitudes and actions are appropriate for creatures but not for the creator (and vice versa). But the very fact that

we are aware of this and agree with it shows that man
is capable of approving standards which are not
typically "human." He is capable of recognizing that
God is not a creature and that this may have radical
consequences for the meaning of righteousness in his
case. In other words it is not unthinkable or unbiblical that a humble, honest person, through a process
of sober reflection on the realities observable in the
world and through Scripture, should conclude that God
has done what he should do in the act of unconditional
election. It is of little concern to me whether one
calls this process of humble, sober reflection
"theodicy."[14] What is of great concern is that in our
haste to deny that Paul was a Leibniz[15] we not distort
him into an anti-rational twentieth-century existen-
tialist. For in doing this we may blind ourselves to
the exegetical realities of the text.

This leads us to the other factor at work in the
frequent protests against theodicy, namely, the difficulty of construing Rom 9:15-18 as a compelling argument for 9:14. At least on the surface of 9:14-18
there is no evidence for Nygren's and Munck's assertion
that Paul "disallows the question" or "rejects the
issue." Mueller (Gottes Gerechtigkeit, 84) is right
that "Paul does not forbid the Jew . . . the right to
speak; nor does he rebuke him for presumptuousness."
The frequent denial that in 9:15ff Paul aims to defend
the position taken in 9:14 fails to do justice to the
text,[16] at least to the surface structure of the text
in which 9:15 is joined to 9:14 by γάρ.[17]

But the real stumbling block is not the surface
structure but the content of the verses. How is it an
argument to say: God is not unrighteous in election
because he says to Moses, I will have mercy on whomever I have mercy? Varying attempts have been made to
make the argument work. Origen's view, in which he was
followed by Diodore, Theodore of Mopsuestia and
Chrysostom, was that 9:15-18 were the words of Paul's
opponent who used the OT quotations in 9:15,17 to
deduce assertions (9:16,18) which Paul then rejected
in 9:19ff.[18] This is no longer taken seriously since
it is scarcely discernible from the text and contradicts Paul's normal technique (see note 17). Pelagius
gave the γάρ its full force but threw away the Pauline
meaning of 9:11-13 so that there was no reason to
object in the first place. Following some early
rabbinic exegesis (see note 3) he translates 9:15 "I
will have mercy on the one whom I foreknow will deserve
mercy, so that I have already had mercy on him"

(Schelkle, Lehrer der Vaeter, 344). Charles Hodge
(Romans, 312) represents a much more widely held view
(cf Stoeckhardt, Roemer, 434) when he appeals simply
to the authority of Scripture:

> It will be remarked that these arguments of
> the apostle are founded on two assumptions.
> The first is, that the Scriptures are the
> Word of God; and the second, that what God
> actually does cannot be unrighteous. Con-
> sequently any objection which can be shown
> to militate against either an express decla-
> ration of Scripture or an obvious fact in
> providence, is fairly answered. And if, as
> is almost always the case, when it militates
> against the one, it can be shown to militate
> against the other, the answer is doubly
> ratified.

Ulrich Luz (Geschichtsverstaendnis, 74) registers a
legitimate protest that this use of the OT flies in the
face of Paul's normal use of Scripture. To be sure the
OT is authoritative for Paul, but do we not expect him
to use it to render more intelligible his denial of the
conclusion that God is unrighteous, rather than using it
to offer an authoritative repetition of the stumbling block?
Therefore, we are inclined to probe more deeply to see
whether Paul's use of Ex 33:19 (in Rom 9:15) does in
fact illuminate and support Paul's claim that God is
not unrighteous when he uses his free sovereignty in
unconditional election.

The conclusion of our exegesis of Ex 33:19 in its
OT context was that the words, "I will have mercy on
whomever I have mercy and I will have compassion on
whomever I have compassion," are a proclamation of
God's name or a manifestation of his glory which consists in his propensity to show mercy and his sovereign
freedom in its distribution (Chapter Four, p 67). There
is a prima facie case, then, for thinking that Ex 33:19
carried this same meaning for Paul and was of use to
him here for that reason. The case is strengthened by
Rom 9:17 (= Ex 9:16): "For the Scripture says to
Pharaoh, 'For this very thing I raised you up: that I
might demonstrate by you my power; and that my name
might be proclaimed in all the earth.'" The inference
Paul draws from this text is, "Whom God wills he
hardens" (Rom 9:18). Why did he not cite one of the
numerous texts from Ex in which it is actually said
that God "hardened" Pharaoh's heart? Why choose a text
in which the very word "hardening" is missing? The

probable answer will show how far off Hodge was in saying that these OT texts are cited simply to show from an authoritative record that God did in fact act in such and such a way. For the answer seems to be that Paul chose this text from Ex because his chief interest lay in the purpose clauses: "to demonstrate my power and proclaim my name" (Räisänen, Hardening, 31). As Mueller (Gottes Gerechtigkeit, 31 note 25) observes, "It is no accident that the key word ὄνομα appears also in verse 17." It is no accident because in both Ex 33:19 and Ex 9:16 Paul has found OT texts in which the exercise of God's sovereign freedom, in mercy and in hardening, is the means by which he preserves and displays the glory of his name.

This suggests strongly, then, that in Rom 9:15-18 Paul is defending the righteousness of God in predestination by referring to two OT texts which reveal that God proclaims his name (i.e. his character) and demonstrates his glorious power in the world by exercising his sovereign freedom to show mercy and to harden. The unstated premise of this argument is that when God acts righteously he must use his freedom in this way; or, to put it another way, God's righteousness consists in his unswerving commitment always to act for the glory of his name--a name which according to Ex 33:19 implies a propensity to show mercy and a freedom from all human distinctives in determining its distribution. So the crucial exegetical question at this point (and the test of our emerging interpretation) is: Does Paul in fact hold to this unstated premise? That is, does he conceive of God's righteousness as his unswerving faithfulness always to preserve and display the glory of his name? The earlier excursus on ἀδικία in Paul pointed precisely in this direction (cf p 73). But since the importance of this question can scarcely be exaggerated I will devote the next three chapters to an effort to try to answer it.

The path of our investigation will be as follows: In Chapter Six I will explore the most likely source of (or influence upon) Paul's conception of divine righteousness, the OT. The reason for this broad effort is that any interpretation of the Pauline conception of divine righteousness will gain intelligibility and credibility if it can be shown to have its roots in the Hebraic-Biblical soil. Then in Chapters Seven and Eight I will examine in detail two of the most important texts in Paul where the righteousness of God is at issue: Rom 3:1-8 and 3:25,26. In these two chapters we will test whether the conception of divine

78

righteousness which seems to be assumed in the logic of Rom 9:14,15, is in fact a conception which Paul embraces. After this necessary three-chapter detour we will return to Rom 9:14-18 and try to see the integrity of the whole unit and its relation to the rest of the chapter.

CHAPTER SIX

THE RIGHTEOUSNESS OF GOD IN THE OLD TESTAMENT

1. The question and method

Our analysis of Ex 33:19, the logic of Rom 9:14,15 and Paul's use of ἀδικία have conspired to suggest that Paul presupposed that God's righteousness is his unswerving commitment to preserve and display the glory of his name. If this is the case the quotation of Ex 33:19 in Rom 9:15 as an argument for the righteousness of God in his unconditional election becomes more intelligible; for, as we saw, Ex 33:19 is a proclamation of God's name and a manifestation of his glory--the glory of his sovereign freedom in having mercy on whomever he wills. The question to be answered here, then, is whether or not the OT pictures God's righteousness in such a way as to support the probability that Paul, who bases so much of his thought on the OT,[1] could have had such an understanding of God's righteousness.

At the outset a number of methodological considerations are in order. First, over ninety per cent of the places in the LXX where δικαιοσύνη translates a Hebrew equivalent, the equivalent belongs to the צדק word group. Therefore, the usage of this word group in the Hebrew OT has provided the basis of my research. Second, Hans Schmid (Weltordnung, 1) said in 1968, "Only a few concepts in OT language have been treated in monographs as often as the concept of 'righteousness.'" This creates an acute problem, especially for a Neutestamentler like me, but fortunately the most recent treatments provide useful references to and interactions with the major positions being taken.[2] My own approach will be to present the major positions and their representatives and to discuss the work of others at those points where it is especially helpful in answering my particular question.

Third, I will avoid making literary-critical distinctions within the OT text itself which would have been foreign to the way St. Paul read the text. For example, it may be of historical interest to try to determine the semantic development of the word צְדָקָה within the so-called Isaiah ("Deutero-Isaiah" and "Trito-Isaiah"), as H. Schmid and F. Cruesemann have done (see note 2), but this would be irrelevant and misleading for my present question. As Brevard Childs ("Prophetic Literature," 54) contends, "Much of the problem of understanding the New Testament's use of the Old Testament prophets lies in the failure to take seriously the canonical perspective common to both Jews and Christians in the first century." Instead of looking for what distinguishes the different OT traditions I will have an eye to what they have in common when they discuss righteousness.

Fourth, I will not assume with N. Snaith[3] and K. Koch[4] that צֶדֶק and צְדָקָה mean the same thing, nor with F. Cruesemann[5] that צְדָקָה is always a deed while צֶדֶק is an abstract quality. Neither will I assume with von Rad that "No radical transformation or development of the ancient Israelite idea of Jahweh's righteousness is discernible."[6] Rather my method will be as far as possible to allow the immediate context to determine the meaning of the term each time it is used. For my purposes it is not required that all the uses of "righteousness" fit into one precise mold. All that is necessary is to demonstrate an understanding of God's righteousness in the OT sufficiently well-attested as to render plausible its influence on Paul. There is little certainty and a good deal of disagreement about what the original meaning of the stem צדק was in Hebrew.[7] This is probably not as great a loss as it may at first seem, since it is precarious to interpret a concept on the basis of its etymology: "Often a word will move so far away from its original sense that the etymology is more of a hindrance than a help to interpretation."[8] Therefore my interpretation of the concept of righteousness will proceed from usage, not from etymology.

2. Norm versus relationship

If we leave to the side many popular notions about righteousness in the OT and consider only the scholarly debate on this concept over the past century the basic disagreements seem to be ones of emphasis rather than mutually exclusive ideas. Most modern studies refer to the work of E. Kautzsch in 1881. His emphasis was that the cluster of words built on צדק refer to "adherence to a norm" (Normgemaessheit): צדקה/צדק signify "the state of corresponding to an objective norm" (Derivate, 28ff, 41ff). This insight has not been abandoned by many contemporary exegetes.[9] But with Hermann Cremer's book Die paulinische Rechtfertigungslehre (1899) a new emphasis emerged. Cremer argued that "the concept of righteousness is in fact a concept of relationship (Verhaeltnisbegriff). It does not have to do with a relationship to an ideal norm but refers to a

relationship between two persons who bring to the
relationship their own claims. Righteousness is the
mutual fulfilment of these claims" (53). This insight
has found agreement among most contemporary scholars.
Gerhard von Rad gives Cremer the tribute of breaking
through to a new way of thinking (less Western and more
Hebraic) "which has so far been rightly accepted as
proven . . . As we now see, the mistake lay in seeking
and presupposing an absolute ideal norm, since ancient
Israel did not in fact measure a line of conduct or an
act by an ideal norm, but by the specific relationship
in which the partner had at the time to prove himself
true."[10]

The reason I say that this disagreement among
scholars is mainly one of emphasis and that the two
sides do not exclude each other is that most of the
scholars who refer to the idea of a norm today do not
mean by it an "absolute ideal norm." David Hill, for
example, who thinks that the basic idea of righteousness is "conformity to a norm" goes on to say, "but not
an absolute ethical norm by which all behavior is
measured nor an ideal standard of 'rightness' for
objects. The norm is furnished by the objective standard of the thing itself."[11] One of the reasons
(besides etymology) many exegetes do not abandon the
idea of norm is the usage of "righteousness" exempli-
fied, for example, in Lev 19:36, "You shall do no wrong
in judgment, in measures of length or weight or
quantity. You shall have just balances (literally:
"balances of righteousness,' מֹאזְנֵי צֶדֶק), just weights,
a just ephah and a just hin . . ." (cf Ezek 45:10;
Prov 17:15). Here the meaning of a "righteous weight"
seems to be a weight that conforms to a standard
measure, i.e., an objective norm.

But the emphasis on righteousness as faithfulness
to the particular claims of a relationship
(Gemeinschaftstreue) has provided a helpful corrective
to the view that righteousness is merely conformity to
the norm of distributive justice in which each person
is rewarded according to his merits. Many texts simply
rule out the idea of "just recompense" and clearly
imply unmerited faithfulness. After David has allowed
his enemy Saul to escape unhurt, Saul confesses, "You
are more righteous (צַדִּיק) than I, for you have repaid
me good, whereas I have repaid you evil" (1 Sam 24:17).
David is righteous not because his behavior conformed
to the ideal ethical norm of a iustitia distributiva
but because, out of respect to "the Lord's anointed"
(24:10), he treated Saul mercifully and thus did his

part to maintain a sound relationship. Later in David's
famous psalm of contrition (51:14) he prays,

> Deliver me from bloodguiltiness, O God, thou
>> God of my salvation,
> And my tongue will joyfully sing of thy <u>righteous-
> ness</u>.

Here it appears that God's righteousness is his
"deliverance" (RSV) in spite of David's guilt. This
element of mercy is even clearer in Ps 143:1,2.

> Hear my prayer, O Lord,
> Give ear to my supplication!
> Answer me in thy faithfulness, in thy righteous-
> ness;
> And do not enter into the judgment with thy
>> servant,
> For in thy sight no man living is righteous.

Here the psalmist virtually equates God's righteousness with his faithfulness to him even though he
himself is not righteous. It necessarily implies mercy.
Thus is ruled out the idea that God's righteousness is
an impartial conformity to a norm by which each man gets
his due. Again in Ps 69:27 the psalmist appeals to God
against his enemies,

> Do thou add iniquity to their iniquity
> And may they not come into thy <u>righteousness</u>.

If God's righteousness were a strict conformity to
distributive justice, the second line would be
just the opposite. But again God's righteousness here
involves mercy and salvation for undeserving men by
which they enter into a right relationship with him.
The psalmist did not want his enemy to experience this.
This same aspect of divine righteousness is evident in
the association of the term righteousness with other
relational and salvific terms in Ps 33:4; 36:5,6,10;
40:10; 88:11,12; 116:5; 145:17; Hos 2:19.

Another feature of righteousness in the OT that
distinguishes it from the more Greek or western concept
is that the term "righteousness" (צְדָקָה) occurs fifteen
times in the plural. This fact accents the functional
and, as we shall see in the following examples, the
salvific aspect of righteousness. Probably the oldest
usage of the plural צְדָקוֹת occurs in the song of Deborah
and Barak (Jud 5:11). After "the Lord routed Sisera"

84

(4:16) and "subdued Jabin the King of Canaan" (4:23)
Deborah and Barak say,

> Sing, you who ride on white donkeys,
> You who sit on rich carpets
> And you who walk by the way.
> At the sound of those who divide flocks among the
>   watering places,
> There they shall recount the righteous deeds of
>   the Lord,
> The righteous deeds of his peasantry in Israel.

The RSV translates these two occurrences of צְדָקוֹת as
"triumphs" for the reference is surely to the deeds God
has just performed for and through the peasants of
Israel, saving them from their enemy in war.[12] Along
the same lines in 1 Sam 12:6-8 Samuel says to the
people,

> It is the Lord who appointed Moses and Aaron
> and who brought your fathers up from the land
> of Egypt. So now take your stand that I may
> plead with you before the Lord concerning all
> the righteous acts of the Lord which he did
> for you and for your fathers. When Jacob
> went into Egypt and your fathers cried out to
> the Lord, then the Lord sent Moses and Aaron
> who brought your fathers out of Egypt and
> settled them in this place.

Here the צְדָקוֹת (RSV "saving deeds") of the Lord are all
the mighty acts by which he faithfully brought his
chosen people out of Egypt, preserved them in the
wilderness and gave them the promised land. The same
usage is found in Mic 6:5. Noteworthy in these three
instances are not only the plural צְדָקוֹת and the saving
character of the concept but also that here the relationship at stake is not between God and an individual
(as in Ps 143:1f etc.) but between God and Israel.

Accordingly God's righteousness in the OT is often
referred to as his "covenant faithfulness"
(Bundestreue). The comment by David Hill (Greek Words,
88) is representative of this viewpoint:

> Not only is the norm by which the nation's
> צְדָקָה is determined provided by the covenant-
> relation and its responsibilities, but in
> fact these are regarded, to some extent, in
> Israel's thought as normative for Yahweh's
> צְדָקָה. In other words, when both Yahweh and

85

his people are fulfilling their covenant-
obligations to one another, things are
ideally 'as they should be'; and the state
of affairs indicated by צְדָקָה obtains.

Some, however, understand this covenant faithfulness as
a strictly saving gift, while others argue that it
embraces the punitive acts of God toward Israel as well.
As we shall see both of these views omit a very significant OT emphasis which Paul seems to pick up.

3.   Is God's righteousness always a saving gift?

From texts like those we have just examined some
scholars have concluded that there is no <u>punitive</u> divine
righteousness in the OT.   Von Rad is usually quoted in
this regard because he states the position so force-
fully:

> From the earliest times onwards Israel cele-
> brated Yahweh as the one who bestowed on his
> people the all-embracing gift of his righ-
> teousness.   And this צדקה bestowed on Israel
> is always a saving gift.   It is inconceivable
> that it should ever menace Israel.   No
> references to the concept of a punitive צדקה
> can be adduced - that would be a <u>contradictio
> in adiecto</u>.[13]

I am not alone in disagreeing with von Rad on this
point.   H. Schmid in his book <u>Gerechtigkeit als
Weltordnung</u> (1968) has a section entitled "Is there a
'punitive righteousness' in the Old Testament?" Here
he surveys the works on both sides, citing L. Diestel,
G.H. Dalmann, E. Kautzsch, H. Cremer and F. Noetscher
among those who answer his question in the affirmative.
His own conclusion which I will cite further on is also
affirmative.   Among English-speaking scholars David
Hill states his conclusion as follows.

> Thus within the action of the divine righ-
> teousness, there is a place for deliverance
> and for condemnation, a place for salvation
> and for punishment . . . Time after time
> this righteous action effected deliverance,
> but at other times, it could mean the oppo-
> site, condemnation and resulting captivity
> (cf Is 10:22).   At Lam 1:18, the city of
> Jerusalem, defeated, looted and destroyed,
> is made to exclaim, not 'The Lord is unjust,'

but 'The Lord is in the right (צַדִּיק):   I have
rebelled against his word.'[14]

Besides Lam 1:18, Hill cites Is 10:22 in support
of a punitive divine righteousness. F. Cruesemann
("Jahwes Gerechtigkeit," 448 note 105), who agrees with
von Rad, refers to this text as the one which "again
and again is referred to as the most important evidence
for an ostensible punitive righteousness." Thus we
should examine it carefully in its context (Is
10:20-23).

> 20. In that day the remnant of Israel and
> the survivors of the house of Jacob will no
> more lean upon him that smote them, but will
> lean upon the Lord, the Holy One of Israel,
> in truth.   21. A remnant will return, the
> remnant of Jacob, to the mighty God.   22.
> For though your people Israel be as the sand
> of the sea, only a remnant of them will
> return. Destruction is decreed, overflowing
> with righteousness (שׁוֹטֵף צְדָקָה).   23. For the
> Lord, the Lord of hosts, will make a full
> end, as decreed, in the midst of all the
> earth.

Cruesemann maintains rightly that the preservation of a
remnant in verse 20 is a saving act. The word "only"
in verse 22, which might suggest the contrary, is not in
the Hebrew original. But he goes on to say that the
phrase "overflowing with righteousness" (verse 22)
refers precisely to this saving act of God in preserving
a remnant and thus contrasts with the phrase, "Destruction is decreed." Three exegetical considerations
stand in the way of this interpretation. First, taken
literally, the two phrases are in apposition: "Destruction decreed! Overflowing righteousness!" This simple
juxtaposition of destruction and righteousness suggests
no contrast but rather that the destruction is a manifestation of overflowing righteousness.

Second, verse 23 is given as a ground (כִּי) for
what precedes. But verse 23 refers only to what has
been "decreed" (חרץ in verses 22,23), namely the destruction (cf כָלָה in verse 23 and כִּלָּיוֹן in verse 22). This would
suggest that only destruction is referred to in verse
22b since only destruction is supported in verse 23.
Third, of the seven other occurrences of the verb שׁטף
("overflow" in Is 8:8; 28:2,15,17; 30:28; 43:2; 66:12)
all but one (66:12) refer to a menacing destructive
stream of some kind. Therefore, Otto Kaiser (Prophet

<u>Jesaja</u>, 118) is, I think, justified in saying of Is
10:22b, "Yahweh's righteousness will pour itself out
over the whole earth like a river that destroys all
sinners." Contrary, then, to Cruesemann and von Rad
this text very probably does refer to "a swell of the
<u>penal</u> righteousness of God" (Keil and Delitzsch, <u>Isaiah</u>,
I, 273).

It is not surprising, therefore, to find another
reference to God's penal righteousness in Is 5:16. In
5:13,15-17 God announces,

> 13. Therefore my people go into exile for
> lack of knowledge; and their honorable men
> are famished, and their multitude is parched
> with thirst . . . 15. Man is bowed down
> and men are brought low, and the eyes of the
> haughty are humbled. 16. But the Lord of
> hosts is exalted in judgment and the holy
> God shows himself holy in <u>righteousness</u>.
> 17. Then the lambs will graze as in their
> pasture, and aliens shall eat the ruins of
> the rich.

There is no sign at all in these verses that God's
action "in righteousness" means less than the desolation of Jerusalem (verse 14). Peter Stuhlmacher
(<u>Gerechtigkeit Gottes</u>, 135 note 8, cf 131 note 7),
who wants to preserve the "basically positive" sense of
צדקה as "saving might" (<u>heilschaffende Macht</u>), nevertheless admits that "according to the present wording
the character of צדקה in Is 5:16; 10:22, namely as
dividing judgment, can scarcely be disputed."[15]

Another instance of punitive righteousness occurs
in Neh 9:33. Ezra intercedes for the people in prayer
(Neh 9:6-37) to God, recounting how faithful God had
been to Israel from Abraham on, but how stiff-necked
the nation had been so that more than once God had
"given them into the hands of their enemies" (verse
27). Now in view of the present distress he prays
(verses 32f),

> 32. Now therefore, our God, the great and
> mighty and terrible God, who keepest covenant
> and steadfast love, let not all the hardship
> seem little to thee that has come upon us,
> upon our kings, our princes, our priests, our
> prophets, our fathers and all thy people,
> since the time of the kings of Assyria until
> this day. 33. Yet thou hast been righteous

(צַדִּיק) in all that has come upon us, for thou hast
dealt faithfully but we have acted wickedly . . .

Von Rad (Theology, I, 377 note 17) of course draws
attention to the statement, "for thou hast dealt faithfully," and says that this is the meaning of God's
righteousness here. But this seems to overlook that it
is "in all that has come upon us," namely, in all this
"hardship" that Yahweh is righteous. The ground (כִּי)
clause of verse 33b supports God's punitive righteousness in that it shows how deserving Israel was of
punishment: even though Yahweh had repeatedly rescued
and blessed her, nevertheless Israel was wicked; therefore Yahweh is righteous to bring hardship on Israel.[16]
This interpretation takes into account both the reference to God's faithfulness and the words "in all that
has come upon us." Other texts which refer with more
or less certainty to God's punitive righteousness are
2 Chron 12:6 and Dan 9:14 (cf Ps 119:75; 141:5).

4. An alternative interpretation

     It is evident from David Hill's position (see
quotes on pp 85 and 86) that to view divine righteousness as "covenant faithfulness" does not necessarily
involve one in a strictly salvific view of righteousness. The terms of the covenant can be understood so
as not to commit God to act savingly regardless of
Israel's behavior. But rather than try to buttress
such a view of divine righteousness, I would like to
raise the question whether this whole emphasis on
covenant faithfulness does not overlook a deeper
dimension of God's righteousness and thus obscure what
is ultimate by focusing on the penultimate.

     K. Koch (THAT, II, 516) and F. Cruesemann ("Jahwes
Gerechtigkeit," 430) have pointed out how seldom the
concept of God's righteousness is found in context with
the term "covenant." Cruesemann can cite only five
places (Ps 50:6/5,16; 89:15,17/4,29,35,40; 111:3/5,9;
132:9/12; 103:6/17,18). Moreover Koch (THAT, II, 520)
draws attention to several references in the OT where
God's righteousness is related to the work of creation
prior to any covenant with Israel: "The arrival of צֶדֶק
on the earth had happened first, without any precon-
ditions, in the event of creation (Ps 33:4-6; 89:11-17)."
These two observations at least sound a warning against
too easily defining the righteousness of God in the OT
solely in terms of "covenant faithfulness."

But the most important evidence for an alternate interpretation is the array of texts in the OT in which we find men appealing to God's righteousness as something basic to, rather than equivalent to, covenant faithfulness. It is on the basis of these texts that I want to argue that, while God's allegiance to the covenant is a real manifestation of God's righteousness, nevertheless the most fundamental characteristic of God's righteousness is his allegiance to his own name, that is, to his honor or glory.[17] His commitment to Israel is penultimate. His commitment to maintaining the glory and honor of his name is ultimate. His saving acts are "righteous acts" not merely because they uphold the covenant promises, but because they preserve and display the honor of God's name. As R. Gyllenberg (Rechtfertigung, 59) puts it in describing the covenant relationship: "The two partners are not equal. Yahweh is God, the Israelites are men. Therefore his honor must determine the relationship between them." Therefore, the maintenance and display of God's honor is the most fundamental determination of his righteous relations with Israel.

In support of this thesis we may first look at Ps 143 which, we have already seen, establishes beyond doubt that God's righteousness is not a mere distributive justice but manifests itself often in mercy to the unrighteous (verses 1b,2):

> Answer me in Thy faithfulness, in Thy righteousness;
> And do not enter into judgment with Thy servant,
> For in Thy sight no man living is righteous. [NASB]

To what is the psalmist really appealing--to God's allegiance to Israel? Verse 11 makes plain, I think, how the psalmist conceived of God's righteousness in saving the unrighteous:

> For the sake of Thy name, O Lord, revive me.
> In Thy righteousness bring my soul out of trouble.

The parallelism here suggests that, for the psalmist, an appeal to God's righteousness was most basically an appeal to God's allegiance to his own name. God's commitment to revive his servant (verse 11) who trusts in him (verse 8) is a penultimate commitment and is grounded in the ultimate commitment to his name. It is apparently with this commitment that the psalmist identifies God's righteousness. "If God cared nothing

for his name . . . we might have doubts of His salvation" (Kidner, Psalms 73-150, 476).

A similar thought connection is found in Ps 31:1-3:

1. In Thee, O Lord, I have taken refuge;
   Let me never be ashamed;
   In Thy righteousness deliver me!
2. Incline Thine ear to me, rescue me quickly;
   Be Thou to me a rock of strength,
   A stronghold to save me!
3. For Thou art my rock and my fortress;
   For Thy name's sake Thou wilt lead me and
      guide me. [NASB]

The thought-parallel between verses 1 and 3 provides the
connection between the righteousness of God and his
acting for his own name's sake: in verse 1 the psalmist
declares that he has taken refuge in God and appeals to
God's righteousness for deliverance; in verse 3 he confesses that God is his rock and fortress (i.e. refuge) and
then expresses his confident hope that God will act on
his behalf for his own name's sake. Thus in the
psalmist's mind the righteous deeds of God are deeds
done out of respect to his own honor and glory.

We turn now to a very instructive passage in
Daniel (9:7,13-19) where Daniel confesses the sins of
Israel, ascribes righteousness to God, and appeals to
him for his anger to turn away from the exiles and his
holy city:

7. Righteousness belongs to Thee, O Lord,
   but to us open shame, as it is this day . . .
   13. As it is written in the law of Moses,
   all this calamity has come on us; yet we
   have not sought the favor of the Lord by
   turning from our iniquity and giving attention to Thy truth. 14. Therefore, the Lord
   has kept the calamity in store and brought it
   on us; for the Lord our God is righteous with
   respect to all His deeds which He has done,
   but we have not obeyed His voice. 15. And
   now, O Lord our God, who hast brought Thy
   people out of the land of Egypt with a mighty
   hand and hast made a name for Thyself, as it
   is this day--we have sinned, we have been
   wicked. 16. O Lord, in accordance with all
   Thy righteous acts, let now Thine anger and Thy
   wrath turn away from Thy city Jerusalem, Thy
   holy mountain; for because of our sins and

91

the iniquities of our fathers, Jerusalem and
Thy people have become a reproach to all
those around us. 17. So now, our God, listen
to the prayer of Thy servant and to his supplications, and for Thy sake, O Lord, let Thy
face shine on Thy desolate sanctuary. 18. O
my God, incline Thine ear and hear! Open
Thine eyes and see our desolations and the
city which is called by Thy name; for we are
not presenting our supplications before Thee on
account of our righteousness but on account of Thy
great compassion. 19. O Lord, hear! O Lord,
forgive! O Lord, listen and take action! For
Thine own sake, O my God, do not delay,
because Thy city and Thy people are called by
Thy name. [NASB]

Concerning the meaning of God's righteousness in this
text H. Schmid (Weltordnung, 143) says, "Yahweh is in
the right; what he has brought upon Israel it deserved.
The nation is not צדיק, it has no צדקה. The connection
here with juridical ideas is clear . . . What is
remarkable is that in the same context, after Yahweh's
צדקה designates his 'right' (Recht) in verse 7, it
refers to 'divine mercy' in verse 16 and is used parallel to רחם (verse 18b)." In other words here we have
in a single prayer a capsule of the contrast we saw
earlier between a punitive and a merciful righteousness.
But Daniel apparently does not feel any tension. One
could argue that the tension is resolved in the concept
of covenant loyalty, if God's punishment is seen as an
expression of his loyalty to the conditionality of the
covenant, and his future mercy is seen as an expression
of his loyalty to his promise to forgive the repentant.
But in fact when Daniel asks that God's anger be turned
away "in accordance with all Thy righteous acts" his
explicit and repeated ground for this is that the honor
of God's name is in jeopardy (verses 15,17,18,19).

This, I would suggest, is the aspect of God's
righteousness that provides the unity between its punitive and merciful manifestations. By punishing Israel
he magnified his glory by showing that idolatry is a
dreadful evil worthy of destruction. One need only
think of the awful theme of coming judgment running
through the early chapters of Ezekiel--a judgment whose
purpose is to reassert the Lordship of Yahweh which the
people have so grossly dishonored: "Then you will know
that I am the Lord, when their slain are among their idols
around their altars . . . I will make the land more
desolate and waste than the wilderness toward Diblah;

thus they will know that I am the Lord" (Ezek 6:13f).[18]
On the other hand, since Jerusalem and Israel are
"called by his name" (Dan 9:17,18,19), to save them and
restore their prosperity after a time of punishment
will magnify God's name and remove the reproach into
which it has fallen among the nations (verse 16). Thus
"the Lord is righteous in all his deeds" (verse 14):
he has never swerved from acting for his own name's
sake, even when the people have acted as if his name
were worthless. When Daniel prays that Israel's
deliverance accord with God's "righteous acts" (verse
16) and that it be "for Thine own sake" (verses 17,19),
he implies that the most fundamental characteristic of
divine righteousness is God's unswerving allegiance
always to act for his own name's sake.

It is generally recognized that in the second half
of Isaiah[19] the righteousness of God signifies God's
"predicted new and eschatological saving act."[20] God's
righteousness and his coming salvation seem almost
interchangeable:

I bring near my righteousness, it is not far off;
And my salvation will not delay (46:13a).

My righteousness is near,
My salvation has gone forth,
And my arms will judge the peoples (51:5).

Do not fear the reproach of man . . .
For the moth will eat them like a garment . . .
But my righteousness shall be forever
And my salvation to all generations (51:7b,8).

Hermann Cremer (Rechtfertigungslehre, 80) grapples with
the problem: On what ground can this coming righteous-
ness/salvation be expected? His answer is that the
hope of salvation rests only in Israel's "free divine
election." "Not the fulfilling of God's commandments
is the final reason that God upholds his election
(בחר עוד ; ἔτι ἐκλέγεσθαι, Is 14:1), but rather only the
election itself. For its sake God forgives his people
at the decisive hour, Is 43:20-44:2 . . ." The reaffir-
mation of God's election is alluded to in Is 41:8,9;
43:7; 44:1; 49:7. Cremer is right, I think, but more
can be said about the ground or reason for the election
of Israel and its maintenance. This will lead to a deeper
understanding of divine righteousness.

In Is 43:6,7 God declares to the dispersed people:

I will say to the north, "Give them up!"

And to the south, "Do not hold them back."
Bring my sons from afar,
And my daughters from the ends of the earth:
Everyone who is called by my name,
And whom I have created for my glory,
Whom I have formed, even whom I have made.

Again in 49:3 the same purpose is stated:

And he said to me, "You are my servant,
    Israel,
In whom I will show my glory."

According to these texts and others (43:21; 44:23;
46:13 etc), God was moved to create or elect Israel for
the sake of his glory. But what so often goes unmen-
tioned in the discussions of God's saving action, or
his righteousness, in Isaiah is that this fundamental
motive of God's initiating a relationship with Israel
also governs the continuation of that relationship. It
is a distortion of large portions of the OT when the
impression is given that the ground of God's saving
action and the touchstone of his righteousness is his
allegiance to Israel's welfare. Note, for example, the
following:

For the sake of my name I delay my wrath,
And for my praise I restrain it for you,
In order not to cut you off.
Behold I have refined you but not as silver;
I have tested you in the furnace of affliction.
For my own sake, for my own sake I will act;
For how can (my name) be profaned?
And my glory I will not give to another (Is
    48:9-11).

I, even I, am the one who wipes out your trans-
    gressions for my own sake,
And I will not remember your sins (Is 43:25).

I would suggest from these texts that if in Isaiah
Israel's salvation is an expression of God's righteousness (see above p 93), then his righteousness is an
expression of his unswerving commitment to act for his
own glory. God's faithfulness to Israel is real and
sure, but it is so only because it is grounded in the
more profound faithfulness of God to the preservation
(Is 48:11) and display (Is 49:3) of his own glory. In
discussing the concept of God's righteousness in Is
40-66, Walther Eichrodt expresses what has not been
given sufficient emphasis in the scholarly discussions
of God's righteousness:

The close connection between God's righteousness and his holiness, of which the righteousness is a revelation, anchors Yahweh's
intervention for the restoration of the
covenant-people firmly in the nature (Wesen)
of God as Lord of the universe. In this way
Yahweh's [righteous] intervention is freed from
all egoistic limitations of national self-
interest and is given its proper place within
the world-wide purposes of the divine sovereignty (Walten).[21]

In passing we should observe also that this way of
thinking about God's saving activity is typical of
other OT writers while it may not always be explicitly
related to the term righteousness. According to
Jeremiah, "The Lord declares, 'For as the waistband
clings to the waist of man so I made the whole household of Israel cling to me that they might be for me a
people, a name, a praise and a glory" (13:11; cf Is
43:7; 49:3). Thus the purpose of God in binding this
people to himself is that his name might be exalted and
his glory displayed. That this purpose of God grounds
his saving intervention for Israel is shown in two
ways. First, Jeremiah quotes God as saying, "I will
cleanse them from all their iniquity by which they have
sinned against me and I will pardon their iniquities . . . and thus this city will be to me a name of
joy, a praise and a glory before all the nations of the
earth which shall hear of all the good that I do for
them . . ." (33:8,9). In other words the ground of
God's initial binding relationship to this people
(13:11) continues to be the ground or motive of his
commitment to restore and maintain that relationship
(33:8f). Second, Jeremiah prays in 14:7,9,20f:

Although our iniquities testify against us,
O Lord, act for Thy name's sake!
. . . .
Why art Thou like a man dismayed,
Like a mighty man who cannot save?
Yet Thou, O Lord, art in our midst,
And we are called by Thy name;
Do not forsake us!
. . . .
We know our wickedness, O Lord,
The iniquity of our fathers, for we have sinned
    against Thee.
Do not despise us, for Thy name's sake;
Do not dishonor Thy glorious throne;
Remember, and do not break Thy covenant with us.

[NASB]

Here it is clear that God's covenant-faithfulness is a
penultimate, not the ultimate, ground for God's saving
intervention. Israel was chosen to be a name, a praise
and a glory for God (13:11). Therefore it is precisely
this deepest faithfulness of God to which Jeremiah
appeals for salvation, namely, God's faithfulness to
his name, to the honor of his glorious throne. A contemporary[22] of Jeremiah expressed it similarly as he
saw the defiled temple and Jerusalem in ruins:

> Help us, O God of our salvation, for the glory of
> Thy name,
> And deliver us, and forgive our sins, for Thy
> name's sake (Ps 79:9).

What about another major prophet, Ezekiel? How
does he present the ground of God's covenant-keeping
faithfulness? That he sees the promised restoration of
the exiled people in terms of God's covenant-keeping is
shown by Ezek 16:59-63:

> For thus says the Lord God: I will deal with
> you as you have done, who have despised the
> oath in breaking the covenant, yet I will
> remember my covenant with you in the days of
> your youth, and I will establish with you an
> everlasting covenant . . . I will establish
> my covenant with you, and you shall know that
> I am the Lord, in order that you may remember
> and be confounded and never open your mouth
> again because of your shame, when I forgive
> you all that you have done, says the Lord God.

The "new covenant"[23] by which God will forgive Israel
for her sins has a very clear and remarkably theocentric ground in Ezek 36:20-32. Speaking of exiled
Israel God says:

> When they came to the nations where they went,
> they profaned my holy name . . . But I had
> concern for my holy name, which the house of
> Israel caused to be profaned among the nations
> to which they came. Therefore, say to the
> house of Israel, Thus says the Lord God: It
> is not for your sake, O house of Israel, that
> I am about to act, but for the sake of my holy
> name, which you have profaned among the nations . . .
> and the nations will know that I am the Lord, says
> the Lord God, when through you I vindicate my
> holiness before their eyes. [Here the "new

covenant" is described--verses 24-30.] Then you
will remember your evil ways, and your deeds
that were not good; and you will loathe your-
selves for your iniquities and your abominable
deeds. It is not for your sake that I will
act, says the Lord God. Let that be known to
you. Be ashamed and confounded for your ways,
O house of Israel.

It could scarcely be more strongly expressed that the
reestablishment of the covenant and its accompanying
salvation are grounded most fundamentally in God's
allegiance to the holiness of his name.[24] This motif
is employed to account not only for the mercy of the
new covenant but also for all the past merciful acts of
deliverance from the exodus onwards. One can see this
most clearly in the fourfold repetition in Ezek 20 of
the words, "I acted for the sake of my name" (verses
9,14,22,44).

While on the one hand Isaiah, Daniel and the psalms
which we looked at brought the righteousness of God and
his allegiance to the honor of his name into direct
connection, Ezekiel and Jeremiah on the other hand do
not make this connection explicit, because explicit
reference to divine righteousness is seldom found in
Jeremiah, and in Ezekiel not at all.[25] But the idea of
God's covenant-faithfulness and his saving acts, to
which divine righteousness is elsewhere so closely
connected, are in these prophetic writings grounded
likewise in God's commitment to always act for the sake
of his glorious name.

Therefore these prophetic writings, along with many
other texts,[26] impress upon the careful reader of the
OT that all God's saving deeds spring ultimately from
his loyalty to his own name. This impression then
functions to confirm for the reader the insight derived
elsewhere from numerous explicit connections that the
righteousness of God consists most basically in God's
unswerving commitment to preserve the honor of his name
and display his glory. Thus if God ever abandoned this
commitment and no longer sought in all things the mag-
nifying of his own glory, then there indeed would be
unrighteousness with God.

Excursus - Implications for human righteousness

To treat adequately the implications of this
thesis for the righteousness of man in the OT
would require too much space here. So I will only

97

cite several texts which provide pointers and, I
think, indirect confirmations of my argument. The
basic implication as I see it is that man's righteousness will be seen now as radically God-
centered. The relational accent is in no way
diminished, but it receives a distinct orientation:
the righteousness of man in relation to God is
(reflecting God's righteousness) to love the honor
of God's name, to esteem above all things God's
glory (especially as it has been mercifully
experienced in his saving deeds), and, finally, to
do only those things which accord with this love
and esteem. Thus human actions may be described
as righteous not because they conform to an "ideal
ethical norm" (like impartial distributive justice,
though this may often be righteous), but rather
because they are fitting expressions of man's
complete allegiance to maintain the honor of God's
name and display his glory.

> But let all who take refuge in thee rejoice,
> Let them ever sing for joy;
> And do thou defend them,
> That those who love thy name may exult in
>   thee.
> For thou dost bless the righteous, O Lord,
> Thou dost cover him with favor as with a
>   shield.

In this passage from Ps 5:11f "the righteous" and
"those who love thy name" are interchangeable.
The righteous man esteems God as a trustworthy
refuge (Ps 34:21f; 37:39f; 64:10) and loves his
name. Thus one might conclude that to do righteousness is to act out of love to God's name, out
of a desire that his name be honored. This would
be confirmed by Ps 23:3 where the psalmist confesses, "He leads me in paths of righteousness for
his name's sake." This verse expresses what we
would expect from our discussion of God's own
righteousness: since a fundamental characteristic
of it is his commitment to act always for his own
name's sake, then it is only natural that the
righteousness into which he would lead his people
would have the same orientation. To walk in righteousness is to seek in everything to honor God's
name because one loves it so much and esteems it
so highly.

Human righteousness is the fitting response
to a true knowledge of God. Jeremiah indicates
this in 22:15f:

> Do you become a king because you are competing
>   in cedar?
> Did not your father eat and drink,
> And do justice and <u>righteousness</u>?
> Then it was well with him.
> He pled the cause of the afflicted and needy;
> ، Then it was well.
> <u>Is not that what it means to know me</u>?
> <u>Declares the Lord.</u>

The "knowledge of God," as is well known, means
much more in the OT than mere cognitive awareness.
It is "almost identical with the fear of God" and
implies that God is "recognized and respected"
(<u>TDNT</u>, I, 698). It is out of a recognition of and
respect or esteem for God that true human righteousness flows. They are so connected that if one does
not do righteousness (in this case, plead the cause
of the poor) then it can be said that he does not
know God.

The same theocentric thrust appears in 2 Sam
23:3f in the parallelism:

> He who rules over men <u>righteously</u>,
> Who rules <u>in the fear of God</u>,
> Is as the <u>light</u> of the morning when the sun
>   rises.

In 1 Sam 24:17 and 26:23f where David is described
as more righteous than Saul (see p 83), it is stated
that David acted as he did "because of the Lord"
(24:6). Out of respect for "the Lord's anointed"
(24:6,10; 26:23) David spared Saul's life. His
righteous deed derives from his high esteem of the
Lord and his anointed. Finally, one could consider
Mal 3:16-18 where the righteous are the ones "who
fear the Lord and esteem His name"[27] (cf also
Is 51:1; Prov 18:10).

In short then, the effect upon human righteousness of construing divine righteousness as
God's faithfulness to his own name is that human
righteousness is seen as radically God-centered
and consisting fundamentally in valuing God above
all and acting for his name's sake.

99

5. Conclusion

The conclusion reached earlier in Chapter Four ran as follows: as a preliminary declaration of the verbal theophany to follow in Ex 34:6,7 the divine words,

> I will be gracious to whom I will be gracious,
> And I will show compassion on whom I will show compassion,

are a manifestation of God's _glory_ (33:18), a "passing by" of his _goodness_ and a proclamation of his _name_. Thus God's glory and his name consist fundamentally in his propensity to show mercy and his sovereign freedom in its distribution. Or, to put it more precisely still, it is the glory of God and his essential nature mainly to dispense mercy (but also wrath, Ex 34:7) on whomever he pleases apart from any constraint originating outside his own will.[28] This is the essence of what it means to be God.

The conclusion I have reached in this chapter is that there is a broad basis for understanding the righteousness of God as his unswerving commitment to preserve the honor of his name and display his glory (p 97). The connection between Ex 33:19 and divine righteousness, therefore, seems to be this: Ex 33:19 in its OT context defines the nature of God's glory and the essence of his name and thus specifies what God must preserve and display in order to maintain his righteousness. If the righteousness of God is most basically his commitment to act unswervingly for his own name's sake and thus display his glory, and if the name and glory of God consist in his sovereign freedom from all external constraints in showing mercy, then God must preserve and display his sovereign freedom from all human claims in the bestowal of his mercy. He must always act out of a full allegiance to the infinite value of his own glorious and sovereign freedom: therein consists his unimpeachable righteousness and therein does the contrite heart who flees to him for refuge find hope (Ps 71:1-5; 143:1f,11).

This connection of thought in the OT offers a key to the understanding of Paul's argument in Rom 9:14,15. When Paul said that God chose to bless Jacob over Esau apart from any basis in their actions but simply on the basis of his choice (ἐκ τοῦ καλοῦντος, Rom 9:12), his opponent objected that this would call God's righteousness into question (9:14). Paul denies this and in support of his denial he cites Ex 33:19 (Rom 9:15).

If we assume that Paul's thinking here (unlike his opponent's) is based on an OT concept of divine righteousness like the one developed in this chapter, then the argument (γάρ "for") of Rom 9:15 is not only a real and valid argument, but it is virtually the only one possible. If we paraphrase and bring out the implicit understanding of righteousness, the argument runs like this: since God's righteousness consists basically in his acting unswervingly for his own glory, and since his glory consists basically in his sovereign freedom in the bestowal and withholding of mercy, there is no unrighteousness with God (Rom 9:11f). On the contrary, he must pursue his "electing purpose" apart from man's "willing and running," for only in his sovereign, free bestowal of mercy on whomever he wills is God acting out of a full allegiance to his name and esteem for his glory.

In answer to the question raised at the beginning, the picture of divine righteousness we have found in the OT does indeed support the probability that in Rom 9:14,15 Paul is arguing in the manner just described. But in order properly to confirm this interpretation we must try to show that in the key texts outside of Rom 9 Paul does in fact hold to a view of God's righteousness like the one described in this chapter. The next two chapters are devoted to this effort.

CHAPTER SEVEN

THE RIGHTEOUSNESS OF GOD IN ROMANS 3:1-8

1. Purpose and orientation

The purpose of this chapter is to investigate
whether in fact Paul had an understanding of God's
righteousness like the one we discovered in the OT
(Chapter Six)--an understanding which would confer on
the argument of Rom 9:14,15 much more coherence and
force than it is often thought to have (Chapter Five).

The more recent discussion of Paul's understanding
of the righteousness of God can be surveyed conveniently
in the articles by Guenther Klein (IDB, Supplement,
750-2) and Manfred Brauch ("Perspectives on God's Righteousness," 523-42). It is clear from this discussion
that the recovery of a more Biblical-Hebraic concept of
righteousness in OT studies (Chapter Six, Section 2)
has influenced the way Paul is understood. Accordingly,
the righteousness of God in Paul, Leonhard Goppelt
(Theologie, II, 468) argues, does not refer to any sort
of "distributive justice" but rather to God's saving
"covenant faithfulness." On the other hand, a group of
German scholars influenced in part by Ernst Kaesemann[1]
understand Paul's debt to the OT and Jewish apocalyptic
differently. Christian Mueller (Gottes Gerechtigkeit,
112) argues that "Paul replaced the concept of covenant
with the concept of creation," so that, as Wolfgang
Schrage ("Roemer 3:21-26," 86) puts it, the righteousness of God is "the faithfulness of the creator to his
creation." My own effort to understand Paul's conception of God's righteousness will involve an interaction
with this recent discussion.

Rom 3:1-8, though it has not received much detailed
attention outside the commentaries,[2] commends itself for
special attention for at least three reasons. First,
the "righteousness of God" in 3:5 clearly does not refer
to God's gift or imputation to man, but rather to his
being righteous and thus parallels the concept in Rom
9:14. Second, the terminology of Rom 3:1-8 (with
references to God's πίστις, ἀλήθεια, δικαιοσύνη, δόξα)
makes the passage a very auspicious source of insight
into Paul's understanding of God's righteousness.
Third, the μὴ ἀδικία παρὰ τῷ θεῷ ("there is no unrighteousness with God, is there?") of Rom 9:14 has its
closest parallel in the μὴ ἄδικος ὁ θεός ("God is not
unrighteous, is he?") of Rom 3:5. Both reject, with the

words μὴ γένοιτο, the idea that God could be unrighteous. The specific goal of this investigation of Rom
3:1-8 is, therefore, not to elucidate every part of it
but to grasp, if possible, Paul's concept of God's
righteousness which finds expression here. An effort
will be made to avoid the errors which I think have
misled many interpreters: 1) the failure to define
precisely how Paul's rhetorical opponents are arguing,
and 2) the failure to distinguish Paul's view of God's
righteousness from the view of his Jewish interlocutors.

2. The text

1   What advantage then does the Jew have, or what
    profit is circumcision?
2a Much in every way.
 b First, they were entrusted with the oracles of
    God.
3a For what if some disbelieved?
 b Their unbelief does not abrogate the faithfulness
    of God, does it?
4a No indeed! Let God be true, and every man a liar!
 b As it is written, "So that you might be justified
    in your words, and conquer when you enter into
    judgment."
5a If our unrighteousness shows the righteousness of
    God, what shall we say?
 b God is not unrighteous who inflicts wrath, is he?
    (I am speaking like a mere man.)
6a No indeed!
 b Otherwise how would God judge the world?
7a For if the truth of God abounds to his glory in
    my falsehood,
 b then why am I still judged as a sinner,
8a and shall we not do evil in order that good may
    come (as we are blasphemed and as some claim that
    we say)?³
 b Their condemnation is just.

Throughout the passage Paul is arguing, as it were,
with Jewish objectors whom he no doubt encountered in
many synagogues as he disputed with his kinsmen about
the gospel. What gave rise to this particular dialogue
in Rom 3:1-8 was the apparent leveling out of all distinctions between Jews and Gentiles in Rom 2. The
unbelieving Jew precedes the Gentile into God's judgment (2:9); the Gentile who keeps the law will judge
the Jew who does not keep it (2:27); in fact it is the
Gentile who may be the true Jew (2:28f). Such ideas
naturally give rise to the question that leads into our
text: "What advantage then does the Jew have?" (3:1).

In answer Paul begins a list of advantages which he picks up and completes only in Rom 9:1-5. The only advantage he names here is that the Jews were entrusted with the words (λόγια), that is, the promises of God.[4] In verses 1-4 Paul argues that the unbelief of some Jews (an understatement in view of 11:14) does not abrogate God's faithfulness to these promises (cf 11:29). Then in verses 5-8 Paul deals with objections which his dialog partners raise because of the things Paul says. My concern is not primarily with the advantages of Israel in this text but with Paul's understanding of God's righteousness as it emerges in the argument of the dialog.

It is helpful to note the parallels in the terminology of this passage. They are as follows.

verse 3	our ἀπιστία	does not abrogate	God's πίστιν
verse 4	every man is ψεύστης	but	God is ἀληθής
verse 5	our ἀδικία	shows up	God's δικαιοσύνην
verse 7	my ψεύσματι	causes to abound	God's ἀλήθεια

3. The position of the opponents

With these data before us the most fruitful place to begin our analysis is in verse 5 with an attempt to reconstruct as precisely as possible how Paul's opponents were arguing. The rhetorical question suggests that the opponents think they have trapped Paul in a contradiction. Literally verse 5 reads, "If our unrighteousness shows (συνίστησιν)[5] the righteousness of God, what shall we say? God is not unrighteous, who inflicts wrath, is he? (I speak like a mere man)." The second question expects the answer, No (interrogative with μή). Commentators[6] generally recognize, rightly, that this is not the way Paul's opponents would have formulated their question. Theirs would have been: "Then, on your grounds, surely God is unrighteous to inflict wrath on us, isn't he?" But Paul, even though he admits that he is speaking as a mere man ("whose mental horizon takes in only what is human"),[7] nevertheless cannot bring himself to pose a question which seems to impugn the righteousness of God. (See p 70.) But the basic outline of the opponents' argument is still clear. They are saying: "If our unrighteousness shows up God's righteousness, then God is

105

unrighteous to inflict wrath upon us for our unrighteousness."[8]

The question that needs to be answered with more
precision than is usually found in the commentaries is:
What did the opponents mean by "the righteousness of
God" in Rom 3:5? The most common answer is that the
righteousness of God in 3:5 refers to God's distributive
justice[9] (according to which he renders to each his
due). The support for this view is at first glance
fairly strong. It could be sketched as follows.

The opponents' rhetorical question (3:5) is most
naturally construed as a response to what Paul just
said in 3:4b. He has just quoted Ps 51:4 (LXX 50:6):
"Just as it is written,

> So that you might be justified in your words,
> And conquer when you judge."

The "so that" (ὅπως) of the Psalm quote shows that God's
(= "you") vindication is the result[10] of the preceding
statement in the psalm:

> Against you and you only have I sinned,
> And done what is evil in your sight,
> So that you might be justified in your words,
> And conquer when you judge.

"Your words" refer to God's expected words of judgment
on David,[11] and the middle voice of κρίνεσθαι ("when
you judge") is to be preferred to the passive voice
("when you are judged")[12] because of the poetic parallelism[13] and the general sense of the following verses,
which refer to God's judgment. Therefore it is fair to
conclude that Paul is using this psalm quote in 3:4b to
show that man's sin vindicates God's judgment upon
it.[14] Accordingly since the opponents' response to
Paul follows immediately, one could easily conclude
that for them the righteousness of God in 3:5 refers to
God's "activity of judging"[15] and thus includes punishment or retribution towards his people.

But I would like to argue that this is a premature
conclusion, for if this is the meaning of divine righteousness which the opponents have in mind in
3:5, then their objection loses all its plausibility.
(I assume that while a rhetorical objection need not
be--indeed cannot be--entirely valid, yet it must, at
least on the face of it, have a measure of plausibility.) I will try to show in the following why this

106

view of divine righteousness depletes the opponents' objection of all plausibility and rules itself out. In the process a different view of the opponents' conception of righteousness will emerge.

Let us try to reconstruct the opponents' argument on the assumption that by "the righteousness of God" in 3:5 they meant a punitive, retributive justice. They would be saying, "If our unrighteousness shows up God's <u>punitive</u> righteousness (by giving him a just cause to judge us), then he is unrighteous to punish us for our unrighteousness." That is so obviously self-contradictory that it has no plausibility. It is like saying: "Since my sin justified God's judgment upon me, therefore he is unjust to judge me." Surely this cannot be the argument of the opponents. Therefore it is wrong to construe the meaning of "the righteousness of God" in 3:5 as the distributive justice of God manifest in his act of judging. There must be a measure of plausibility in the opponents' objection.

The same thing emerges when we reconstruct the opponents' argument in verse 7. Literally the text reads, "If by my falsehood the truth of God abounds to his glory, why am I still judged as a sinner?" The similarity to verse 5 is clear from the following table of parallels.

Verse 5	Verse 7
	If the truth of God
If our unrighteousness	in my falsehood
shows	abounds
the righteousness of God	to his glory,
What shall we say? God is not unrighteous who inflicts wrath, is he?	then why am I still judged as a sinner?

"My falsehood" stands in the place of "our unrighteousness"; God's "truth" and "glory" stand in the place of God's "righteousness"; and being "judged" stands in the place of incurring "wrath." The change to first person singular ("my falsehood") from first plural ("our unrighteousness") is not significant as far as I can see, especially since the singular phrase ("I am judged") of verse 7 is recalled in verse 8b by "their (plural) judgment." The argument is thus virtually the same as that of verse 5 except that it is strengthened: my falsehood does not just "<u>show</u>" God's truth but more--it

107

causes God's truth to "abound" to his glory; therefore he would be unjust to punish me as a sinner. (This is the force of the rhetorical question, "Why am I still judged as a sinner?")

This confirms that the meaning of God's righteousness in verse 5 is not mere retributive justice, since the "truth" (ἀλήθεια) of God (verse 7a) is parallel to his "righteousness" (verse 5a) but in all likelihood refers to his "truthfulness . . . in keeping his promises" (Sanday and Headlam, Romans, 73). Thus, as Peter Stuhlmacher (Gerechtigkeit, 83) argues, the faithfulness of God in verse 3 which man's unbelief does not abrogate, the righteousness of God in verse 5 which the unrighteousness of man highlights, and the truth of God in verse 7 which the falsehood of man causes to abound all refer basically to the same thing. Since the "faithfulness" of God in verse 3 is that which grounds the "advantage" (verse 1) of Judaism, its primary meaning in this passage is something mainly positive and gracious rather than punitive. This then is probably the main force which each of the three parallel terms (πίστις, δικαιοσύνη, ἀλήθεια) carries throughout (but as we shall see, we must be prepared to allow for differences between Paul's definitions and those of his opponents).

This receives added confirmation when we examine the third and final argument of Paul's opponents in verse 8. They claim that Paul's teaching leads to the untenable conclusion: "Let us do evil that good may come." In conjunction with the preceding arguments of verses 5-7 this would mean: "Let us be as 'unrighteous' and as 'false' as we can so that God's righteousness and truth might abound to his glory." But the opponents would never say this (even hypothetically) if "the good" they hoped for (i.e. the glorification of God's righteousness and truth) included their own judgment. Therefore the truth and righteousness of God which would abound through "doing evil" is something beneficial, not punitive. This is supported by Rom 6:1 where Paul cites the same slander, but with the words, "Shall we continue in sin that grace may abound?" We may be reasonably sure, then, that Paul's opponents construed the righteousness of God in Rom 3:5 as saving and gracious, not retributive.

Now let us test this conclusion by trying again to reconstruct their argument in verse 5. It would apparently run like this: "If our unrighteousness shows up God's saving righteousness (in that it gives him an

occasion to be more gracious), then God is unrighteous
to inflict us with wrath (for that would mean that he
fails to take advantage of an opportunity to magnify
his grace)." Similarly the opponents' argument in
verse 7 would be: "If the truth of God (which is manifest in his saving me in spite of my falsehood) thus
abounds to his glory by my falsehood, then God should
not judge me as a sinner but save me and thus magnify
his gracious truth." That this argument is indeed
plausible further validates our conclusion that for
Paul's opponents the righteousness of God in Rom 3:5
refers to God's gracious saving action which should
guarantee their salvation (escape from God's "wrath")
even if they are "false"[16] toward God.

Therefore, when Paul's opponents react to his
reference to judgment in 3:4b (= Ps 51:4) they are
claiming to have caught Paul in a contradiction. On
the one hand they agree with 3:1-4a that the unbelief
of some does not abrogate the faithfulness (= the righteousness) of God and that even if all become liars (=
unbelievers)[17] God would remain true to his promises.
But, on the other hand, as Bornkamm ("Teufelskunst,"
143) keenly points out, they draw the false conclusion
that "the faithfulness of God would completely exclude
any judgment at all upon the covenant people." And,
therefore, when Paul says in 3:4b that God would be
righteous (δικαιωθῇς) in judgment even upon David, the
opponents think Paul has contradicted himself.

That this is the sequence of the opponents'
thought can also be shown by pointing out the parallels
between verse 4 and verse 7.

Verse 4	Verse 7
Let God be <u>true</u>	If the <u>truth</u> of God abounds to his glory
and every man a <u>liar</u>. As it is written, "So that you might be justified in your words and conquer when	by my <u>lie</u>,
<u>you judge</u>."	why am I still <u>judged</u> as a sinner?

These parallels show how the Jewish opponents construe
Paul's words: on the one hand they see a claim that
man's falsehood, i.e. unbelief, does not abrogate God's
truthfulness but magnifies it. They take this to

guarantee their own security even if they themselves
should be the ones who are false. But on the other
hand they hear Paul say that Jews can be judged for
what they thought magnified his truthfulness. Therefore, their accusation that Paul is contradicting himself finds expression in the rhetorical question: If
our unrighteousness shows up God's <u>saving</u> righteousness
(= truth) as you imply in 3:1-4a, then God is unrighteous to inflict wrath as you suggest he could do in
3:4b.

We may conclude then that when the opponents use
the term "righteousness of God" in 3:5 they mean by it
a strictly saving commitment of God to his covenant
people.[18] It excludes a punitive or retributive dimension at least in relation to themselves.

4. Paul's position and the function of Romans 3:4b

What has become evident now is that the validity
of the opponents' objection hangs on the twofold assumption that the righteousness of God in Rom 3:5 is his
strictly saving commitment to Israel and that it was
Paul's intention in 3:1-4a to enunciate such a commitment, which then contradicted his use of Ps 51:4 in
3:4b. The fault with this assumption is that 3:1-4a
does not necessarily imply that for Paul the righteousness of God is strictly saving for Israel. To find out
how Paul <u>does</u> conceive of the righteousness of God we
should ask how 3:1-4a and the Psalm quote in 3:4b
cohere, rather than assuming (with the opponents) that
we already know Paul's view and then finding a contradiction to it in 3:4b. Therefore we must now try to
give an account of how the Psalm quote functions for
<u>Paul</u> in this context--a problem the solution of which
will help clarify more precisely Paul's underlying concept of God's righteousness. I call it a problem
because the logical relationships of verses 2-4 are not
readily obvious. To show this let us paraphrase the
four steps of the argument:

Step 1: the Jews have been blessed with the
promises of God (verse 2).

Step 2: the unbelief of some does not abolish
God's faithfulness to keep those promises
(verse 3).

Step 3: for nothing man can do will abrogate
God's truthfulness (verse 4a, see note
17).

Step 4: just as Scripture says: the sin of man
justifies God's judgment upon it (verse
4b).

The problem here is how step 4 functions in the argument. Since Paul is stressing in steps 1-3 God's
gracious faithfulness to his promises in spite of man's
sin, why does he introduce an OT quote (step 4) that
asserts God's righteousness in punishing sin? It does
not seem to fit. I have already given the reasons why
I cannot follow Kaesemann who solves the problem by
seeing in the psalm quote not a reference to punishment
but to the justification of the ungodly (see note 14).
Such a view seems to smooth out the logic of verses 1-4
but it makes the references to wrath and judgment in
verses 5-7 (and thus the opponents' objections) inexpli-
cable as far as I can see.

How then shall we understand the relationship
between step 4 and the preceding steps? The phrase "as
it is written" is used by Paul ten times in Rom,[19]
always to refer to an OT text which supports the point
he is making. What Paul wants to support in Rom 3:2-4a
is that man's sin of unbelief does not abrogate God's
faithfulness. The unusual way Paul chooses to support
this is by citing an OT text which shows what effect
man's sin does have on God. Far from impugning God's
faithfulness and truth it highlights the righteousness
of God's punitive judgment. In other words Ps 51:4 is
a support for what sins do not do to God (abrogate his
faithfulness) by showing what in fact they do do to
God (justify his judgment).

But here we get a crucial insight into Paul's
understanding of God's righteousness. Paul's OT
support has force only if the righteousness of God
embraces both his merciful faithfulness and his punitive judgment. Only if God's judgment because of sin
and his merciful faithfulness in spite of sin cohere in
one concept of divine righteousness, can Paul argue
that the righteousness of judgment, highlighted by the
gravity of sin, supports the merciful faithfulness of
God to his promises in spite of man's sin. The
sequence, "God is faithful" (verse 3), "God is true"
(verse 4a), just as it is written, "God is shown righteous" (verse 4b), indicates that God's righteousness
embraces his truth and faithfulness. But since the way
he is "shown righteous" is through the gravity of sin
vindicating his judgment, therefore, we should conclude
that in Paul's mind God's righteousness also embraces
his punitive judgment.[20] Paul found himself thus in

111

conflict with a Judaism whose erroneous view of its own solidarity[21] and of God's faithfulness contradicted the Pauline message of justification by free grace through faith alone. Consequently I cannot follow the scholars who maintain that _for Paul_ the righteousness of God is the opposite of his wrath and is always a saving, never a punitive, reality.[22] They have, in my judgment, failed to distinguish in Rom 3:5-8 between Paul's view and the view of his opponents. The view of divine righteousness which they ascribe to Paul is precisely the one upon which his opponents base their argument and which Paul rejects on the basis that it excludes punitive judgment.[23]

What then is Paul's understanding of the righteousness of God reflected in Rom 3:1-8? The reference to the glory of God in verse 7 indicates that Paul's opponents had probably heard Paul defend God's actions as righteous in that they displayed God's glory.[24] So they responded: "If the truth of God by my lie abounds to his _glory_ then God would be _unrighteous_ to judge me" (verse 7). The truth in this argument is that God's righteousness _is_ manifested when his truthfulness abounds to his glory. The error is the twofold assumption: 1) that God's truthfulness would abound to his glory even if he indefinitely spared persistent unbelievers from judgment, and 2) that his glory would not abound if God judged unbelieving Israel.

It emerges from Rom 3:1-8, therefore, that _for Paul_ God's righteousness is neither a strict distributive justice nor a merely saving activity. It is more fundamental to God's nature than either of these and thus embraces both mercy and judgment. It is God's inclination always to act so that everything abounds to his glory.

In accord with the logic of 3:2-4 God's righteousness embraces both his gracious faithfulness to his promises and his punitive judgment upon sin. As far as individual man is concerned, what determines whether he glorifies God one way or the other is not his belonging to Israel, as the opponents thought, but his faith in the promises of God. Thus God manifests his righteousness in keeping his promises to those who believe, for in this he displays the value of his glory by blessing those whose stance of faith renders his glory most conspicuous (Rom 4:20). But he also manifests his righteousness in punishing those who remain in unbelief because unbelief is the gravest assault on God and to bless it indefinitely would be to deny the infinite value of his glorious trustworthiness.

In conclusion, then, our first exegetical effort to test whether Paul had a conception of righteousness like the one we discovered in the OT (Chapter Six) has turned up a positive answer. God's unswerving commitment to preserve and display his own glory in salvation and judgment is precisely the conception of righteousness which accords best with Paul's view in Rom 3:1-8 and which renders the argument here most intelligible.

CHAPTER EIGHT

THE RIGHTEOUSNESS OF GOD IN ROMANS 3:25,26

1. The text and the thesis

Rom 3:21-26 is "the center and heart"[1] of the book
of Romans. Accordingly "the central concept of Pauline
theology" (Kaesemann, Romans, 320), the righteousness
of God, is used here in a unique concentration (verses
21,22,25,26). But "the concept of God's righteousness
in Rom 3:25,26 carries a new and special accent as over
against verses 21,22" (Kuss, Roemerbrief, I, 117). It is
not to be equated with the gift of God received by the
believer in justification but rather is a description
of God's character manifest in the way he acts. Therefore, Rom 3:25,26, along with Rom 3:1-8, offers another
close analogy to Paul's usage in Rom 9:14. It will not
be surprising, then, if the understanding of the righteousness of God which emerges from these verses is the
same as the one we found in Rom 3:1-8 (Chapter Seven).
This is in fact the thesis of the chapter, namely that
the righteousness of God in Rom 3:25,26 refers most
basically to the characteristic of God's nature or the
unswerving inclination of his will (see note 29) which
precedes and grounds all his acts and gifts. It is his
inviolable allegiance to act always for his own name's
sake--to maintain and display his own divine glory. I
will use the following subdivision of the verses:

3:21a   But now apart from the law the righteousness
        of God has been manifested,
   b   being attested by the law and the prophets,
  22a   that is, the righteousness of God through
        faith in Jesus Christ for all who believe.
   b   For there is no distinction,
  23a   for all sinned
   b   and lack the glory of God,
  24   being justified freely by his grace through
        the redemption which is in Christ Jesus;
  25a   whom God put forth as a propitiation through
        faith, in his blood, for a demonstration of
        his righteousness
   b   on account of the passing over of sins done
        beforehand (26a) in the forbearance of God;
  26b   for a demonstration, I say, of his righteous-
        ness in the present time,
   c   in order that he might be righteous even in
        justifying the man who believes in Jesus.

115

2. The use of tradition in Romans 3:24-26

Since the rise of form-criticism we have been much more sensitive to the so-called "deep dimension of Scripture,"[2] that is, the traditions out of which the Scriptures grew. It is generally recognized that Paul's disclaimer in Gal 1:12 does not mean that he rejected all tradition. On the contrary he preserved, handed on, and adapted much early Christian tradition in various forms (cf 1 Cor 15:3; 11:2,23; 2 Thess 2:15; 3:6).[3] The form-critical judgment that in Rom 3:24-26a Paul is using a "traditional statement which perhaps can be traced back to the earliest church" begins with Rudolf Bultmann. He reckons the following to be pre-Pauline (with Pauline additions in parentheses):

> (24) . . . justified (by his grace as a gift) through the redemption that is in Christ Jesus, (25a) whom God put forward as an expiation by his blood (to be received by faith); (25b) this was to show God's righteousness, because he passed over former sins (26a) in his divine forbearance.

His arguments for this judgment are that 1) the designation of Christ as the ἰλαστήριον occurs only here in Paul; 2) it is not Paul's habit elsewhere (except Rom 5:9 and the traditional passages, 1 Cor 10:16; 11:25,27 [if one rejects Eph 1:7; 2:13; 6:12; Col 1:20 as non-Pauline]) to speak of "the blood" of Christ but rather of the cross; 3) "the idea found here of the divine righteousness demanding expiation for former sins is otherwise foreign to him" (Theology, I, 46).

It was Ernst Kaesemann's development of Bultmann's position in a 1951 article entitled "Zum Verstaendnis von Roemer 3,24-26"[4] which caused this form-critical judgment to prevail in German scholarship. Here and in his recent commentary he supplements Bultmann's arguments with the following. 1) The participial construction in verse 24 is such a "harsh breaking off" from the syntax of verse 23 that "it can be explained only by assuming Paul is now quoting a hymnic fragment" (Romans, 96f; "Roemer 3,24-26," 96). 2) This assumption accounts for the piling up of terminology which is not characteristic of Paul: πάρεσις, προγεγονότα, ἀμαρτήματα, προτίθεσθαι in the sense of manifesting, δικαιοσύνη as a divine attribute (verse 25), and ἀπολύτρωσις as a designation for an accomplished redemption (Rom 8:23 refers to the future, and 1 Cor 1:30; Col 1:14 are traditional) ("Roemer 3, 24-26," 96).

116

3) The "overladen style of the verses with their genitive constructions and prepositional connections . . .
is the characteristic of hymnic, liturgical tradition"
("Roemer 3, 24-26," 96). 4) In verse 25, διὰ πίστεως
interrupts the flow of the sentence and reveals itself
as a Pauline insertion (Romans, 97f).

   5) The fifth argument to support a traditional
formula in Rom 3:24-26a is, for Kaesemann, decisive: a
different conception of the righteousness of God is
found in this unit than we have in verse 26b, where
Paul, through the parallel construction beginning with
πρὸς τὴν ἔνδειξιν, "corrects" the tradition. In the
tradition "one sees oneself standing in continuity with
the people of God, holding to the history of Israel as
one's own, and counting the new covenant as the restitution of the old one" ("Roemer 3,24-26," 99). Thus
the righteousness of God is here (verse 25) God's
faithfulness to his covenant. But this is precisely
what moves Paul to add his "correction," since "for him
the righteousness of God is not primarily, if at all,
the restitution of the old covenant . . . The present
καιρός (verse 26b) is not viewed in relation to the
redemptive history begun by Moses but rather over
against the fallen world which is under God's wrath. . .
Since he is thinking universalistically and no longer
in terms of the covenant people, he speaks immediately
at the end of verse 26 of the individual believer"
("Roemer 3, 24-26," 100). In this way Paul gives his
own interpretation to the "righteousness of God":   "it
becomes God's faithfulness to his whole creation and
his right which is established in this relationship."[5]

   It is precisely this fifth argument of Kaesemann
that makes the whole form-critical issue relevant for
my specific question concerning the righteousness of
God. If Kaesemann is right, then verses 25-26a cannot
be used, as they have been traditionally, to interpret
Paul's own understanding of the demonstration of God's
righteousness, since Paul's own view is given in a
"correcting addition" in verse 26b. So we turn now to
an assessment of this form-critical position.

   First, the inclusion of verse 24 in the traditional
unit has been widely rejected. Eduard Lohse pointed
out that not only the words δωρεὰν τῇ αὐτοῦ χάριτι were
from Paul (which Kaesemann recognizes) but also the
designation Χριστῷ Ἰησοῦ, "since this phrase is not
found prior to Paul."[6] Gerhard Delling (Kreuzestod
Jesu, 12) argues further that δικαιούμενοι is a good
Pauline word and need not come from the tradition.

117

That leaves only the un-Pauline character of
ἀπολυτρώσεως and the awkward syntactical connection
with verse 23 as arguments for including verse 24 with
the tradition. But Klaus Wengst (<u>Christologische
Formeln</u>, 87), in explicit opposition to Kaesemann,
argues that the coordination of participles with finite
verbs (as in verses 23,24) is something Paul "loves" to
do. Heinrich Schlier (<u>Roemerbrief</u>, 107) in support of
this gives 2 Cor 5:6; 7:5; 8:18 as examples. Finally
Wengst (<u>Christologische Formeln</u>, 87) argues that
ἀπολύτρωσις is not <u>so</u> unusual for Paul (Rom 8:23; 1 Cor
1:30; Eph 1:7,14; 4:30; Col 1:14) that it can definitely
be ascribed to the tradition; nor has Kaesemann proven
that Paul's use of it in 1 Cor 1:30 is a "gepraegte
Formel." I regard these arguments as weighing heavily
in favor of not counting verse 24 as part of the early
Christian "traditional formulation."

But the traditional character of Rom 3:25,26a has
been much more widely accepted[7] though not universally.
While sporadic voices try to solve the syntactical
unevenness and parallel structure of these verses by
reference to later glosses or interpolations,[8] a number
of scholars have seen good reasons for reckoning all of
Rom 3:24-26 as Paul's own work. First of all, Heinrich
Schlier (<u>Roemerbrief</u>, 109) argues that the relative
clause which begins verse 25 <u>could</u> (as in Rom 4:25;
Phil 2:6; Col 1:13) signal a traditional unit, but that
one ought not draw this conclusion in the absence of
clear stylistic and rhythmic features which set the
unit off from Paul's own way of writing. This corrob-
orating evidence is missing here. The quotation is too
short to reveal any rhythm and the grouping of prepositional phrases is not so distinctive as to argue
strongly against Pauline origin.

Secondly, with regard to the argument from non-
Pauline terminology, since πάρεσιν and προγεγονότων
are <u>hapax legomena</u> in the New Testament and ἱλαστήριον
occurs only here and in Heb 9:5, it is an argument from
silence that they belonged to the earliest Christian
tradition. Moreover other important terms in these
verses are not foreign to Paul. Delling (<u>Kreuzestod
Jesu</u>, 13) points out that the key term ἔνδειξις is
found in the NT <u>only</u> in Paul (Rom 3:25,26; 2 Cor 8:24;
Phil 1:28) and with a sense similar to the one here.
The word ἀνοχή is found only here (verse 26a) and in
Rom 2:4. Ἁμάρτημα is genuinely Pauline in 1 Cor 6:18
and, while προέθετο has a meaning in verse 25 different
from its use in Rom 1:13 and Eph 1:9, this is also true
of προγράφω in Gal 3:1 (in contrast to Rom 15:4; Eph

3:3) which no one denies to be Paul's. In short, the
argument from non-Pauline terminology is not as strong
as some have thought. Word statistics are too ambiguous
to settle the issue.[9] And even if we grant the presence
of traditional terms that are not <u>uniquely</u> Pauline, this
would not betray the quotation of a pre-Pauline formulation but only the adoption of familiar traditional
terminology (Schlier, <u>Roemerbrief</u>, 109).

Thirdly, and most decisive in my judgment, Otto
Kuss and C.E.B. Cranfield have objected that it is
highly unlikely that in this "vital and central paragraph" Paul would have proceeded in the way Kaesemann
suggests. Cranfield (<u>Romans</u>, I, 200, note 1) argues
that

> to accept Kaesemann's account of these verses
> requires a very great deal of credulity. In
> the construction of a paragraph as vital and
> central to his whole argument as this para-
> graph is, Paul is scarcely likely to have
> gone to work in the way Kaesemann would have
> us envisage. It is very much more probable
> that these verses are Paul's own independent
> and careful composition reflecting his own
> preaching and thinking (cf Cambier, <u>L'Evangile
> de Dieu</u>, 784) and that the overladen style is
> the result, not of the incorporation of a
> <u>Vorlage</u> and the need to provide it with
> connectives, but of the intrinsic difficulty
> of interpreting the Cross at all adequately
> and perhaps also, in part, of the natural
> tendency to fall into a more or less litur-
> gical style when speaking of so solemn a
> matter.

Otto Kuss (<u>Roemerbrief</u>, I, **161**) shows even more precisely
why Kaesemann's "purely hypothetical construction" is
to be rejected. "Absolutely nothing in the context
points up an intention in verse 26b to correct verses
25-26a." How are we to imagine that Paul intended his
Roman readers (lacking contemporary form-critical tools,
like concordances and other NT documents for comparison)
to discover that Rom 3:25-26a is corrected in verse
26b? The issue at stake in these verses (the ground of
justification) is simply too important for Paul to have
omitted some kind of adversative particle in verse 26b if
he intended his readers to <u>contrast</u> it with verses
25-26a. As it stands it is far more probable that εἰς
ἔνδειξιν τῆς δικαιοσύνης αὐτοῦ διὰ τὴν πάρεσιν τῶν
προγεγονότων ἁμαρτημάτων ἐν τῇ ἀνοχῇ τοῦ θεοῦ (verses

25,26a) gives the reason in the past why such a demonstration was necessary (see below p 129) and verse 26b (πρὸς τὴν ἔνδειξιν . . .) gives the present purpose of the demonstration. There is no need to assume that Paul is correcting a limited Jewish-Christian view of righteousness. Therefore I conclude with Kuss and others that even if Paul was using tradition here "doubtless in this central text he presents theological sentences which to an especially high degree he has made his own."[10] Accordingly in the rest of this chapter I will not assume that the righteousness of God in Rom 3:25 has a different meaning from the same term in verse 26b.

3. Critique of the prevailing view

There are two fundamentally different views of the demonstration of God's righteousness in Rom 3:25,26. The one is associated with Anselm's satisfaction view of the atonement (Cur Deus Homo?). It distinguishes between the righteousness of God in verses 21,22 and the righteousness of God in verses 25,26. The latter is an attribute of God's nature (usually equated with his strict distributive justice); the former is the imputed divine righteousness appropriated by the believer in the event of justification or the action of God in justifying. For the other view, which rejects any identification with Anselm and which claims to have more Biblical-Hebraic presuppositions than he, the demonstration of the righteousness of God is his eschatological saving action in accomplishing redemption through the death of Jesus.[11]

While this second view has, to be sure, gained the ascendancy in recent decades, the dispute is by no means at an end. By way of example: Herman Ridderbos argues in his book on Paul that the righteousness of God in Rom 3:25f refers to "the vindicatory righteousness of God."[12] And, on the other side, Stuhlmacher ("Roemer 3, 24-26," 317) takes him to task for "brushing aside not only any attempt at an analysis of the tradition but also the whole newer discussion of the Semitic background of the expression 'righteousness of God.'" My aim is not to defend Ridderbos, even though I think his view is not as wrong as Stuhlmacher does. But, while avoiding the criticisms leveled against Ridderbos, I do want to argue for an alternative to the prevalent view of the righteousness of God in Rom 3:25,26.

One of the most seminal studies of Rom 3:25,26 which interprets God's righteousness as his saving action in justification is W.G. Kuemmel's "Πάρεσις und ἔνδειξις, ein Beitrag zum Verstaendnis der paulinischen Rechtfertigungslehre" (1952).[13] Subsequent studies regard this work as foundational. Therefore I will examine Kuemmel's arguments in some detail and allow my alternative position to emerge as the evidence points in that direction.

Kuemmel's interpretation may be summed up as follows: the demonstration of the righteousness of God in Rom 3:25,26 is "an exact exposition" of the manifestation of God's righteousness in verses 21,22 (160). The twofold ἔνδειξις of verses 25,26, which refers to an active showing (Erweis) rather than to a factual proof (Beweis), corresponds exactly to the active manifestation (πεφανέρωται) of God's righteousness in verses 21,22 and to the justification (δικαιούμενοι) of verse 24 (160f). In keeping with this view the prepositional phrase διὰ τὴν πάρεσιν . . . is rendered not as a causal phrase ("on account of the passing over of sins done beforehand"), but rather as an instrumental phrase ("through the pardon of sins done beforehand"). Therefore, we are not to think that the passing over of sins calls God's righteousness into question so that he now must prove himself righteous by punishing sin in the death of Jesus; on the contrary God's righteousness is shown forth precisely in the pardon (Erlass) of those sins (165). Accordingly the righteousness of God in verses 25f refers not to a quality or attribute of God which must be preserved but rather to the saving action of God which justifies sinners. "Therefore the satisfaction theory of Anselm does not even have a starting point in Paul's teaching" (166).[14]

Now let us examine Kuemmel's key arguments in support of this interpretation. After doing a lexical study of the key words πάρεσις and ἔνδειξις outside Rom 3:21-26 Kuemmel concludes with regard to both words that "only the context can decide" which of the possible meanings Paul intends here (158f). Thus all his arguments are based on grammatical and theological considerations of the immediate and wider Pauline context.

Kuemmel's first and main argument is that up to this point in Romans, and most importantly in the near context of 3:21,22, the righteousness of God has referred to the action of God in justifying sinners--to "Gottes rechtfertigendes, Gerechtigkeit schaffendes, den Menschen gerecht sprechendes Handeln" (to "the justifying, righteousness-creating, human-acquitting

121

action of God," 161). Therefore to construe the righteousness of God in 3:25,26 as an <u>attribute</u> of God would be "contrary to the preceding usage" (161). A serious flaw in this argument is Kuemmel's omission of any reference to the meaning of God's righteousness in Rom 3:5 and his consequent assumption that the term δικαιοσύνη θεοῦ has a uniform meaning throughout. Bultmann ("<u>ΔΙΚΑΙΟΣΥΝΗ</u>," 12) and others[15] have warned against the contemporary tendency to limit this term to only one meaning. Moreover, in Chapter Seven I tried to show that <u>Paul's</u> understanding of the righteousness of God in <u>Rom</u> 3:5 does <u>not</u> refer simply to the action of God in justifying sinners. Therefore Kuemmel's argument from the uniformity of the meaning of God's righteousness in Rom 1-3 is weak since the meaning of the term in 3:25 may be more similar to the meaning in 3:5 than it is to the meaning of 3:21f.

The rest of Kuemmel's arguments are attempts to show the error of the alternative "<u>Anselmsche</u>" interpretation. But I question whether the precise form of that interpretation which he defeats is really his strongest opponent. He argues that the interpretation of ἔνδειξις as "proof" (<u>Beweis</u>) is untenable "because it is not at all clearly expressed to whom God should want to prove his righteousness" (161). Moreover "in view of Rom 9:19f, it is foreign to Paul's theology that any man could put God's action into doubt and that God could see himself obligated to <u>prove</u> that such doubt is unfounded" (162f). Here he is arguing against the view which says, in the words of John Murray (<u>Romans</u>, I, 119f), that "the forbearance exercised in past ages [3:25b,26a] tended to obscure in the apprehension of men the inviolability of God's justice" and this "passing over" of sin "made it necessary for [God] to demonstrate his inherent justice" by punishing sin in the death of Jesus.

In response to Kuemmel one could argue, in view of Rom 2:23 where Paul picks up the OT theme of how God's name is held in derision among the nations (cf Ezek 36:20; 22:16; Is 52:5), that it would accord perfectly with God's holy zeal for his own name if he should act to clear his name and <u>prove</u> that such derision is folly. This would not contradict Pauline theology at all.

But such an argument is unnecessary because the alternative to Kuemmel's interpretation does not necessarily involve the concept of <u>proof</u> which he chides. One could translate ἔνδειξις as "a showing forth" or "an expression" and not lose anything essential to the "satisfaction theory" which he is opposing.[16]   One would simply argue that what was showing itself in the death of Christ is God's exacting demand of a recompense for sin. Therefore, Kuemmel does not strengthen his view by trying (unsuccessfully I think) to eliminate the idea of "proof" from the term ἔνδειξις in Rom 3:25f.

Perhaps the best response to Kuemmel's argument comes from C.E.B. Cranfield, who draws attention to the very important grammatical fact that the ultimate object of God's "showing" his righteousness is given with the words "in order that he himself might be righteous" (3:26c). Cranfield (Romans, I, 213) argues that "The words εἰς τὸ εἶναι αὐτὸν δίκαιον mean not 'in order that He might show that He is righteous' [contra Barrett (Romans, 80)] , but 'in order that He might be righteous.' . . . Paul recognizes that what was at stake was not just God's being seen to be righteous, but God's being righteous." If the purpose of God in the ἔνδειξις of his righteousness is that he might be righteous then the ἔνδειξις is not a mere "proof" or a mere "showing" but an establishment of righteousness. Without the death of Christ as a propitiation[17] for sins the problem would not have been the false accusations of men but the real unrighteousness of God. (More on this below, pp 129f.)

The next argument, which has to do with the meaning of πάρεσις (verse 25b), seems also to miss the target. Kuemmel rejects the meaning "passing over" or "letting go" (hingehenlassen) or "over-looking" (uebersehen) and opts for "pardon" or "forgiveness" (Erlass)--a forgiveness granted in the death of Christ for the sins of old. He argues, "It is in no way the opinion of Paul that during the time of God's ἀνοχή [verse 26a] he overlooked sins" (163). Rather from Rom 1:24; 2:4; 6:23; and 7:13 he concludes, "The ἀνοχή of God in the period before the sending of Christ consisted not in overlooking (uebersehen) of sins but in a punishment which did not destroy but aimed to bring about repentance (Rom 2:4) . . ." (163).

With this criticism Kuemmel does not weaken his opponent at all. For these reasons: Kuemmel's and Kaesemann's[18] insistence that Paul views the time before Christ not as a time of leniency but a time of wrath (1:18-3:20) is an oversimplification of Pauline theology. To be sure in Rom 2:4,5 (the only other use of ἀνοχή in the NT) men are storing up wrath for

themselves in the patience of God, but Paul still calls
this period a period of the "kindness of God" (χρηστὸν
τοῦ θεοῦ, 2:4). Kuemmel himself refers to the sins of
this period as "not completely punished" (nicht
endgueltig gestraft, 165). This concession is all that
is required to validate the interpretation he is opposing. For the scholars who hold to a "satisfaction
theory" do not claim that the period of God's ἀνοχή was
all leniency and that sins were ignored. What is argued,
in the words of Leon Morris (Apostolic Preaching, 278),
is that "God had not always punished sin with full
severity in the past." The "kindness" of withholding
full judgment (not to mention the blessings given, cf
Acts 14:16; 17:30; Mt. 5:45) was not deserved by sinful
man and precisely this provides the basis of the satisfaction theory which claims that God's apparent injustice must be rectified.

But even more can be said to show the weakness of
Kuemmel's argument. Suppose πάρεσις does mean "pardon"
or "forgiveness" in verse 25. Even this does not
contradict, but accords with, the satisfaction theory.
The OT is replete with the mercies of God "who forgives
iniquity and transgression and sin" (Ex 34:7) and, for
example, angers his prophet Jonah with his mercy toward
Nineveh. It may well be the justifying forgiveness
shown to the OT saints which constitutes the πάρεσις of
3:25. Paul certainly thought that men of faith like
David (Rom 4:6-8) and Abraham (Rom 4:9) had received
forgiveness before Christ. But this remitting of sins
creates the same problem for justice that leniency of
punishment does. Therefore the "satisfaction theory"
cannot be refuted by showing that πάρεσις means pardon.
One would have to go further and demonstrate that διά
τὴν πάρεσιν does not have its usual causal force ("on
account of [past] pardon") but rather has a rare instrumental force ("through the [present] pardon [in Christ] ").
I will discuss this problem further on (see pp 127-9).

The basic reason why Kuemmel and others view the
righteousness of God in Rom 3:25,26 as God's saving
action is not any exegetical detail or contextual clue.
The factor that weighs most heavily in their exegesis
is the conviction that has been growing ever since
Hermann Cremer enunciated it in his book Die
paulinische Rechtfertigungslehre (1899), namely, that
the righteousness of God in the OT is not his conformity
to an ideal ethical norm (like strict retributive
justice) but is his faithfulness within the dictates of
a given relationship, especially his covenant with
Israel.[19] This view has been supported by most OT

scholars (see Chapter Six). Together with the proper
conviction that the Pauline doctrine of righteousness
can be understood only against an OT background, this
conviction has exerted tremendous power in the interpretation of the righteousness of God in Paul. Accordingly Anselm and all his contemporary followers are
accused of importing Greek (Stuhlmacher, Gerechtigkeit,
88 note 6) or Germanic (Goppelt, Theologie, II, 424)
concepts of law into the Hebraic-Biblical view of God's
righteousness.

Since Kuemmel's 1952 article, in which he treated
this relational view of God's righteousness as a
"presupposition" (Voraussetzung, 162) for the interpretation of Rom 3:25,26, Kaesemann has provided the fore-
most illustration of how strongly the findings of
history-of-religions research influence the interpretation of Paul. He has stressed that late Jewish apocalyptic had a profound influence on Paul. It is "the
mother of Christian theology" ("Christian Apocalyptic,"
137) and it is "the driving force of Pauline theology
and practice" (Romans, 306). The specific concept of
righteousness out of which Rom 3:25f grew, he claims,
is summarized in two key texts. The first is from
Qumran (1 QS 11:12-15):

> And if I stagger, God's mercies are my salva-
> tion forever; and if I stumble because of the
> sin of the flesh, my justification is in the
> righteousness of God which exists forever. . .
> He has caused me to approach by His mercy.
> And by His favors He will bring my justifica-
> tion. He has justified me by His true justice
> and by His immense goodness He will pardon all
> my iniquities. And by His justice He will
> cleanse me from the defilement of man and of
> the sins of the sons of men, that I may
> acknowledge His righteousness unto God and His
> majesty unto the Most High.20

The second text providing a summary statement of the
Jewish-apocalyptic background of Paul's understanding
of God's righteousness is 4 Ezra 8:31-36:

> For we and our fathers have passed our lives
> in ways that bring death: but thou because
> of us sinners art called compassionate. For
> if thou hast a desire to compassionate us
> who have no works of righteousness then
> shalt thou be called 'the gracious One'.
> For the righteous who have many works laid

up with thee, shall out of their own deeds
receive their reward. But what is man that
thou shouldest be wroth with him? Or what
is a corruptible race that thou canst be so
bitter towards it? For in truth there is
none of the earth-born who has not dealt
wickedly, and among those who exist who has
not sinned. For in this, O Lord, shalt thy
<u>righteousness</u> and goodness be declared, if
thou wilt compassionate them that have no
wealth of good works.[21]

It is fairly obvious from these texts as well as
many in the OT (cf Chapter Six) that the righteousness
of God in Jewish literature does not always mean strict
retributive justice: it embraces mercy. This view of
righteousness as <u>iustitia salutifera</u> has come to be
seen as the peculiarly Jewish-Biblical view and thus
functions for many scholars as an <u>assumption</u> in dealing
with Pauline texts.

More than a few scholars, however, have seen the
hermeneutical pitfalls of such a use of the history of
a concept. Kaesemann and Stuhlmacher especially have
come in for methodological criticism on this point. In
reaction to the Kaesemann-Stuhlmacher interpretation of
God's righteousness, Hans Conzelmann and Guenther Klein
have both stressed "the priority of interpretation over
any deductions from history-of-religions research or
history-of-tradition research . . . Decisive is not the
history of a concept but the Pauline context"
("Gottesgerechtigkeit," 227; <u>IDB</u>, <u>Supplement</u>, 751).
"The evidence in Paul should be assessed on the basis
of his own usage" (Conzelmann, <u>Theology</u>, 218).
Because of his doubt that the righteousness of God is a
technical term in the late Jewish literature (as
Stuhlmacher maintains, <u>Gerechtigkeit</u>, 175) and because
he is alert to a peculiar, Pauline usage of the term,
Conzelmann admits that in Rom 3:25f the righteousness
of God "can (as in the Jewish usage) mean the covenant
faithfulness of God. But that is not certain. It can
also be understood as <u>iustitia distributiva</u>."[22]

Thus the interpretation of God's righteousness in
Rom 3:25,26 which Kuemmel and others espouse is in my
judgment based mainly on the assumption that Paul
stands in the stream of the OT-Jewish tradition and
that the OT-Jewish view of God's righteousness, as a
relational term embracing mercy, rules out the satisfaction theory of the atonement in which God's righteousness demands punishment for sins. The implicit

126

danger here of minimizing Paul's originality[23] has already been mentioned. But the greatest objection to Kuemmel's supposedly Biblical-Hebraic conception of God's righteousness is that it does not go to the heart of divine righteousness which the OT itself reveals. I have argued in Chapter Six (p 90) that to focus on "covenant faithfulness" as the fundamental meaning of righteousness in the OT obscures a deeper dimension of God's righteousness, namely his faithfulness in upholding the honor of his name. His commitment to Israel is penultimate; his commitment to maintain his own glory is ultimate. His saving deeds are "righteous" not merely because they uphold the covenant promises, but basically because they preserve and display the honor of God's name. If this is the way Paul read his OT,[24] then the major bulwark of Kuemmel's exegesis falls. So we must ask: Does the logic of Rom 3:25,26 confirm or contradict our thesis that Paul does work with a concept of divine righteousness like the one just sketched?

4. An alternative interpretation of Romans 3:25,26

There are two pivotal phrases in Rom 3:25,26 which receive their most coherent and least strained interpretation against the OT background I have developed. The first is διὰ τὴν πάρεσιν τῶν προγεγονότων ἁμαρτημάτων: "on account of (or through) the passing over (or pardon) of sins done before." One can at least say from this phrase that man's sins have created the need for God to put Christ forth as a propitiation by his blood.

What is the essential character of these sins? Rom 1:21-23 together with 3:23 gives the best answer to this question. "All sinned and are lacking the glory of God" (3:23). Most recent commentators are probably right that this loss of glory reflects the Jewish tradition[25] according to which Adam was divested of his glory when he sinned. How Paul conceives of this loss is seen in Rom 1:21-23. "Although they knew God they did not glorify him as God or thank him . . . they exchanged the glory of the incorruptible God for the likeness of the image of corruptible man and birds and four-footed beasts and reptiles." One can hear an echo of Jer 2:11, "Has a nation changed its gods, even though they are no gods? But my people have changed their glory for that which does not profit" (cf Ps 106:20). Not to glorify him as God and thank him is the primal sin: the esteeming of the creature above the creator and the consequent belittling of the creator's glory.

127

This "foolish" exchange results, as 1:24ff shows, in a swell of dishonorable and demeaning attitudes and acts. Thus, according to Rom 1:24ff all sins are an expression of dishonor to God, stemming as they do from the evil inclination of man's heart to value anything above the glory of God.

For God to condone or ignore the dishonor heaped upon him by the sins of men would be tantamount to giving credence to the value judgment men have made in esteeming God more lowly than his creation. It is not so much that he would be saying sins do not matter or justice does not matter; more basically, he would be saying that he does not matter. But for God thus to deny the infinite value of his glory, to act persistently as if the disgrace of his holy name were a matter of indifference to him--this is the heart of unrighteousness. Thus if God is to be righteous he must repair the dishonor done to his name by the sins of those whom he blesses. He must magnify the divine glory man thought to deny him.[26]

It is pointless to object here that God never is trapped in a situation where he must do something. This is pointless because the only necessity unworthy of God is a necessity imposed on him from causes not originating in himself. To say that God must be who he is, that he must value what is of infinite value and delight in his infinite beauty, this is no dishonor to God. On the contrary what would dishonor God is to deny that he has any necessary identity at all and to assert that his acts emerge willy-nilly from no essential and constant nature.

Nor is it a legitimate objection here to say that "Greek" or "Germanic" ideas of justice are being brought in and that the Semitic background is being ignored. The point is not that God is somehow forced to conform to an ideal ethical norm. The point--in good OT fashion--is simply that God must be God and will brook no belittling of his glorious name.

In view of the nature of sin as dishonor to the glorious name of God and in view of the most basic OT aspect of God's righteousness as his unswerving faithfulness to act always for his own name's sake in preserving and displaying his glory, there is no reason whatever to construe the prepositional phrase beginning with διά (verse 25b) any way but in its usual causal sense.[27] Given this perfectly Jewish thought connection we need not follow Kuemmel ("Πάρεσις," 164) and

Kaesemann (Romans, 99) in the unlikely view that here
διά with the accusative is instrumental and means
"through." Thus the sense of the prepositional phrase
is that since God has not required from all individual
sinners a loss of glory commensurate with their debase-
ment of God's glory, therefore to preserve and display
the infinite value of his own glory, God set forth
Christ as a propitiation whose death for sinners so
glorified God (Rom 15:7-9) that God's righteousness was
preserved and made known.

The second pivotal phrase in Rom 3:25f is verse
26c,εἰς τὸ εἶναι αὐτὸν δίκαιον καὶ δικαιοῦντα τὸν ἐκ
πίστεως Ἰησοῦ. The interpretation by Kaesemann
(Romans, 101), following C. Blackman ("Romans 3:26b,"
203f), to the effect that the καί here is explicative
(or intensive) and that God is δίκαιος precisely as he
is ὁ δικαιῶν, is very awkward in view of what precedes.
The awkwardness of this interpretation stems from its
failure to distinguish clearly 1) the demonstration
(ἔνδειξις, verse 26b) of God's righteousness, 2) his
being (εἶναι, 26c) righteous and 3) his justifying
believers (verse 26c). According to Kaesemann, the
first and third of these--the demonstration of God's
righteousness at the present time and the justification
of the one who trusts Jesus--refer to the same thing:
"the eschatological saving action" of God. But
Kaesemann does not say how we are to understand God's
being righteous in distinction from this active demon-
stration.28 It may be that he sees no distinction.
But that would involve not taking Paul's purpose construction (εἰς τό plus the infinitive εἶναι) seriously.
For Paul the demonstration of God's righteousness and
God's being righteous are not the same; the latter is
the outcome and purpose of the former. But this means
that the action of God in justifying believers (verse
26c) is also not interchangeable with God's being
righteous. Therefore the καί is not intensive and one
should not construe verse 26c to mean that God is
"just" insofar as he is "justifier" or that his righteousness consists in justifying.

If we grant full force to the purpose construction
(εἰς τὸ εἶναι) and thus to the distinction between
demonstration and being, a coherent interpretation
emerges against the backdrop of the OT view of divine
righteousness sketched above. In putting Christ
forth as a propitiation God acts for the sake of his
glory, i.e., he actively demonstrates inviolable
allegiance to the honor of his name in order that his

129

inexorable love of his own glory may not be weakened, i.e., in order that he might remain and be righteous.[29]

In this context the justification of sinners through faith (verse 26c) and the passing over (or pardoning) of former sins (verse 25b) both seem to imply that God is disregarding his glory (and would indeed imply this if it were not for God's setting Christ forth as a propitiation by his blood). "Therefore the καί [of verse 26c] must be understood . . . as an adversative and is to be translated 'it was to prove at the present time that he himself is just and yet the justifier of him who has faith in Jesus" (Ladd, Theology, 432). Or as Cranfield (Romans, I, 213) translates it: "that God might be righteous even in justifying." Understood in this way this pivotal purpose clause at the end of verse 26 is a fitting and perfectly clear climax to verses 25,26a. God has accomplished his twofold purpose of sending Christ: he has manifested and preserved his own righteousness and yet[30] has justified the ungodly merely through faith. The glorification of God and the salvation of his people are accomplished together.

In conclusion, therefore, I find confirmed that in Rom 3:25,26 the concept of God's righteousness as his absolute faithfulness always to act for his name's sake and for the preservation and display of his glory provides the key which unlocks the most natural and coherent interpretation of this text.

CHAPTER NINE

THE JUSTIFICATION OF GOD: ROMANS 9:14-18
PART II

In Chapter Five the first steps were taken in
trying to understand how Paul intends to defend the
righteousness of God in predestination. The suggestion
put forward tentatively there was that on the basis of
Ex 33:19 (= Rom 9:15) and Ex 9:16 (= Rom 9:17) Paul
argues that God's name or his glory consists in the
sovereign exercise of his freedom to show mercy and to
harden. This insight, however, could function for Paul
as a defense of God's righteousness in predestination
only if Paul's conception of divine righteousness was
such that it consisted basically in God's unswerving
commitment always to act for the glory of his name. As
Chapters Six-Eight have shown, this is in fact the case.

What must be done now is to pursue our analysis of
Rom 9:14-18 to see whether or not the parts which we
have not yet examined confirm and cohere with our
emerging interpretation, and also to see how this unit
fits into the flow of Paul's argument in the rest of
the chapter. (For my verse divisions of the text see
p 69).

1. "It is not of the one who wills or runs" (Rom 9:16)

Paul uses the word "run" (τρέχω) in 1 Cor 9:24,26;
Gal 2:2; 5:7; Phil 2:16; 2 Thess 3:1. The usage is not
uniform in meaning. Running can refer to the normal
good progress of daily Christian living (Gal 5:7); to
the successful spread of the Gospel as the word runs
and is glorified in reaching the goal of faith (2 Thess
3:1); and to Paul's apostolic ministry with all the
spiritual effort it involves (1 Cor 9:24-26; Gal 2:2;
Phil 2:16). In the latter case it parallels the sport
of boxing on the one hand (1 Cor 9:26) and the toil of
labor on the other (Phil 2:16)--the former stressing
Paul's reward for finishing his course (cf 2 Tim 4:8)
and the latter stressing the happy completion of the
thing he was laboring on.

The explicit allusion to the sport of running in
1 Cor 9:24-26 inclines most commentators to construe
the running of Rom 9:16 as a similar allusion with the
focus being on the exertion required to run. But Adolf
Schlatter raised a question whether in fact Paul
intends any reference to the stadium here

(Gerechtigkeit, 300), and Bent Noack ("Celui qui court," 113-16) and Gerhard Maier (Mensch und freier Wille, 368-70) have developed compelling arguments against an athletic, Hellenistic background and in favor of a Jewish one. Their arguments may be summarized as follows.

1) The immediate and wider context of Rom 9:16 is marked by a distinctly Jewish concern (cf 9:1-5) and there is no hint (excepting the one word "run") of an athletic metaphor. 2) The phrase, "not of the one who wills neither of the one who runs," translates back into Hebrew as לא ביד הרוצה ולא ביד הרץ and reveals a possible word play or alliteration between הרוצה and הרץ, which suggests that we do well to consider the use of רוץ in the OT as the background for Rom 9:16. 3) Ps 119:32 (LXX 118:32) commends itself readily as an indication of how Paul may have understood running here: "I will run the way of your commands." In other words, not the physical effort of the Greek games, but the moral resolve to keep the law may well be the background of Paul's metaphor.[1] 4) The allusion to "running the way of the commandments" would cohere very closely with Rom 9:30f where the similar word διώκω appears: "the Gentiles who did not pursue righteousness attained righteousness, the righteousness from faith; but Israel, though pursuing a law of righteousness, did not reach the law" (cf also Phil 3:14-15). 5) Noack (115) gives two rabbinic references to confirm the Jewish usage: b. Ber. 28b: "I run and they run; I run toward the life in the world to come, they run toward perdition"; b. Pes. 112a: "Be courageous as the panther, swift as the eagle, run like the deer, and be strong like the lion to do the will of your Father who is in heaven." 6) Maier (p 53f) argues that Paul expresses himself in conscious opposition to the widespread Pharisaic viewpoint expressed in Ps Sol 9:4f (quoted in Chapter Three, note 59) and Sir 15:14f: "It was [the Lord] who created man in the beginning and he left him in the power of his own inclination." The substance of Paul's response[2] falls within the line of thought developed to its logical conclusion in Qumran: "For is man the master of his way? No, a man does not establish his steps, for his justification belongs to God and from his hand comes perfection of way. By his knowledge all things are brought into being, by his purpose every being established, and without him is nothing done" (1 QS 11:10f; cf Chapter Three, notes 57, 58). That Paul's mind is moving in this thought-world lessens the probability that with the word "run" he has reached for a Greek athletic metaphor rather than a Jewish metaphor

132

of moral attainment. 7) Finally, Maier (368) correctly observes that verse 16 is "a sharpened repetition of the thesis of predestination in 9:11f." More specifically, the "not from works but from him who calls" in 9:12 corresponds precisely to "not of him who wills or of him who runs but of God who has mercy" in 9:16. Therefore, we are to understand willing and running as an expression of "works" which according to Rom 9:32 is the way Israel was "pursuing" (i.e., running after) the law. I conclude, therefore, with Noack and Maier that Paul draws his metaphor from a Jewish background in which, for some, human willing and acting in pursuit of the law were regarded as finally decisive in determining God's merciful blessing.

But we must be careful not to place an unintended limitation on Rom 9:16 as if Paul wanted to say merely that only some willing and running (i.e., "works") do not initiate God's decision to show mercy while another kind of willing and running (e.g., the "work of faith"; cf Gal 5:7; 1 Thess 1:3) do initiate God's decision to show mercy. There are at least three reasons why not just some but all human willing and running are excluded here as determinative in God's decision to show mercy. First, the fact that, as we have seen, 9:16 repeats the point of 9:11f proves that all willing is intended in 9:16 since in 9:11 God's decision to show a special mercy to Jacob and not Esau happened before they were born. Neither the bad willing/running of "works" nor the good willing/running of faith had any influence at all on God's decision to show mercy.

Second, 9:16 is an inference from Ex 33:19 ("I will have mercy on whomever I have mercy"), but one cannot infer from this text that God's decision to have mercy is determined by some acts of human willing/ running but not others. Such an interpretation would have to be read into the text by those who have already decided that Paul must leave room here for human self-determination. What really follows from "I will have mercy on whomever I have mercy" is precisely what Paul says: not any attitude or act of men, but God alone determines his bestowals of mercy. Third, the closest analogy in Paul to the phrase οὐ τοῦ θέλοντος οὐδὲ τοῦ τρέχοντος in Rom 9:16 is Phil 2:13: "God is the one who works in you both the willing and the working"(τὸ θέλειν καὶ τὸ ἐνεργεῖν). This text gives the positive counterpart to our text and confirms our interpretation. Man's willing and running do not determine the bestowal of God's mercy (9:16); on the contrary, God's mercy determines man's willing and working (Phil 2:13).

133

And since the "willing and working" referred to in, Phil 2:13 is not evil "works" but the obedience of faith, it follows that the assertion of Rom 9:16 cannot be limited to only some kinds of willing and running. For these three reasons Rom 9:16 should be construed so as to sweep away forever the thought that over against God there is any such thing as human self-determination in Pauline anthropology.[3]

We may be able to refine our understanding of the juxtaposition of θέλειν and τρέχειν still further. In answer to the question why Paul should mention both of these words one might naturally suggest that willing is viewed as the <u>inception</u> of an action (running) and running is viewed as the <u>consummation</u> in behavior of a decision or attitude (willing). Thus Paul aims to say that no processes at all in the psycho-physical life of man determine God's decision to bestow mercy or not. This, I think, is an accurate statement of Paul's inten- tion. But there may be an added nuance of meaning suggested by Paul's analogous uses of θέλω elsewhere. In Rom 7:15 Paul says, "What I will this I do not prac- tice, but what I hate this I do" (οὐ γὰρ ὃ θέλω τοῦτο πράσσω, ἀλλ' ὃ μισῶ τοῦτο ποιῶ; cf Gal 5:17). Here it is evident that Paul knows θέλειν does not always give birth to a deed. This is a common experience and no surprise to us. But in 2 Cor 8:10, where Paul is urging the believers to lay aside money for the poor saints in Jerusalem, he says, "This is best for you who began a year ago not only to do but also to will" (οὐ μόνον τὸ ποιῆσαι ἀλλὰ καὶ τὸ θέλειν). We might have expected just the reverse order. Here Paul treats θέλειν as something over and above ποίειν, something more that makes the ποίειν even better. Evidently θέλειν here stands not for that initial act of will by which all human action is generated but for the <u>cheer- ful</u> and <u>hearty</u> consent commended in 2 Cor 9:7. There- fore, it is possible that one could be "running" (i.e., doing good deeds) but not "willing" (i.e., consenting cheerfully to the deed). If Paul is thinking in these terms in Rom 9:16 then the nuance of meaning not to be overlooked would be: it does not matter whether you perform your deeds with cheer or begrudgingly; God's decision to bestow mercy or not lies wholly within himself. But the progression from willing to running ("neither of the one who wills nor of the one who runs") makes this interpretation less than certain.

2. The scope of God's freedom in Romans 9:16

I have been assuming so far in the discussion of

Rom 9:16 that the implied subject of the sentence is "God's bestowal of mercy": "God's bestowal of mercy is not of the one who wills nor of the one who runs but of God who has mercy." The justification and specification of this assumption must now be given. There are two reasons why virtually all commentators agree that in general the subject is "God's bestowal of mercy." The first is that 9:15 (= Ex 33:19), from which 9:16 is inferred, refers only to God's showing mercy on whomever he wills. It follows from God's freedom in showing mercy on whomever he wills that his bestowal of mercy is not dependent[4] on man's willing or running. The second reason is that verse 16 does not say "not of one who wills nor of one who runs, but of God." Instead it adds a defining participle (of God who shows mercy) which suggests clearly that the subject is "God's bestowal of mercy."

But there the agreement among the commentators ceases. When an attempt is made to specify what bestowal of mercy Paul has in mind the ranks divide along the same issue that we addressed in Chapter Three, Section 3.2. Some want to limit the application to God's favors granted only on the plane of history with no one's eternal destiny at stake.[5] Others see no reason for such a limitation and acknowledge that also the mercy of eternal salvation is "not of one who wills or one who runs" (see Chapter Three, notes 25, 26).

It is very misleading for Forster and Marston (note 5) to argue that since Moses' eternal destiny was not at issue in Ex 33:19, therefore Paul is not concerned in this context with the salvation of individuals. Our exegesis of Ex 33:19 in its OT context (Chapter Four) showed that Ex 33:19 is not a description of how God acted in any particular instance toward Moses in granting him a theophany or toward Israel in renewing the covenant. Rather it is something far more fundamental and far-reaching, namely, a solemn proclamation of God's name and glory. In other words Ex 33:19 means that an essential feature of God's glorious character is his propensity to show mercy and his absolute freedom in bestowing it on whomever he wills apart from any constraints originating outside his will. Furthermore, I have argued, along with U. Luz, C. Mueller and G. Maier (Chapter Four, note 2), that Paul employed Ex 33:19 with precisely this meaning (see pp 77f). In turn this was confirmed by the intelligibility and coherence it lends to the argument of 9:14,15.

Therefore, it is irrelevant to discuss whether
Paul thinks Moses was predestined to salvation, because
what Paul draws from the OT in Rom 9:15 is not a comment
about the condition or treatment of Moses but a declaration of God's character, namely, his sovereign freedom
in dispensing mercy. Therefore, the issue of whether
Rom 9:15,16 has anything to say about the determination
of individuals to their eternal destinies must be
decided on the basis of the scope of God's freedom
implied in Paul's context. The crucial question is:
To what problem does Paul apply this fundamental principle of divine freedom? Or: How does Rom 9:15,16 fit
into the flow of Paul's argument developed from 9:1 to
9:14?

My answer here depends in large measure on the
exegesis of Rom 9:1-13 in Chapters Two and Three. So I
will only summarize the line of reasoning which I
defended there. The basic problem described in 9:1-5
is that many Israelites, to whom, as a nation, saving
promises had been made, are now accursed and cut off
from Christ (9:1-3). The condemnation of so many
Israelites to eternal destruction raises the question
whether God's word has fallen. Paul denies it (9:6a)
and defends his denial in 9:6b-13. In defense of God's
faithfulness to his word, in spite of many Israelites
being accursed, Paul argues that God's "purpose" from
the beginning of Israel's history was a purpose "according to election" (9:11), that is, a purpose not to
save every individual Israelite, as though descent from
Abraham guaranteed that one would be a child of God,
but rather a purpose to "call" a true Israel (9:6b)
into being by choosing some Israelites and not others
"before they were born or had done anything good or
evil" (9:11). It is this Israel for whom the promises
are valid. The unconditional election of Isaac and
Jacob over Ishmael and Esau (whether to eternal destinies or only to historical roles) reveals the principle
of God's freedom in election which is the ultimate
explanation why many of Paul's kinsmen according to the
flesh are accursed and cut off from Christ. As he says
in Rom 11:7, "the elect obtained it [salvation],but the
rest were hardened." For this reason it cannot be said
that God's expressed purpose has fallen (9:6a).

That God, in determining the beneficiaries of his
mercy, does not base his decisions on any human distinctives that a person may claim by birth or effort,
evokes from Paul's rhetorical conversation partner the
charge that God would then be unrighteous (or Paul must
be wrong). Paul denies this (9:14) and in 9:15 cites

Ex 33:19 as support for his denial. I have tried to explain and render plausible the logic of this support in Chapters Four-Eight. In a nutshell it goes like this: Paul's conception of God's righteousness is that it consists basically in his commitment to act always for his own name's sake, that is, to preserve and display his own glory (cf Chapters Seven and Eight). Therefore, since according to Ex 33:19 God's glory or name consists basically in his sovereign freedom in the bestowal of mercy (cf Chapter Four) there is no unrighteousness with God when his decision to bless one person and not another is based solely on his own will rather than on any human distinctive. On the contrary he <u>must</u> pursue his "purpose of election" in this way in order to remain righteous, for only in his sovereign, free bestowal (and withholding) of mercy on whomever he wills is God acting out of a full allegiance to his name and esteem for his glory.

Since Rom 9:15 is brought in to support the righteousness of God which was seemingly jeopardized by his unconditional election in 9:11-13, and since Rom 9:16 is an inference from 9:15 and a virtual restatement of 9:11f, therefore the <u>scope of God's freedom</u> in 9:16 must correspond to the <u>exercise of that freedom</u> in 9:11-13. This means that if our argument developed in Chapter Three and summarized here is right, then the scope of God's freedom in bestowing mercy <u>does</u> embrace his predestination of individuals to their eternal destiny. This conclusion is not based on any conviction about God's dealings with the individual Moses, but rather on the fundamental truth of God's freedom expressed in Ex 33:19 and on the scope of this freedom required by the context to render the sequence of Paul's thought from 9:1 to 9:16 coherent. This conclusion also corresponds to the conclusion of Section 1 (pp 131-134) that "willing and running" cannot legitimately be limited in such a way that <u>some</u> willing, like the act of trusting Christ, does ultimately determine God's bestowal of mercy, namely the mercy of salvation. Faith is indeed a <u>sine qua non</u> of salvation; Rom 9:16, therefore, necessarily <u>implies</u> that the act of faith is ultimately owing to the prevenient grace of God. But this is a theological inference, however true, beyond Paul's explicit concern here. There is no reference at all to faith in Rom 9 until verse 30.

One other question needs to be answered at this point: If Rom 9:15-18 is really intended by Paul to be a coherent and compelling argument for God's righteousness in unconditional election, why is 9:16, which as

an inference (ἄρα οὖν) from Ex 33:19 seems to have
logical primacy, simply a reassertion of the action of
God in 9:11f which called God's righteousness into
question in the first place? Would we not rather
expect in a unit defending the righteousness of God
a series of arguments rather than two OT quotations
(9:15,17) and two restatements of the initial problem
(9:16,18)? Perhaps we would. But we must not insist
that Paul carry through his justification of God's
election the same way we would, especially when a
plausible explanation of his procedure is available.

What we should recall is the nature of the opponent's objection. It must have had a double prong: on
the one hand, Paul is accused of making God out to be
unrighteous; on the other hand, since the opponent no
doubt believes God is righteous, the objection implies
that Paul is wrong about unconditional election. Is
it not plausible, then, that Paul's response will not
only supply the evidence which supports the righteousness of God (as he understands it) in unconditional
election (9:15,17), but will also reassert what is
really being challenged by the objector, namely, the
sovereign freedom of God manifested in that election
(9:16,18)?

3. The γάρ of Romans 9:17

In Rom 9:17 Paul quotes Ex 9:16 as his second OT
support for the righteousness of God in unconditional
election: "For the Scripture says to Pharaoh: 'For
this very thing I raised you up that I might show in
you my power and that my name might be proclaimed in
all the earth.'" Commentators do not agree on how the
verse relates to what precedes. One group[6] sees the
γάρ of 9:17 as parallel to the γάρ of 9:15 and thus
connected as a support to 9:14. The other group[7] argues
that γάρ attaches 9:17 directly to 9:16 as a ground.
Both groups seldom give reasons for their interpretation. But the first group could point to the structure
of the paragraph: just as the ἄρα οὖν of 9:18 corresponds to the ἄρα οὖν of 9:16 so the γάρ of 9:17 corresponds to the γάρ of 9:15. The second group could
argue that it is illegitimate to leap back over two
verses to make the γάρ of 9:17 attach to 9:14 when it
makes good sense to attach it as usual to what immediately precedes. The sense of this second interpretation, as expressed by Sanday and Headlam (Romans, 225),
is: Verse 17 is "additional proof showing that the
principle just enunciated (in 9:16) is true not merely
in an instance of God's mercy, but also of his

138

severity." Hence 9:17 would argue that also in the
matter of divine <u>hardening</u> "it is not of one who wills
nor of one who runs but of God."

On the basis of grammatical rules alone no resolu-
tion is likely to be reached. It seems to me from the
logical structure of Paul's argument that 9:17 relates
to both 9:14 and 16. This will become clearer if we
paraphrase 9:14-16. Verse 16 asserts that God is free
in the bestowal of his mercy: his choices of its
beneficiaries are not conditioned by a man's willing or
running. Verse 14 asserts that God is righteous to act
in this way. Standing in between these two assertions,
verse 15 supports them both by showing from Ex 33:19
that God does in fact exercise such freedom (support
for 9:16), and that this is an essential aspect of his
glorious name which it is righteous to exalt (support
for 9:14). In all probability Paul intends the quotation of Ex 9:16 in Rom 9:17 to provide the negative
counterpart (hardening) to 9:15 (mercy) and to function
in the same way, namely, to support both the assertion
of God's freedom in election (9:16,18) and the assertion
that he is righteous to act this way (9:14). The way
9:18 correlates mercy (from 9:15) and hardening (from
9:17) is in favor of this interpretation. If it is
correct, then the debate over whether the γάρ in 9:17
relates to 9:14 or 9:16 is not so crucial, since
basically it relates to both.

I am suggesting, therefore, that Paul employs Ex
9:16 (= Rom 9:17) as he did Ex 33:19--to further
support his initial claim in 9:14 that God is not
unrighteous in the absoluteness of his unconditional
election. To see precisely how this OT quotation
functions in Paul's argument we should now examine the
OT context in which he read the text. This is all the
more necessary since many commentators, precisely on
the basis of the OT context, construe Paul's meaning in
a way quite foreign to the intention evident in the
context of Rom 9.

4. The hardening of Pharaoh in the OT context

In Ex 4-14 the hardening of Pharaoh's heart is
designated by three different Hebrew words.[8] It will
be helpful to list the occurrences of these with their
Hebrew parsing, grammatical subjects and equivalents
from the LXX.

חזק
4:21, pi imp, God,
   σκληρυνῶ
7:13, q imp c,[9] heart,
   κατίσχυσεν
7:22, q imp c, heart,
   ἐσκληρύνθη
8:15(19), q imp c, heart,
   ἐσκληρύνθη
9:12, pi imp c, God,
   ἐσκλήρυνεν
9:35, q imp c, heart,
   ἐσκληρύνθη
10:20, pi imp c, God,
   ἐσκλήρυνεν
10:27, pi imp c, God,
   ἐσκλήρυνεν
11:10, pi imp c, God,
   ἐσκλήρυνεν
14:4, hiph perf, God,
   σκληρυνῶ
14:8, pi imp c, God,
   ἐσκλήρυνεν
14:17, pi ptcp, God,
   σκληρυνῶ

כבד
7:14, q perf, heart,
   βεβάρηται
8:11(15), hiph inf abs,
   Pharaoh,
   ἐβαρύνθη
8:28(32), hiph imp c,[9]
   Pharaoh,
   ἐβάρυνεν
9:7, q imp c, heart,
   ἐβαρύνθη
9:34, hiph imp c, Pharaoh,
   ἐβάρυνεν
10:1, hiph perf, God,
   ἐσκλήρυνα

קשה
7:3, hiph imp, God,
   σκληρυνῶ
13:15, hiph perf, Pharaoh,
   ἐσκλήρυνεν

In our day critics explain the diverse vocabulary
from the narrator's use of diverse sources.[10] Paul, on
the other hand, probably read the account with its
varying vocabulary as a literary unit with a unified
intent. Therefore, it will be enlightening to survey
Ex 4-14 to see what impact it offers such a reading.

Excursus: The vocabulary of hardening in Ex 4-14

   In all likelihood when Paul uses the word
σκληρύνει in Rom 9:18 he is adopting the word from
the LXX which corresponds to not just one of the
three main Hebrew words but to the synonymous
import of each. Σκληρύνειν translates חזק every-
where except once in Ex 4-14, כבד in 10:1 and קשה
in 7:3 and 13:15. Moreover the wider usage of
each of these Hebrew words shows that they can all
refer to the metaphorical "hardness" that makes a
person insensible to promptings and inflexible in
his will. For example, קשה regularly refers to
the hard or stiff neck (Neh 9:16,17,29; Jer 7:26;
17:23; 19:15; Deut 10:16; 2 Chr 30:8; 36:13; 2 Kgs
17:14; Prov 29:1) but can also refer to the
hardening of spirit (Deut 2:30), heart (Ps 95:8;

140

Ezek 3:7), face (Ezek 2:4) and the whole person
(Is 48:4).

The basic lexical meaning of כבד is "be
heavy." Five times in Ex 4-14 the LXX renders it
with βαρύνειν. But the usage here shows that the
meaning is similar to that of Is 6:10: "Make the
heart of this people fat and make their ears
heavy (הַכְבֵּד) and their eyes shut, lest they see
with their eyes and hear with their ears." The
point is that to be heavy is to be insensible,
unresponsive, deadened, which signifies virtually
the same thing as "hardened." Similarly Zech
7:11,12: "But they refused to listen and gave a
stubborn shoulder, and made their ears heavy so as
not to hear (הִכְבִּידוּ מִשְּׁמוֹעַ). And their heart they
made adamant so as not to hear (שָׂמוּ שָׁמִיר מִשְּׁמוֹעַ
וְלִבָּם)." Note here how the "adamant heart" and the
"heavy ear" correspond and both refer to a willful
inability to hear.

The word חזק very often means "be or grow
strong," a meaning which Forster and Marston (God's
Strategy, 155-77) argue is to be preferred throughout this context, against the LXX. From wider
usage and from the theological premise that
Pharaoh's evil choice must be autonomous, they
argue that to harden means to strengthen someone
in his chosen course.[11] But it is clear from Jer
5:3 that חזק can mean "harden" and not just
"strengthen": "O Yahweh, do not your eyes look
for truth? You struck them but they felt no pain;
you consumed them, but they refused to take correction. They made their faces harder than rock
(חִזְּקוּ פְנֵיהֶם מִסֶּלַע)." The comparison with rock
proves that the metaphorical import of חזק can be
virtually the same as that of קשה. This is confirmed by the alignment with קשה in Ezek 3:7-9:
"The house of Israel is not willing to listen to
you, for they are not willing to listen to me.
For all the house of Israel are of a hard forehead
and a hard heart (חִזְקֵי-מֵצַח וּקְשֵׁי-לֵב) . . . But I have
made as adamant, harder than flint (כְּשָׁמִיר חָזָק מִצֹּר),
your forehead. Do not fear them." The same alignment with קשה also occurs in Ezek 2:4 but here חזק
refers to the heart as in the Exodus context:
"And the sons are hard of face and hard of heart
(קְשֵׁי פָנִים וְחִזְקֵי-לֵב)." The idea of strengthening
has fallen aside in such uses of חזק .

141

That this is the sense of חזק in Ex 4-14 is
shown by two facts. 1) It will become clear in
the following pages that 7:13, 8:15(19) and
9:12,35 in which חזק appears are understood by the
narrator as specific fulfillments of the prediction in 7:3 in which קשה appears. Therefore,
since it was of no concern of the narrator to
coordinate the vocabulary more closely, we may
infer that he understood קשה and חזק to be synonymous. Thus the LXX is fully justified in rendering
both by σκληρΰνειν (except once--7:13). 2) In
7:13,14 and 9:34,35 the words חזק and כבד occur
twice back to back so as to require virtually the
same meaning.

I conclude, therefore, that the narrator of
Ex 4-14 does not see in קשה , חזק , and כבד terms
with fundamentally different meanings. They all
point to a condition of heart which renders it
insensible to promptings and inflexible of will,
and thus, in Pharaoh's case, adamantly opposed to
God's demands. Hence in the following survey I
will render each of the terms by the English
"harden."

Already in God's conversation with Moses at the
burning bush the note of God's sovereign freedom in
dealing with men is sounded. Before getting angry
with Moses' unwillingness to go to Pharaoh (Ex 4:14),
God gives Moses one last argument why he should be confident in speaking God's word to the king: "Who made
man's mouth? Who makes him dumb or deaf or seeing or
blind? Is it not I, Yahweh?" (4:11). To be sure, this
refers to God's readiness and power to enable Moses to
speak. But the divine claim is far more extensive than
that and reveals a God who will work so that "Pharaoh
will not listen to [Moses]" (7:4).

After Moses gets his release from Jethro and heads
for Egypt, God says in Ex 4:21, "When you go to return
to Egypt, behold all the wonders which I have put in
your hand, and do them before Pharaoh, and I will
harden his heart, and he will not send the people away."
In Ex 5:1, therefore, Moses and Aaron approach Pharaoh
and say, "Thus says Yahweh, the God of Israel, send
away my people . . ." But Pharaoh's response concludes
with, "I will not send Israel away" (5:2). The result
of this first encounter with Pharaoh is thus probably
intended to be read as a fulfillment of God's predicted
action in Ex 4:21: "I will harden his heart and he
will not send the people away." The narrator confirms

142

this interpretation to us by showing us that Moses perceives God's hand in this first act of resistance by Pharaoh. For when Pharaoh, instead of sending Israel away, compounds the burden of their labor (5:7-9), Moses says to Yahweh, "Why have you done evil to this people? Why did you then send me?" (5:22). Moses sees the inevitable conclusion, namely, God said he would harden Pharaoh's heart so that he would not send Israel away (4:21); he does just that (5:2), and, therefore, the worsened plight of the Israelites is an "evil"[12] from God.

This makes very unlikely the interpretation of the third-century rabbis[13] which in our day is espoused by Forster and Marston[14] and others.[15] This interpretation argues that, since until after the sixth plague (Ex 9:12) we read only of Pharaoh's heart "being hardened" (7:13,14,22; 8:15 [19]; 9:7) or of Pharaoh's hardening his own heart (8:11 [15]; 8:28 [32]), therefore God's hardening activity did not commence until after Pharaoh had shown himself deserving of this punitive measure through his own self-hardening. A precise analysis of the verb forms (see table on p 140) reveals that before the first active assertion of God's hardening in Ex 9:12 there are two assertions that Pharaoh hardened his own heart (כבד) and after 9:12 there are two assertions that he hardened his own heart (כבד and קשׁה). What follows from this is that Pharaoh's "self-hardening" is equally well-attested before and after the first statement that God has hardened him. From this it cannot be inferred that Pharaoh's "self-hardening" represents his prior, independent sin for which God's hardening is the punishment. In view of the subsequent "self-hardenings" (9:34; 13:15) it is just as probable that "the hardening of man by God appears as self-hardening."[16]

Concerning the six passive references to Pharaoh's "being hardened" five occur before Ex 9:12 and one (9:35) afterwards. But the most important question here is: Who is doing the hardening? Forster and Marston assume it is Pharaoh and not God. But in view of the prediction of 4:21 ("I will harden") this assumption loses its plausibility. This will be confirmed in what follows.

Ex 6:28ff reads like a fresh start after Pharaoh's initial rebuff. As in 4:21 so in 7:2-4a God commissions Moses, "You shall speak all that I command you, and your brother Aaron shall tell Pharaoh to send away the children of Israel from his land. And I will harden

143

the heart of Pharaoh, and I will multiply my signs and
my wonders in the land of Egypt; but Pharaoh will not
listen to you." So in Ex 7:8-13 Moses and Aaron go to
Pharaoh and perform a miracle for him, but the section
ends with the words, "The heart of Pharaoh was hardened
and he did not listen to them just as Yahweh had said."
The explicit connection between 7:13 and 7:3,4a confirms our critique of Forster and Marston's view mentioned above. In 7:3,4a God says he will harden
Pharaoh's heart so that Pharaoh will not listen to
Moses and Aaron. Then in 7:13 the narrator observes
that Pharaoh's heart was hardened so that he would not
listen to them, "just as Yahweh had said." The words,
"just as Yahweh had said," prove that the refusal of
Pharaoh to listen in 7:13 is a fulfillment of the prediction in 7:3,4a; and since this refusal is the intended result of God's hardening in 7:3,4a it would be
unwarranted to construe 7:13 as anything other than a
fulfillment of God's hardening of Pharaoh's heart.
Therefore, Otto Kuss (Roemerbrief,III,724,following M.
Noth) is fully justified in saying, "Since already in
Ex 7:3 it was announced that Yahweh intended to harden
Pharaoh's heart, one must assume that in the narrator's
opinion Yahweh is the one who was at work in this from
the beginning."

Also at this point in the story God's purpose in
hardening Pharaoh begins to emerge: "I will harden the
heart of Pharaoh and I will multiply my signs and my
wonders in the land of Egypt. But Pharaoh will not
listen to you; and I will lay my hand on Egypt and will
bring my hosts, my people, the children of Israel, out
from the land of Egypt with great judgments. And the
Egyptians shall know that I am Yahweh . . ." (7:3-5).
God's intention apparently is that, by hardening
Pharaoh's heart, there be an extended occasion for the
multiplication of God's "signs and wonders" and then a
mighty act of deliverance with "great judgments." In
all of this the name of Yahweh is to be exalted as the
one who has sway over Egypt.

Now after two introductory interplays between
Moses and Pharaoh in which the double prediction of God
(4:21; 7:3f) has been doubly fulfilled (5:2; 7:13) in
God's hardening of Pharaoh's heart, the prerequisite for
the demonstration of God's power ("the multiplying of
signs and wonders") in the ten plagues has been met. This
seems to be the force of Ex 7:14,15a, "And Yahweh said
to Moses: 'The heart of Pharaoh is hardened; he refuses
to send away the people. Go to Pharaoh in the
morning' . . ."

144

So the plagues begin: all the water is turned to blood; but "the magicians of Egypt did so by their secret arts, and the heart of Pharaoh was hardened, and he did not listen to them as Yahweh had said" (Ex 7:22). Again the narrator reminds us that this hardening is owing to what Yahweh said he would do (7:3f). The second plague (frogs) comes without even a mention of Pharaoh's refusal to obey God (between 8:4 and 5; in Hebrew between 7:29 and 8:1). But then Pharaoh entreats for deliverance and lies about letting Israel go (8:8, Hebrew 8:4). Moses (like Elijah) goes an extra mile in making the plague marvelous by letting Pharaoh choose when the frogs will be gone. His purpose echoes the one in 7:3-5: "Be it as you say, so that you may know that there is none like Yahweh" (8:10, Hebrew 8:6). "But when Pharaoh saw that there was a respite he hardened his heart and did not listen just as Yahweh had said" (8:15, Hebrew 8:11). The third plague (gnats or lice) comes upon Egypt with no specific warning (8:17, Hebrew 8:13) and this time the magicians cannot imitate the wonder but instead confess that "this is the finger of God." But "the heart of Pharaoh was hardened and he did not listen to them, as Yahweh had said" (8:19, Hebrew 8:15). Pharaoh lies again to rid himself of the fourth plague (flies). So the flies are removed. "But Pharaoh hardened his heart this time also, and he did not send the people away" (8:32, Hebrew 8:28). After the fifth plague (death of cattle) no remorse or deceit is mentioned; only: "But the heart of Pharaoh was hardened and he did not send away the people"(9:7).

The sixth plague brought boils on all the Egyptians and again with no interaction between Moses and Pharaoh the narrator simply observes (for the first time in this verbal form), "Yahweh hardened the heart of Pharaoh, and he did not listen to them as Yahweh had said" (9:12). The effect of this phrase, "as Yahweh had said," is to unite 9:12 with the prediction in 7:3,4 as well as with the previous fulfillments in 7:13,22; 8:11(15),15(19), where this phrase has occurred. The unity of 9:12 (where God explicitly does the hardening) with 7:13,22 and 8:15(19) (where the passive voice is used) and with 8:11(15) (where Pharaoh hardens his own heart) is another confirmation that for the narrator these three expressions all represent the results of God's initial, expressed intention to harden Pharaoh's heart.

In Ex 9:13-21 God instructs Moses how to prepare for the seventh plague (hail) and what to say to

Pharaoh. It is from this unit (9:16) that Paul takes his quotation in Rom 9:17. Through Moses God says to Pharaoh in Ex 9:14-16, "For at this time I am going to send all my plagues upon your heart and on your servants and on your people so that you may know that there is none like me in all the land. (15) For now I could have stretched forth my hand and smitten you and your people with pestilence and you would have been destroyed from the earth. (16) But for this reason I raised you up: in order to cause you to see my power and to declare my name in all the earth." In trying to judge how Paul construed this text it will be helpful to put his quotation alongside the Hebrew and the LXX of Ex 9:16.

Hebrew Ex 9:16	LXX Ex 9:16	Rom 9:17
וְאוּלָם בַּעֲבוּר זֹאת	καὶ ἕνεκεν τούτου	εἰς αὐτὸ τοῦτο
הֶעֱמַדְתִּיךָ	διετηρήθης	ἐξήγειρά σε
בַּעֲבוּר הַרְאֹתְךָ	ἵνα ἐνδείξωμαι ἐν σοί	ὅπως ἐνδείξωμαι ἐν σοί
אֶת־כֹּחִי וּלְמַעַן	τὴν ἰσχύν μου καὶ ὅπως	τὴν δύναμίν μου καὶ ὅπως
סַפֵּר שְׁמִי	διαγγελῇ τὸ ὄνομά μου	διαγγελῇ τὸ ὄνομά μου
בְּכָל־הָאָרֶץ	ἐν πάσῃ τῇ γῇ	ἐν πάσῃ τῇ γῇ

Before discussing the differences here we must attend to Ex 9:15 because it appears that the LXX of 9:16 results from its peculiar understanding of 9:15. Kautzsch (Gesenius' Hebrew Grammar, Section 106 p) cites Ex 9:15 as an example of perfect tense used "to express actions and facts, whose accomplishment in the past is to be represented, not as actual, but only as possible (generally corresponding to the Latin imperfect or pluperfect subjunctive)." This is how the English translations thus render the verse: "For by now I could have put forth my hand . . . and you would have been cut off" (RSV). But the LXX construes the verbs of 9:15 as futures and the verse as a continuation of the prediction from 9:14 of what God will do instead of a statement of what he could have done: νῦν γὰρ ἀποστείλας τὴν χεῖρα πατάξω σε καὶ τὸν λαόν σου θανάτῳ καὶ ἐκτριβήσῃ ἀπὸ τῆς γῆς. This understanding of 9:15 probably accounts for the LXX's substitution of καί (at the beginning of 9:16) for the "strong adversative" (BDB, 19) אוּלָם. For if 9:15 is a prediction that God will strike Pharaoh there is no adversative

146

relationship between 9:15 and Pharaoh's being "preserved" (διετηρήθης, 9:16) for this demonstration of
power. It follows from this interpretation by the LXX
that the words ἕνεκεν τούτου (9:16) probably look back-
ward to the predicted blow in 9:15: "And on account of
my intention to strike you . . . and drive you out . . .
you were preserved."

        Paul, on the other hand, departs from the LXX and,
with the telic phrase εἰς αὐτὸ τοῦτο, removes the
ambiguity of the LXX and leaves no doubt that he construes τοῦτο to look forward in Ex 9:16 to the demonstration of God's power. That Paul is probably construing Ex 9:16 somewhat differently than the LXX is
confirmed by his use of ἐξήγειρά σε instead of the LXX
διετηρήθης to translate הֶעֱמַדְתִּיךָ . Paul's translation
has a closer lexical correspondence to the Hebrew word
and probably shows that the point he wanted to make
with the quotation was implied more clearly by the
Hebrew text. However, since Paul is not a purist elsewhere in sticking to the Hebrew text, Luz (Geschichtsverstaendnis, 77) is probably right that ἐξήγειρά σε is
not simply a reversion to the Hebrew text but rather
reflects "a dependence on the general Biblical usage
[of ἐξεγείρω]." The usage[17] of ἐξεγείρω to which Luz
refers is that found, for example, in Num 24:19 (a
conqueror shall be raised up from Jacob); 2 Sam 12:11
(God promises to raise up evil for David out of his own
house, i.e., Absalom); Hab 1:6 ("I will raise up
against you the Chaldeans"); Zech 11:16 ("I will raise
up a shepherd in the land"); Jer 27(50):41 ("many kings
shall be raised up from the end of the earth"). To
these could be added the identical use of the simple
ἐγείρω in such texts as Jud 2:16; 3:9,15; Acts 13:22.
On the basis of these texts there is a fairly
large consensus that by ἐξήγειρά Paul means that
God raised up Pharaoh onto the scene of history and
brought him to his place of power.[18]

        Generally it is assumed that this does not however
render the precise meaning of the Hebrew text of Ex
9:16. G. Bush (Notes, I, 116), Keil and Delitzsch (Pentateuch, I, 490) and B. Childs (Exodus, 158) construe
הֶעֱמַדְתִּיךָ to mean "let live" or "preserve safe." In
other words, the sense is: "I could have struck you and
cut you off, but instead I preserved you alive." What
Paul did, then, in choosing the word ἐξεγείρειν[19] was,
according to Meyer (Romans, II, 138), to "expand the
special sense of [הֶעֱמַדְתִּיךָ] to denote the whole appearance
of Pharaoh, of which general fact the particular one
was a part." This interpretation of the Hebrew of Ex

147

9:16 and what Paul has done with it is not impossible,
but there is another plausible way of looking at Paul's
interpretation of Ex 9:16.

It is not at all certain that Paul would have construed העמדתיך as "preserve alive." There is no such
equivalent usage of the hiphil of עמד in the OT. The
closest analogies would be 1 Kgs 15:4; 1 Chr 16:17;
17:14; Prov 29:4; Ps 105:10. But the very common
meaning of the hiphil of עמד is to "appoint" to a task
or to "set up." This meaning also gives a quite intelligible sense to Ex 9:15,16. Ex 9:14, in spite of its
ambiguities (see M. Noth, Exodus, 61f), announces that
there are plagues yet to come and that their purpose,
like the purpose of those gone before (Ex 8:10; Hebrew
8:6), is "that you may know that there is none like
[Yahweh] in all the earth." Then in accord with this
purpose (and as a confirmation of it; cf כי, 9:15) God
says that by now he could have destroyed the Egyptians
from the land but that such an early destruction is not
the purpose for which Pharaoh had been appointed. The
purpose rather, in accord with 9:14, is to cause Pharaoh
to see an extended display of God's power and to exalt
his name in the earth. In other words it is not necessary to assume that Paul understood Ex 9:16 to refer
merely to Pharaoh's being preserved alive, a meaning
which he then "expanded." Lexically and contextually
it is just as likely that he construed העמדתיך to refer
to God's initial historical act of raising up Pharaoh
to be king of Egypt, and that his ἐξήγειρά σε thus
honors the OT context. We will return later to the
questions: What significance do the purpose clauses of
Ex 9:16 have for Paul? and: In illustrating hardening
(Rom 9:18) why does he choose a text in which the term
"hardening" does not even occur? But for now let us
continue our survey of the OT context.

The seventh plague (hail) strikes. After getting
a promise from Pharaoh to release the people Moses
says, "When I go out of the city I will spread out my
hands to Yahweh; the thunder will cease and there will
be no more hail, so that you may know that the earth is
Yahweh's" (9:29). Moses keeps his word. "But when
Pharaoh saw that the rain and the hail and the thunder
had ceased, he sinned again, and hardened his heart, he
and his servants. And the heart of Pharaoh was
hardened and he did not send away the children of
Israel, as Yahweh had said by the hand of Moses"
(9:34f). Three things call for attention here. 1) The
purpose of exalting Yahweh's right and power over all
the earth is achieved not only in the plagues themselves

148

(9:14) but also in the removal of the plagues. Not just the act of final deliverance or the plagues themselves are the means by which God declares his name and shows his power, but the whole complex of events from Ex 4 through 14. 2) In hardening his heart Pharaoh is said to sin (לחטא). This prepares the way for the next question of Paul's opponent in Rom 9:19, "Why then does God still find fault?" The objector knew well that God <u>did</u> find fault with Pharaoh, because he finds fault with <u>sin</u>. 3) In 9:35 we encounter for the last time (in these chapters) the phrase "as Yahweh had said." It has occurred six times since the predictions in 4:21 ("I will harden his heart and he will not send the people away") and in 7:3f ("I will harden the heart of Pharaoh . . . and he will not listen to you"). <u>The repeated reference back to these predictions has shown that the hardening of Pharaoh's heart was understood by the narrator to be God's work from the beginning.</u> Thus behind the passive voice in 9:35 stands Yahweh. But since the hardening of 9:35 is parallel to the self-hardening in 9:34 we are shown again (pp 143-144) that for the ancient writer these three events (self-hardening, being hardened, and God's hardening) are not three but one.

Before sending Moses to threaten Pharaoh with the eighth plague (locusts) God confides to Moses what he has done and why. "Go in to Pharaoh, for I have hardened his heart and the heart of his servants, so that I may set these signs of mine in their midst, and so that you may relate in the ears of your son and your son's son how I have made sport of[20] the Egyptians, and my signs which I have performed among them, and that you may know that I am Yahweh" (10:1,2). This is the clearest statement yet of the purpose of God's hardening. It has significance for Paul's context in at least two regards. 1) It shows that the purpose of God in hardening Pharaoh is virtually the same as the purpose in 9:16 of "raising him up." Paul quoted 9:16 (in Rom 9:17) in which the word "harden" does not occur, and yet in Rom 9:18 he drew the inference from it that God "hardens whom he wills." It is probably the parallel between 9:16 (he raises up Pharaoh to show his power) and 10:1 (he hardens Pharaoh to display his signs) which justifies Paul's inference in Rom 9:18. Since the whole sequence of signs would not have happened apart from God's hardening of Pharaoh's heart (10:1) and since God's raising Pharaoh up was for the purpose of demonstrating his power through those very signs, it follows that in all likelihood the ἐξήγειρά σε of Rom 9:17 necessarily implied (for Paul and all who were

149

familiar with the OT context) the accompanying divine
activity of hardening.[21] This does not yet answer why
Paul chose to quote Ex 9:16 instead of 10:1. This will
be handled later. 2) Unlike the statements of purpose
in 7:5; 8:10(6); 9:14,16,29, the one in Ex 10:1-3 says
that God's revelation of his power is aimed at <u>Israel</u>
and not only at the Egyptians ("that <u>you</u> may tell your
sons . . . that you may know I am Yahweh"). This, as
we shall see later, corresponds in Paul's context to
the revelation of God's glory to the <u>vessels of mercy</u>
(Rom 9:23).

After the eighth plague (locusts) Pharaoh beseeches
that his "sin be forgiven" and that "this death" be
taken away (10:17). But when the locusts were gone,
"Yahweh hardened the heart of Pharaoh and he did not
send away the children of Israel" (10:20). After three
days of darkness when Pharaoh was about to release the
Israelites (10:24), "Yahweh hardened the heart of
Pharaoh and he was not willing to send them away"
(10:27). The final warning of the tenth plague (the
death of all firstborn) is given by Moses in 11:4-8 and
is followed by a word of God to Moses: "'Pharaoh will
not listen to you in order that I might multiply my
miracles in the land of Egypt.' And Moses and Aaron did
all these miracles before Pharaoh, but Yahweh hardened
the heart of Pharaoh and he did not send away the children of Israel from his land" (11:9,10). The purpose
of the hardening is the same as in 10:1 ("I have
hardened his heart . . . so that I may set these signs
of mine in their midst"). But note that not just the
tenth plague is in view here; the text functions as a
summary: "Moses and Aaron <u>did all these miracles</u> . . ."
Both the vocabulary[22] and the content of 11:9,10 recall
the predictions at the beginning of our story (4:21;
7:3f).

Ex 4:21	Ex 11:9,10	Ex 7:3,4
And Yahweh said to Moses:	And Yahweh said:	
As you return to Egypt	<u>Pharaoh will not listen to you</u>	<u>I will harden the heart of Pharaoh</u>,
see <u>all the miracles</u>	in order <u>to mul-tiply my miracles</u>	and I will <u>mul-tiply my</u> . . . <u>miracles</u>
which I have put in	in the land of <u>Egypt</u>.	in the land of <u>Egypt</u>.

150

your hand	And Moses and Aaron	
and <u>do them</u>	<u>did all these miracles</u>	
<u>before Pharaoh.</u>	<u>before Pharaoh.</u>	
<u>But I will harden</u>	<u>But Yahweh hardened</u>	
<u>his heart</u>,	<u>the heart of Pharaoh</u>,	
<u>and he will not send away</u>	<u>and he did not send away</u>	<u>And Pharaoh will not listen to you</u>.
the people.	the children of Israel from his land.	

The underlined portions of 11:9,10 have parallels in
either 4:21 or 7:3,4. The implication of this summary
is that "all the miracles" of Yahweh (not just half of
them, as some say) from the first plague to the last
did not move Pharaoh to release Israel because <u>Yahweh</u>
was hardening Pharaoh's heart.

The plagues are over now and the Israelites have
been released. But the purpose of God's hardening of
Pharaoh is not yet complete. He tells Moses to have
the people camp between Migdol and the sea so that
"Pharaoh will say of the children of Israel: 'They are
entangled in the land, the wilderness has shut them
in.' And I will harden the heart of Pharaoh, and he
will pursue you; and <u>I will get glory over</u> Pharaoh and
over all his armies. And the Egyptians shall know that
I am Yahweh" (14:3,4). Thus when we read in 14:5, "The
heart of Pharaoh . . . <u>was turned</u>[23] against the people,"
we should see at least the beginning of the fulfillment
of God's promise (in 14:3) to harden him. Then when
the chariots and army are gathered, "Yahweh hardened
the heart of Pharaoh king of Egypt and he pursued the
children of Israel" (14:8). The Israelites cry out to
God and against Moses for fear of the Egyptians but God
steadies Moses with these words: "And I, behold I, am
hardening the heart of the Egyptians, and they will go
after them. And I will get glory over Pharaoh and over
all his armies and over his chariots and over his horsemen. And the Egyptians shall know that I am Yahweh
when I get glory over Pharaoh and over his chariots and
over his horsemen" (14:17,18). And thus the Egyptians
were routed, "and Israel saw the great hand with which
Yahweh worked against Egypt; and the people feared

151

Yahweh, and they believed in Yahweh and in his servant Moses" (14:31).

That was God's aim: to so demonstrate his power and glory that his people fear him and trust him always (cf Ps 106:12). But his aim was wider than that: it was also "that his name be declared in all the earth" (9:16). Hence in the song of Moses this achievement is also celebrated: "Now are the chiefs of Edom dismayed; the leaders of Moab seized by trembling. All the inhabitants of Canaan are melted; terror and anguish have fallen upon them. By the greatness of your arm they are silent as a stone, until your people pass through, O Yahweh, until the people whom you have bought pass through" (15:15,16). Thus God's purpose to magnify his name had succeeded far and wide; the demonstration of his glory in Egypt lifted the voices of generations of his own people in praise (Ps 78:12,13; 105:26-38; 106:9-11; 136:10-15) and the news of it went before them into Canaan (Josh 2:9,10; 9:9).

5. "Whom he wills he hardens" (Romans 9:18b)

The inference Paul draws from his quotation of Ex 9:16 is "Whom [God] wills, he hardens" (ὅν δὲ θέλει σκληρύνει). On the surface, it is not clear how this inference follows from the assertion, "I raised you up to show my power . . ." But I have already tried to show (pp 149-150) how Paul can legitimately infer the "hardening" in Rom 9:18 from the "raising up" in Ex 9:16. In short, the divine purpose (ὅπως, Rom 9:17) to be achieved through "raising Pharaoh up" could, according to the OT narrator, be achieved only by repeated hardenings of Pharaoh's heart. Therefore, the raising up of Pharaoh implies, as its necessary accompaniment, God's hardening of Pharaoh's heart.[24] But now we must ask more precisely what the relative clause, ὅν δὲ θέλει σκληρύνει, means.

5.1 The freedom of God to harden

The two halves of Rom 9:18 (not counting the conjunctions) are grammatically identical: ὅν θέλει ἐλεεῖ--ὅν θέλει σκληρύνει. There would have to be a strong contextual warrant (which I cannot see) for construing these relative clauses differently. What is said in 18a about mercy is also said in 18b about hardening. This is helpful in determining the point of 9:18b.

It is generally agreed that 9:18a (ὃν θέλει ἐλεεῖ) restates the assertion of 9:16 (the bestowal of God's mercy is not of one who wills or runs but of God who shows mercy). Nothing new was said about mercy explicitly in 9:17, and therefore the summary statement (ἄρα οὖν) in 9:18 reaches back to 9:15,16 for its inference about mercy (18a) and back to 9:17 for its inference about hardening (18b). The point then of 18a ("On whom he wills, he has mercy") is, according to 9:16, that God is wholly free in determining the beneficiaries of his mercy: his decisions are not ultimately conditioned by man's will or actions. It follows, therefore, from the identical form[25] of 18b ("Whom he wills, he hardens"), that God asserts the same sovereign freedom in determining whom he will harden: his decisions are not ultimately conditioned by man's will or acts.

At this point in our exposition the controversy becomes impassioned--and rightly so, for the theological issue at stake (double predestination or the decretum absolutum reprobationis) reaches to the heart of our understanding of God and man. Therefore, every effort should be made to respect the object of our research and thus let Paul have his say. There is no value in calling all expositors to a disinterested neutrality (even if such a thing were possible), but there is great value in being willing, if the grammatical and historical evidence demands it, to let Paul say something different from what we would initially prefer.

We may look first at the construction of Paul's meaning which J. Munck offers:

> The word given to Moses is a continuation of
> the examples of Isaac and Jacob: God chooses
> whom he wishes and it is not the will or the
> actions of man but solely God's mercy that
> decides whether the Heilsgeschichte shall be
> carried on through one part of a people or
> another, for this is a matter of peoples and
> parts of peoples, and not of individuals; God
> chose Jacob (Israel) and not Edom. Nor is
> Moses conceived of as an individual; he here
> represents Israel, whom God chooses and saves
> in its affliction in Egypt. Over against
> Moses stands Pharaoh, an adversary who like
> Ishmael and Edom is a threat to the contin-
> uance of the Heilsgeschichte. But God's
> sovereign will also rules Pharaoh the repre-
> sentative of Egypt. (Christ and Israel, 44f)

Munck cites Lagrange (Romains, 234) approvingly, who
writes, "To Moses as an example of grace, Paul adds the
case of Pharaoh his adversary, who is a type of all
those who resist God and refuse to obey his commands."
This interpretation seems to me to produce a good deal
more smoke than it does light. By focusing on factors
outside Paul's immediate concern it obscures the crucial
issues.

I have argued in Chapter Three that in Rom 9:6-13
Paul is not just concerned with peoples instead of
individuals; and in Chapters Four and Five (Section 3)
I argued that Ex 33:19 (Rom 9:15) is not cited because
of Moses' significance either as an individual or as a
representative of Israel, but rather because the words
constitute a declaration of God's name. These criticisms of Munck's view need not be repeated here. What
needs attention here is Munck's view of Pharaoh. He
wants to see Pharaoh as "like Ishmael and Edom" (in
9:6-13), namely, as a "threat to the continuance of
Heilsgeschichte," and "a type of those who resist God
and refuse to obey his commands." Thus his overthrow
reveals God's sovereign ability to secure his saving
purposes in redemptive history and to turn all opposition to his own glory. The best clue that these ideas
(no matter how true theologically) are not Paul's
point is that the correspondence between Pharaoh, on
the one hand, and Ishmael and Edom, on the other, is
not what Munck says it is. Ishmael and Edom are not
cited by Paul either as threats to redemptive history
or as those who disobediently resist God. On the
contrary their purpose is to represent the sovereign
freedom of God who rejected them "before they were born
or had done anything good or evil" (9:11). To be sure
Esau was a threat to Jacob later in life, but that
later history is beside the point in Rom 9:10-13 where
the whole transaction concerns God's unconditional
choice of one son over the other before they offered
any "resistance" or posed any "threat" to God's saving
plan. I agree that there is a correspondence between
"Jacob I loved and Esau I hated" (9:13), on the one
hand, and "He has mercy on whom he wills and he hardens
whom he wills" (9:18), on the other hand (Michel,
Roemer, 241). But for Paul the implication that must
then follow is that God's act of hardening is just as
unconditional as the loving and hating of 9:13, which
God determined "before they were born or had done anything good or evil." It is irrelevant and misleading
to focus on Pharaoh's disobedience and his threat to
God's people, for neither of these receives any attention at all by Paul. Both the correspondence between

154

mercy and hardening in 9:18, and the correspondence
between the hardening of 9:18b and the hating of
9:13b, show that Paul's point is the unconditional
freedom of God in determining whom he will harden.

It is a theological premise not an exegetical
insight when Lagrange (Romains, 234) says, "It is certain that the verb σκληρύνω (verse 18) supposes an
antecedent evil disposition," and when Murray (Romans,
II, 29) says, "The hardening . . . presupposes ill-
desert and in the case of Pharaoh, particularly the ill-
desert of his self-hardening."[26] Sometimes support for
this assertion is sought in the Exodus narrative which,
it is argued, describes God's act of hardening as a
reaction to Pharaoh's self-hardening (Stoeckhardt,
Roemer, 438). But in Section 4 (pp 143-144) I
have argued that this is not at all the intention of
the OT narrator. Not once in Ex 4-14 is the assertion
of God's hardening of Pharaoh grounded in any attitude
or act of Pharaoh. Instead, again and again the reason
given for the hardening is God's purpose to demonstrate
his power and magnify his name. Paul picks up precisely
this theme in Rom 9:17 and heightens it by altering the
ambiguous LXX (ἕνεκεν τούτου, Ex 9:16) to the more telic
εἰς αὐτὸ τοῦτο in 9:17: "for this very purpose (and
for nothing else)[27] I raised you up." With this
selection and adaptation of Ex 9:16 Paul indicates his
understanding of the Exodus context: the action of God
in Pharaoh's life is determined ultimately by the
purposes of God, not Pharaoh's willing or running. This
understanding of God's treatment of Pharaoh is the
basis of the inference about hardening in 9:18: since
God's hardening of Pharaoh's heart (which is implied in
his "raising up" of Pharaoh, cf pp 149-150) is ultimately determined by God's purposes (and not by
Pharaoh's willing or running), therefore, God evidently
always acts this way and thus chooses to harden not
simply "those who have met the condition" but "whom he
wills." In 9:11f God chose to love Jacob and hate Esau
not on the basis of any good or evil done by them but
ἵνα ἡ κατʼ ἐκλογὴν πρόθεσις τοῦ θεοῦ μένῃ, i.e., to
accomplish a purpose. In 9:17 the two ὅπως clauses
serve the same function as the ἵνα clause in 9:11: not
on the basis of any good or evil done by Pharaoh[28] did
God raise him up and harden him, but rather it was to
accomplish a purpose. I conclude, therefore, with U.
Luz (Geschichtsverstaendnis, 78 note 211) that "an
exegesis which looks to Pharaoh's life for the grounds
of his being hardened fails to give heed to the scope
of Paul's statement."[29]

In sum then I have tried to demonstrate with three arguments that the phrase, "Whom he wills he hardens," describes God's freedom to choose the recipients of his hardening apart from any ground in their willing or acting. First, the parallel between 18a and 18b shows that the freedom of God to harden is parallel to his freedom to show mercy, which according to 9:16 has no ground in a person's willing or running. Second, the correspondence between the pairs, mercy/hardening (9:18) and love/hate (9:13), shows that Paul does not intend for us to view the hardening as a "divine reaction" to sin, since the divine decision to "hate" Esau was made "before they were born or had done anything good or evil" (9:11). Third, Paul's selection and adaptation of Ex 9:16, which summarizes the theme of Ex 4-14, show that he understands God's activity to be grounded in his own purposes, not in the plans or actions of men.

5.2 The meaning of "hardening"

The next question to be answered is: What does Paul have regard to in his own context when he asserts God's free and unconditioned hardening? The commentators generally divide along the lines that have been set in their exegesis of Rom 9:6-13. Munck (Christ and Israel, 45), Lagrange (Romains, 235), Zahn (Roemer, 452), and Beyschlag (Theodicee, 48) all agree that it is exegetically unjustified and theologically blasphemous to say that Paul has regard to the eternal destinies of individuals. On the other side Michel (Roemer, 241f), Luz (Geschichtsverstaendnis, 77 notes 207, 208), Maier (Mensch und freier Wille, 370), Kaesemann (Romans, 268f), and Kuss (Roemerbrief, III, 723) all agree that the connection of thought and alignment with "mercy" require that hardening refer to eternal reprobation. The evidence is decisively in favor of the latter view.

Generally, the approach taken to refute the view that hardening refers to an individual's eternal destiny is that this cannot be proved from the OT in the case of Pharaoh. There is even a rabbinic tradition based on Ex 9:15f and 15:11 that Pharaoh was saved from the debacle at the sea and repented (Strack-Billerbeck, I, 647). In short Ex 4-14 is concerned with God's guiding events within history, not with God's determining anyone's eternal destinies. As a description of the meaning of Ex 4-14 this objection is basically sound. It would probably be more accurate to say that in reality the hardening of Pharaoh could have consigned him to eternal punishment but that this is an argument from silence since the eternal destinies of individuals were not a consideration of the OT narrator. He did not express himself one way or the other on this issue. But to infer from the narrator's concern with God's work within history that Paul does not mean something more by hardening is not valid. Whether he does and how it is justified must be decided mainly from considerations within the Pauline context.

Rom 9:18 is the only place Paul uses the verb σκληρύνω. The noun σκληρός he does not use at all. The only other etymologically related word in Paul is σκληρότης used once in Rom 2:5: "According to your hardness and unrepentant heart you are storing up for yourself wrath on the day of wrath and the revelation of the righteous judgment of God." Here hardness (of heart) represents a condition of will that is unresponsive to God's (Rom 2:4) call, and thus bound for final judgment under the wrath of God. Eph 4:18 shows that πώρωσις is a synonym of σκληρότης: ". . . alienated from the life of God on account of the ignorance which is in them on account of the hardness of their heart." In Eph 2:1-4, persons in this condition are described as "dead in sins" and as "children of wrath" whose only hope is a revivifying act of God who is rich in mercy (πλούσιος . . . ἐν ἐλέει, cf Rom 9:23). The verb πωρόω in 2 Cor 3:14 signifies basically the same thing: "The minds [of the Israelites] were hardened" so that they could not apprehend that which would overcome their alienation from God and keep them from "perishing" (cf 2 Cor 4:3f). What is evident from this survey of Paul's vocabulary for "hardening," as Beyschlag (Theodicee, 47) and Schmidt (TDNT, V, 1030) point out, is that σκληρύνω and πωρόω are synonyms.

Πωρόω and πώρωσις are each used one other time in Paul (Rom 11:7,25). According to Rom 11:25: "A hardening has come upon part of Israel, until the full number of the Gentiles comes in." This hardening is a condition that leaves part of Israel unresponsive to the gospel and so excludes them from salvation, as Rom 11:5-8 shows:

> There is in the present time a remnant according to the election of grace. But if it is by grace, it is no longer by works since then grace would no longer be grace. What then? What Israel was seeking, this it did not obtain; the elect obtained it, but the rest were hardened (ἐπωρώθησαν), just as it is written:

157

                    God gave them a spirit of stupor,
                        eyes so as not to see
                        and ears so as not to hear,
                    unto this very day.

Paul speaks here of a hardening given by God which
prevents Israel from obtaining what it sought. What
they sought according to Rom 9:30 was the righteousness
which would allow them to stand in the judgment. What
is at stake, therefore, in Rom 11:5-8 is clearly salvation and destruction. The "remnant" referred to are
the "saved" in Israel (cf 11:14), and their status as
such accords with an election based on grace not works.
Thus "the elect obtained [the righteousness that leads
to salvation] but the rest were hardened [i.e. shut up in
a condition which excludes them from salvation]" (11:7;
cf 11:25,32).

        There is good reason to think that, when Paul says
"God hardens whom he wills" in Rom 9:18b, he is describing an act just like the hardening of 11:7. In the
first place, hardening is the counterpart to mercy, a
word (ἐλεέω/ἔλεος) which characteristically for Paul
refers to the decisive, eschatological salvation of God
rather than to non-salvific historical beneficence (Rom
9:23; 11:30,31,32; 15:9; 2 Cor 4:1; Eph 2:4; 1 Tim
1:13,16; 2 Tim 1:16,18). It is likely then that ἐλεέω
in Rom 9:18a has this sense and that σκληρύνω thus
means the opposite. In the second place, four verses
after coordinating mercy and hardening, Paul coordi-
nates "vessels of mercy" and "vessels of wrath." Since
the vessels of wrath are "prepared for destruction"
(ἀπώλεια) it is clear that they are excluded from salvation[30] (cf Chapter Ten). Consequently hardening appears
to constitute one as a vessel of wrath as opposed to a
vessel of mercy. Rom 2:5 confirms this connection:
"According to your hardness and unrepentant heart you
are storing up wrath for yourself on the day of wrath
and the revelation of the righteous judgment of God."

        In the third place, and most importantly, the flow
of Paul's thought in the chapter up to this point
demands that being hardened refer to a condition outside salvation. If Paul were concerned, as so many
say, to show only that God rules the historical affairs
of men, raising one king for his purposes and casting
down another, then why should he choose to use the word
"harden" at all? It did not even occur in the text he
cited from Ex 9:16 ("For this very purpose I raised
you up . . ."). Why did he not say, "Whom he wills he
raises up"? One answer commends itself above all

                            158

others: he had never lost sight of the problem he posed at the beginning of the chapter (9:1-5), nor of the solution he had begun to give in 9:6-13. The word "harden" serves the flow of this argument far better than "raise up" would have.

Briefly, the problem posed in 9:1-5 was that God's word of promise, his saving purpose with Israel, seems to have fallen because many of Paul's kinsmen according to the flesh are accursed and cut off from Christ. The first stage of Paul's solution to this apparent problem is to argue that not all those from Israel are (true) Israel. For God's purpose was never to guarantee salvation to every individual child of Abraham, as if human descent made one a "child of God." Rather his purpose was an "electing purpose" (ἡ κατ᾽ ἐκλογὴν πρόθεσις) which has not "fallen" but "remains" (9:11c). Hence the explanation for the unbelief and condemnation of so many of Paul's kinsmen is not the failure of God's purpose but, as typified by Jacob and Esau, the explanation is God's sovereign and unconditional election of "some" (cf 11:14) Israelites while (to use the words of 11:7) "the rest were hardened."

In 9:14-18 Paul is answering an objector who says that if God acts this way he is unrighteous. The thread of Paul's thoughts, therefore, requires that 9:14-18 concern itself with the divine action described in 9:6-13, namely with God's choosing to save some within Israel while rejecting others, or as 9:13 puts it, with his loving some and hating others. Nothing else but the demands of this flow of thought explains so clearly why Paul in 9:14-18 treats the two sides of God's sovereign activity and why he chooses to use the word "harden" in 9:18. Must we not conclude, therefore, that the hardening in Rom 9:18 has reference, just as the hardening in 11:7, to the action of God whereby a person is left in a condition outside salvation and thus "prepared for destruction" (9:22)?[31]

One final objection to be dealt with is that this view of hardening cannot be legitimately inferred (ἄρα οὖν, 9:18) from Ex 9:16 (= Rom 9:17). My answer is basically the same as the one I gave in Chapter Three to a similar objection concerning Paul's use of Jacob and Esau. What Paul infers (rightly) from the Exodus story is the principle of God's freedom to harden whom he wills, i.e., unconditionally, guided only by his purposes, not by man's running or willing (cf Section 5.1). Since the principle is established in the case of Pharaoh's recalcitrance, Paul applies it to his immediate concern, namely the recalcitrance and condemnation of his kinsmen according to the flesh. Paul may or may not have thought that Pharaoh was eternally condemned. But the legitimacy of his application hangs not on that, but on whether the principle of God's freedom from determination by human autonomy applies only to certain areas of divine action and not to others. Paul apparently saw no grounds for restricting the principle.

6. The justification of God

The one task remaining in this chapter is to complete our exposition of how Paul intends for Rom 9:15-18 to defend the claim that God is not unrighteous in unconditionally predestining some Israelites to salvation and some to condemnation. This we began to do in Chapter Five, Section 3, and pp 136ff of this chapter. Up through Rom 9:16 the defense goes like this: Paul's conception of God's righteousness is that it consists basically in his inclination to act always for his own name's sake, that is, to maintain and demonstrate his glory (cf Chapters Six-Eight). In accord with its OT intention Paul understands Ex 33:19 (= Rom 9:15) as a solemn declaration of God's name, or a pronouncement of the essence of his glory (cf Chapter Four). The function of Rom 9:15, therefore, is to prove that God's glory or name consists in his sovereign freedom to bestow mercy on whom he wills. It follows then that, since God's righteousness is his unswerving allegiance to his own name, and since that name consists in his sovereign freedom to show mercy on whomever he wills, therefore, God is not unrighteous when his decision to have mercy on one person and not another is based solely on his own will rather than any human willing or running. On Paul's premises, then, the quotation of Ex 33:19 is indeed a penetrating defense of God's righteousness against the objection of his opponent in 9:14.

In Chapter Five, pp 77f, I suggested how the quotation of Ex 9:16 (= Rom 9:17) is integral to Paul's line of defense. At this stage in our exposition the role of 9:17 merits somewhat more development. A question that came up in Section 4 but which was not answered was: If Paul wanted to infer from an OT quotation that God hardens whom he wills, why did he choose to cite Ex 9:16 in which the word "harden" is missing? The partial answer suggested was that Paul's inference about God's freedom in hardening is based on the purpose clauses of Ex 9:16 which show that God's actions are determined by his own sovereign designs, not by the autonomous willing or running of men. This is only a partial answer because in Ex 4-14 (cf Section 4) there are numerous other statements of the purpose of Pharaoh's being hardened which Paul might have quoted but did not. To complete the answer we must show what makes the purpose clauses[32] of Rom 9:17 especially apt in the flow of Paul's argument.

One observation that makes 9:17b apt is that it is exploited again in 9:22.

Rom 9:17b	Rom 9:22
ὅπως ἐνδείξωμαι	θέλων . . . ἐνδείξασθαι τὴν ὀργὴν
ἐν σοὶ τὴν δύναμίν μου	καὶ γνωρίσαι τὸ δυνατὸν αὐτοῦ

We will probe this parallel more fully in the next chapter, but the least we can say here is that these purpose clauses (in Rom 9:17) are not taken over un-thinkingly; they were the object of deep reflection and are made to carry a tremendous theological load.

A second observation that makes 9:17 an apt quota-tion in the flow of Paul's argument is made by C. Mueller (Gottes Gerechtigkeit, 31 note 25), who argues as I do that Ex 33:19 is a declaration of God's name. He observes, "It is no accident that the key word ὄνομα appears also in verse 17." This may well be the chief reason why Ex 9:16 commended itself so strongly to Paul at this place in his argument. It can scarcely be overemphasized that, for the sake of Paul's defense of God's righteousness, in Rom 9:15 and 17 Paul employs OT texts in which the exercise of God's sovereign freedom, in mercy and in hardening, is the means by which he declares the glory of his name! This is the heart of Paul's defense: in choosing unconditionally those on whom he will have mercy (love) and those whom he will harden (hate) God is not unrighteous, for in this "electing purpose" he is acting out of a full allegiance to his name and esteem for his glory.

In summary, Paul has answered in Rom 9:14-18 the two-pronged objection of his opponent (cf p 138). The objection sprang from the unconditional election and rejection taught in 9:6-13. The objector says in effect: if you are right, Paul, then God is unrigh-teous (that is one prong). But God is not unrighteous, so you are wrong about God's freedom (that is the other prong). Paul responds that God is not unrighteous (9:14) and defends this assertion, as I have tried to show, by quoting two OT texts (9:15,17) which show that God's freedom from human "willing and running" is at the very heart of what it means to be the all-glorious God. This OT revelation is a justification of God because the divine righteousness consists in God's unswerving commitment to preserve and display his glory.[33] That is Paul's answer to the first prong. In 9:16 and 18 Paul restates in different words the freedom of God which was implied in 9:11-13. That is the answer to the second prong: since unconditional election does not at all imply that God is unrighteous, God does elect unconditionally: "He has mercy on whom he wills and he hardens whom he wills." Or: "Jacob I loved and Esau I hated."[34]

CHAPTER TEN

THE RIGHTS AND PURPOSES OF THE CREATOR

ROMANS 9:19-23

The basic concern of this chapter is to inquire whether the thought of Rom 9:19-23 coheres with the interpretation of Rom 9:1-18 which I have developed, or if it requires a revision of that interpretation. In the course of this inquiry I will explain why I conclude the study at 9:23 (Section 1), offer a preliminary summary exposition of 9:19-23 (Section 2) and then in Sections 3-5 interact with those who construe these verses differently. I conclude in Section 5.4 with a summary explanation of how Paul brings his justification of God to a close in a way which accords with the concept of divine righteousness developed in the preceding chapters.

1. Delimiting the text

The final unit to be examined is Rom 9:19-23, to which I will refer in accord with the following verse divisions. Peculiarities of the translation will be discussed in the exegesis.

19a You will say to me then, "Why does he still find fault?
b For who has ever resisted his will?"
20a O man, on the contrary, who are you to dispute with God?
b Shall the thing made say to its maker, "Why did you make me thus?"
21 Or does not the potter have authority over the clay to make from the same lump one vessel for honor and another for dishonor?
22a So then what if God, in order to fulfil his desire to demonstrate wrath
b and to make known his power,
c sustained and tolerated with much patience the vessels of wrath made for destruction,
23 also for the purpose of making known the wealth of his glory on the vessels of mercy which he prepared beforehand for glory?

The assumption of this monograph is that Rom 9:14-23 is a distinct unit with its own unique function within Rom 9-11. Rom 9-11 in general (beginning with 9:6) aims to render an account of how God can be

163

reckoned faithful to his word of promise when most
Israelites in Paul's day are "accursed and cut off from
Christ" (Rom 9:3). Paul's answer comes in three steps.
Step one: Paul answers in Rom 9:6-13 that the promise
was never intended to guarantee salvation to every
individual Israelite and that physical descent from
Abraham offers no security. Step two: in chapter 11,
Paul answers further that nevertheless there is a
remnant of ethnic Israel in the church (11:1). And
finally, step three: at the end of the age, Christ
will banish ungodliness from Jacob and "all [corporate,
ethnic] Israel will be saved" (11:26). Within the first
step (9:6-13) of this three-step defense of God's
faithfulness to his word of promise, Paul reaches for
the <u>ultimate</u> explanation of why some Israelites are
"children of God" (9:8) and some are not (9:3). The
explanation he gives is the <u>unconditional election</u> of
some and not others (9:11-13). What makes Rom 9:14-23
distinct as a unit is that here Paul's justification of
God deals <u>specifically</u> with <u>this</u> issue - not <u>generally</u>
with the issue of God's faithfulness to his promise to
Israel. To be sure the two issues are not separate in
reality, for God's unconditional election is always the
foundation of the fulfillment of his promises. But it
is legitimate and fruitful at times to examine a foundation for itself, and that is the reason for my
limited focus in this book on Rom 9:14-23 (with 9:1-13
providing the necessary setting; cf Chapters Two and
Three).

A legitimate question may be raised as to why I
close the unit at 9:23 instead of 9:24, especially
since 9:24 is a relative clause attached to 9:23.
According to my construction, the relative clause of
9:24 would begin, "These he also called . . ." (οὓς καὶ
ἐκάλεσεν). "In substance the relative clause becomes a
main clause" (Schlier, <u>Roemerbrief</u>, 303). My rationale
for this is as follows. While the καί in 9:24a probably
correlates "he called" with "he prepared beforehand"
in 9:23 (ἃ προητοίμασεν εἰς δόξαν, οὓς καὶ ἐκάλεσεν),
nevertheless the masculine οὓς does not agree in gender
with its antecedent ἃ (which had the neuter σκεύη as
its own antecedent). This grammatical disjunction
reveals that there is a shift here in Paul's thought
away from the metaphor of "vessels" to a new application, namely, the assertion that these vessels of mercy
are "us" (ἡμᾶς), the church "from Jews and from Gentiles" (9:24). The following verses (9:25-29) are OT
texts cited precisely to ground this assertion in 9:24,
so that this verse gains a kind of independent weight
over against what precedes and should be kept closely

164

attached to 9:25-29. I thus follow Meyer (Romans, II, 153) and numerous others[1] who argue that "the interrogative conditional sentence forming an aposiopesis [having begun in verse 22] terminates with verse 23 and is not to be extended to verse 24 since all that follows from verse 25 onward belongs to the topic started in verse 24."

Romans 9:24 arches back, as it were, to 9:6-8 (where it was asserted that not all, but only some, from Israel are children of God); but then 9:24 goes further[2] and makes explicit that Gentiles too are included among the "called" (compare ἐκάλεσεν, 9:24, with καλοῦντος, 9:12, and κληθήσεται, 9:7). It seems to me, therefore, that Paul concludes his justification of God's unconditional election with the unfinished sentence of 9:23 and then with 9:24 returns to the level of 9:6-8 which had given rise to the issue of unconditional election. Since every study must end somewhere, it seems less unjust to Paul's intention to close our detailed analysis with 9:23 than to sever 9:24 from its OT support in 9:25-29.

2. Preliminary exposition of Romans 9:19-23

Lest we get lost among the many disputed points of Rom 9:19-23, I propose in this section to outline Paul's meaning as I see it without stopping to give detailed arguments or discuss alternatives. Then in the following sections all the important objections to this interpretation will be discussed and its exegetical support will be presented in detail.

In 9:19 Paul anticipates the next objection to what he has just said in 9:15-18. The objector reasons like this: if, as you say, a person's hardness is owing ultimately to God's will and not to a man's "willing or running," then it is unrighteous of God to condemn a man for that very hardness. In your view, Paul, nobody has ever successfully resisted the divine will, because even when they are resisting God's commands (as Pharaoh did), they are still fulfilling God's secret purposes. So God is wrong to find fault with men, since without the freedom of self-determination men cannot justly be condemned for their choices.

The extended reflection on this problem which Paul offers in 9:21-23 shows that he does not reject a humble inquiry into the ways of God. But in 9:20 he does reject the attitude of presumption which he perceives in the objection of 9:19. The objection was not

165

a humble "How can these things be?" (cf Lk 1:34), but an indignant declaration that these things ought not to be. This is the generally accepted meaning of ἀνταπο-κρινόμενος in 9:20a (TDNT, III, 945; cf Lk 14:6). Paul's emphatic "O man" at the beginning of 9:20a and his emphatic "to God" at the end of 9:20a assign to the objector his proper place: "as a mere man you have no right to accuse God of unrighteousness." Paul has no objection when a person seeks to understand as much of God's dealings as possible, but he objects strenuously when a person criticizes and rejects the truth which he discovers.

The rhetorical question of 9:20b gives the reason why a person like Pharaoh (or his advocate in 9:19) should not question God's ways: man is creature; God is creator. For man to advise God about how he ought to act is as out of place as for a statue to advise a sculptor how to chisel. The presumption that a man's sense of values is ultimate and can prevail against God's sense of values is as ludicrous to Paul as a ranting figurine.

The rhetorical question of 9:21 ("Or does the potter not have authority over the clay . . .?") expects a positive answer and thus aims to introduce something obvious enough to render the point of 9:20b even more certain. The obvious thing is that in a relationship between potter and vessel, that is, between creator and creature, the sole authority for determining what sorts of vessels it is right to make belongs to the potter-creator. It is the right, perhaps even the duty, of a great and gifted craftsman and artist to display the full range of his powers in the various sorts of vessels he makes and the purposes for which he designs them. He has the right to take a single lump of clay, which in itself is no more suitable for one purpose than another, and by his own free choice make vessels for honorable use and vessels for dishonorable use. Because the creator has this unassailable right (9:21), no creature has the right to oppose the sovereign choices of God (9:20b), and, therefore, the objector of 9:19 has no grounds for disputing God's righteousness in "hardening whom he wills."

Paul could have concluded his defense at this point. But since he does not, we see that he is not averse to reflecting even more deeply on the problem of God's sovereignty in hardening some and having mercy on others. Romans 9:22,23 is Paul's final insight into

the whys and wherefores of unconditional election, and
(together with 9:15-18) it is probably the closest that
the Bible ever comes to offering us a justification of
the mysterious ways of God with man. The if-clause
that begins in 9:22 and continues through 9:23 has no
explicit then-clause. This need not mean that Paul
lost his train of thought, because there are analogous
instances where a rhetorical question begins with an if-
clause, then breaks off with the expectation that the
reader can supply the inference (cf John 6:62; Acts
23:9; Rom 2:17ff). The inference to be supplied in this
case would be something like, "Will you then still con-
test God's rights?" (Bornkamm, "Anakoluthe," 90). In
other words Paul intends in 9:22,23 to give insight
into God's way of acting which will show that man cannot legitimately dispute God's right to act the way
Paul says he acts in Rom 9:18: "He has mercy on whom
he wills and he hardens whom he wills," that is, he
makes from one lump vessels for honor and vessels for
dishonor (9:21).

Grammatically the main assertion of 9:22,23 is,
"God sustained and tolerated in much patience vessels
of wrath made for destruction" (9:22c). Since "vessels"
is plural here, the reference is not only to Pharaoh;
yet he serves as the type of all other vessels of wrath.
God tolerated, as it were, a ten-fold recalcitrance
from Pharaoh and sustained him alive instead of bringing
destructive judgment on him right away. He did this
even though he himself had hardened Pharaoh and destined
him for destruction.

Most important for Paul, however, is God's purpose
in acting this way. This purpose finds expression in
the θέλων clause with its two subordinate infinitive
phrases in 9:22ab, and in the ἵνα-clause of 9:23.
To be precise, θέλων is a causal participle:
"Because God desires . . . he sustained and tolerated . . ." What he desires is to accomplish a
purpose, namely, "to demonstrate wrath and to make
known his power." Therefore, by revealing a twofold
purpose which God desires to accomplish, Rom 9:22ab
answers the question why God sustains and tolerates
vessels of wrath. Evidently by doing this God's
sovereign power and terrible wrath can be demonstrated
even more vividly than if God were to bring down final
judgment on vessels of wrath at the very outset of
their disobedience.

It behooves every great artist to demonstrate in
the variety of his work the full range of his skill and

167

power. And, according to Paul, it is God's right and
his great desire to manifest the full range of his
character in the things that he does. This includes
wrath and tremendous power in its execution. Since God
is the absolutely sovereign creator, his creatures cannot legitimately find fault with him if he so disposes
all things that there are in fact persons set for
destruction on whom God can fulfill his will to demonstrate almighty wrath. For a man to argue that this is
wrong for an eternal, sovereign creator to do, he must
also argue that it is right for the creator never to
reveal to his creation certain aspects of his person-
hood. But for Paul God's righteousness, as we have
seen, consists most fundamentally in his unswerving will
to preserve and display his glory. To argue that God
should not give open display to his wrath is to imply
that it is not in fact glorious, that God is not in
fact as he should be. But how can a creature advise
the eternal, never-becoming, always-perfectly-being
God what he should be like? He cannot. It is unthinkable (9:20).

Therefore, the only way Paul can even attempt to
justify God's sovereign hardening is not to show that
it accords with normal human values, nor that it
follows from the ways humans regularly employ their
reason, but rather that it follows necessarily from
what it means to be God. It is precisely the incompre-
hensible distinction between the never-having-begun
givenness of the infinite God and the utterly dependent
brevity of human life that makes it so hard for us,
especially with our incorrigible bent toward self-
exaltation, to affirm the ways of God. But I do not
doubt that Paul cherished the hope that, perhaps not
many, but some would see what it means to be God and
would "justify him" (cf Lk 7:29,35) in all lowliness
and trust.

Now in 9:23 Paul takes one last step into the
divine mystery. There is another, final purpose which
God aims at in patiently tolerating vessels of wrath
made for destruction. By this he aims "to make known
the wealth of his glory on vessels of mercy which he
prepared beforehand for glory." Paul's great hope as a
believer is that at the day of Christ the glory of God
will open upon his view with a power and beauty that so
completely transform and satisfy his soul forever
that the troubles of this life will seem as nothing
(Rom 2:10; 8:17,30; 2 Cor 4:17; Col 1:27; 3:4; 1 Thess
2:12; 2 Tim 2:10). This is the revelation of glory
referred to in Rom 9:23. The remarkable thing is that

168

the revelation of this treasure of glory which the church (cf 9:24) will experience as mercy, is accomplished, at least in part, by God's patiently sustaining and tolerating vessels of wrath set for destruction.

The καί at the beginning of 9:23 seems to <u>coordinate</u> this third purpose with the first two purposes expressed in the infinitives of 9:22ab (cf the grammar of 1 Cor 14:5). But its position as the last of three purposes and its distinct introduction with ἵνα (and not an infinitive) suggest that the purpose clause in 9:23 is <u>ultimate</u> and that the two purposes of 9:22ab are subordinate to this ultimate one. Therefore, Cranfield (<u>Romans</u>, II, 496) is right to argue as follows:

> There is no question of an equilibrium between God's will to show His wrath and God's will to manifest the riches of His glory on the vessels of mercy, as though He sometimes willed the one thing and sometimes the other. The former purpose must be understood as subordinate to the latter. The ἵνα clause indicates the one ultimate, gracious purpose of God, for the sake of which He also wills to show his wrath. The relations between the statement ὁ θεός . . . ἤνεγκεν . . . and the three statements of purpose may therefore be expressed as follows: God has endured . . . for the sake of purpose 3, and also (since the fulfillment of purpose 3 requires the fulfillment of the two other purposes) for the sake of purposes 1 and 2.

Therefore, Paul's justification of God does not stop with the demonstration that God, as God, must display the whole panorama of his character in order to be righteous; he goes on to assert that there is a <u>unity</u> in this display in that the various manifestations of all God's attributes stand in the service of his mercy, and thus function to heighten the revelation of glory for the vessels of mercy and to intensify their appreciation of it. The revealed character of God has integrity: it is not fragmented or contradictory. The acts of God come forth not in continuous reaction to autonomous external stimuli but from a unified, sovereign purpose. They cohere to achieve one great end-- the magnification of God's great glory for the eternal enjoyment of his chosen people. The fact that this purpose "requires" (as Cranfield says) the demonstration of wrath upon vessels of wrath will no doubt be disputed by men to the end of the age. But for Paul it was beyond dispute. (See below Section 5.4.)

3. Has the objector in Rom 9:19 interpreted Paul correctly?

I have assumed with most commentators that the objection in Rom 9:19 is based on a sound interpretation of 9:18. That is, Paul agrees with the objector that no one can[3] resist God's will and that nevertheless God still finds fault (as God did with Pharaoh, Ex 7:16; 10:3; etc). What Paul rejects is the presumptuous objection which the opponent registers to this divine action.[4] But there are a few scholars who do not agree that the objection of 9:19 is based on a correct interpretation of 9:18.

In **1888 James Morison (Exposition, 149)** argued that the objector "fails to discriminate" and thus reads into Paul's theology a meaning for hardening which Paul did not intend. Morison counters, "God, it is true, has to do with men's hardness of heart. Insofar as the hardness is penal, it is right that God should take to do with it. But if it be penal, it must come after transgression. And if it come after transgression, surely . . . it is right." In other words the objection of 9:19 is without force because it fails to realize that "he hardens whom he wills" (9:18) really means: "he punitively hardens those who first commit transgression." Before we respond to Morison's interpretation let us get before us a more recent but similar explanation.

In 1973 R.T. Forster and V.P. Marston published an exegetical critique of the Augustinian-Calvinistic explanation of God's Strategy in Human History. Their interpretation of Rom 9:19 goes as follows (God's Strategy, 80):

> Paul's critic had willfully misunderstood the gospel of grace in Romans 3. Likewise he makes out in Romans 9 that Paul is saying that God's will for an individual is irresistible. Paul has pictured God as moving in history: He has mercy on whom He will and whom He will He hardens. Yet Paul does not say here (or anywhere else) that God's plan or will for an individual is irresistible-- and Luke in his inspired text[5] plainly says they are not. We have seen that the Exodus story to which Paul alludes is far from

170

implying any "irresistible will". It is true
that God will ultimately achieve his plan for
the world in spite of those who resist it,
but the individual still has his own moral
choice of whether or not to reject God's plan
for him. The question of Paul's critic in
Romans 9:19--"Why does he still find fault?
For who can resist his will?" (RSV)--is based
on a flagrant misunderstanding of Paul's
teaching.

One would suppose that, if Rom 9:19 represented as
blatant a misunderstanding of 9:18 as Morison and
Forster and Marston claim, Paul would very simply have
set the objector straight and removed the bogus stumbling block. Thus Murray (Romans, II, 32, following
Calvin[6]) is right to argue that, "If in the matter
concerned, the determinative will of God were not ultimate, if the differentiation of verse 18 were not due
solely to God's sovereign will, then the apostle would
have to deny the assumption on which the objection is
based. This he does not do." Forster and Marston are
pressed by the weight of this argument to give a unique
and wholly improbable interpretation of Paul's response
in 9:20. They argue in the following way:

> Yet Paul's angry reply: "Nay, but O man, who
> are you that replies against God?" itself
> demonstrates the stupidity of such a misrepre-
> sentation. How could the man reply against
> God if, as he supposed, he could not resist
> God's will? Therefore, Paul says, "Nay,
> rather, you yourself are resisting it now!"

What is evident from this remarkable construction
is that the objector of Rom 9:19 understands Paul much
better than Forster and Marston do. For when they ask
rhetorically, How could a person reply against God
without resisting God's will? the objector could very
simply answer, Because my reply is a fulfillment of the
hardening will of God. In other words Forster and
Marston have not grasped as well as the objector that
Paul sees Pharaoh's "resistance" of God's commands as a
fulfillment of God's hardening decree. They view God's
will in such a way that, if God says to Pharaoh, "Let
my people go," and Pharaoh says, "No," then we have
proof that men can and do resist God's will, and the
objector has erected a bogus difficulty that does not
really exist in Paul's theology.

171

Against this interpretation stands first, as we have seen, the fact that Paul, unlike Morison and Forster and Marston, does not give the slightest trace of disagreement with the objector's interpretation of Rom 9:18. On the contrary, his response in 9:20-23 not only affirms but heightens (if that is possible) the absoluteness of God's sovereign will in disposing all things. Secondly, the conclusion of our own exegesis in Chapter Nine, if it is correct, confirms that objector's interpretation of Rom 9:18, not Forster and Marston's. Accordingly when Paul rebukes the objector, he accuses him not of misconstruing Rom 9:18 but of presuming to question the rightness of God's dealing (Barrett, Romans, 187; Schlatter, Gerechtigkeit, 303; Gifford, Romans, 172; Meyer, Romans, II, 143). "It is precisely because the objection has the character of insolence rather than anguish that Paul responds so sharply" (Lagrange, Romains, 236).

To be sure, Pharaoh said "No" to God's command that he send the Israelites into the wilderness. This can reasonably be called "resisting" God (cf Acts 7:51). But this is so obvious to everyone that it is utterly implausible that the objector would be affirming that no one has ever resisted God in this sense. Everyone has. But Paul's point was that even this resistance is in one sense willed (θέλει, 9:18) by God as hardness. The objector sees clearly that Paul is saying: God wills that Pharaoh resist God's own commands.[7]

This fact has compelled both exegetes[8] and systematic theologians[9] to speak of God's will in two different senses. These two senses have sometimes been designated as God's signified will and effectual will, or as God's revealed will and secret will, or as his will of command and will of decree. What is important for us here is to note that it is the second member of each of these pairs which the objector says cannot be resisted. And indeed this is a necessary and legitimate inference from Paul's teaching in Rom 9:14-18. Perhaps Paul chose the unusual word βούλημα in 9:19b (although he had used θέλει in 9:18) to stress that what cannot be resisted is precisely the effectual will or decree of God.[10] Probably the will referred to is the πρόθεσις of 9:11 which stands firm because it is established "apart from works" (9:12) and before Jacob and Esau were born (9:11).[11]

Therefore, what the objector correctly sees is that God, not man, holds final sway even in the lives of unbelievers. But his premise is that, unless man

has the power of self-determination over against God,
his evil acts cannot justly be faulted, i.e., he cannot
be judged as a sinner (cf Rom 3:7). From this premise
he opposes Paul's description of how God acted with
Pharaoh and by implication the way he acts with all
people in all times. In all likelihood the historical
reality behind this (formally familiar)[12] objection is
the same pharisaical standpoint countered by Paul in
Rom 9:11, as described and located by Gerhard Maier[13]
(see Chapter Three, notes 16, 59).

4. The authority of the creator: Romans 9:20,21

Paul's response to the objection raised in Rom
9:19 seems to ascribe to God the same absolute control
over the destinies of individual men that we have seen
in 9:11-13 and 9:16,18. "Does not the potter have
authority over the clay to make from the same lump one
vessel for honor and another for dishonor?" Nevertheless this is denied by some here, as it was earlier,
and so it is necessary that I interact with them and
thus try to demonstrate the validity of the interpretation suggested in Section 2.

E. H. Gifford (Romans, 173) argues that for Paul
the "distinction between 'one vessel unto honor and
another unto dishonor' is applied, like the rest of
the figure of which it forms a part, to God's absolute
freedom in dealing with one nation [Israel] and another
[Gentiles]. This reference of the passage to national,
not individual election is required by the whole purpose of St. Paul's argument and placed beyond doubt by
vv 24-26." Similarly, J. Munck (Christ and Israel, 58)
says, "The image [of 9:21] should not be interpreted as
referring to the creator's shaping of individual human
beings; it is used rather in political and heilsgeschichtliche context where God is dealing with the
Gentiles and the chosen people. We find this most
clearly expressed in Jer 18:6-10." Others are willing
to admit that Paul is not dealing merely with different
nations, but also is dealing with different individuals
within those nations. For example, Forster and Marston
(God's Strategy, 82) say, "The unrepentant portion of
Israel has become a vessel unto dishonor and the
faithful part a vessel unto honor." But they do not
infer from this that God predestines individuals to
their eternal destinies. Accordingly Cranfield (Romans,
II, 492 note 2) argues, "εἰς ἀτιμίαν implies menial use,
not reprobation or destruction. The potter does not
make ordinary, everyday pots, merely in order to destroy
them." Or as Lagrange (Romains, 238) says: "The most

modest vessel is never a vessel of wrath destined to be destroyed."

In this series of quotes three arguments emerge to support the view that Paul is dealing with nations and/ or temporal roles rather than the eternal destiny of individuals: 1) the OT texts quoted in 9:20-21 deal with the nation Israel, not individuals; 2) the whole purpose of the argument in Rom 9 and especially the verses 24-29 demand this corporate view; 3) the meta-phor will not allow the view of individual reprobation since no potter makes a vessel just to destroy it. In what follows I will try to test these arguments by the text and see as well if there are other data which would support or contradict this corporate-historical view.

4.1 The traditions behind Romans 9:20,21

In response to the first argument we should make at least six observations about the traditions from which Paul may be drawing.

4.11

It is true that the image of potter and vessel in Is 45:9-11 and Jer 18:1-6 has reference to God's dealings with Israel as a nation and that in Jer 18:7f the potter responds to the repentance of the "clay."

> Woe to him who strives with his maker (MT; cf LXX: ποῖον βέλτιον κατεσκεύασα ὡς πηλὸν κεραμέως;). A vessel among vessels of earth! Shall the clay say to its maker, "What are you doing?" (LXX: μὴ ἐρεῖ ὁ πηλὸς τῷ κεραμεῖ τί ποιεῖς;). Or: "Your work has no handles!" Woe to him who says to a father: "What are you begetting?" Or to a woman: "With what are you in travail?" Thus says Yahweh the Holy One of Israel and his maker: "Do you ask me about things to come, about my sons and about my hands do you command me?" (Is 45:9-11).

> The word which came to Jeremiah from Yahweh saying: "Arise and go down to the potter's house, and there I will cause you to hear my words." So I went down to the potter's house and behold he was making a work on the wheel. And the vessel he was making in clay

174

was spoiled in the potter's hand. So again he
made it another vessel, as it seemed good in
the eyes of the potter to make. And the word
of Yahweh came to me, saying: "Am I not able
to do to you, O house of Israel, as this potter
did?" says Yahweh. "Behold as clay in the
potter's hand, so are you in my hand, house of
Israel (LXX: ἰδοὺ ὡς ὁ πηλὸς τοῦ κεραμέως
ὑμεῖς ἐστε ἐν ταῖς χερσίν μου). When I speak
against a nation and against a kingdom to
uproot or pull down or destroy, and that
nation which I spoke against turns from its
evil, I will repent of the evil which I
intended to do to it" (Jer 18:1-8).

It is also true that Paul shares some of the
terminology of these texts (e.g. κεραμεύς, πηλός) and
that the rhetorical question of Is 45:9 is similar to
the question of Rom 9:20b (though not as similar as Is
29:16, see below). Nevertheless what would have to be
shown is that the point of comparison between these OT
texts and Paul's similar use of language is any more
than a shared metaphor and perhaps the point from Is
45:9-11 that what is made cannot dispute with its
maker. It is possible that Paul's allusion to the
potter is intended to communicate all the aspects
of the prophet's meaning; but whether or not it is
probable must be shown on other grounds than the use of
a common metaphor, especially since that metaphor is
very widespread in later Jewish literature as well as
elsewhere in the OT.

4.12

In fact, if Paul is quoting any OT text in Rom
9:20b it is Is 29:16, for here we find the closest
verbal parallel.

Woe to those who go deep to hide their counsel from Yahweh, whose works are in the dark,
and who say, Who sees us? and, who knows us?
O your perversity! Shall the potter be
counted as the clay? For shall the work say
of its maker, "He did not make me"? Or what
is formed say of its former, "He does not
understand"? (LXX: μὴ ἐρεῖ τὸ πλάσμα τῷ
πλάσαντι Οὐ σύ με ἔπλασας; ἢ τὸ ποίημα τῷ
ποιήσαντι Οὐ συνετῶς με ἐποίησας;) (Is
29:15-16).

The underlined portion is identical to Rom 9:20b,
but what the πλάσμα says is not the same in Paul and
Isaiah. This suggests that Paul is not so much citing
a text for authority as he is adapting a common metaphor for his own purpose. But should someone want to
press for an OT meaning behind Paul's image, then Is
29:16 offers the most probable source. But here Isaiah
is <u>not</u> speaking of the nation as a corporate whole, but
of the "perverted" wise men (cf 29:14) in Israel, who
in their presuming to hide counsel from God, act as if
they were God. They can no more keep secrets from God
than a clay vessel can instruct its potter or deny that
he made it. What is clear from the use of the potter/
clay image in Is 29:16; 45:9-11 and Jer 18:1-7 is that
it is a very flexible metaphor that can be used in
various contexts to imply different things. It is
futile therefore to appeal to any given usage of the
image as a proof of what Paul meant by it. But lest we
abandon too quickly the help which the traditional
background may give, we should note the other close
parallels in the Jewish literature of Paul's day.

4.13

Probably the most remarkable, yet frustrating,
parallel is found in the Wisdom of Solomon 15:7.

For when a potter kneads the soft earth he
laboriously molds each vessel for our service.
But from the same clay he molds (ἀλλ' ἐκ τοῦ
αὐτοῦ πηλοῦ ἀνεπλάσατο) some vessels to serve
clean uses (τά τε τῶν καθαρῶν ἔργων δοῦλα
σκεύη), some for contrary uses, all in like
manner (τά τε ἐναντία, πάντα ὁμοίως). But
what shall be the use of each of these the
worker in clay decides. (τούτων δὲ ἑτέρου
τίς ἑκάστου ἐστὶν ἡ χρῆσις, κριτὴς ὁ
πηλουργός.)

What is remarkable about this is that the potter's
making two different sets of vessels for clean and
unclean uses from the same clay is so close in thought
to Rom 9:21 as to seemingly demand some sort of allusion to this text on Paul's part. But what is frustrating is that the <u>meaning</u> of Wis 15:7 has almost
nothing in common with Paul's meaning. The context has
to do with idolatry and the potter illustrates the
idol-maker who makes a god from the same clay as all
his other vessels (15:8). The point is the absurdity
of idol worship because the idol-maker "is better than
the object he worships" (15:17).

176

But there may be a link in Wis 15:8 which brought this text to Paul's mind at this point in his argument, and thus provided him with language if not with meaning. The writer comments further on the idol-maker: "With misspent toil he forms a futile god from the same clay-- this man who was made of earth a short time before and after a little while goes to the earth from which he was taken, when he is required to return the soul that was lent him." The underlined portion of this verse is pointed irony: the idol-maker makes of earth a god to worship, forgetting all the while that he was made of that same earth and therefore should be worshipping his maker. In retrospect then the potter/clay image of Wis 15:7 might very well raise in the careful reader's mind the question whether God, who shaped the idol-maker (15:8,11), may not also make from the same clay vessels for opposite uses. Whether Paul in fact says this of individuals cannot be proved from Wis 15:7, but at least we can say (as in the case of Is 29:16) that this text, which probably supplies some of the surface structures of Paul's language, does not point in the direction of a corporate, national interpretation of "vessel."

4.14

In Sir 33:7-13 the potter/clay image is used to describe God's determination of individual destinies. Moreover 33:13 is a much closer allusion to Jer 18:6 than Rom 9:21 is. This shows that by no means can the similarity of language between Rom 9:21 and Jer 18:6 prove Paul is thinking of nations instead of individuals.

7) Why is any day better than another, when all the daylight in the year is from the sun?
8) By the Lord's decision they were distinguished, and he appointed the different seasons and feasts;
9) Some of them he exalted and hallowed and some of them he made ordinary days.
10) All men are from the ground and Adam was created of dust.
11) In the fullness of his knowledge the Lord distinguished them and appointed their different ways;
12) some of them he blessed and exalted and some of them he made holy and brought near to himself; but some of them he cursed and brought low, and he turned

177

them out of their place.
13) As clay in the hand of the potter--
(ὡς πηλὸς κεραμέως ἐν χειρὶ αὐτοῦ, cf Jer
18:6)
for all his ways are as he pleases--
(πᾶσαι αἱ ὁδοὶ αὐτοῦ κατὰ τὴν εὐδοκίαν
αὐτοῦ)
so men are in the hand of him who made
them
(οὕτως ἄνθρωποι ἐν χειρὶ τοῦ ποιήσαντος
αὐτοὺς)
to give them according to his judgment
(ἀποδοῦναι αὐτοῖς κατὰ τὴν κρίσιν αὐτοῦ).

This offers a remarkable parallel in substance to
Rom 9:21. Four elements in these verses have substantial counterparts in Paul. 1) There is the idea, both
with respect to differing days (33:7) and differing
persons (33:10), that they are all from the same origin
(cf "from the same lump," Rom 9:21). 2) Therefore, days
and persons owe their differences not ultimately to
different sources but to the sovereign decision or
knowledge of God who distinguishes and appoints days
and persons to different ends (33:8,11; cf the ἐξουσία
of God in Rom 9:21 and the θέλει in 9:18). 3) In the
case of persons, God blesses and exalts some but curses
and lowers others (33:12), and no ground for this is
given in the persons themselves; but rather the explanation is given that God relates to individual persons
as potter to clay (33:13; cf κεραμεὺς in Rom 9:21).
4) Finally, the parenthetical comment in 33:13 gives
the intended sense of the potter metaphor: "all God's
ways accord with his (sovereign) good pleasure." The
point is that his choices in determining which vessels
or which persons serve which ends are based on his own
secret wisdom, not on the free choices of men (cf Rom
9:11, κατ' ἐκλογήν, as well as 9:20,21).

Therefore, when Paul uses metaphorical language
common to Jer 18:1-6 and Sir 33:13, it cannot be
assumed that he intends that language to carry all the
nuances of Jeremiah rather than the nuances of Sirach.
He does not claim to be quoting Scripture.[14] Thus far
in our analysis, I would say (with Maier, Mensch und
freier Wille, 376) that it is much more likely that
Paul intends the image of the potter and clay to be
understood the way Sir 33 does (individually) than the
way Jer 18 does (nationally).

4.15

The only other place Paul uses the word πλάσσω (Rom 9:20b) is 1 Tim 2:13 with reference to God's creating Adam. Significantly, this confirms Luz's view (Geschichtsverstaendnis, 239) that "Plassō, on the basis of OT usage, is a term referring to the action of God in creation." Gen 2:7f uses it for Adam's creation, and it is used in this sense in 2 Macc 7:23; Philo, Op M, 137; Josephus, Ant I, 34; Sib Or 3,24; 1 Clem 33:4; Diog 10:2; cf 1 Clem 38:3; Bar 19:2. It is likely therefore that when Paul uses the potter/clay metaphor he is thinking of God as creator and man as creature.[15] Sirach had moved very naturally from God as creator of Adam (33:10) to God as "maker" (ποιήσαντος, 33:13; cf ἐποίησας in Rom 9:20b) of every individual man. This was natural because in the OT God is viewed as the one who creates and shapes the individual and his heart. For example: Job 10:9, "remember that you have made me as clay" (ὅτι πηλόν με ἔπλασας); Ps 33(LXX 32):15, " . . . he who fashions the hearts of them all" (ὁ πλάσας κατὰ μόνας τὰς καρδίας αὐτῶν); Ps 119(LXX 118):73, "Your hands made me and formed me" (αἱ χεῖρές σου ἐποίησάν με καὶ ἔπλασάν με); Ps 138:5(LXX), "Behold, Lord, you know all things, the end and the beginning; you formed me (σὺ ἔπλασάς με) and put your hand on me." We may infer from this that there is good OT and Jewish precedent for viewing God as the creator and shaper of every individual and that the use of πλάσσω and ποιέω in Rom 9:20 to refer to God's activity is what we would expect if this were Paul's intention.

4.16

In Chapter Three (pp 53f) I cited Gerhard Maier's very helpful work, Mensch und freier Wille nach den juedischen Religionsparteien zwischen Ben Sira und Paulus. He develops the plausible argument 1) that Paul stands within the tradition of predestination rooted in the OT, which developed through Sir 33:7-13 to its most radical form (embracing individuals and their eternal destinies) in Qumran (cf 1 QS 3:15-4:26; 11:10f) and 2) that from this position Paul formulates his argument in Rom 9 in conscious opposition to the common pharisaic insistence (expressed, e.g., in Ps Sol 9:4,5) that human free will is the prerequisite of accountability if God is to be righteous. Two minor observations now from Rom 9:20,21 add credence to this view.

179

First, Maier (378) observes that not only does Paul
share an unconditional election of individuals with
Qumran (cf Chapter Three), but also the πηλοῦ of Rom
9:21 has its counterpart in the common designation of
man in Qumran as "creature of clay" (יֵצֶר הַחֲמָר, cf 1 QH
1:21; 3:23; 4:29; 11:3; 12:26,32; 18:12). And the
vessels made for honor and dishonor (Rom 9:21) correspond to the two groups whose end is either glory
(כָּבוֹד) and honor (הָדָר) or endless reproach (וְחֶרְפַּת) and
shame (כְּלִמַּת) (1 QS 4:7,8,12,13).

Second, Maier (376) points out that the very words
which Ps Sol uses to defend man's power of self-
determination Paul turns around and ascribes to God.
Ps Sol 9:4 says, "Our works are subject to our own
choice and authority . . ." (τὰ ἔργα ἡμῶν ἐν ἐκλογῇ καὶ
ἐξουσίᾳ). We saw in Chapter Three how Paul took the
term ἐκλογή and used it in 9:11 to describe the sovereign free choice of God, not man, in determining the
destinies of Jacob and Esau. Here in Rom 9:21 Paul
does the same thing with ἐξουσία: it is the potter,
not the clay, who has the authority to determine the
destinies of his creatures.

We may conclude from these six observations that
the argument for a national/temporal interpretation of
Rom 9:20f on the basis of its traditional background is
not persuasive. On the contrary our survey suggests
much more strongly that Paul stands in a tradition in
which the image of God as potter and man as clay implies
the sovereign rights of the creator to determine the
destinies of all his individual creatures. So now we
must ask whether the Pauline context bears this out.

4.2   The context of Romans 9:20,21

The second argument for the national/temporal view
of Rom 9:20f is in fact an argument from this context.
For example, Gifford (Romans, 173) argues that the
"reference of the passage to national, not individual
election is required by the whole purpose of St. Paul's
argument and placed beyond doubt by verses 24-26."
This quote from Gifford is indicative of one of the
greatest problems in discussing Rom 9--there is an
amazingly widespread propensity to make vague, sweeping,
general statements about "the context" with the assumption that almost any reference to a corporate entity
will suffice to settle the issue of whether this chapter
has a bearing on individual predestination. Therefore,
over against Gifford's bald claim I appeal to the
preceding eight chapters of this book that "the whole

180

purpose of St. Paul's argument" in Rom 9:1-18 does not exclude, but definitely includes God's eternal dealings with individuals, and that, if anything, the context of 9:19-23 encourages us to interpret this unit with reference to individuals and their eternal destinies.

With regard to 9:24ff the implication seems to be just the opposite of what Gifford claims. To be sure there is reference to "Jews" and "Gentiles" (9:24), but the point is that the "vessels of mercy" are identical to neither of these corporate entities but have been "called . . . from Jews and from Gentiles" (9:24). Since the vessels of mercy consist of Jewish individuals and Gentile individuals, there is no basis for arguing that Paul's contrast between vessels of mercy and vessels of wrath (or between vessels for honor and vessels for dishonor) is a contrast between nations. The argument from the preceding and following contexts is all in favor of the view that Rom 9:19-23 concerns individuals and their eternal destinies.

4.3 The metaphor of potter and vessels

The third argument for the national/temporal view of Rom 9:20f is that the metaphor will not allow the view of individual reprobation, since no potter makes a vessel just to destroy it. To make a vessel "εἰς ἀτιμίαν implies menial use, not reprobation or destruction" (Cranfield, Romans, II, 492 note 2).

In order to make this argument stand, Lagrange,[16] Munck[17] and Cranfield must maintain that the pair "vessel unto honor" and "vessel unto dishonor" in 9:21 does not have its substantial parallel in the pair "vessel of mercy which God prepared before for glory" and "vessels of wrath prepared for destruction" in 9:22f. Cranfield (Romans, II, 495 note 4) argues "that σκεύη ὀργῆς and σκεύη ἐλέους are not to be taken as interpreting the vessels made εἰς τιμήν and εἰς ἀτιμίαν, respectively, of verse 21. Had Paul intended this allegorical interpretation of verse 21 he should have put the definite articles with σκεύη ὀργῆς and σκεύη ἐλέους. σκεῦος is used in verses 22,23 metaphorically . . . probably--in our view--without any special thought of the literal use of the word in verse 21." But, against Cranfield, can we really imagine that Paul did not intend his reader to see a substantial parallel between the pair of vessels in 9:21 and the pair in 9:22f? In view of the proximity of 9:21 to 9:22f the similar vocabulary and (apparently) similar thought, Cranfield's contention is very improbable.

181

Meyer (Romans, II, 147) is surely much closer to the mark than Cranfield when he says that the two kinds of vessels in 9:22f "are necessarily the same as those meant in verse 21 . . . This is shown by the retention of σκεύη as well as by the attributes κατηρτισμένα and ἃ προητοίμασεν corresponding to the ποιῆσαι of verse 21, just as εἰς ἀπώλειαν aptly corresponds to the εἰς ἀτιμίαν and εἰς δόξαν to the εἰς τιμήν, verse 21." As far as I can see there is no reason (except theological aversion) to deny that the image of two sorts of vessels in 9:21 is continued in 9:22f.[18] Cranfield does assert that if Paul wanted the σκεύη pair of 9:22f to refer back to the pair of 9:21 he should have used definite articles with the pair in 9:22f. This argument has no force for two reasons: 1) there are no such rigorous grammatical laws governing the way one must employ a metaphor and its application; and 2) even where a noun in NT Greek is definite the article is often omitted if the noun has a genitive modifier (Blass-Debrunner, 259; cf Rom 2:5, ἐν ἡμέρᾳ ὀργῆς; Phil 4:3, ἐν βίβλῳ ζωῆς, etc).

Therefore, it is highly probable that the vessel made for dishonor in 9:21 is the same as the vessels prepared for destruction in 9:22. If so then "dishonor" is further illuminated by "destruction" (ἀπώλεια). Most commentators agree that "εἰς ἀπώλειαν indicates clearly the eternal perdition" (Lagrange, Romains, 240). Beyschlag (Theodicee, 61) tries to restrict the reference of ἀπώλειαν in 9:22 to historical rather than eternal destruction on the basis of the parallel to Pharaoh's fate in 9:17. But Meyer (Romans, II, 150 note 1) is right that "the employment of εἰς δόξαν in contrast is decisive against this view." That is, in Paul's thinking the experience of the wealth of God's glory (9:23) comes at the end of the age when Christ is revealed (see Chapter Two, pp 18,19), and therefore the negative counterpart to this glory, namely "destruction," must be final eschatological judgment. This is recognized as the normal sense of ἀπώλεια in the NT.[19]

Therefore, contrary to Cranfield, Lagrange and Munck, it is very probable that when Paul says in 9:21 that God has the right to make a vessel "unto dishonor," it means he has the right to fit vessels for destruction (9:22). Cranfield's objection that potters simply don't make vessels to destroy them is based on an unnecessary conception of destruction as shattering. Oepke (TDNT, I, 396) says concerning the concept of destruction in Paul, "In contrast to σῴζεσθαι or to ζωὴ αἰώνιος, ἀπόλλυσθαι is definitive destruction, not merely in the sense of the extinction of physical existence, but rather of an eternal plunge into Hades and a hopeless destiny of death in the depiction of which such terms as ὀργή, θυμός, θλῖψις and στενοχωρία are used (Rom 2:8f)." In other words there is no reason to force "destruction" in Rom 9:22 to mean that the vessels are shattered. It is just as likely that we should picture a vessel placed outside the house and used, say, as an incinerator ("where the worm does not die, and the fire is not quenched," Mk 9:48). Destruction is not the opposite of existence; it is the opposite of glorious existence (9:22f). And that is all that the metaphor of 9:21 requires. If ἀπώλεια means an eternal inglorious existence in hell, then the objection that God could not make persons for such ἀπώλεια, since potters do not do that sort of thing, is not true. For potters do make vessels which are fit for inglorious uses outside the house. I conclude therefore that the arguments against interpreting Rom 9:21 as a reference to the predestining of individuals to their respective eternal destinies are not compelling. The evidence points the other way.

4.4 Summary

What, in sum then, are the pointers that lead the reader to construe Rom 9:20f as a reference not merely to nations and historical roles but to individuals and eternal destinies?

4.41

First of all the flow of the argument from Rom 9:1-18 requires that the issue of individual destiny be addressed. This is the issue raised in Rom 9:1-5 (where it is implied that many of Paul's kinsmen are accursed and cut off from Christ) and it is the issue that Paul has been addressing all along. The support for this contention is Chapters Two-Nine of this book.

4.42

The objection in 9:19 to which 9:20f is addressed is formulated with reference to an individual: "Who (τίς) can resist his will?" The objector perceives rightly that individual accountability is at stake when he asks, "Why does God still find fault?" Moreover Paul's response to the objection in 9:20 deals apparently with the individual objector: "Will the thing formed say to its maker, why did you make me thus?" Even though this rhetorical question implies a general principle, it probably has immediate reference to the

183

individual objector. If so then it is even more clear that the πλάσμα in 9:20 and the σκεῦος in 9:21 refer, in Paul's mind, to individuals in their relation to God.

4.43

The parallels between 9:21 and 9:22f, as we have just seen, suggest that the image of the vessels in 9:21 is being continued and applied[20] in 9:22. Rom 9:24 then makes it clear that the "vessels of mercy" in 9:23 are not any one nation but are those individuals "from Jews and from Gentiles" who are called. The thought is similar to the thought in 1 Cor 1:24 where "the called" are distinguished from Jews and Greeks and are distinguished as "those who are being saved," as opposed to "those who are perishing" (1 Cor 1:18). Therefore, both the "vessels of mercy" in 9:23 and its parallel in 9:21 ("vessel for honor") have reference not to ethnic or national groups but to those individuals from all ethnic groups who are called (in the sense of Rom 8:30) and thus saved.

4.44

In Section 4.3 we saw that the "destruction" mentioned in 9:22 refers to eternal perdition not historical defeat. This conclusion was based on the normal NT usage of ἀπώλεια and its particular usage in 9:22 as the opposite of (eschatological) glory. If, then, the image of 9:21 is illuminated by its application in 9:22f, it is very probable that the dishonorable use of the vessel in 9:21 and the destruction (= eternal perdition) of the vessels in 9:22 are in reality the same event. This, then, is another reason not to construe 9:20ff as though it were dealing with nations and their historical roles. Rather, the meaning of ἀπώλεια and its parallel in 9:21 suggest that the issue at stake is the eternal destinies of individuals.

4.45

"Does not the potter have authority over the clay to make from the same lump one vessel for honor and another vessel for dishonor?" The various types of vessels which the potter chooses to make are not at all determined by what the clay itself is, apart from the potter's shaping.[21] Had the vessel for honor and the vessel for dishonor been made from different lumps of clay one might argue that it was some distinctive

184

quality in the different lumps which caused the potter
to appoint one vessel for dishonorable use and another
for honorable use. But Paul rules that out with the
phrase "from the same lump."

With this phrase Paul recalls the example of
Rebecca and her two sons in 9:10-13. In distinction
from the Sarah-Isaac example in 9:9 the stress in
9:10-13 falls on the fact that Rebecca conceived her
two sons "by <u>one man</u>, Isaac" (ἐξ ἑνὸς κοίτην ἔχουσα).
In the case of Isaac and Ishmael the parents were not
the same: Isaac was born to Sarah and Ishmael was born
to Hagar the Egyptian. So it was not perfectly clear
in this case that the distinction God made between
these two was due only to his "purpose according to
election." So Paul gives the better example of Jacob
and Esau who had exactly the same parents, occupied the
same womb at the same time and were appointed for their
respected destinies before they were born. In other
words from "<u>the same lump</u>" God made one vessel for
honor and another for dishonor.

It is clear therefore that in 9:21 Paul still has
in mind the issue of unconditional election raised in
9:6-13. For those who remain unconvinced that Paul was
concerned with the predestination of individuals to
salvation and perdition in 9:6-13 this observation will
not strengthen the case for seeing predestination of
individuals in 9:21. But if our argument in Chapter
Three was sound, then the link between 9:21 and 9:10 is
another argument in favor of construing 9:21 as a
reference to the eternal destiny of individuals.

4.46

Though it is of little help in interpreting Rom
9:21 we should probably discuss briefly the significance of 2 Tim 2:20 which has very similar language.
Paul warns Timothy of

Hymenaeus and Philetus 18) who have swerved
from the truth by holding that the resurrection is past already. They are upsetting the
faith of some. 19) But God's firm foundation
stands, having this seal: "The Lord knows
those who are his," and, "Let everyone who
names the name of the Lord depart from
iniquity." 20) In a great house there are not
only vessels of gold and silver but also
wooden and clay ones, <u>and some for honor and
some for dishonor</u> (ἃ μὲν εἰς τιμὴν ἃ δὲ εἰς

185

ἀτιμίαν). 21) Therefore, if someone cleanses himself of these, he will be a <u>vessel for honor</u>, sanctified, pleasing to the Lord, prepared for every good work.

It might be possible to argue that since the vessels in 2 Tim 2:20 refer to individuals, the vessels in Rom 9:21 do too. But the differences in context and in the metaphor itself make such an argument unwarranted. In 2 Tim the vessels are not of "the same lump." They are not even all of clay; some are silver and gold. The different vessels refer probably to the faithful in the church ("the Lord knows those who are his!") and to the unfaithful false teachers like Hymenaeus and Philetus. Alford (III, 386), Ellicott (<u>Pastoral Epistles</u>, 146) and Schlatter (<u>Erlaeuterungen, VI</u>II, 220) are probably right that Paul's point is the same one Jesus was making in the parable of the dragnet (Mt 13:47-50). There are "genuine" (1 Cor 11:19) and false brethren in the visible church. Most commentators are therefore right in leaving 2 Tim 2:20 out of account when trying to explain Rom 9:21.

5. Four problems in Romans 9:22,23

22) And if God, desiring to show his wrath and to make known his power, bore in much long-suffering vessels of wrath fitted for destruction, 23) and that he might make known the wealth of his glory on vessels of mercy which he prepared before for glory . . .

In discussing now Rom 9:22,23, my purpose is not to deal with every exegetical ambiguity but rather to show as clearly and briefly as I can why I think the interpretation offered above in Section 2 is the most probable. Only the grammatical and lexical difficulties necessary to that end will be treated. The key questions are these: 1) How does God's "desire" to show his wrath relate to his enduring the vessels of wrath (concessively or causally)? 2) How can God be said to endure "in much long-suffering" those whom he has hardened for destruction? 3) If God has prepared both vessels of wrath for destruction and vessels of mercy for glory, why is a passive verb (κατηρτισμένα) used to describe the preparation of vessels of wrath and an active verb (προητοίμασεν) used to describe the preparation of vessels of mercy? 4) What is God's chief aim in his sovereign work, and how does this answer the objection of Rom 9:19, "Why does he still find fault?"

5.1 The logical relationships of the clauses

Generally it is assumed that Rom 9:22,23 is an if-
clause for which the then-clause is unstated. The
then-clause usually supplied[22] is a rhetorical question
like "Will you still dispute with Him?" (Bornkamm,
"Anakoluthe," 90). As Cranfield (Romans, II, 493) says,
"The point here is that to reckon with the truth . . .
expressed in verses 22-24 will make a big difference to
our understanding of God's right to act in the way
indicated in verse 18, going beyond what has already
been established by verses 20b-21." That is, in
9:22,23, Paul goes on "to justify the actual course of
[God's] dealing" with man (Gifford, Romans, 173).

But not all scholars agree that 9:22,23 is an if-
clause without a then-clause. G. Staehlin (TDNT, V,
426), T. Zahn (Roemer, 461), C. Plag (Weg, 15) and A.
Nygren (Romans, 372) are among those who construe 9:23
as the then-clause. Thus the sentence would read
(following Staehlin):

> 22) But if God tolerated in great long-
> suffering the vessels of wrath which were
> made for destruction, because he willed to
> manifest his wrath and declare his power in
> them, 23) (he did it) also in order that
> he might make known the riches of his glory
> in the vessels of mercy, which he had pre-
> pared long before for glory.

So instead of adding a then-clause after 9:23, this
verse is itself made the then-clause by adding the
words "he did it."

The arguments against this construction, however,
are weighty. First, the sense is very awkward: "if
he endured them to show wrath and power then he also
endured them to show glory." The then-clause of this
construction does not seem to follow from the if-clause.
Second, as Cranfield (Romans, II, 492) says, the
"ellipsis of the apodosis of a conditional sentence is
fairly common in classical Greek and occurs several
times in the NT" (cf Jn 6:62; Acts 23:9; Blass-
Debrunner, 482). Third, Murray (Romans, II, 35) makes
the very plausible suggestion that the ἵνα clause of
9:23 is coordinate with the two infinitive phrases of
9:22 and thus the ἵνα clause is dependent on θέλων.
Hence: εἰ δὲ θέλων ὁ θεὸς ἐνδείξασθαι . . .
καὶ γνωρίσαι . . . καὶ ἵνα γνωρίσῃ . . . In support of
this construction Murray points out that ἵνα does intro-

187

duce the object of verbs of willing (Mt 7:12; Mk 9:30; 10:35; Jn 17:24, etc; cf Bauer, 378). But even more persuasive is the analogy in 1 Cor 14:5 where Paul says, θέλω δὲ πάντας ὑμᾶς λαλεῖν γλώσσαις, μᾶλλον δὲ ἵνα προφητεύητε. "I desire you all to speak in tongues, and even more that you prophesy." Here θέλω is followed by an infinitive phrase and a ἵνα clause in a way similar to the infinitive phrases and ἵνα clause following θέλων in Rom 9:22-23.[23]

Probably then Calvin (Romans, 211), Cranfield (Romans, II, 496) and others are right in saying that the two infinitive phrases of 9:22 and the ἵνα clause of 9:23 give three purposes which God "desires" (θέλων) to achieve in sustaining and enduring the vessels of wrath. If this is correct, then the participle θέλων almost certainly should be construed as the cause of God's enduring vessels of wrath rather than as a concession in spite of which he endures them. That is, you cannot say, "Although God desires . . . he endured . . ." if part of what he desires is "to make known the wealth of his glory on vessels of mercy" which he achieves precisely in enduring vessels of wrath. This desire to reveal glory to vessels of mercy is not adversative to God's enduring vessels of wrath but causal. Therefore if the θέλων governs not only the two infinitive phrases of 9:22 but also the ἵνα clause of 9:23 it can scarcely be given a concessive meaning ("although he desired . . ."). Rather the three things God "desires" constitute his goals in enduring vessels of wrath, and so his desire to achieve those goals is the motive or cause for the endurance.[24]

Most commentators[25] (not all, see note 24) do construe θέλων as a causal clause, and the most compelling reason is the parallel in thought and language between 9:22 and 9:17.

Rom 9:17	Rom 9:22
εἰς αὐτὸ τοῦτο ἐξήγειρά σε	εἰ δὲ θέλων ὁ θεὸς
ὅπως ἐνδείξωμαι ἐν σοὶ	ἐνδείξασθαι τὴν ὀργὴν
τὴν δύναμίν μου.	καὶ γνωρίσαι τὸ δυνατὸν αὐτοῦ.

Though Paul is now speaking more generally about "vessels of wrath," the words of God to Pharaoh in Ex 9:16 are still serving as the pattern for the way God acts. God's raising up Pharaoh and enduring him through a ten-fold recalcitrance was not in spite of his desire

to show his power but <u>because of</u> his desire to show it.
God could have destroyed Pharaoh after any one of his
acts of disobedience, and the reason he did not was
that he might "multiply his wonders in the land of
Egypt" (Ex 11:9). By "sustaining and tolerating"[26]
Pharaoh again and again God accomplished his purpose to
show his power in the plagues and finally to win renown
in Pharaoh's overthrow at the Red Sea (cf the purpose mentioned in Ex 7:3-5; 9:14-16; 10:1; 11:9; 14:4,17-18).
Therefore, since Rom 9:22 uses the same language as
9:17, it is more probable that God's desire to show his
wrath and make known his power is the <u>cause</u> of his sustaining and tolerating vessels of wrath than that this
sustaining and tolerating are <u>in spite of</u> that desire.

5.2 God's patience with the vessels of wrath

The strongest argument against saying that God
sustains and tolerates vessels of wrath <u>in order to</u>
show his wrath and power is that this seems to contradict the fact that God is sustaining and tolerating
these vessels "in much long-suffering" (ἐν πολλῇ
μακροθυμίᾳ). This argument gains force also from Rom
2:4,5: "Or do you despise the wealth of his kindness
and forbearance and long-suffering (μακροθυμίας), not
knowing that the kindness of God is leading you to
repentance? But according to your hardness and unrepentant heart you are storing up for yourself wrath on the
day of wrath and the revelation of the righteous judgment of God." From this text it appears that God's
long-suffering is an expression of his kindness and has
the purpose of leading men to repentance.[27]

The problem encountered here is the same as the
one we encountered in connection with the hardening of
Pharaoh and discussed in Section 3 (pp 172f). God
addresses Pharaoh through Moses: "Let my people go."
This corresponds to the kindness and long-suffering of
pointing the way to repentance (Rom 2:4). Nevertheless,
God has already told Moses that he is going to harden
Pharaoh's heart so that he will not let the people go.
This corresponds to the intention of God expressed in
9:22 to show his wrath precisely by means of enduring
in much long-suffering vessels of wrath. If God's
command to Pharaoh can be thwarted by God's own decree
to harden Pharaoh's heart, then in the same way God's
command to men to repent and the time he gives them to
obey (Rom 2:4) can also be thwarted in the case of the
vessels of wrath by God's decree to harden whom he
wills and thus show his wrath on the day of judgment.

189

One could argue as Beyschlag (<u>Theodicee</u>, 63) does
that Rom 2:4,5 constitute "an acknowledgment of the
real freedom men have--a freedom whose highest decision
cannot be predicted even by God." But if Romans 9:14-23
is taken seriously and if Paul has not contradicted himself, then such an inference from Rom 2:4,5 is premature. Is it not possible that what Paul means in Rom
2:4 is that in the interval of life given to men and
nations everything in nature (Rom 1:18-23; Acts 14:17)
and history (Acts 17:26f) and the human conscience (Rom
2:15) is pointing (i.e. "leading") men to repentance and
faith? God has not left himself without a witness and
has not left man without an occasion to respond. No
man will ever be able to say that God did not provide an
opportunity for him to repent, nor that God did not give
evidence that should have led him to do so. That God
should then act, as he did with Pharaoh, so that some
are hardened and do not come to repentance and are yet
held to be blameworthy is not an idea forced onto Paul
by Calvinistic exegetes. Rather it is precisely what
the spokesman in Rom 9:19 saw in Paul's theology and so
strongly objected to. Therefore, the summons to repentance in Rom 2:4 (even more pointedly expressed in
10:21) must not be used to silence the absoluteness of
God's sovereignty expressed in Rom 9:21-23. Such a
procedure (followed by Beyschlag) is based on a philo-
sophical conception of the prerequisites of human
accountability which Paul evidently did not share. In
its haste to preserve the free will of the creature it
fails to perceive the complexity (and far deeper unity)
of the will of the creator.

But we have yet to answer the question why Paul
says the vessels of wrath are endured "in much patience"
if he does not mean that they are being given time for
repentance (which the context seems to rule out), but
that they are only storing up wrath for themselves (as
2:5 says) in order that God's "desire to show his wrath"
(9:22) might be fulfilled in them.[28] Is there any
evidence that μακροθυμία could mean patiently holding
back judgment with a view to a greater display of wrath
and power?

There are several analogies of "patience" being
exercised in this way. From IV Ezra (probably first
century) we read,

> For this reason, therefore, shall all the
> sojourners in the earth suffer torture,
> because having understanding they yet wrought
> iniquity, and receiving precepts they yet

kept them not, and having obtained the law
they set at naught that which they received.
What then will they have to say in the judgment, or how shall they answer in the last
times? For how long a time hath the Most
High been long-suffering with the inhabitants of the world--not for their sakes
indeed, but for the sake of the times which
he has ordained! (7:72-74)

The least this passage shows is that among Jews of the
first century it was not unheard of to speak of God
being patient with man for some reason other than man's
good.

Another helpful analogy comes from 2 Macc 6:12-14.
In this context the Jews had been brutally treated by
the Seleucids and the writer says,

Now I urge those who read this book not to be
depressed by such calamities but to recognize
that these punishments were designed not to
destroy but to discipline our people. In
fact, not to let the impious alone for long,
but to punish them immediately is a sign of
great kindness (εὐεργεσίας). For in the case
of other nations the Lord waits patiently to
punish them until they have reached the full
measure of their sins; but he does not deal
this way with us. (οὐ γὰρ καθάπερ καὶ ἐπὶ
τῶν ἄλλων ἐθνῶν ἀναμένει μακροθυμῶν ὁ δεσπότης
μέχρι τοῦ καταντήσαντος αὐτοὺς πρὸς
ἐκπλήρωσιν ἁμαρτιῶν κολάσαι . . .).

Here the patience of God with the nations has a view to
giving them an occasion to fill up their sins and make
their judgment worse.

Finally, we may look at an example of human
patience used in a similar way. From 1 Macc 8:1-4 we
read:

Now Judas heard of the fame of the Romans
that they were very strong and were well dis-
posed toward all who made an alliance with
them . . . Men told him of their wars and of
the brave deeds which they were doing among
the Gauls, how they had defeated them and
forced them to pay tribute, and what they
had done in the land of Spain to get control
of the silver and gold mines there, and how

191

they had gained control of the whole region
by their planning and <u>patience</u> (τῇ βουλῇ
αὐτῶν καὶ τῇ μακροθυμίᾳ), even though the
place was far distant from them.

Here we see expressed what is commonly known: that in
a conflict, a measure of patience and restraint at one
point in the battle may secure a greater victory later.

This insight into the patience of a military commander may help explain how it is that God's "desire to
show his wrath and make known his power" motivates him
not immediately to overthrow the enemy but rather to
patiently sustain and tolerate him. The glory and power
of a commander are more remarkably displayed in a combination of calm, patient restraint and swift decisive
advance than they would be if he were capable of only
one or the other. And when one reads Ex 4-14 this is
just the impression one gets. God endures the repeated
insults of Pharaoh's disobedience, yet turns every
moment of patient restraint into an occasion to display
his power. Finally in Ex 14:1-4 God maneuvers his
people into an impossible position and incites Pharaoh
to pursue. God tells Moses why: "I will harden
Pharaoh's heart, and he will pursue them and I will get
glory over Pharaoh and over all his host; and the
Egyptians shall know that I am the Lord" (14:4). So
Moses says to the fearful people, "The Lord will fight
for you, and you have only to be still" **(14:14)**. And
thus by his patient restraint the great Warrior of
Israel draws Pharaoh and his hosts into an awesome
display of wrath and power which had been long in
coming.

Since the language of Rom 9:22 is so clearly
reminiscent of 9:17 where God's dealings with Pharaoh
are in view, there is good reason, therefore, to infer
that the divine action of 9:22 is indeed the action of
a mighty commander who wills to display his power and
wrath in defeating his enemies (the "vessels of wrath")
for the sake of his people, the "vessels of mercy."
Against this contextual backdrop the idea of sustaining
and tolerating the enemy <u>in much patience</u> is not inconsistent with, but conducive to, God's "desire to show
his wrath and make known his power."

5.3 "Fitted for destruction"

The next question raised against the interpretation
put forward above in Section 2 is this: does not the
use of the passive voice in the phrase "vessels of wrath

fitted (κατηρτισμένα) for destruction" suggest that Paul does not attribute their condition to God's doing, especially since he uses the active voice in the phrase "vessels of mercy which he prepared before for glory"?

Elsewhere in Paul (1 Cor 1:10; 2 Cor 13:11; Gal 6:1; 1 Thess 3:10), and indeed in the whole NT, καταρτίζω has the positive meaning of repair, prepare, equip or complete. It refers once to the divine act of creation--Heb 11:3. In Ps 16:5 (LXX) it probably means ordain. Delling (TDNT, I, 476) suggests the meaning "foreordain" in Rom 9:22. That is quite uncertain. In view of the clay/potter analogy in 9:21 "created" or "prepared" would seem most natural. But to settle the question of the meaning of κατηρτισμένα one must first address the question of agency: who is doing the action?

There are at least four views: 1) God is the one who fits (or creates) the vessels of wrath for destruction;[29] 2) the voice is middle not passive and thus means that the vessels of wrath have fitted themselves for destruction (Bengel, Gnomon, II, 86; Beyschlag, Theodicee, 65); 3) the participle is to be construed adjectivally as "fit for destruction" with no implication intended about who did the fitting (Lagrange, Romains, 240; Cranfield, Romans, II, 495f; Sanday and Headlam, Romans, 261; Schlier, Roemerbrief, 301); 4) the passive is intended to express a mystery no human can break through.[30]

The least likely of these is the second according to which κατηρτισμένα is construed as "having fitted themselves." In a context where the sovereignty of God as a potter over clay has been stressed, Paul would have had to use a clearer grammatical construction to signify all of a sudden that man's destiny is self-determined. And indeed the well-known reflexive use of ἐτοιμάζειν ἑαυτόν (Rev 8:6; 19:7) lay ready for such use if Paul had intended such.

The third and fourth views are similar, in that both assert that Paul did not intend to inform the reader about who did the "fitting for destruction." The fourth view says this is because he did not know the answer to that question; the third view says it is because, though he may have known the answer, it was beside the point in Rom 9:22 to give it. The point was only to say that those who are ultimately judged are in a condition that makes this judgment fitting or appropriate. That the fourth view contradicts the context

of what Paul claims to know in Rom 9 and that the third
view is true but does not go far enough, I will try to
show by the following observations.

It seems to me that, after the clear and powerful
statements of double predestination in Rom 9, it is
grasping at a straw to argue that the passive voice of
κατηρτισμένα proves that Paul denied divine agency in
fitting men for destruction. "Jacob I loved and Esau I
hated" (9:13). "He has mercy on whom he wills and he
hardens whom he wills" (9:18). "He makes from the same
lump a vessel for honor and a vessel for dishonor"
(9:21). Is it really plausible after such assertions
to argue that the differences between "vessels of wrath
fitted for destruction" and "vessels of mercy which he
prepared before for glory" are such that Paul is now
denying or even trying to conceal the divine agency in
the former? Paul has just stated unabashedly that God
makes from the same lump vessels for dishonor (9:21).
I cannot escape the implication that anti-Calvinistic
apologetic is in control when in the next verse we are
forbidden to suggest that the divine Potter is at work
in the phrase "vessels of wrath fitted for destruction."
Moreover in view of the parallels between Rom 9:22 and
9:17 (see above p 188) a most natural suggestion is
that Pharaoh serves as an example of a "vessel of wrath
fitted for destruction." And since Paul's inference
from the Pharaoh story is that "God hardens whom he
wills" (9:18), the most natural suggestion from the
context is that "fitted for destruction" (9:22) refers
precisely to this divine hardening.

Besides these contextual considerations we may also
recall how closely related Paul's thought has proved to
be to the apocalyptic tradition reaching its climax in
the double predestination of Qumran. (See Section 4.16
and Chapter Three, p 53, and Maier, Mensch und freier
Wille, 381.) The word καταρτίζω (cf Rom 9:22) translates the Hebrew כון three times in the LXX (Ps 67:9;
73:16; 88:37). This lends even greater credence to the
suggestion that Paul is at home with the Essene doctrine
of predestination[31] for we find the word כון used in
predestinarian contexts which resemble the thought of
Rom 9:22f. For example, 1 QH 15:12-22 (translation
from Dupont-Sommer):

> And I, because of Thine understanding, I know
> that [the righteousness of man] is not in the
>   hand of flesh
> [and] that man [is not] master of (13) his way
> and that mankind cannot strengthen his step

(לְהָכִין עֲצָדוֹ).

And I know that the inclination of every spirit
is in Thy hand
(14) [and that] Thou hast ordained [the way of
every man]
before creating him (הֲכִינוֹתָה בְּטֶרֶם בְּרָאתוֹ).
And how can any man change Thy words?
Thou alone hast created (15) the just
and established him (הֲכִינוֹתוֹ) from his mother's
womb unto the time of good-will (cf Rom 9:23)
that he may be preserved in Thy covenant
and walk in all Thy way . . .
And Thou hast raised up (17) his glory from
among flesh
whereas Thou hast created (בְּרָאתָה) the wicked
[for the time of] Thy [wr]ath
and hast set them apart from their mother's
womb for the Day of Massacre . . .
(19) Thou hast created all [them that despise]
Thy [will]
to execute judgment against them (גְּדוֹלִים
הֲכִינוֹתָם לַעֲשׂוֹת בָּם שְׁפָטִי)
(20) in the eyes of all Thy works
that they may serve as a sign and wo[nder unto]
everlasting [generations]
that [all] may know Thy glory (cf Rom 9:23) and
awful might (cf Rom 9:22).

This use of כּוּן (which can be rendered by καταρτίζω) in
a context so much like Paul's (cf also 1 QS 11:10,11)
increases the probability that with κατηρτισμένα Paul
has in view the divine agency.

To the Qumran analogies may also be added at least
one example of a rabbinic conception of predestination
which, though late (about 340), may reflect early
tradition. According to Midrash Esther 1,1 (829) a
rabbi said,

From the beginning of the creation of the
world God <u>prepared</u> (התקין) what he chose:
Adam (he prepared) to be the first creature,
Cain to be the first murderer, Abel to be
the first one murdered, Noah to be the first
one saved, etc. (cf Strack-Billerbeck, I, 982).

I conclude, therefore, primarily from the context of
Rom 9 (but also with some corroboration from Paul's
Jewish milieu; cf also Apoc Abr 22) that it accords
best with Paul's intention to see the divine agency
behind the passive κατηρτισμένα in Rom 9:22.

We can only guess why Paul used this passive verb
in reference to vessels of wrath and an active verb
(προητοίμασεν) in reference to vessels of mercy. Since
the grammar of Rom 9:22,23 is awkward it is not unrea-
sonable to suggest that a shift occurred in Paul's
thought as he was writing the sentence. Thus at first
he may have intended to express the divine action in
both cases with the passive voice. But then as he
began to formulate 9:23 he also conceived how he would
continue it in 9:24 ("whom he also called . . .").
This continuation may have been suggested to him by the
earlier sequence in Rom 8:30 (οὓς δὲ προώρισεν, τούτους
καὶ ἐκάλεσεν)--a sequence which commended not only the
active voice for προητοίμασεν but also the relative
clause and the prefix προ-.

Another possible explanation for the passive
κατηρτισμένα, if we assume a good bit more grammatical
reflection on Paul's part, is that he really does want
to make a statement about the way God works: though
God does accomplish all things by the counsel of his
will he does not bring about all things in the same
way. In the accomplishment of some things he employs
intermediary agents perhaps. Or to put it another way,
his heart is engaged differently in different acts,
loving some deeds in themselves and inclining to others
only as they are preferable in relation to greater ends
(cf Lam 3:33). If this is the case Paul would be
implying that not wrath but mercy is the greater, over-
arching goal for which God does all things.

5.4 The justification of God in his ultimate purpose

With that suggestion we have arrived at our final
question, namely, What is God's chief aim in his sovereign activity over man and how, at last, does this aim
answer the objection raised at Rom 9:19 (Why does he
still find fault?)? I have already cited above on p
169 the excellent quote from Cranfield to the effect
that among the three purposes of God mentioned in Rom
9:22,23, the purpose to "make known the wealth of his
glory on the vessels of mercy" is primary. As K.
Mueller puts it, "God's wrath is put into the service
of his mercy" (Zuvorersehung, 16). This ordering of
God's aims is generally recognized.[32] Cranfield
(Romans, II, 496) sums up the arguments for this
position as follows:

> We now turn to the three statements of pur-
> pose contained in this passage. That the
> last of these (ἵνα γνωρίσῃ κ.τ.λ.) is

dominant is clear. It alone is introduced by
ἵνα; and it is given special emphasis by its
position in the sentence, by the fact that it
is extended by means of the two relative
clauses which follow, and by the fact that
verses 25-29 focus further attention on it.
Above all its content marks it off from the
others; for the manifestation of the wealth
of the divine glory is nothing less than the
ultimate purpose of God.

This purpose statement (9:23) probably has its closest
parallel in Eph 2:7 where God's purpose in redemption
is "that he might show (ἐνδείξηται) in the coming ages
the surpassing wealth of his grace in kindness on us
(ἐφ' ἡμᾶς; cf ἐπί in Rom 9:23) in Christ Jesus." God's
chief end in creation and redemption is to display for
the benefit of his elect the fulness of his glory,
especially his mercy.

Now what about the objection raised in Rom 9:19,
namely, If God sovereignly "has mercy on whom he wills
and hardens whom he wills" (9:18), why does he still
find fault? Has Paul really answered it? To see that
he has requires a remarkable degree of openness to the
text and freedom from inherited notions about the
righteousness of God. I know of no one who has labored
to open himself to Paul's way of thinking more than
Prof. Daniel Fuller, from whom so much of the stimulus
for this book has come. Therefore, I would like to
quote at length his effort[33] to understand the integrity of Paul's answer to the objector in Rom 9:19.

> To this objection Paul replies that men
> have no more right to call God into question
> for his dealings with them than clay has in
> telling a potter into what shape he should
> form it. Needless to say, Paul's reply here
> is considered by many to be unacceptable.
> James Denney in his commentary on Romans in
> the Expositor's Greek Testament says (ad loc),
> "To this objection [cf 9:19] there is really
> no answer, and it ought to be frankly admit-
> ted that the apostle does not answer it."
> Likewise C.H. Dodd in the Moffatt New Testa-
> ment Commentary says (ad loc), " . . . the
> objector is right. Paul has driven himself
> into a position in which he has to deny that
> God's freedom of action is limited by moral
> considerations. 'Has the potter no right
> over the clay?' It is a well-worn

197

illustration. But the trouble is that a man
is not a pot; he <u>will</u> ask, 'Why did you make
me like this?' and he will not be bludgeoned
into silence. It is the weakest point in the
whole epistle."

The trouble with these commentators, however, is that they construe Paul's reply to
the objector to mean that men have no right to
question God but must blindly accede to what
he does <u>without seeing any reason for it</u>. But
it should be observed that in verses 22
through 24 Paul does set forth the purpose
which controls God's exercise of his sovereignty. To be sure, men have no right to ask
God to cease to be God by surrendering any of
his sovereignty (9:20-21). But men are not
asked to submit to this sovereignty blindly,
for God's exercise of it is as purposeful and
non-arbitrary as the way a potter uses clay.
Just as it is altogether right for a potter
to use clay so that he may make evident the
full range of his skill as a potter, so it
can only be right for God to deal with men in
such a way that the full range of his glory
becomes externalized. Thus while Paul does
not surrender one iota of God's sovereignty,
he does show that its exercise is not arbitrary but purposeful, and in so doing Paul's
argument is anything but weak; neither is he
bludgeoning men into submission, but is
rather showing the reasonableness of it all.

Verses 22-24 assert that it is only
right for God to display the full range of his
glory in his sovereign dealings with men.
[These verses are a rhetorical question which
when] shaped into a declarative statement
assert that it is right for God to work with
his creation so that it will externalize all
aspects of his glory, his wrath and power on
the one hand, and his mercy on the other.
But God has a greater purpose than simply to
show the full range of his glory. He would not
be showing himself as he really is if he set
forth his wrath and power as coordinate and equal
to his love and mercy. God delights more in
his mercy than in his wrath, but in order to
show the priority of his mercy, God must place
it against a backdrop of wrath.[34] How could
God's mercy appear fully as <u>mercy</u> unless men

198

were in a plight that would call for mercy?
It would be impossible for men to share with
God the delight he has in his mercy unless
they see clearly the awfulness of the almighty wrath from which his mercy delivers
them. Thus to show the full range of his
glory, God not only prepares beforehand vessels of mercy but also vessels of wrath in
order that the riches of his glory in connection with the vessels of mercy might thereby
become manifest.

Thus it is surely right for God to prepare vessels of wrath, for it is only by so
doing that he is able to show the exceeding
riches of his glory, the capstone of which is
his mercy. For God not to prepare vessels of
wrath would mean that he could not fully show
himself as the merciful God that he is. As a
result it would be impossible for creation to
honor him for what he is. But if creation
does not render God the honor due his name,
then he has been unrighteous, for in the act
of creation he has done something which is not
consonant with the full delight he has in his
own glory. God would be unrighteous were he
to do anything inconsistent with his own purpose to find full delight in his glory.

But God is not only righteous in preparing vessels of wrath but also in finding fault
with such vessels and visiting wrath upon
them. Were God to prepare vessels deserving
of wrath, and then not visit wrath upon them,
he would obviously act in complete inconsistency with his love for his own glory. God
acts consistently with his love for his own
glory only as he opposes all who oppose finding
delight in his glory. Consequently he is only
righteous in that he prepares vessels for wrath
and then visits them with the wrath they
deserve. Were he not to do these things in the
world which he freely created, he would cease to
be God. Hence the objection of 9:19 that God
should not find fault with those whom he hardens is shown to be without substance.[35]

199

CHAPTER ELEVEN

CONCLUSION

I have attempted in this book to do objective, historical-grammatical exegesis of Rom 9:1-23. Objectivity does not mean for me disinterested detachment. It means that I have tried to submit my preconceptions to what Matthew Arnold called the "severe discipline" of following another person's line of thought on its own terms. I do not regard the work as a theology of election nor as a fully rounded justification of the sovereign decrees of God. But I do consider it a needed foundation stone of such a theology and such a justification. In conclusion then I will try to sketch briefly the contours of that stone discovered in the course of the study.

The roots of this study go back to my perplexity about how Rom 9:15 ("For God says to Moses: I will have mercy on whomever I have mercy and I will be gracious to whomever I will be gracious") could be an argument (γάρ) for Rom 9:14 ("There is no unrighteousness with God, is there? No indeed!"). How could this quote from Ex 33:19 support Paul's assertion of God's righteousness? What is Paul's justification of God?

To answer this question it was necessary to clarify as precisely as I could just what had called God's righteousness into question. This required an exegesis of Rom 9:6b-13 (Chapter Three). But this unit is Paul's support for his assertion in 9:6a that "It is not as though the word of God has fallen." In order to accurately understand Paul's defense of the fidelity of God's word it was also necessary to inquire from Rom 9:1-5 what had called God's word into question (Chapter Two).

The upshot of this ground-laying in Chapters Two and Three was this: the painful fact that had called God's word into question was that many Israelites, having rejected their Messiah, are accursed and cut off from Christ. How could this be, if they are the people to whom irrevocable divine promises were made? Can God's word of promise fall? All of Rom 9-11 is written with a view to showing that God has not been and will not be unfaithful to his word. Rom 9 alone is only part of Paul's demonstration of the truth of God. Rom 11 on the future salvation of "all Israel" is an

201

essential part of the demonstration. But this part of his response lay outside our immediate concern.

Paul's preliminary defense (Rom 9:6-13) of the truthfulness of God's promise is to argue from the OT that the promises of God never were intended to guarantee the salvation of every individual Israelite. His promise gave expression to an "electing purpose" (9:11) by which God aims to preserve his complete freedom in determining who will be the beneficiaries of his saving promises, who will be the "Israel" within Israel (9:6b). His purpose is thus maintained by means of the predestination of individuals to their respective eternal destinies. I tried to assess as fully and fairly as I could the view which sees only national election in these verses, but found the view exegetically (not dogmatically) untenable. Paul's solution, then, to the problem posed in 9:1-5 is that "all those from Israel are not Israel" (9:6b). Within the context of Rom 9 this means that God maintains his sovereign "purpose of election" by determining, before they are born, who will belong to the "saved" among Israel. And this determination is, therefore, not based on what a person wills or does (9:11,12,16), but solely on God whose "call" effects what he purposes (9:12). For this reason Paul is confident that God's word has not fallen but is in fact working out God's sovereign purpose even in the unbelief of Paul's kinsmen.

Between Rom 9:13 and 14 we may imagine an objection being raised. It apparently sounded like this: if God, in determining who will be the beneficiaries of his mercy, does not base his decisions on any human distinctives that a person may claim by birth or effort, then he is unrighteous. The assumption seems to be that divine righteousness would require that God elect persons on the basis of their real and valuable distinctives whether racial (Jewishness) or moral (keepers of the law).

Paul denied in Rom 9:14 that God is unrighteous. I argued, therefore, that evidently Paul does not share this conception of divine righteousness. How Paul does conceive of God's righteousness we begin to see as we struggle to understand its defense in Rom 9:15ff. The defense begins with the puzzling quotation of Ex 33:19 ("I will have mercy on whomever I have mercy . . ."). Therefore I devoted Chapter Four to an effort to understand Ex 33:19 in its OT context as Paul may have understood it.

202

From the OT context I concluded that Ex 33:19, as
a brief, preliminary declaration of the verbal theophany
which follows in Ex 34:6,7, constitutes a manifestation
of God's glory (Ex 33:18), a "passing by" of his goodness (33:19a) and a proclamation of his name (33:19b).
These three realities overlap in the Ex context so that
we can say God's glory and his name consist fundamentally in his propensity to show mercy and his sovereign
freedom in its distribution. Or to put it more precisely, it is the glory of God and his essential nature
mainly to dispense mercy (but also wrath, Ex 34:7) on
whomever he pleases apart from any constraint originating outside his own will. This is the essence of
what it means to be God. This is his name.

If this is the meaning that Ex 33:19 had for Paul
when he quoted it in Rom 9:15, the question then arises:
How does an affirmation that God's glory (or name) consists largely in his sovereign freedom to show mercy on
whom he wills function as an argument for the righteousness of God in election? The thesis that I formulate
in Chapter Five in answer to this question is that for
Paul the righteousness of God must be his unswerving
commitment always to preserve the honor of his name and
display his glory. If this is what it means for God to
be righteous, and if his glory (or name) consists
mainly in his sovereign freedom to have mercy on whom
he wills, then the quotation of Ex 33:19 as an argument
for the righteousness of God in unconditional election
does in fact make good sense.

So the crucial question became: Does Paul really
have this view of the divine righteousness? To answer
this question I first inquired in Chapter Six whether
there is an OT precedent for such an understanding of
the righteousness of God. This was a crucial step
because so much of Paul's theology has its roots in the
OT. The conclusion I reached was that there is indeed
a broad basis for understanding the righteousness of
God as his unswerving commitment to preserve the honor
of his name and display his glory. So the next step
was to test whether in the crucial Pauline texts this
understanding of God's righteousness is evident. My
investigation both of Rom 3:1-8 (Chapter Seven) and Rom
3:25,26 (Chapter Eight) confirmed that Paul does share
this view of the righteousness of God.

With that conclusion I returned in Chapter Nine to
complete my treatment of Rom 9:14-18. Here the scope
of God's freedom to show mercy and to harden was
described in more detail and the reference in Rom 9:17

to God's purposes in dealing with Pharaoh was found to cohere remarkably with our interpretation of Ex 33:19. In 9:17 Paul cites Ex 9:16: "For the Scripture says to Pharaoh: For this very thing I raised you up, that I might show in you my power and that I might proclaim my name in all the earth." It can scarcely be overemphasized, for the sake of Paul's justification of God, that in Rom 9:15 and 17 Paul employs OT texts in which the exercise of God's sovereign freedom, in mercy (Ex 33:19) and in hardening (Ex 9:16), is the means by which he declares the glory of his name! This is the heart of Paul's defense: in choosing unconditionally those on whom he will have mercy and those whom he will harden God is not unrighteous for in this "electing purpose" he is acting out of a full allegiance to his name and esteem for his glory.

Paul's justification of God does not end at Rom 9:18, because someone registers another objection in 9:19: "Why does God still find fault since no one can successfully resist his sovereign will?" That is, if God is in absolute control of whether men are hardened or not, then he has no right to condemn them for their hardness. How Paul responds to this final objection is the subject of Chapter Ten and the climax of our study. God is our creator and as such has as much right to make of us what he wills as a potter has over his clay to make from the same lump a vessel for honor and a vessel for dishonor (9:21). We have no right to dispute with God our maker. Yet Paul does not stop with a reprimand, for man is not asked to submit to God's sovereignty without seeing some justification for why he does what he does.

The final statement of this justification of God's ways is given in Rom 9:22,23. God's desire is "to show wrath and make known his power." But even more he desires "to make known the wealth of his glory on his people, the vessels of mercy." The ultimate aim of God is to show mercy. But to do this he must place it against a backdrop of wrath. For "how could God's mercy appear fully as mercy unless men were in a plight that would call for mercy? It would be impossible for men to share with God the delight he has in his mercy unless they see clearly the awfulness of the almighty wrath from which his mercy delivers them. Thus, to show the full range of his glory [and therefore be righteous], God not only prepares beforehand vessels of mercy but also vessels of wrath in order that the riches of his glory in connection with the vessels of mercy might thereby become manifest" (Fuller, <u>Unity of the Bible</u>, pp xx,5).

For those who, like myself, confess Rom 9 as Holy Scripture and accord it an authority over our lives, the implications of this exegesis are profound. We will surely not fall prey to the naive and usually polemical suggestions that we cease to pray or that we abandon evangelism. If we did that we would only betray our failure to be grasped by this theology as Paul was who "prayed without ceasing" (1 Thess 5:17) and who labored in evangelism "harder than any of the other apostles" (1 Cor 15:10). On the contrary we will be deeply sobered by the awful severity of God, humbled to the dust by the absoluteness of our dependence on his unconditional mercy, and irresistibly allured by the infinite treasury of his glory ready to be revealed to the vessels of glory. Thus we will be moved to forsake all confidence in human distinctives or achievements and we will entrust ourselves to mercy alone. In the hope[1] of glory we will extend this mercy to others that they may see our good deeds and give glory to our Father in heaven.

ENDNOTES

NOTES FOR CHAPTER TWO

Notes from pp 3,4

1. See Luz, Geschichtsverstaendnis, 19-25, for a discussion of the various views on the relationship
   between Rom 1-8 and 9-11. Also Mueller, Gottes
   Gerechtigkeit, 54f, and Kuemmel, "Probleme von
   Roemer 9-11," 15-28.

2. J. Jervell, "The Letter to Jerusalem," 61ff.

3. A. Suhl, "Der Konkrete Anlass des Roemerbriefes,"
   Kairos 13, 1971, 119ff.

4. Romans, 241. "The question forced on Paul is
   whether the promises are still valid, since they
   were made to a people now repudiated. The whole
   security of the promise is thus challenged, and
   thus the whole doctrine of justification by faith.
   At the same time the continuity and unity of the
   people of God, of which the apostle wishes to con-
   vince the readers, becomes insecure. How could
   the young church feel conscious of belonging to
   the old trunk of which Abraham is the stem, if the
   new dispensation develops outside the framework of
   the elect people of God?" (242). Similarly Nygren,
   Romans, 357.

5. "Israel und die Kirche," 181: "If God's word,
   which calls Israel to become his people and
   expresses his election of them (Rom 9:6; 11:28),
   has fallen then the ground of Christian hope, the
   climax of Rom 1-8, has also collapsed: 'Those whom
   he predestined, these he also called; and those
   whom he called, these he also justified; and those
   whom he justified, these he also glorified' (Rom
   8:30). Accordingly the question about Israel in
   Rom 9 grows out of the line of argument in Rom 1-8
   just as it does out of the situation of church and
   mission that confronted Paul at the end of his
   work in the eastern half of the empire (Rom
   15:19-33)."

6. J. Munck, Christ and Israel, 35: "If God has not
   fulfilled his promises made to Israel, then what
   basis has the Jewish-Gentile church for believing
   that the promises will be fulfilled for them?"

209

7. Kaesemann, Romans, 261: "The problem of this
   entire section is here formulated." See references to other literature here. In addition Rese
   ("Vorzuege," 218) argues: "What in Rom 3:3 was
   only a query has now in Rom 9:6a become the decisive question and theme of Rom 9-11." Zeller,
   Juden und Heiden, 113: "Rom 9:6a has the effect
   of a title." Cf Corley, "The Jews," 45.

8. Mueller, Gottes Gerechtigkeit, 54f: "If Israel,
   to whom God has granted the υἱοθεσία, and to whom
   belong the ἐπαγγελίαι and the διαθῆκαι and the
   κλῆσις, can perish (9:4), then the υἱοθεσία of the
   Christians (8:14ff), their election and call
   (9:29f), has become unsure and their salvation
   uncertain. We are confronted again with the stead-
   fastness of God, which for believers is a matter
   of life and death. It is inseparably connected
   with the problem of Israel." Luz, Geschichtsverstaendnis, 28: "The unbelief of Israel brings
   God's own trustworthiness into question" (cf also
   21, 36). Cf Rese, "Vorzuege," 215.

9. Most commentators follow the United Bible Societies' and Nestle's Greek New Testament which print
   the plural (X C K Ψ 33 81 614 1739 Byz Lect etc)
   instead of the singular ἡ διαθήκη (p46 B Dgr etc).
   Metzger (Textual Commentary, 519) explains the
   preference of the Bible Societies' text (with a
   probability level of C in the 3rd edition): "(a)
   copyists would have been likely to assimilate the
   plural to the pattern of instances of the singular
   number in the series, and (b) plural covenants may
   have appeared to involve theological difficulties
   and therefore the expression was converted to the
   singular number. Certainly there is no good
   reason why the singular, if original, should have
   been altered to the plural." Luz (Geschichtsverstaendnis, 272 note 24) agrees that the plural
   may be the harder reading but suggests that it may
   be accounted for by assimilation to the plural
   ἐπαγγελίαι (9:4b). Cerfaux ("Privilège," 348)
   argues for the singular by pointing out that
   Paul's normal usage is singular (Rom 11:27; 1 Cor
   11:25; 2 Cor 3:6,14; Gal 3:15,17) and that the two
   instances of plural (Gal 4:24; Eph 2:12) refer to
   the Old and New Covenants, which, he says, is
   impossible here in Rom 9:4. But his exegesis of
   Eph 2:12 ("strangers to the covenants of promise")

as well as Rom 9:4 is unconvincing, as will appear
in the course of our discussion. Both Luz and
Cerfaux stress that the external evidence appears
to favor the singular διαθήκη: "In all other
cases this fact decides the best text. Why not
here?" (348). While certainty is not possible, I
am inclined to the plural because of how much more
probable it seems that a copyist would assimilate
the plural to Paul's common singular usage, and
because I think the parallel with ἐπαγγελίαι is
Paul's intention, not a copyist's (see below p 6).

10. Alford, II, 404: "Not only on their relationship
to himself does he ground this sorrow and his self-
devotion: but on the recollection of their ancient
privileges and glories." Kaesemann, Romans, 258
(German 246: "οἵτινες begruendet zugleich"). Cf
Paul's use of οἵτινες in Rom 2:15 and Michel's
(Roemer, 80) comment: "The relative connector
οἵτινες (cf 1:25,32) is always given emphasis by
Paul and has the effect of a demonstrative pronoun."

11. One might try to construe πατέρες in 9:5a as the
antecedent of ἐξ ὧν in 9:5b, but Meyer (Romans, II,
117) is surely correct in saying: "The καί before
ἐξ ὧν forbids the reference of the latter to οἱ
πατέρες."

12. Meyer (Romans, II, 116) ignores all grammatical and
formal features in arguing from content for an
intended chiasmus in the terms διαθῆκαι, νομοθεσία,
λατρεία, ἐπαγγελίαι. In fact, even with regard to
content, the three rhyming pairs go well together:
the rabbis saw a close connection between Israel's
adoption and the giving of the law (Huonder, Israel
Sohn Gottes, 44); the tent of worship was sanctified by God's glory (Ex 29:43); and the covenants
are, according to Paul, "covenants of promise"
(Eph 2:12).

13. Michel, Roemer, 228: "The artful structure of this
list and the reference to the christological confession [9:5c] at the end suggest that Paul has
reworked in verse 4 older Hellenistic-Jewish con-
fessional material, especially since the language
is not typically Pauline but is elsewhere used
differently by Paul." This last remark will, I
think, have to be qualified in view of our

Notes from p 7

exegesis. Moreover I cannot reconcile this argument of Michel with his comment on 227 note 2:
"The artful structure of verses 4 and 5 shows the
great significance which these verses are accorded
by Paul." How can the artful structure be both an
argument for the unit's traditional character and
a reflection of the significance the unit has for
Paul (presumably as careful artisan)? Cerfaux,
"Privilège," 340: "If Saint Paul possesses in all
these expressions some originality, it does not
reside in the enumerating of the prerogatives of
the chosen people. There is no end to the litanies
which, in the Old Testament and literature of
Judaism, constantly recall and multiply these
prerogatives." But the "litanies" which Cerfaux
cites bear no formal resemblance to Rom 9:4,5 (1
Kgs 8:33-66; Is 56:3-7; 63:7-18; Ps 104(105):5-11;
Sirach 24:8-12; 36:16-19; 2 Macc 2:17f; Sib Or III,
218-295; 4 Ezra 3:13-24; 5:23-30; 6:58f; 8:51; 2
Bar 21:24f; 57:1-3; 59:1-2; 61:1-2). Cerfaux presents the same argument in The Church, 25. See
also Dietzfelbinger, Heilsgeschichte, 16f.

14. The dialogical interaction with his opponents'
views, for example, in 2:1-5, 17-24; 3:1-8;
6:1,2,15; 9:14,19,20, supports this view. Dinkler,
"Praedestination," 85, observes that "in a certain
sense the whole letter to the Romans must be read
as a dialogue between the Christian church and the
synagogue." But this is too sweeping, since significant portions of the letter reflect concerns
inside the church itself (e.g. 12-14) as well as
the concern that the Greek Christians not boast
over the broken-off branches (11:20) or "become
wise in themselves" (11:25).

15. The earliest known instances of the word are in
second century B.C. inscriptions, with the social,
legal meaning of adoption. In the Greek world
there are no instances of υἱοθεσία in a theological
sense. TDNT, VIII, 397-9. Strack-Billerbeck, III,
261 note concerning υἱοθεσία: "A corresponding
abstract formation is missing in the rabbinic
writings."

16. Luz, Geschichtsverstaendnis, 270 note 13: "Above
all, similar expressions in Judaism are almost
completely missing. The nearest parallels known to
me are found in 4 Ezra 3:32f; 5:23ff; cf 10:21f

212

(but in a totally different sense). See also 2
Macc 1:25 and the inscription from the Bar Cochba
time in ThW III 362. To my knowledge the Judaism
of that day never spoke of the prerogatives quite
like this, in an indicative, present sense.
Therefore one should view Rom 9:4 as Paul's own
formulation and recognize his rhetorical art." In
the same vein see Rese, "Vorzuege," 212, who inter-
acts with those who think Paul is speaking here
more as a Jewish patriot (e.g. Wrede, Paulus, 74)
than as an apostle.

17. After the εἰσιν of 9:4a the three modifying relative clauses are without verbs. But in such cases
the time of the subordinate clause is always determined by the time of the main verb. It would be
wholly without grammatical warrant to construe the
relative clauses to mean "whose were the sonship . . . whose were the fathers . . ." etc.

18. I will argue below that if Paul were merely saying
that Israel's privileges applied only to the
former times, then the word of God would not be so
severely jeopardized as it seems to be in 9:6a.
The problem presented in 9:1-5 is not how the
Church can take Israel's place (see next three
notes) but how Paul's kinsmen can be both anathema
and privileged at the same time.

19. Munck (Christ and Israel, 30) offers no support
for his assertion that "all the benefits mentioned
in 9:4,5 as evidence of God's graciousness toward
Israel belong to the early times of Israel's history." Compare Otto Kuss (Roemerbrief, III, 678) who
describes Rom 9:4f as "the unique theocratic position of Israel."

Cerfaux ("Privilège") goes beyond Munck and argues
that these privileges used to belong to Israel
according to the flesh but now have passed over to
the Church. As far as the Jews are concerned "in
Rom 9:4 one has in view only the Old Testament"
(348). But after that "episode of waiting" "the
Christ came, Israel was done away with" (363).
Therefore, "all the prerogatives of Israel were
essentially temporary and insecure" (364), with
the result that "the privileges of Judaism find
their fulfilment in the Christian church" (341).
His support for this position is a general survey

of labels which Paul attached to the Church. He sums up as follows: "In conclusion, we observe therefore the tendency of Saint Paul to separate the most characteristic and religious appellations (Israel, seed of Abraham, elect, called, beloved) from the concrete people, or more explicitly from the Jewish generation which rejected the Messiah, in order to make of them theological appellations which from now on apply to the church. This is a pointer for the interpretation of the privilege of Israel" (347). With this assumption then he approaches Rom 9:4,5 and thus cannot own up to the very probable intention of Paul to assign these privileges not to the Church but to his "kinsmen according to the flesh" in the present.

20. See G. Eichholz (Theologie des Paulus, 289-300) on the unity of Rom 9-11. "Against the analysis of Erich Dinkler, we understand the flow of thought in Rom 9-11 as a unity and not collapsed in contradictions."

21. Gutbrod (TDNT, III, 387) argues rightly concerning the privileges of Israel in Paul: "that there can be no transfer of the title to the new community at the expense of the old is shown particularly clearly by the image of the olive tree in Rom 11:17ff; Israel is the one community of God into which the Gentiles are now engrafted." He tries to show that Gal 6:16 and 1 Cor 10:18 are only partial exceptions. Cf also Eichholz, Theologie des Paulus, 291: "These privileges are not taken from Israel by Paul--not with one single syllable." Mueller, Zuvorersehung, 12: "If only individual Israelites are to be saved, then in spite of everything there would be a breach in God's promise. Therefore in chapter 11 Paul describes the divine guidance of the peoples which finally must lead to the salvation of Israel as a people (11:26)."

22. "Vorzuege," 219: "It cannot reasonably be questioned that for Paul the advantages of Israel cannot be abolished through temporal priority nor can Yahweh's election 'simply be transferred over to the church (as eschatological Israel).' Church and Israel are for Paul two distinct but interdependent realities. God and his promises are true. Therefore, even after Christ, Israel remains

214

the elect people of God--now as the already saved
remnant of Jewish Christians [cf Rom 11:1ff] , and in
the future (after the fullness of the Gentiles
comes in) as the yet-to-be-saved people of Israel.
For the fall of Israel is the God-intended enabling
of the mission to the Gentiles and the redemption
of the world. Church and Israel exist, therefore,
also after Christ, side-by-side as two distinct
but interdependent realities" (221). The latter
half of this article is marred, I think, by Rese's
attempt to show that a radically different view of
Israel and the Church is given in Eph 2:12:
Israel's peculiarity is transferred to the Church.
But his argument is mainly from the silence there
about a future for historical Israel. He does not
seem to see how similar the picture in Eph 2 is to
the olive tree analogy in Rom 11:17ff.

23. Geschichtsverstaendnis, 273f. The privilege of
Israel is a gracious gift. "Precisely in this
lies the possibility that the privileges of Israel
can also be fully ascribed to unbelieving Israel.
Precisely the fact that Israel's advantages are
God's gift prevents Paul, unlike the writers of
Apocalyptic, from pushing the promises of God into
the future and from complaining about the unreality
of God's word. Paul can ascribe to the unbelieving
Israel of the present its status as Israel fully
and completely. He can speak so positively about
Israel (unlike anything I know in contemporary
Judaism) because he knows: God does not give up
his freedom vis-à-vis unbelieving Israel. Therefore in the end it is precisely the freedom of God
which is Israel's privilege."

I think Luz has been carried by his eloquence to
overstate the case. To say that Paul ascribes to
the present generation of Israel her privileges
"fully and completely" and that he, unlike the
writers of apocalyptic, "does not push the promises of God into the future," does not reflect an
adequate appraisal of Rom 11. The great benefit
of Israel, its corporate salvation, is indeed post-
poned "until the fullness of the Gentiles comes
in" (11:25f). And in the present, Israel does not
obtain what it sought (11:7). It is in a condition
of transgression and loss (11:12). Only "some"
are being saved (11:14). It is rejected now, but
will in the future be accepted (11:15). Therefore

215

Notes from pp 15-17

> Luz's stress that the unbelieving Israel of the
> present possesses Israel's privileges "fully and
> completely" is true only in the sense that there
> is an ethnic and religious continuity from genera-
> tion to generation in Israel such that one may
> refer to the experience of a future generation as
> belonging to the people of the present.

24. In the NT the term is used only in John 1:47; Acts
    2:22; 3:12; 5:35; 13:16; 21:28; Rom 9:4; 11:1; 2
    Cor 11:22. On the difference between Israel(ite)
    and Jew see TDNT, III, 360ff.

25. Huonder, Israel Sohn Gottes, 54: "We can call this
    text Ex 4:22f the classic passage of Scripture for
    grounding Israel's sonship." Huonder's book is a
    convenient and helpful collection of early and late
    rabbinic discussion of Israel's sonship organized
    around the key OT texts. The material is presen-
    ted under the following texts and titles:

    > Ex 4:22f; Is 63:8; Hos 11:1--The firstborn son
    > Deut 14:1--The exercise of sonship
    > Deut 32:5--Sons or not-sons
    > Deut 32:19; Is 43:6--Sons and daughters
    > Deut 32:20; Is 1:2,4; 30:1,9; Jer 3:14,19,22;
    >   4:22--Sonship in crisis
    > Is 45:11; Jer 31:20; Hos 2:1--The future of
    > sonship

26. Rese, "Vorzuege," 216: "Just before this, in Rom
    8:15, Paul had described sonship as something
    belonging to the salvation of Christians.
    . . . All the more astounding is it then when Paul
    now in Rom 9:4f calls 'sonship' the privilege of
    unbelieving Israel without any qualification" ("ohne
    jeden Abstrich," my emphasis).

27. The same line of thought could be developed also
    from Eph 2:18,19 where Gentiles and Jews become
    reconciled to the same Father and Gentiles become
    "members of God's household." Similarly Gal
    3:16,26-29 connects Christian sonship to the
    Jewish promise.

28. For citations see TDNT, VIII, 360; Strack-
    Billerbeck, I, 220; III, 18; and especially
    Huonder, Israel Sohn Gottes, 41, 85, 98f, 126,
    143, 161, 174.

29. Roemerbrief, 286: "Here it is said concretely that
    to them belongs 'the sonship' in which now also
    the Christians are included."

30. Geschichtsverstaendnis, 271: "The Christian com-
    munity has now taken over this privilege. All the
    more striking is it then that Paul here allows
    Israel to keep it and ascribes the sonship to the
    unbelieving Israel of the present with no hesita-
    tion. There can be no talk of a historical aban-
    donment in favor of the church."

31. Sanday and Headlam, Romans, 230; Michel, Roemer,
    227; Murray, Romans, II, 5; Schlatter, Gerechtig-
    keit, 294; Kaesemann, Romans, 258; Munck, Christ
    and Israel, 31.

32. The other places in Paul where δόξα (with modi-
    fiers) refers to eschatological glory are Rom 5:2;
    8:21; 9:23; 1 Cor 2:7; Eph 1:18; Phil 3:21; 1
    Thess 2:12; 2 Thess 1:9; 2:14; Tit 2:13. In the
    synoptic gospels δόξα is usually Christ's coming
    glory (Mk 8:38 par; 10:37 par; 13:26 par; Mt 25:31
    par).

33. TDNT, II, 241f (von Rad). Within the later rabbi-
    nic literature "express statements concerning
    participation in the glory of God are rare" (TDNT,
    II, 246). Moreover, "We are not aware of any
    example in the rabbinic literature in which כבוד
    and יקרא are used absolutely with no addition of a
    divine designation" (Strack-Billerbeck, III, 262).

34. On the textual question of whether the singular or
    plural variant is original see note 9. Paul uses
    the plural in one other place--Eph 2:12--and
    singular in Rom 11:27; 1 Cor 11:25; 2 Cor 3:6,14;
    Gal 3:15,17.

35. As cited in Alford, II, 404, both Augustine and
    Jerome construed "covenants" in Rom 9:4b to
    include the old and new covenants.

36. Murray, Romans, II, 6; Munck, Christ and Israel, 32
    note 15; Michel, Roemer, 227; Rese, "Vorzuege,"
    216; Luz, Geschichtsverstaendnis, 272; Kaesemann,
    Romans, 259.

37. Calvin (Romans, 195), Alford (II, 404), and Kuss
    (Roemerbrief, III, 676) admit that either one implies
    the other.

38. See his "Paul and the Works of the Law" and Gospel
    and Law: Contrast or Continuum, chapter 4.
    Others developing a similar line of argument are
    Felix Flueckiger, "Christus, des Gesetzes telos,"
    and C.E.B. Cranfield, "Some Notes on Romans
    9:30-33."

39. "The Mosaic Law Preaches Faith."

40. In 1 Macc 2:19-22 λατρεία, διαθήκη and νόμος are
    almost synonymous: "Mattathias answered and said
    in a loud voice: 'Even if all the nations that
    live under the rule of the king obey him, and have
    chosen to do his commandments, departing each one
    from the λατρεία of his fathers, yet I and my sons
    and my brothers will live by the διαθήκη of our
    fathers. Far be it from us to desert the νόμον
    καὶ δικαιώματα. We will not obey the king's words
    by turning aside from the λατρείαν to the right
    hand or to the left.'" Lagrange (Romains, 226)
    sees an essential connection in the sequence of
    νομοθεσία, λατρεία: "Paul envisages the law
    itself as able to be counted among the privileges
    of Israel inasmuch as it regulates the λατρεία,
    the only cult which in antiquity was rendered to
    the true God."

41. The rabbinic word for promise is הַבְטָחָה, a nomen
    actionis from הִבְטִיחַ. "The choice of this expres-
    sion as a designation of God's promise shows that
    its characteristic attribute was regarded as
    unconditional certainty or dependability" (Strack-
    Billerbeck, III, 207).

42. Alford (II, 404) tries to limit the promises to
    those to the patriarchs since "the next two
    clauses place the patriarchs and Christ together
    without any mention of the prophets. So Abraham
    is described, Heb 7:6, as τὸν ἔχοντα τὰς
    ἐπαγγελίας." But once you have mentioned the
    privilege of having "the promises" it is redundant
    to mention the prophets! Thus most commentators
    speak generally of promises and especially "those
    which found their focus on the Messiah" (Murray,
    Romans, II, 6; Sanday and Headlam, Romans, 231;

Hodge, <u>Romans</u>, 299; Lagrange, <u>Romains</u>, 226;
Michel, <u>Roemer</u>, 227; Kaesemann, <u>Romans</u>, 259;
Schlier, <u>Roemerbrief</u>, 287).

43. "The ancient synagogue also knew Abraham as the
     heir of the whole world" (Strack-Billerbeck, III,
     209; texts cited here). Cf Sirach **44:21**, "There-
     fore the Lord assured him [Abraham] by an oath that
     the nations would be blessed through his posterity;
     that he would multiply him like the dust of the
     earth, and exalt his posterity like the stars, and
     cause them to inherit from sea to sea, and from
     the River to the ends of the earth."

44. A similar explanation could also be offered for
     how Paul comes to view the "blessing of Abraham"
     as summed up in "the promise of the Holy Spirit"
     (Gal 3:14).

45. Barrett (<u>Romans</u>, 178) is right (though he did not
     make much of it) when he says, "It is worth noting
     that all the privileges mentioned in verse 4 can
     be understood as promises. For adoption and glory
     see Rom 8:15,23; 2:7. The past covenants point to
     the new covenant (Jer 31:31; 1 Cor 11:25). The
     temple worship suggested the language of 3:26 and
     the law itself, rightly understood, pointed for-
     ward to the Gospel, as did the patriarchs."

46. This is the usual interpretation. However Murray
     (<u>Romans</u>, II, 6) argues, "It would not be proper to
     restrict the denotation to these patriarchs (cf
     Mk 11:10; Acts 2:29; 1 Cor 10:1; Heb 1:1; 8:9).
     The next clause would require the inclusion of
     David. In 1:3 Paul had spoken of Jesus as 'born
     of the seed of David according to the flesh.' It
     would not appear reasonable to exclude the father
     expressly mentioned in 1:3. Thus we should have
     to extend the time beyond Jacob and conclude that
     the fathers of distinction in redemptive history
     from Abraham onwards are in view." It seems
     inconsistent to me, on the one hand, to say that
     9:5b "requires" the inclusion of David since the
     Christ was born of David, and yet, on the other
     hand, to argue (correctly, see above note 11) as
     he does further on that the antecedent of ὧν in
     9:5b is not "the fathers" in 9:5a but "Israelites"
     in 9:4a.

47. Especially helpful on the "Merits of the Fathers"
    is Solomon Schechter, Rabbinic Theology, 170-89,
    who quotes many original sources: "Generally it
    may be stated that the Zachuth of the fathers
    still retained its hold on Jewish consciousness,
    at least in its aspect of the covenant, if not at
    all times. In fact the two aspects are closely
    combined. Thus we are told that God removes the
    sin of Israel on account of the Zachuth of the
    conditions (of the covenant) which he made with
    Abraham, their father (between the pieces)" (180;
    cf Cant R I. 14). See also the excursus in Sanday
    and Headlam, Romans, 330-32.

48. This is probably reflected in the word of John the
    Baptist addressed to the multitudes in Lk 3:8, "Do
    not begin to say to yourselves, 'We have Abraham
    as our father,'" as though that would shield them
    from wrath.

49. It is remarkable how many commentators pass over
    this privilege with a brief comment such as this.
    Cf e.g. Hodge, Romans, 229; Gifford, Romans, 168;
    Michel, Roemer, 227f.

50. Kaesemann (Romans, 258) fails, I think, to reckon
    with the "mysterious" complexity of Paul's view of
    Israel's salvation when he finds a contradiction
    between Rom 9:5a and chapter 4. "The relationship
    of the Christian world to Abraham is now extended
    to all Israel in opposition to the context of
    chapter 4." My response to this supposed contra-
    diction is essentially the same as my response to
    Dinkler's supposed contradiction between 9:6-13
    and 11:1-32. See Excursus, pp 9-15.

51. Rom 11:1 is most to the point: ἐγὼ Ἰσραηλίτης
    εἰμί, ἐκ σπέρματος Ἀβραάμ. Note, he does not say
    "from Abraham" but "from the seed of Abraham"
    which is virtually the same as saying "from
    Abraham's descendants," i.e., "from Israelites."
    The two phrases, "I am an Israelite" and "I am
    from the seed of Abraham," are synonymous. Cf in
    the same sense Rom 16:10, τοὺς ἐκ τῶν Ἀριστοβούλου,
    and 16:11, τοὺς ἐκ τῶν Ναρκίσσου, and probably 9:6b,
    οἱ ἐξ Ἰσραήλ (not the father, but the people).

52. Meyer (Romans, II, 116) points in the same direc-
    tion: "Now after the first relative sentence with

its six theocratic [sic] distinctions, two other
relative clauses introduce the mutually correla-
tive persons, on whom the sacred-historical
calling of Israel was based and was to reach its
accomplishment."

53. Except for John 8:15 the phrase κατὰ σάρκα occurs
only in Paul: Rom 1:3; 4:1; 8:12; 9:3,5; 1 Cor
1:26; 10:18; 2 Cor 1:17; 5:16; 10:2,3; 11:18; Gal
4:23,29; Eph 6:5; Col 3:22.

54. They refer to "Rom 9:5 where the addition of the
article strongly accents the limitation (insofar as
the flesh comes into view)." Moule (Idiom-Book,
III, p 14) cites Rom 12:18 (τὸ ἐξ ὑμῶν) as an
essential parallel.

55. The problem of punctuating in Rom 9:5bc and the
arguments pro and con whether θεός refers to Christ
have been discussed again and again. I have
nothing new to add except to say that my analysis
of κατὰ σάρκα as well as my demonstration of the
saving, eschatological orientation of all of Rom
9:4,5 renders it very plausible that Paul is concluding in a climactic way with the exaltation of
the Messiah to a point where the condemnation of
Israel (9:3) appears as paradoxical as possible.
Beyond this I will simply cite the literature where
the best arguments on both sides appear. Suffice
it to say I find the arguments in favor of
referring θεός to Christ most powerful. Otto Kuss
(Roemerbrief, III, 677-96), Ernst Kaesemann (Romans,
259f), Hans Lietzmann (Roemer, 90), Eduard Schweizer
(TDNT, VII, 128 note 238) and C.K. Barrett (Romans,
179) argue that Rom 9:5c is a doxology to God, not
a reference to Christ. On the other side see
Meyer, Romans, II, 116-22; Alford, II, 405f;
Sanday and Headlam, Romans, 233-38; Stoeckhardt,
Roemer, 419-23; Schlatter, Gerechtigkeit,
296; Munck, Christ and Israel, 33; Murray, Romans,
II, 6f, 245-8; Lagrange, Romains, 227f; Michel,
Roemer, 228f; Cullmann, Christology, 312f; Schlier,
Roemerbrief, 288. See Luz, Geschichtsverstaendnis,
27 note 44, for bibliographies on this text.

56. Moule (Idiom-Book, 72) cites 2 Thess 1:9 and Rev
12:14 as parallels to the use of ἀπό in Rom 9:3.
Rev 12:14 also clearly means separation.

Notes from pp 29,30

57. The promise of Rom 8:35-39 also helps account for
the imperfect tense of Paul's wish (ηὐχόμην) in
9:3a. The wish <u>cannot</u> be carried through because
it is theologically impossible. "The sense of the
imperfect in such expressions is the proper and
strict one (and no new discovery, but common enough
in every schoolboy's reading): the act is unfinished, an obstacle intervening" (Alford, II, 403).
Cf Moule, <u>Idiom-Book</u>, 9, and Moulton, III, 65. For
a larger treatment of the whole verse in its context see Michel, "Opferbereitschaft," who, however,
misses the point as I see it. The rabbinic formula,
"May I be an atonement for so and so," does not, I
think, have much effect on Paul's meaning. Cf
Strack-Billerbeck, III, 261; Lietzmann, <u>Roemer</u>, 89;
Munck, <u>Christ and Israel</u>, 2a.

58. According to the surface logic of the text the
expression of grief in 9:2 would be the main point
of 9:1-5 because 9:3 grounds (γάρ) 9:2 and 9:4,5
grounds (see note 10) 9:3. But surface logic is
not always decisive.

59. Liechtenhan, <u>Vorherbestimmung</u>, 43: "The grief of
the apostle stems not merely from Israel's loss of
her unique place in redemptive history, but also
from her loss of salvation itself. When Paul
expresses his willingness to be cast away in order
to bring salvation to his kinsmen, he shows that
in fact they are excluded from salvation."
Kuemmel ("Probleme von Roemer 9-11," 19-22) like so
many others misses this crucial point of Rom
9:1-5.

60. The whole of Rom 9-11 was written to define in
precisely what sense.

NOTES FOR CHAPTER THREE

1. On the concept of "theodicy" see Chapter Five, pp 74ff.

2. The construction οὐχ οἷον δὲ ὅτι is unique in Paul. Its closest analogy is the use of οὐχ ὅτι . . . ἀλλά (e.g. "Not that we lord it over your faith, but we work with you for your joy," 2 Cor 1:24; cf 3:5; Phil 4:11,17; 2 Thess 3:9). Whenever Paul uses this he is guarding against a possible misunderstanding of something he has just said. Bauer (Lexicon, 565), Blass/Debrunner (section 480) and Turner (Grammar, III, 47) conjecture that the phrase in 9:6a is a combination of this common Pauline construction with οὐχ οἷον which is Hellenistic for οὐ δήπου and means "by no means!" The sense of Rom 9:6a then is this: "Regardless of what my words in 9:1-5 imply to you, by no means do they really imply that God's word has fallen."

3. This is the most common view: Calvin, Romans, 197; Alford, II, 406; Hodge, Romans, 305; Munck, Christ and Israel, 34; Murray, Romans, II, 9; Barrett, Romans, 180; Kaesemann, Romans, 262; Mueller, Gottes Gerechtigkeit, 29.

4. E. Guettgemanns, Heilsgeschichte, 41. David Kotansky ("A Note on Romans 9:6") argues that ὁ λόγος τοῦ θεοῦ is a "terminus technicus to describe [Paul's] own ministry and the proclamation of the gospel of faith" (24). So it is Paul's message that has not fallen. In favor of this view is the fact that the term "word of God" elsewhere in Paul always means the apostolic message about Christ (with the possible exception of 1 Tim 4:5). Kotansky's fault is his allowing Paul's general usage to outweigh the two close and essential analogies, namely, τὰ λόγια τοῦ θεοῦ in Rom 3:2 and ἐπαγγελίας ὁ λόγος in 9:9a, neither of which refers to Paul's gospel. Also, as we shall see below, Rom 9:11c is probably the positive counterpart to 9:6a.

5. Michel, Roemer, 231, "In this context the phrase λόγος τοῦ θεοῦ is an expression of the purpose and will of God."

6. Liechtenhan, Vorherbestimmung, 43: "The word of
   God which Paul says has not fallen sums up all the
   prerogatives of Israel in verse 4, namely salvation."

7. So Meyer, Romans, II, 132; Alford, II, 407; Murray,
   II, 14f.

8. The other close analogy in the NT is Lk 16:17 (not
   one letter of the law will fall, πεσεῖν). None of
   the other uses of ἐκπίπτω (except in Rom 9:6) has
   God's word or anything like it as the subject.
   However in the LXX διαπίπτω offers some close
   analogies: Judith 6:9; Josh 21:45; 1 Sam 3:19;
   2 Kgs 10:10.

9. I say "not so easily" because the problem would
   still remain as to how Israel as a corporate whole
   would experience the fulfillment of the promises
   (as I argued in the previous chapter it must).
   This is why chapter 11 is as essential in the
   support of 9:6a as is chapter 9. For in chapter
   11 we get the whole picture of how the present
   hardening of Israel will lead eventually to her
   salvation (11:26).

10. I see no reason (against Schlier, Roemerbrief, 292,
    and others) to construe verse 11 as a parenthesis.
    The absence of a verb in Rom 9:10bc does not mean
    this broken-off sentence is picked up again in
    9:12c, especially since the nominative Rebecca
    (9:10b) cannot be the subject of ἐρρέθη in 9:12c.
    We must simply supply a verb in 9:10bc as we do in
    9:10a. So Murray, Romans, II, 14.

11. Roemer, 430. He follows Luther and Hofmann: Rom
    9:12ab is not "an addition to the purpose clause,
    which would be a very awkward construction and
    thought connection."

12. Romans, II, 132. Ἐρρέθη αὐτῇ in 9:12c "already has
    its defining clause in μήπω κ.τ.λ., and that a
    clause after which οὐκ ἐξ ἔργων κ.τ.λ. annexed to
    the ἐρρέθη αὐτῇ as a definition of mode, would be
    something self-evident and superfluous." See also
    Lagrange, Romains, 230.

13. K.H. Schelkle has gathered the material very con-
    veniently with all the sources documented in Paulus

Lehrer der Vaeter: Die altkirchliche Auslegung
von Roemer 1-11. On p 337 he cites the sources
for Origen's eccentric view that to avoid ascribing
injustice to God one had to assert that election is
based on the works of the preexistent soul of man.
The more common view, held, e.g., by the Greek
fathers, Acacius of Caesarea (d. 366), Diodore
(d. 390), Theodore of Mopsuestia (d. 429) and John
Chrysostom (d. 407), was that "God determined in
advance, in that he knew men's decisions in
advance. For his choice is not unjust but agrees
with the decision of man" (Theodore). The same
view was held by the Latin fathers, Hilarion (d.
371), the early Augustine and Pelagius, who said
of our text, "Before they were born, they were
different to God through the merit of future faith,
so that the decision of God to choose the good and
reject the bad already consisted in his foreknowledge" (Schelklc, 338). Schelkie is right to
observe (337) that in this view Paul's meaning is
virtually turned inside out: "here ἵνα ἡ κατ'
ἐκλογὴν πρόθεσις τοῦ θεοῦ μένῃ stands for ἡ κατὰ
πρόθεσιν ἐκείνων ἐκλογή (= God's choice according
to the prior purpose of those men)." With regard
to the appeal to "foreknowledge" as the ground of
predestination in Rom 8:29, this "knowing" is not
mere prior recognition but knowing in the sense of
setting one's favor on (cf Amos 3:2; Ps 1:6). See
especially Murray, Romans, I, 315-18. Odeberg
(TDNT, II, 954) points out that already before the
NT the Jewish solution to Jacob's precedence over
his elder brother was solved "along the lines that
his privilege was invalidated by his evil works.
In this respect future works, both his own and his
descendants', were foreseen and taken into account.
At the very most, therefore, we have here only a
praedestinatio de praeviso. The Jewish standpoint
is typically expressed in Jubilees 35:13 ['And
Isaac said to her: I too know and see the deeds
of Jacob who is with us, how that with all his
heart he honors us; but I loved Esau formerly more
than Jacob, because he was the firstborn; but now
I love Jacob more than Esau, for he has done manifold evil deeds and there is no righteousness in
him, for all his ways are unrighteousness and
violence . . .']."

14. O. Kuss, Roemerbrief, III, 709. The phrase "not from
works but of the one who calls" "does not allow the

Notes from p 36

smallest crack through which one could slide in
any sort of human participation. Therefore, when
one maintains that faith is an obvious but tacit
presupposition of our text or condition of God's
purpose (ἡ πρόθεσις τοῦ θεοῦ), one thus completely
overlooks the fact that 'not on the basis of works
but on the basis of the one who calls' means something essentially different than 'not on the basis
of works but on the basis of faith.'"

15. The term ἐκλογή does not occur in the LXX. In the
NT it occurs in Acts 9:15 (Paul is a "vessel of
election" = chosen vessel); Rom 11:5 ("a remnant
according to the election of grace"); 11:28
("according to election they are beloved on account
of the fathers"); 1 Thess 1:4 ("knowing, beloved
by God, your election"); 2 Pt 1:10 ("be eager to
make firm your call and election"). Of the fifteen
uses of ἐκλογή in Polybius, seven are in the phrase
κατ' ἐκλογήν (TDNT, IV, 176). Schrenk notes that
"when κατ' ἐκλογήν is used the principle of selection is usually added" as for example in Rom 11:5,
κατ' ἐκλογήν χάριτος ("chosen according to the
principle of grace"). In Rom 9:11c-12b the
"principle of selection" is designated by οὐκ ἐξ
ἔργων ἀλλ' ἐκ τοῦ καλοῦντος, which is virtually
synonymous with χάριτος in 11:5 (cf 11:6, εἰ δὲ
χάριτι οὐκέτι ἐξ ἔργων). God's choices are not
grounded in or constrained by anything outside his
own creative purposes. See following note.

16. G. Maier (Mensch und freier Wille, 359-62) has confirmed this common conclusion with his attempt
"to shed light on the problem from the Jewish
doctrines of predestination and freedom which are
known to us." He argues "that with the term
πρόθεσις τοῦ θεοῦ Paul really wanted to render
מחשבת אל [God's predestining plan]" (360, see especially the use of this term in 1 QS 3:15,16; 11:11
etc). On the term ἐκλογή Maier stresses the
pharisaic background: "We encountered in the preceding study of Ps Sol [9:4] the emphatic pharisaic
point of doctrine: 'Our works are in the free
choice (ἐκλογή) and authority (ἐξουσίᾳ) of our
soul, to do righteousness and unrighteousness is
in the works of our hands' [see note 59]. We
recognized there in ἐκλογή a pharisaic terminus
technicus which aims to express free will. [So used
by Josephus also, Jewish Wars II, 165] . . .

226

Everything suggests that the rabbinically schooled
Paul in such an important part of his epistle,
where he disputes the Jewish viewpoint before
Jewish readers, has used the traditional Greek
equivalent for the pharisaic terminus technicus for
free will. The application of the term to God is
no hindrance to this assumption. The only appropriate translation of ἐκλογή therefore in Rom 9:11
is 'free will', 'freedom'. Accordingly Paul has
put together skillfully the two Jewish termini
technici for free will [ἐκλογή] and predestination
[πρόθεσις] in order to express that God determined
his purpose in complete freedom uninfluenced by
any works at all" (361f).

17. G. Maier (Mensch und freier Wille, 358) criticizes
    Munck on this point too: "Paul does not reflect
    on the precise point in time when the πρόθεσις was
    formed, nor does a predestinatio gemina presup-
    pose an abstract concept of God" (as Munck asserts).

18. E. Weber, Problem der Heilsgeschichte, 29. "The
    explosive point clearly lies in the question:
    temporal or eternal?"

19. For example Munck (Christ and Israel, 70): "Paul
    is throughout this passage speaking of peoples and
    parts of peoples . . . God's actions do not exclude
    the actions of men, as in so much modern talk of
    determinism and indeterminism. We do not have the
    material for an exposition of Paul's views upon
    this modern problem." But see Maier's historical
    study of the problem in the Jewish milieu of Paul's
    day, Mensch und freier Wille. He remarks, "Could
    it not be that 'this modern problem'--determinism
    and indeterminism--is not so modern after all?"
    (352).

20. See his article "Erwaehlung und Freiheit im
    Roemerbrief nach der Auslegung der Vaeter" and his
    book Paulus Lehrer der Vaeter.

21. On the Freedom of the Will, 69. "Now let us look
    at the other passage about Esau and Jacob, of
    which an oracle had spoken before they were born,
    'The greater shall serve the lesser' as Gen., ch.
    25, has it. But this does not properly apply to
    the salvation of man." Then on Mal 1:2 = Rom 9:13
    he says, "It seems that the prophet is speaking

227

there not of the hate whereby we are damned eternally, but of temporal misfortune, as when one speaks of the wrath and fury of God."

22. On the Bondage of the Will, 251-3. Luther denies Erasmus' interpretation of both Gen 25:23 and Mal 1:2.

23. In his commentary on Romans (199) he states Paul's "first proposition" in Rom 9:6-13: "As the blessing of the covenant separates the people of Israel from all other nations, so also the election of God makes a distinction between men in that nation, while he predestines some to salvation and others to eternal condemnation."

24. E. Gordon Rupp, who coedited the Luther/Erasmus debate for the Library of Christian Classics, writes, "When somebody gives us a definitive edition of the debate about Free Choice and Grace between John Eck and Andrew Karlstadt, it may very likely turn out to be a better piece of historical theology and show that these two stuck rather more closely to their subject" (Luther and Erasmus, 1).

25. See Franz Leenhardt, Romans, 249f: "The names mentioned certainly do not connote individuals so much as peoples who are thus named after their eponymous ancestors according to the OT practice. It is best to understand the names in this way since the argument which they are quoted to support concerns the destiny of Israel as a whole, and not the destiny of individuals who compose Israel." H. Lietzmann, Roemer, 91: "One should keep in view that the theme of Paul is not really the predestination of individuals but of whole peoples, which in fact accords with his way of thinking. Cf Rom 15:19." H.L. Ellison, Mystery of Israel, 43: "So in his discussion on predestination he is not looking at the eternal destiny of the individual but at the manner in which God's purposes are worked out in this world by the individual or people of His choosing" (cf 46, 48). See also Forster and Marston, God's Strategy, 61; F. Godet, Romans, 351; James Strauss, "God's Promise and Universal History," 195; T. Zahn, Roemer, 446.

26. T. Hoppe, Idee der Heilsgeschichte, 128: "The attempt to construe the hardening and rejection

only in a temporal sense has no basis in the text."
E. Dinkler, "Praedestination," 88: "In Rom 9:14-23
Paul defends the divine election and makes clear
that its real meaning is to be seen not in the
election of an empirical people as a whole but in
the election of individuals." "A praedestinatio
gemina is demonstrated by the examples of the sons
of Abraham, the twins of Rebekah, and Pharaoh
(9:7-13,17)" (92). U. Luz, Geschichtsverstaendnis,
76 note 199: "The remarkably frequent allegations
in the commentaries that eternal blessedness or
damnation is not in view (e.g. Pharaoh) are
foreign to the text. Does this concern for
Pharaoh spring from the true subject matter of the
text or from a humanism that is inadmissible when
measured by the righteousness of God?" E.
Kaesemann, Romans, 264f: "Paul is no longer concerned with two peoples and their destiny but time-
lessly (against Gaugler) with the election and
rejection of two persons who are elevated as
types . . . Thus one may not already here explain
reprobation as historically limited in the light
of chapter 11. It is a softening as well when a
person following the cited text in its original
meaning sees it speaking of nations not of individuals . . . Clearly the aim of expositors who proceed along such lines is to save human responsibility, and the same is true when they relate
verses 12b-13 simply to leadership in relation to
human enterprises . . . The presence of a strong
concept of predestination cannot be denied,
although only here does Paul present double predestination." See also Hodge, Romans, 310; E.
Weber, Problem der Heilsgeschichte, 29ff; H.A.W.
Meyer, Romans, II, 132; M. Dibelius, Paulus, 31;
O. Michel, Roemer, 235 note 2; G. Maier, Mensch
und freier Wille, 357f.

27. Most commentators agree that the OT quotations in
Rom 9:6-13 assume an acquaintance with the whole
story of which they are a part and that without
this knowledge the isolated quotations would be
virtually unintelligible as part of the argument.
Cf Luz, Geschichtsverstaendnis, 64.

28. Probably Paul chose to cite Gen 18:10,14 in Rom
9:9 (instead of say, Gen 17:21) because here God's
promise is expressed with an emphasis on God's own
powerful activity. This indicates that for Paul

the "promise" or "word" of God is not merely a
wise prediction based on foreknowledge but is an
expression of his intention to act so as to
achieve what is promised. This relates the "promise" of Rom 9:9 closely to the "calling" of 9:12b.
As Rom 4:17 shows, God's call is not a mere invi-
tation but a creative act that accomplishes what
it purposes and promises. This is why Paul has
such confidence that "the word of God has not
fallen."

29. Stoeckhardt, Roemer, 430: "We also assume that
many of the descendants of Ishmael and Esau . . .
were saved."

30. There is ample evidence that this view was com-
monly held among first-century Jews, though it was
not the only view. Cf Mt 3:9 ("We have Abraham as
our father!"). For texts consult Sanday and
Headlam, Romans, 55, 249, 330ff; Davies, Paul and
Rabbinic Judaism, 84; Moore, Judaism, II, 95, 285,
351, 387f; Strack-Billerbeck, I, 117-21; III, 263f;
Huonder, Israel Sohn Gottes, 85f, 161, 174.
Justin Martyr in his Dialog with Trypho (L. Schopp,
Writings of Saint Justin Martyr, 363) said of
Jewish teachers in his day, "Besides this, those
teachers deceive both themselves and you when they
suppose that those who are descendants of Abraham
according to the flesh will most certainly share
in the eternal Kingdom, even though they be faithless sinners and disobedient to God, suppositions
which the Scriptures show have no foundation in
fact."

31. The promise cited by Paul from Gen 21:12 ("In
Isaac shall your seed be called") was given even
after Isaac was born.

32. The Hebrew of the phrase Paul cites in Rom 9:12c
is וְרַב יַעֲבֹד צָעִיר . רַב is rare as a reference to
"older" but צָעִיר is common in the sense of younger
especially as opposed to "first born" (הַבְּכוֹר); cf
Gen 43:33; 48:14; Josh 6:26; 1 Kgs 16:34; Job 32:6.
A synonym of רַב (הַגָּדֹל) is used in Gen 10:21; 29:16
for "older."

33. Paul Althaus, Roemer, 102: "The example of Jacob
and Esau comes into view only as a proof of the
principle expressed in verses 11b and 12a. The

emphasis falls on this principle. Therefore one
may not expand upon this example so as to argue
that Paul here teaches a pre-temporal double predestination of men to salvation or damnation."

34. This positive view of Esau is not impossible but
would contradict the accepted Jewish view represented also in Heb 12:16 that Esau was a godless
and unrepentant person. Cf 1 Enoch 89:11,12;
Jubilees 37:22f; 4 Ezra 3:16. For the rabbinic
references see Odeberg, TDNT, I, 605; Strack-
Billerbeck, III, 267f, where Esau is even excluded
from the age to come.

35. Artur Weiser, Das Buch der zwoelf kleinen Propheten, II, 191: "From a human standpoint Jacob
and Esau were equals (verse 2); the basis for
their different destinies lay solely in God who
gave Jacob the preference simply because in his
sovereign freedom he willed it to be so."

36. Appeal is made, for example, to Lk 14:26 par; Gen
29:31,33; Deut 21:15-17; 22:13,16; 24:3; Judges
14:16; Is 60:15. Forster and Marston (God's
Strategy, 60f) argue that "when the Bible uses the
word hate as a contrast to love, it intends us to
understand it to mean 'love less than.'"

37. Sanday and Headlam, Romans, 247: "There is no
need to soften these words as some have attempted,
translating 'loved more' and 'loved less.'"

38. How else could Paul have argued from the OT for
the principle of God's freedom in election, since
the eternal salvation of the individual as Paul
teaches it is almost never the subject of discussion in the OT? Therefore Paul's selection of
texts may reflect the limited scope of his sources
rather than a desire on his part to guard against
the implication of predestination unto individual
salvation.

39. Problem der Heilsgeschichte, 29f: "The thesis to
be opposed is that Paul is speaking here merely
of historical role rather than eternal destiny.
Does the ἀπώλεια of verse 22 really refer only to
the judgment of historical destruction as Beyschlag
and Goebel so confidently maintain? May one really
say that in the whole discussion personal

blessedness is not at stake? . . . As if the
stumbling block to be overcome were this
historical guidance of Israel! But one asks with
amazement: Would the unbelief of Israel in this
case really require such earnest wrestling for a
solution? Would the pain of the apostle be natural
if it were not the unavoidable destiny of eternal
lostness which stood before his soul? . . . In the
way that Paul proceeds, it is clear that the
problem of the eternal lostness of Israel stands
over the whole ninth chapter. The subject matter
is the (apparent) exclusion of Israel from salvation. From this all inferences about the divine
mercy and hardening receive their tone . . . The
conclusion that the inferences of the chapter
relate only to historical position is completely
foreign to the context." Liechtenhan
(Vorherbestimmung, 43) argues similarly.

40. Against numerous commentators, like Mueller,
Gottes Gerechtigkeit, 29, who usually give no
justification for their construction.

41. H. Schlier, Roemerbrief, 291: "The principle that
finally and basically God and God's word make
'Israel' out of Israel has been realized only once,
but it is a general and always valid principle."
O. Kuss, Roemerbrief, III, 702: "Evidently then there
is a 'principle', active in both cases. It is Yahweh's
'way' so to act." In a similar way Liechtenhan
(Vorherbestimmung, 43) speaks of a "law" and a
"rule."

42. Michel, Roemer, 199: "When Paul in Rom 8:14-16
speaks both of 'sons' and 'children' he is following the Semitic way of speaking which signifies
no theological difference between the two." Contrast Sanday and Headlam, Romans, 202.

43. This restricted use by Paul is not surprising.
While Israel as a whole was known as God's son in
the OT (see Section 2.12 in the preceding chapter)
Jesus (following the initiative of the OT prophets)
limited the concept of sonship to those who had
the faith and character of a son (cf Mt 5:9; 5:45;
Lk 20:36).

44. H.A.W. Meyer, Romans, II, 126: "It is evident from
the relation of v. 8 to v. 9 that [Paul] limited

the saying to the person of Isaac himself . . ."
U. Luz, Geschichtsverstaendnis, 69: "Verse 9b
shows that with the phrase ἐν Ἰσαάκ (verse 7),
Paul is thinking primarily of the individual."

45. Sanday and Headlam, Romans, 241: "σπέρμα is used
collectively [in 9:7b] to express the whole number
of descendants, not merely the single son Isaac."

46. Lagrange, Romains, 229: "The principle of which
the election of Isaac is an application remains
always the same; the right of the flesh does not
count. God remains free to call whom he wills."
Cf Murray, Romans, II, 10.

47. With the surprising exception of Barrett (Romans,
180f) almost all commentators recognize that
σπέρμα is used in two different senses in Rom 9:7a
and 9:8b. Cf Gifford, Romans, 169; Meyer, Romans,
II, 125; Althaus, Roemer, 101; Kuss, Roemerbrief,
III, 701, etc.

48. Lietzmann (Roemer, 91) probably overstates his case,
but surely points in the right direction when he
says, "Verse 8 is really understandable only for
the one who has Gal 4:21-31 in mind." Others who
argue for viewing Rom 9:8 in the same light as Gal
4:21-29 include Stoeckhardt, Roemer, 424f; Meyer,
Romans, II, 127; Althaus, Roemer, 101; Gifford,
Romans, 169.

49. Meyer, Romans, II, 127. He points out also that
this interpretation allows the genitive ἐπαγγελίας
in Rom 9:8b to correspond with the genitive σαρκός
in 9:8a. He also cites (without reference)
Chrysostom: ἡ τῆς ἐπαγγελίας ἰσχὺς ἔτεκε τὸ
παιδίον. See also Hodge, Romans, 306f; Lietzmann,
Roemer, 91; Murray, Romans, II, 11, "those in whom
the promise takes effect."

50. Geschichtsverstaendnis, 68f: "'Epanggelia' is
always understood by Paul to be 'deed-word' of
God, believed by men but not at their disposal . . ."

51. Numerous interpreters suggest rightly, I think,
that Isaac functions for Paul here as a type. I
have avoided the word, however, because it may
imply too much precision. On Isaac as a type see

Meyer, Romans, II, 126; Stoeckhardt, Roemer, 425; Althaus, Roemer, 101; Michel, Roemer, 233.

52. The combination of λογίζομαι and εἰς occurs in the NT in Acts 19:27; Rom 2:26; 4:3,5,9,22; 9:8; 2 Cor 12:6; Jam 2:23. Of the seven instances in Paul, four are based on Gen 15:6 (Abraham's faith was reckoned to him for righteousness). Rom 2:26 is the closest parallel to Rom 9:8.

53. Kaesemann, Romans, 263: Paul "returns in v. 8b to the λογίζειν, which in non-Greek fashion stresses God's freedom (Barrett) and means acceptance in his judgment." Also Mueller, Gottes Gerechtigkeit, 28f.

54. The Greek words in parentheses are Cranfield's (Romans, I, 175) suggestions for filling in the ellipses of Rom 2:28. Another telling grammatical parallel to Rom 9:6b and 8a is Gal 3:7, οἱ ἐκ πίστεως, οὗτοι υἱοί εἰσιν Ἀβραάμ.

55. So also Mueller, Gottes Gerechtigkeit, 32 note 33: "Paul speaks of rejection unto eternal damnation (εἰς ἀπώλειαν) . . . The attempt to exploit the passive form (κατηρτισμένα) for indeterministic purposes ('they have prepared themselves,' or the like) is not admissible."

56. Maier cites, for example, Is 45:5-7. The Lord addresses Cyrus: 5) "I am Yahweh and there is no other; besides me there is no God. I clothe you though you do not know me 6) that they may know me, from the rising of the sun and from the setting, that there is none besides me. I am Yahweh and there is no other 7) forming light and creating darkness, making peace and creating evil (עֹשֶׂה שָׁלוֹם וּבוֹרֵא רָע). I Yahweh do all these things." Of course one would have to mention, above all, the texts Paul himself refers to, namely Gen 21:12; 18:10,14; Mal 1:2; Ex 33:19; 9:16; Is 29:16; 45:9; Jer 18:6.

57. The text of Sirach 33:7-15 (RSV).

> 7) Why is any day better than another,
> when all the daylight in the year is from the sun?
> 8) By the Lord's decision they were distinguished,

and he appointed the different seasons and
feasts;
9) some of them he exalted and hallowed,
and some of them he made ordinary days.
10) All men are from the ground,
and Adam was created from the dust.
11) In the fullness of his knowledge the Lord
distinguished them
and appointed their different ways;
12) some of them he blessed and exalted,
and some of them he made holy and brought near
to himself;
but some of them he cursed and brought low,
and he turned them out of their place.
13) As clay in the hand of the potter--
for all his ways are as he pleases--
so men are in the hand of him who made them,
to give them as he decides.
14) Good is the opposite of evil,
and life the opposite of death;
so the sinner is the opposite of the godly.
15) Look upon all the works of the Most High;
they likewise are in pairs, one the opposite of
the other.

58. The text of 1 QS 3:15-17 (from Dupont-Sommer,
Essene Writings): "From the God of knowledge comes
all that is and shall be, and before (beings) were,
He established all their design. And when they
are, they fulfill their task according to their
statutes, in accordance with His glorious design,
changing nothing within it. In His hand are the
laws of all (beings) and He upholds them in all
their needs." 1 QS 3:25-4:1: "Truly, the Spirits
of light and darkness were made by Him; upon these
(Spirits) He has founded every work, upon their
[counsels] every service, and upon their ways [every
Visit]ation. The one, God loves everlastingly,
and delights in all his deeds forever, but the
counsel of the other He loathes, and He hates all
his ways forever."

59. Text of Ps Sol 9:4f: "Our works are in the free
choice and authority of our soul (τὰ ἔργα ἡμῶν ἐν
ἐκλογῇ καὶ ἐξουσίᾳ τῆς ψυχῆς ἡμῶν); to do righteousness and unrighteousness is in the works of
our hands. And in your righteousness (δικαιοσύνῃ)
you visit the sons of men: the one who does righteousness treasures up life for himself with the

Note from p 53

Lord, and the one who does unrighteousness, he is guilty of his soul in destruction (ἀπώλεια). For the judgments of the Lord are in righteousness (δικαιοσύνη) according to a man and his house."

NOTES FOR CHAPTER FOUR

Notes from pp 55-60

1. The same interpretation is found in Stoeckhardt,
   Roemer, 433; Zahn, Roemer, 448; Gifford, Romans,
   171; Godet, Romans, 352.

2. U. Luz, Geschichtsverstaendnis, 75; Mueller,
   Gottes Gerechtigkeit, 31; G. Maier, Mensch und
   freier Wille, 367.

3. Therefore, while I have consulted, I have not been
   helped in my immediate purpose by Walter Beyerlin,
   Herkunft und Geschichte der aeltesten Sinaitradi-
   tion, and Erich Zenger, Die Sinaitheophanie.
   Untersuchung zum jawistischen und elohistischen
   Geschichtswerk as well as the sections on "Liter-
   ary and Traditio-Historical Analysis" in Brevard
   Childs, Exodus, 555f, 584-6, 604-10.

4. H.J. Schoeps, Paul, 32. Earle Ellis (Paul's Use,
   150-2) notes only thirteen cases where Paul seems
   to agree with the LXX against the Hebrew. Our
   analysis of Rom 9:17 will show that Paul made use
   of both the Hebrew and the Greek.

5. The function of 33:7-11 in its present context is
   apparently to illustrate the point that God cannot
   abide in the midst of Israel (33:3,5). Hence the
   tent of meeting where he talks with Moses face to
   face is outside the camp. So George Bush, Notes, II,
   227, and Brevard Childs, Exodus, 592. Childs sees
   other functions of the pericope but I think he is not
   right when he views the worshipful behavior of the
   people in 33:10 as a "warrant" for Moses' continued
   intercession for them (592). Moses never bases his
   appeal to God on any good quality in the people.
   On the contrary his final appeal is grounded (γάρ/
   כִּי, 34:9c) in the unchanged fact that Israel is
   stiff-necked but God loves to pardon.

6. Earlier in 33:14 God has already promised, "My
   presence will go and I will give you rest." Why
   did Moses "seem to pass roughshod over the concession" (Childs, Exodus, 594) in his further
   request in 33:15,16? Both Childs (595) and J.P.
   Lange, Exodus, 140, draw attention to the fact that
   the promise of 33:14 still attaches to the person
   of Moses (as in 32:10) since the "you" is singular

(14b). So Moses presses on to procure the blessing for the whole people (cf "I and your people"
in 33:16 twice). In view of this progression of
thought God's promise in 33:17 is a full agreement
to do all that Moses asked. Now the only thing
left is for Moses to look into the depths of God's
goodness for the assurance he needed to believe
such an amazing concession.

7. "To bestow a perpetuity of blessing on a people
wavering now and again into disobedience, was a
problem that seemed to task the highest intelligence, to transcend the ordinary ways of providence and call into exercise some inner and higher
reaches of the eternal mind. Moved by a wish to
do his duty with intelligence [and, I would add,
assurance], Moses ardently desires some insight
into this profound mystery and he feels that it
touches the very center of the divine nature and
involves the sublimest manifestations of his
glory. Hence his . . . grandest petition. 'Show
me now thy glory'" (John Hall, Exodus, 217).

8. The Hebrew conjunction כִּי can be used concessively
(BDB, 473) but this is not nearly so common as the
ground usage. Moreover the LXX renders it with
γάρ. Keil and Delitzsch, Pentateuch, II, 241,
also construe the כִּי as a ground. But they are
wide of the mark I think when they argue on the
analogy of Gen 8:21 that God's wrath was mitigated
because being stiff-necked was Israel's "natural
condition." This interpretation of the ground
clause misses the point that in this context grace
and mercy are being exalted rather than the evil
deserts of man being diminished.

9. Moses does not try to ground God's favor toward
him (34:9a; 33:12d,13a,17b) in any merit on his
part. On the contrary in 34:9d he reckons himself
among those who need forgiveness ("our iniquities
and our sins").

10. The Hebrew grammatical construction here in 34:9de
is ambiguous. The verbs "you shall forgive"
(וְסָלַחְתָּ) and "you shall take us for an inheritance"
(וּנְחַלְתָּנוּ) are perfects with waw connectives. They
may thus continue the imperative sense of 34b or
they may simply state Moses' conviction of what
will be. Even if they are to be construed as

imperatives (as e.g. in Ex 20:9) nevertheless the
preceding context makes plain that the forgiveness
requested is a forgiveness of which Moses is
confident.

11. This does not contradict 33:13bc which says,
"Cause me to know, please, your way and I will
know you." If there is a necessary connection
between God's person and his acts so that the
former grounds the latter, then one can, con-
versely, know the person of God by attending to
his "way." This is in fact the characteristic
mode of revelation in the OT. Cf G. Ernest
Wright, God Who Acts, 11: biblical theology "is a
theology of recital or proclamation of the acts of
God, together with the inferences drawn therefrom."

12. E. Kautzsch, Gesenius' Hebrew Grammar, Section
67ee cites Ex 33:19cd as examples of perfects with
waw consecutives. See 49h for the usage of waw
consecutive with perfects.

13. Kautzsch, Sections 107a, 49h.

14. TDNT, IX, 378. Neubauer's view is found in Der
Stamm ch n n im Sprachgebrauch des Alten Testaments, 55, 145.

15. Similarly, see N. Glueck, Das Wort hesed im
alttestamentlichen Sprachgebrauche, 38.

16. Also defending the view which sees 33:19cd as an
explanation of the name of Yahweh: A. Dillmann,
Exodus, 385, and H.J. Stoeve, THAT, I, 595.

17. Concerning 34:6f Childs (Exodus, 612) says, "In the
present context the actual theophany is portrayed
as a fulfillment of Moses' request in the previous
chapter to see God's glory (33:17ff). The repetition of the key words 'pass by' and 'proclaim
the name' establishes the author's intention."

18. For the frequent stereotyped usage of the name
formula see Num 14:18; Neh 9:17; Ps 86:15; 103:8;
111:4; 112:4; 116:5; 145:8; Joel 2:13; Jon 4:2;
Nah 1:3; 2 Chr 30:9.

19. The translation of the phrase וְנַקֵּה לֹא יְנַקֶּה (literally "clearing he shall not clear") is disputed.

Notes from p 65

The usual translation is "but he will by no means clear the guilty" (RSV). The ambiguity lies in the grammatical construction itself. Concerning this Kautzsch (Gesenius, Section 113n) says, "The infinitive absolute [is] used before the verb to strengthen the verbal idea, i.e. to emphasize in this way either the certainty . . . or the . . . completeness of an occurrence." The usual translation of our phrase here construes it to negate the uncertainty of retribution. My translation construes it to negate the completeness of absolution. Kautzsch cites Jud 1:28 ("they did not utterly drive them out") and Amos 9:8 ("I will not utterly destroy") which illustrates negation of the idea of completeness. A. Dillmann (Exodus, 387) translates the phrase in Ex 34:7 "but not left completely unpunished." George Bush (Notes, I, 247) develops a long, and to my mind persuasive, argument for my translation, using the close analogies in Jer 30:11; 49:12; 25:29; Is 30:19. He illustrates his view as follows, "Though prone to pardon, yet it was to be known that Yahweh could and would punish, whenever his wisdom saw that the occasion required, even in those cases where, on the whole, his mercy was predominant. Thus in the case of David, while his great sin was forgiven . . ., yet in 'clearing he was not wholly cleared.' A series of chastisements and afflictions followed him to his dying day, that he might learn how bitter and evil a thing it was to turn away from God as he had rashly done."

20. The usual English translation, "he will by no means clear the guilty," obscures the indefiniteness of the Hebrew construction, which has no counterpart to "guilty" (וְנַקֵּה לֹא יְנַקֶּה). The LXX also does this: καὶ οὐ καθαριεῖ τὸν ἔνοχον. See note 19.

21. On the relation between the name and the self in the OT, see B.W. Anderson's article, "God, Names of," in IDB, II, 407-17. "It could be said soberly of anyone that his name is his very self" (408). Cf Ex 34:14. See also TDNT, V, 257, "The name stands for the person." Cf Ps 7:17; 9:10; 18:49; Is 25:1; 26:8; 56:6; Mal 3:16 etc. THAT, II, 956, "Der Name Yahweh als Wechsel Begriff fuer Yahweh" (Section 4d).

22. If verse 5 is viewed in isolation it is not clear
whether this "he" is Moses or Yahweh. But in view
of the same Hebrew phrase in 33:19b I agree with
Childs (Exodus, 611) that "v 5 now receives its
clearest interpretation from what follows in v 6.
Clearly God is the one who pronounces the divine
name." In agreement with this: TDNT, V, 260;
THAT, II, 950. Dillmann (Exodus, 387) thinks
Moses is the subject in 34:5.

23. Bush (Notes, I, 237f), Driver (Exodus, 362), Dillmann
(Exodus, 385) and others construe טוּבִי as "beauty"
or "goodliness" as for example in Gen 39:6; Ex 2:2
etc. They argue 1) that a moral attribute could
not be said to "pass by" (33:19a), 2) the LXX
renders טוּבִי with δόξη and thus shows it was considered to be a visible display of beauty, 3)
Moses' request was to see God's glory and so since
the request was for the visible, we may expect the
answer to grant the visible. This first objection
is probably overly literal. The hiphil of עבר
(19a) is often used of non-sensible objects (sin--
2 Sam 12:13; time--Jer 46:17; mischief--Es 8:3;
reproach--Ps 119:39). All the sentence needs to
mean is, "I will cause you to perceive in a direct
way how good I am." With regard to the relationship between "glory" and "goodness" see Section 6.3.
Childs (Exodus, 596), Hall (Exodus, 217), and Hyatt
(Exodus, 317) construe טוּבִי as moral rather than
aesthetic.

24. Ex 33:20-23, which begins (20a) and ends (23c) with
God's refusal to show Moses his "face," and which
speaks of God covering Moses with his hand in the
cleft of the rock as his glory passes by (22), is
almost wholly neglected in the fulfilment scene of
34:5-7. The emphasis shifts completely from a
dazzling vision of God's "back" to revelatory
encounter through God's personal word. Childs
(Exodus, 595) suggests that another tradition is
being used in 33:20-23. The function of it in the
present context, judging from the repeated, "You
shall not see my face," is to stress that, while
God is granting a profound revelation of himself
to Moses, yet there remains an intensity of glory
which would consume a man if he saw its fullness.
Thus the passage functions as a warning against
presumption.

25. George Bush's comment here is well-balanced and
    worth citing at length (<u>Notes</u>, I, 238): "The most
    gorgeous and dazzling exhibition of a merely <u>sen-
    sible glory</u> would leave the mind unsatisfied,
    except so far as it could be regarded as a kind of
    outward reflection of mental and moral attributes
    of corresponding character . . . A glorious though
    partial disclosure should indeed be made to his
    sight; but he should withal be enabled by means of
    a supernatural illumination to pierce beyond the
    sensuous imagery and comprehend its interior
    meaning. He should have a mental perception of
    those divine perfections which were so illus-
    triously displayed in connection with the sublime
    spectacle of the Shekinah . . ."

26. <u>Works</u> I, 118 (cf Sections IV and VI). See next
    endnote for his arguments.

27. In a section entitled "Der Name Jahwehs als
    Inbegriff der Herrlichkeit Jahwehs" (950) he says,
    "Since Yahweh's name is bound up with his fame,
    (t^ehillā) (Ps 48:11), šēm Jhwh can be used as a
    synonym for Yahweh's glory (kābōd, Is 59:19; Ps
    102:16; cf Ps 72:19; Neh 9:5)." We may summarize
    the arguments for identifying the name and glory
    of God as follows: 1) They are interchangeable in
    synonymous parallels (Ps 8:1; 102:15; 148:13; Is
    48:9,11; 59:19); 2) Israel is said to exist for
    God's glory (Is 43:7; 46:13) and for his name (Jer
    13:11); 3) the terms occur in construct with each
    other--"the glory of his name" (Ps 79:9; 29:2;
    66:2; 96:8) and "the name of his glory" (Ps 72:19;
    Neh 9:5); 4) when men are called to "give God the
    glory due his name" (Ps 29:2) the only reason is
    that there is a glory in the name worthy of such
    glorification.

28. Cf the Midrash Tanhuma (Vienna, 1863) 3^b cited in
    Strack-Billerbeck, IV/1, 489. "As Moses stood and
    spoke to God: 'Let me see your glory' (Ex 33:18),
    what he said was, 'Lord of the world, let me know
    by what guideline you rule your world'; as it says,
    'Let me know your ways' (Ex 33:13). God answered
    him, 'Yes, I will show you; I will let all my good-
    ness pass by before you, etc' (Ex 33:19). God
    said to him: 'I am not obligated to any man; what-
    ever a man might do by way of fulfilling the com-
    mands, I still recompense him out of grace (חנם);

not that I owe man anything, but rather I reward
him out of grace' (חַנָּם); as it says, 'I will be
gracious to whom I will be gracious, and I will be
merciful to whom I will be merciful'" (Ex 33:19).
See also the Rabbah on Deut (Venedig, 1545) 2
(197[b]).

NOTES FOR CHAPTER FIVE

Notes from pp 69-71

1. The introductory phrase, τί οὖν ἐροῦμεν, is found
   exactly in Rom 4:1; 6:1; 7:7; 8:31; 9:30 and par-
   tially in Rom 3:5; 6:5. The closest analogies are
   6:1 and 7:7 because these are the only two which
   entertain a false inference from the preceding
   exposition and then reject it with μὴ γένοιτο.
   Therefore, as in those two places, what Paul is
   doing is beginning a kind of excursus which deals
   with problems raised in what he has just said.
   His approach in all three cases is to let his
   rhetorical opponent voice an objection (though the
   phrasing reflects Paul's answer already), then to
   deny it and answer it.

2. Mueller, Gottes Gerechtigkeit, 30 note 22, suggests
   similarly that "The formulation can be attributed
   to Paul's hesitancy to bring God and adikia
   together."

3. It is unnecessary for our purposes to identify the
   opponent precisely. Mueller, Gottes Gerechtigkeit,
   30, says, "A Jew would surely have seen God's
   adikia in this free hating and loving." But this
   sentence must be qualified because it is too
   sweeping. It is not valid, for example, in the
   case of the Qumran Jews whose doctrine of predestination is as absolute as Paul's (cf 1 QS
   3:15-4:26; 11:10f). Nor when we consult the Jewish interpretations of Ex 33:19 do we find a uniform position towards the freedom of God in showing
   mercy. See the texts in note 28 of the preceding
   chapter, but contrast Targum Jerusalem I on Ex
   33:19: "I will spare him who is worthy to be
   spared and I will show mercy on him who is worthy
   of mercy." We need not over-generalize about "the
   Jewish interpretation of the matter" (Munck, Christ
   and Israel, 14 note 48). All that is necessary to
   give historical credibility to our interpretation
   is to show that the objection of Rom 9:14 which we
   can reconstruct from Paul's argument does in fact
   have representatives in the Judaism of his day.
   Cf Strack-Billerbeck, III, 268.

   G. Maier's contention in Mensch und freier Wille,
   367, that "One does best to understand 'unrighteousness' as an offense against behavior that

accords with the covenant" is formally correct but lacking in precision. It simply raises the further question, What does "accord with the covenant" mean?, because the rabbis did not agree on what God had committed himself to do for Israel in the covenant. Some tended to think all Israelites would be saved (W.D. Davies, Paul, 84; G.F. Moore, Judaism, II, 95, 285, 387) while others restricted salvation to the righteous in Israel (Moore, Judaism, II, 313, 315, 362 note 6, 369, 377; cf 4 Ezra 7:49-6:1; 8:1,3). "Behavior that accords with the covenant" would vary according to one's conception of what the covenant relationship guarantees. I have tried to describe Paul's opponent's view of divine righteousness broadly enough to cover any view of covenantal commitment which grounds God's election in human distinctives, whether racial or moral. In other words the opponent could be on either side of the dispute as to whether all Jews will be saved.

4. Michel, Roemer, 238, speaks of Paul's "deeper meaning": "One must understand the term righteousness . . . in a deeper sense: As Creator God sets his own right." Mueller, Gottes Gerechtigkeit, 85, argues for two distinct conceptions, one for the opponent and one for Paul. For the opponent "God is righteous when he binds himself as impartial judge to the norm of the law and recognizes the erga of men. Paul on the other hand understands adikia not as an attribute but as action . . ." Whether or not Michel and Mueller are right about the nature of righteousness for Paul, they are right that Paul's conception is not the same as his opponent's.

5. U. Luz (Geschichtsverstaendnis, 73) points out how Paul, unlike the LXX and the normal Hellenistic usage, restricts himself to the singular form of ἀδικία so that it cannot be conceived as a sum of unrighteous acts. It has the character of a power which vies with other powers in determining a person's relationship to the truth of God.

6. With some qualification this position is not unlike E. Kuehl's, Theodicee, 18, "Adikia does not mean unrighteousness in the sense of unjust partiality, but in the sense that God is just if he acts in accord with the norms that lie in his own

246

essence. So one would have to attribute <u>adikia</u> to him if he offended these norms." Mueller, <u>Gottes Gerechtigkeit</u>, 85, and others register strong protest against attributing to Paul a concept of righteousness "as <u>justitia distributiva</u>, or, more exact, as 'correspondence to a norm.'" And rightly so, if one means that the "norm" is set for God by anything other than his own character. But, as will become evident in the following chapters, it is not unbiblical or unpauline to speak of God's truth, his glory, his name as that to which God must be faithful if he is to be righteous. It is of little consequence to me whether we use the word "norm." Therefore, with this qualification I approve of Kuehl's statement.

7. G. Schrenk (<u>TDNT</u>, I, 156) points out the contrast between ἀδικία and truth in John 7:18 and comments, "ἀδικία is present when we do not seek God's glory but our own reputation" ("the one who seeks the glory of the one who sent him is <u>true</u> and there is no ἀδικία in him"). This goes for Paul's use too. And it implies that if God did not always preserve and display his own glory (for there is no higher glory for him to seek) he would be unrighteous.

8. E. Kuehl, <u>Zur paulinischen Theodicee</u> (1897); W. Beyschlag, <u>Die paulinische Theodicee</u> (1868); E. Weber, <u>Das Problem der Heilsgeschichte nach Roemer 9-11. Ein Beitrag zur historisch-theologischen Wuerdigung der paulinischen Theodizee</u> (1911); R. Liechtenhan, <u>Vorherbestimmung</u>, 46 note 2 (1922), defends the use of the word with qualifications.

9. <u>Roemer</u>, 103: "He does not ground God's action; he simply shows that in redemptive history God has never acted otherwise."

10. <u>Israels Weg zum Heil</u>, 15: "Verses 19-21 repeat later that for this kind of action there can be no ground at all."

11. <u>Roemer</u>, 255: "Paul does not really ground the rejection of God's unrighteousness which he just raised. He rather reads out of the Scripture that God's action does not change."

12. <u>Roemerbrief</u>, III, 720: "Characteristically the Apostle does not in the least try to 'save' God through a

'theodicy.'" 722: "Paul offers no proofs for his argumentation."

13. "Probleme von Roemer 9-11," 19: "Rom 9:6-29 treats the Israel question. The problem of theodicy is not discussed, and predestination in the sense of God's saving plan is not in view."

14. If "theodicy" simply meant the humble attempt to show as best we can from Scripture and reason that God is right and good in all that he does and allows done, then I think the task is an admirable one with Biblical precedent. But, like most catch-phrases, the term "theodicy" is loaded with a history of philosophic connotation which if applied to Rom 9 could import extraneous and misleading concerns. It is understandable then that many would want to avoid the term as Christian Mueller (Gottes Gerechtigkeit, 18) does in these careful sentences on Rom 9:14: "Is the problem of theodicy really raised here, that is, the question about the origin and meaning of evil, and about the dishar- mony of the world in view of a postulated harmony? For Paul, the question of God's adikia rises not out of the disharmony of the world but out of God's free grace, which he gives to one and denies to another (9:13). The slant of the Pauline text is quite otherwise. One should therefore not speak of Rom 9-11 as a Pauline theodicy."

15. The term "theodicy" stems from Gottfried Wilhelm Leibniz (1646-1716) whose book, Essais de théodicée sur la bonté de Dieu, la liberté de l'homme et l'origine du mal (1710), indicates its philosophic scope and different orientation from Rom 9.

16. C.K. Barrett, Romans, 185; E. Weber, Problem der Heilsgeschichte, 57: "One hardly does this text justice when one assumes that Paul simply uses Bible texts to knock down any objection."

17. That the γάρ does in fact introduce a ground is supported by the fact that Paul's normal technique of argumentation is to give reasons after he has denied an objection with μὴ γένοιτο (Rom 3:6; 6:2,15; 7:7; 11:1,11).

Note from p 76

18. Cited in K.H. Schelkle, <u>Lehrer der Vaeter</u>, 341f, with references to the original.

NOTES FOR CHAPTER SIX

Notes from pp 81,82

1. It is generally recognized that "The Pauline
   doctrine of righteousness can be understood only
   against an OT background" (George Ladd, "Righteousness in Romans," 6). The best evidence is the
   sheer fact that Paul quotes the OT so frequently
   in this regard (besides Rom 9:15,17 see Rom 4).
   Hans Schmid, Gerechtigkeit als Weltordnung, 2, note
   2, presents a bibliography supporting this view.

2. Besides Schmid (Weltordnung, 1 note 1) another
   recent treatment is Frank Cruesemann, "Jahwes
   Gerechtigkeit (sᵉdāqā/sădăq)," 427-50 (see especially his footnote 2). Also among the more
   recent works that interact with the wider literature are Klaus Koch's article in THAT, II, col.
   507-30; Rafael Gyllenberg, Rechtfertigung und
   Altes Testament bei Paulus; Peter Stuhlmacher,
   Gerechtigkeit Gottes bei Paulus, 113ff; David
   Hill, Greek Words and Hebrew Meanings, 82ff.

3. The Distinctive Ideas, 72: "There is no difference in meaning. The choice is independent of
   date, and is a matter of style or caprice."

4. THAT, II, 507. But Koch seems to renege in col.
   518 when he acknowledges an apparent difference in
   meaning in Ps 40:10f.

5. "Jahwes Gerechtigkeit," 431. One of the arguments
   for maintaining a difference in meaning is that the
   feminine צדקה occurs fifteen times in the plural
   ("righteousnesses" = righteous deeds) but the
   masculine צדק never does. But on the other hand
   (as Koch points out) how do we account for the
   fact that צדקה in 2 Sam 22:21 becomes צדק in the
   parallel text Ps 18:20?

6. Theology, I, 372. Cruesemann, "Jahwes Gerechtigkeit," 428, undertakes to demolish this idea with
   a history-of-traditions study of Yahweh's righteousness. Whether he is successful depends on
   what von Rad meant by "radical (tiefgreifende)
   transformation," for there is a unity in the concept but that does not rule out development.

7. W. Eichrodt, Theology, I, 240: "It is a decided obstacle to any attempt to define the concept of divine righteousness, that the original significa- tion of the root sdq should be irretrievably lost" (p 240). David Hill (Greek Words, 83) is slightly less sceptical; on the basis of Ugaritic, Phoenician and Arabic texts he says, "The most we can say is that they suggest that the fundamental idea of צדק available to us is that of conformity to a norm which requires to be defined in each particular case." H. Schmid, however (Weltordnung, 66), following A. Jepsen, argues that צדק is "an impor- tant, ontologically relevant Canaanite concept" which is an expression of "world order" in various manifestations.

8. Gerhard Friedrich, "Pre-History of the Theological Dictionary of the New Testament," in TDNT, X, 659.

9. N. Snaith, Distinctive Ideas, 77: "Tsedeq, with its kindred words, signifies that standard which God maintains in the world. It is the norm by which all must be judged." Hill, Greek Words, 84: "צֶדֶק basically connotes conformity to a norm." Schmid, Weltordnung, 183, gives a larger biblio- graphy of scholars who stress the norm-character of righteousness.

10. Theology, I, 371. Others who have stressed the relational aspect of righteousness are E. Achtemeier, "Righteousness in the OT," IDB, IV, 80-85; W. Eichrodt, Theology, I, 240; G. Schrenk, TDNT, II, 195; K. Koch, THAT, II, 514; D. Hill, Greek Words, 84ff; H. Schmid, Weltordnung, 185, who also gives a longer bibliography on this point.

11. Greek Words, 84. Similarly G. Ladd ("Righteous- ness in Romans," 6) following N. Snaith (Distinc- tive Ideas, 77) defines righteousness in terms of conformity to a norm and then goes on to interpret this norm relationally. Even E. Kautzsch (Derivate, 53) escapes von Rad's criticism when he says that the "Normierende" may be "viewed some- times in an external standard (a conventional, fixed weight or volume or fact or objective com- mand) and sometimes in generally valid ethical presuppositions, and sometimes in the idea of a person, thing or even action."

12. F. Cruesemann, "Jahwes Gerechtigkeit," 436: "The s^{e}dāqōt Jahwes are acts of war which brought deliverance and salvation for all Israel."

13. Theology, vol 1, 377. Most recently F. Cruesemann ("Jahwes Gerechtigkeit," 488f) has come to the same conclusion as von Rad. He gives a substantial bibliography.

14. Greek Words, 90. Another more recent voice for the punitive aspect is Andreas Nissen, Gott und der Naechste im antiken Judentum, 247.

15. Von Rad (Theology, I, 377 note 17), says, "Even Is 5:16 cannot bear the onus of proof." But he gives no argument to support this.

16. Keil and Delitzsch, Nehemiah, 248: ". . . concerning all that has befallen us; because their sins deserved punishment, and God is only fulfilling His word upon the sinners."

17. See THAT, vol 2, 958, for the relationship between the name and the glory of God.

18. The same phrase "You shall know that I am the Lord" is given as the purpose of judgment on Israel in Ezek 6:7,10; 7:9,27; 11:10,12; 12:15,16,20; 13:9,14; 14:8; 15:7; 20:26.

19. In accordance with the methodological guidelines on pages 81f, I will not make the literary-critical distinctions between a second and third Isaiah.

20. F. Cruesemann, "Jahwes Gerechtigkeit," 444. See also D. Hill, Greek Words, 91; W. Eichrodt, Theology, I, 245; von Rad, Theology, I, 372, who says that this idea is not created by Isaiah but is much older.

21. Theologie des Alten Testaments, Teil 1, 117 (my translation). Compare Theology, I, 245.

22. Ps 79 is generally thought to stem from the period of Jerusalem's fall in 587 B.C. D. Kidner, Psalms 73-150, 286; R.E. Murphy, "Psalms" in: The Jerome Biblical Commentary, 590.

Notes from pp 96-100

23. In Ezek 36:24-28 the phrase "new covenant" is not
    used, but the parallel with Jer 31:31ff shows that
    this is the sense. As von Rad (Theology, II, 235)
    says, "The fact that the word 'covenant' is not
    here mentioned means nothing--there are other
    passages where he did designate the saving event
    as covenant (Ezek 34:25; 37:26)--for the content
    of the passage shows it to be closely parallel,
    feature by feature, to Jeremiah's pericope on the
    new covenant (Jer 31:31ff)."

24. Recall Eichrodt's comment (p 95) that God's righ-
    teousness is a revelation of his holiness. This
    comports well with God's deliverance being an
    expression of his allegiance to his holy name even
    though Ezekiel does not refer to the righteousness
    of God at all. On Ezekiel's view of God Curt Kuhl
    (The Prophets of Israel, 129) argues that "Concern
    for His name and His reputation among the nations
    is thus the sole raison d'être for His grace."

25. The only references in Jer are 4:2; 9:24; 11:20;
    12:1; 23:5f = 33:15f. Both, especially Ezek,
    have other references to the righteousness of men.

26. See, for example, Ex 14:4 ("I will harden Pharaoh's
    heart, and he will pursue them and I will get glory
    over Pharaoh"); 1 Sam 12:22 (The Lord will not
    abandon his people on account of his great name);
    2 Sam 7:23 (he redeemed his people to make a name
    for himself); 2 Kgs 19:34 = 20:6 ("I will defend
    this city for my own sake"); Ps 25:11 ("For thy
    name's sake, O Lord, pardon my guilt"); Ps 106:8
    (he saved them for the sake of his name).

27. The rendering of וּלְחֹשְׁבֵי שְׁמוֹ in the RSV (following
    BDB, 363) as "and thought on his name" seems much
    less likely in this context than the equally pro-
    per meaning in the sense of esteem, value, regard.
    Keil and Delitzsch, The Minor Prophets, II, 467,
    cite the parallel usage in Is 13:17 and 33:8: "to
    consider or value the name of the Lord."

28. N. Snaith (Distinctive Ideas, 138) has a keen sen-
    sitivity to this OT teaching. He has a section
    entitled "Is God's Love Irrational?" In response
    to the accusation that God's love is arbitrary, he
    points out that the word arbitrary "can mean that
    it depends solely on the will of the agent. In

254

this sense God's love is certainly arbitrary. It is arbitrary in the sense that it is unconditioned by anything outside the Nature of God. Men can give no reason for it. God's thoughts are not our thoughts, neither are his ways our ways. They are 'things too wonderful for me, which I know not' (Job 42:3)."

NOTES FOR CHAPTER SEVEN

Notes from pp 103,104

1. Kaesemann's contention (over against the existential interpretation of Paul, i.e. Bultmann) is that Paul's theology "has a universal thrust and is thus oriented to the antithesis of Adam and Christ, of the first and last creation" (Romans, 79). Within this universal orientation the righteousness of God, which is "the central concept of Pauline theology" (320), takes on a special meaning: it is "the power which establishes its right to the creature" (84). It is no longer "covenant faithfulness" because "when Paul thinks of the covenant he no longer thinks of Moses and Sinai, but in a transferred sense of the creation of the world. . . God's righteousness is the power which has its legal title in this first and most comprehensive covenant of creation and which therefore eschatologically reestablishes and enforces its law in this covenant as its sphere of lordship" (80). Cf also Peter Stuhlmacher, Gerechtigkeit Gottes bei Paulus.

2. One exception I am aware of is Guenther Bornkamm, "Theologie als Teufelskunst, Roemer 3:1-9," 140-8. Other treatments that have tangentially treated the righteousness of God in Rom 3:1-8 include R. Bultmann, "ΔΙΚΑΙΟΣΥΝΗ ΘΕΟΥ," 12-16; Guenther Klein, "Gottes Gerechtigkeit als Thema der neuesten Paulus-Forschung," 229; Eduard Lohse, "Die Gerechtigkeit Gottes in der paulinischen Theologie," 223; Karl Kertelge, 'Rechtfertigung' bei Paulus, 63-70. See also the appropriate sections in Stuhlmacher, Gerechtigkeit, 85ff, and Mueller, Gottes Gerechtigkeit, 49f, 65f, 110f.

3. This translation and punctuation follow the interpretation of H. Ljungvik, "Zum Roemerbrief 3:7-8," 207-10, and A. Fridrichsen, "Nochmals Roemer 3:7-8," 306-8. Verse 8a is construed not as Paul's response to the opponents in verse 7 but as a continuation of the opponents' own objection. Cranfield (Romans, I, 186) objects that this leaves the objections unanswered and that it results in "a very awkward combination of the first person singular and the first person plural in the same question." But perhaps Paul does not want to be diverted here and so postpones his answer until

257

6:1. And is not verse 6 at least a partial answer?
Cranfield's second objection is stronger and makes
a final decision uncertain. I would only point
out that the ὧν τὸ κρίμα of verse 8b which definitely refers to the plural τινες of verse 8a also
refers to the singular κρίνομαι of verse 7. Thus
the "I" of verse 7 and the "we" of verse 8 may be
viewed simply as two ways of expressing the objectors' identity. The main arguments of this essay
do not, in any case, rest on this uncertainty.

4. The reason the logia of God are generally interpreted as promises is that the following verse (3)
refers to Jewish unbelief and to God's faithfulness
both of which make best sense in relation to a word
of promise.

5. See Rom 5:8; Gal 2:18; 2 Cor 6:4; 7:11 for Paul's
use of this verb.

6. Hans Lietzmann, Roemer, 45; C.K. Barrett, Romans,
64; C.E.B. Cranfield, Romans, I, 184.

7. Lietzmann, Roemer, 45. Cf 1 Cor 9:8; Gal 3:15;
Rom 6:19.

8. This is the most common reconstruction of the opponents' position. Guenther Bornkamm, "Teufelskunst,"
144, states their argument as follows: the opponent in verse 5 attacks the righteousness of God
"because it needs our unrighteousness as a backdrop in order to be put in the proper light, and
he infers that therefore the basis of God's punishment is taken away. A God who is dependent on
the unrighteousness of man in order to show himself
righteous would be unrighteous to judge this very
unrighteousness of men." See the quote by H.
Thyen in note 22.

9. R. Bultmann, "ΔΙΚΑΙΟΣΎΝΗ," 13; G. Bornkamm,
"Teufelskunst," 145; Charles Hodge, Romans, 72.

10. John Calvin, Romans, 61: "The particle that is
not final and does not refer to a farfetched consequence, but suggests the conclusion, 'Against
thee only have I sinned, therefore thou wilt
punish me justly.'" Similarly John Murray, Romans,
I, 95. Cranfield (Romans, I, 183) gives no support
for his peculiar idea that the ὅπως is "dependent

not on the preceding half-verse but on verse 3
(LXX: 5)."

11. Calvin, <u>Romans</u>, 61. "By the <u>words</u> of God David
means the judgments which he pronounces upon us.
It is too forced to understand by this, as is commonly done, the promises of God."

12. So A. Schlatter, <u>Gottes Gerechtigkeit</u>, 116; C.K.
Barrett, <u>Romans</u>, 63. Kaesemann's (<u>Romans</u>, 81)
defense of the passive meaning on the basis of the
passive κρίνομαι in verse 7 seems to me to prove
the opposite: if man "is judged" then <u>God</u> must be
judging. See note 13.

13. O. Michel, <u>Roemer</u>, 96: "The parallelism of the
double ἐν speaks more for the middle than for the
passive meaning of κρίνεσθαι."

14. Compare Ps Sol 9:2f: "Among every nation were the
dispersed of Israel according to the Word of God,
<u>that Thou mightest be justified, O God, in Thy</u>
<u>righteousness by reason of our transgres-</u>
<u>sions</u> . . ." E. Kaesemann's (<u>Romans</u>, 81f) view of
the significance of the Psalm quote is radically
different from mine. He too thinks it is of great
relevance for Paul but not because it speaks of
God's retributive justice. Rather "with these
quotes the <u>justificatio impii</u> . . . was asserted"
(82). "God's victory [referred to in the Psalm
quote] is achieved over the faithless and, as 11:32
sums up, over rebels. It is continually, as 4:5
will say, the justification of the ungodly" (82).
Thus Kaesemann argues that the Psalm quote is a
statement that God justifies the ungodly and this,
he says, is correctly understood by Paul's pious
opponents. I cannot follow Kaesemann for at least
two reasons: 1) his view demands the possible, but
in this case wholly unnecessary, assumption that
Paul has ignored the basic OT meaning of the Psalm
and would seem to offer no explanation for the
ὅπως; 2) I cannot see how an assertion of the justification of the ungodly gives rise to the opponents' reference to wrath (verse 5) and judgment
(verse 7) upon them. See Section 4 for a discussion of how 3:4b functions in Paul's argument.

15. J.A. Ziesler, <u>Righteousness in Paul</u>, 190: "In
verse 5 God's righteousness is opposed to man's

259

wickedness and thus means his own righteousness,
but specifically his activity of judging."

16. The human "unrighteousness" of verse 5 and "falsehood" of verse 7 are virtually the same as the
"unbelief" of verse 3 (or at least broadly overlap
with each other)--Sanday and Headlam, Romans, 72.
This finds support in the fact that when Paul says,
"let . . . every man be a liar" (verse 4b), the
sequence of thought between verse 3 and 4 shows
that "unbelief" and "lie" are basically the same.
Thus when the term "lie" or "falsehood" turns up
again in verse 7 it is likely that the same meaning
is intended, namely unbelief--which is tantamount
to unfaithfulness to God's covenant mercy.

17. The "eloquent progression" (Murray, Romans, I, 95
note 2) from "some" (verse 3a) to "every" (verse
4b) would collapse if "liar" meant less than
unbeliever. All unbelievers are liars in the sense
that they deny the truth of God's promise: unbelief is the false assertion that God is not trustworthy. If the question is raised, how could God
be true to his promises if every man were an
unbeliever, my answer would be that he could not
be. But part of his faithfulness is to preserve a
believing remnant to whom the promises will be
fulfilled. Thus I regard the statement, "Let God
be true and every man a liar," as a hypothetical
case that hyperbolically leaves out of account the
effectual grace of God to preserve a believing
remnant. The point of the statement is to show
that nothing man can do will ever call God's
truthfulness into question.

18. Note that I am not trying to show in general how
the opponents conceived of the "righteousness of
God." I am concerned only with what they mean by
that term in Rom 3:5 which may merely be a
reflection of how they (erroneously!) construe
Paul.

19. 1:17; 2:24; 3:10; 8:36; 9:13,33; 10:15; 11:26;
15:9.

20. When K. Kertelge (Rechtfertigung, 70) objects to a
punitive righteousness here and argues, with
Stuhlmacher (Gerechtigkeit, 85) and others, that
righteousness and wrath are not the same in Rom 3:5

but are opposites, he makes two mistakes I think:
1) he overlooks that the opponents' view, not
necessarily Paul's, is expressed in 3:5 and 2) he
knocks down a straw man, for no one equates God's
righteousness and his wrath. All I am maintaining
is that God's righteousness embraces also punishment, or that punishment is one expression of it.

21. This emerges in the failure of Paul's opponents to
grasp the significance of Paul's "some" in 3:3a
and their false inference from God's faithfulness,
namely, that all Jews will be spared judgment.
Paul attacks this false view of solidarity head-on
in Rom 9:6: "not all Israel is Israel"--that is
why the promises of God have not fallen (9:6) even
though "some" Jews are accursed (9:3).

22. Juergen Becker, Das Heil Gottes, 275 ("always
positive as a term of salvation"); Stuhlmacher,
Gerechtigkeit, 85f; Kaesemann, Romans, 83;
Kertelge, Rechtfertigung, 70. Kertelge seems to
try to have it both ways by saying the wrath and
righteousness of God are in "tension" with each
other but that the one is the "reverse side" of
the other. He cites two works where a punitive
righteousness is defended: O. Olivieri, "Quid ergo
amplius Iudaeo est? (Rom 3:1-8)," and M. Pohlenz,
Vom Zorn Gottes. Hartwig Thyen, Studien zur
Suendenvergebung, 165f, gives a short but pointed
critique of Stuhlmacher's interpretation of Rom
3:1-8. He says, "God shows himself 'righteous' in
that he punishes the adikia with his wrath. Paul's
point is not the 'covenant faithfulness' of God but
the demonstration that judgment is deserved and
therefore righteous" (166). That Paul knew of a
punitive divine righteousness is confirmed, it
seems to me, by 2 Thess 1:5f, "(Your persecution)
is a sign of the δικαίας κρίσεως τοῦ θεοῦ in order
to make you worthy of the kingdom of God for which
you suffer, since it is δίκαιον παρὰ θεῷ to pay
back tribulation to those who oppress you and to
give you who are oppressed rest with us." Parallel to this would be Rom 2:5 where those Jews who
spurn God's mercy store up for themselves "wrath
on the day of wrath and of the revelation of the
δικαιοκρισίας τοῦ θεοῦ."

23. This is the point of 3:6, "Otherwise how will God
judge the world?" In other words: if your view of

God's righteousness prevails, it rules out all
judgment. Therefore since there is judgment, your
view of a strictly saving righteousness is not
correct. Righteousness is not the gracious opposite of punitive judgment but rather finds one
expression precisely in judgment (verse 4b).

24. Kaesemann (Romans, 84) is on the right track when
he says, "It should be noted that God's righteousness and glory are interchanged almost inciden-
tally. The OT and Jewish apocalyptic provide a
basis for this."

NOTES FOR CHAPTER EIGHT

1. Cranfield, Romans, I, 199; Schrage, "Roemer 3:21-26," 65.

2. "The tradition out of which the Scripture has grown is the deep dimension of Scripture" (Leonhard Goppelt, "Tradition nach Paulus," 232).

3. For a recent summary in English see Ralph Martin, New Testament Foundations, II, 248-275.

4. ZNW 43 (1950/51), 150-54. Now in Exegetische Versuche und Besinnungen, vol 1, 96-100.

5. Romans, 101. Guenther Klein, "Gottes Gerechtigkeit als Thema der neuesten Paulus-Forschung," 230, goes even further when he says that Paul was critical of the tradition "not only in the sense of broadening the motif of covenant-faithfulness to that of faithfulness to creation . . . The correction is rather qualitative: a concept of being (εἰς τὸ εἶναι αὐτὸν δίκαιον) becomes a forensic one (καὶ δικαιοῦντα)." See note 10 below for an alternative view.

6. Martyrer und Gottesknecht, 149 note 4. Also Werner Kramer, Christos Kyrios Gottessohn, 140 note 509.

7. Recently, Peter Stuhlmacher, "Zur neueren Exegese von Roem. 3:24-26," 316; Georg Eichholz, Theologie des Paulus, 191 (who still includes verse 24); Klaus Wengst (Christologische Formeln, 87); Hartwig Thyen, Studien zur Suendenvergebung, 164; Wolfgang Schrage, "Roemer 3:21-26," 86; Dieter Zeller, "Suehne und Langmut," 51ff; Eduard Lohse, Martyrer, 140; Christian Mueller, Gottes Gerechtigkeit, 110f.

8. Gottfried Fitzer, "Der Ort der Versoehnung nach Paulus"; Charles Talbert, "A Non-Pauline Fragment at Romans 3:24-26?"

9. H. Schlier, Roemerbrief, 107 note 8: "Concerning fundamental methodology, must the appearance of a concept used elsewhere only seldom or never by Paul really point to the use of tradition?"

10. Roemerbrief, I, 160. E. Lohse, "Die Gerechtigkeit Gottes in der paulinischen Theologie," 222: "Paul takes up this confession with full agreement, but gives it an interpretation which allows its point to emerge with much stronger force." P. Stuhlmacher, "Roemer 3,24-26," 331, concludes that Paul's interpretation of the tradition must be understood "not simply as a criticism, not to mention a qualitative correction, but with Lohse as a consistent expansion and extension." Walter Maier, "Paul's Concept of Justification," 254, concludes that Rom 3:24-26 is not a pre-Pauline formulation.

11. The following representatives do not necessarily agree in all exegetical details: A. Schlatter, Gottes Gerechtigkeit, 148f; A. Nygren, Romans, 365; O. Michel, Roemer, 107; J.A. Ziesler, Righteousness in Paul, 194; L. Goppelt, Theologie, II, 194.

12. Paul, 167, 189: "In Christ's death the righteousness of God thus reveals itself in the demanding and vindicatory sense of the word. His blood as atoning blood covers the sin which God until now had passed over, when as yet he kept back the judgment. All that men wish to detract from the real character of Christ's propitiatory death signifies a devaluation of the language of Romans 3:25,26, which is unmistakable in its clarity."

13. ZThK 49 (1952), 154-67. The page numbers in the text refer to this essay.

14. Goppelt (Theologie, II, 424) and Stuhlmacher (Gerechtigkeit, 88) also make explicit their rejection of Anselm's view.

15. For example, E. Lohse, "Die Gerechtigkeit Gottes in der paulinischen Theologie," 223. See also Cranfield, Romans, I, 97.

16. "Whether one speaks here of a proof (Beweis) or a demonstration (Erweis) does not make a substantial difference," O. Kuss, Roemerbrief, I, 158.

17. It is not necessary for my present purpose to enter the debate over the precise meaning of ἱλαστήριον. The older controversy between Roger Nicole ("C.H. Dodd and the Doctrine of Propitiation") and C.H. Dodd ("ΙΛΑΣΚΕΣΘΑΙ, Its Cognates,

Derivatives and Synonyms in the Septuagint") has
recently been revived: See R. Nicole, "Hilaskesthai Revisited." For a recent and thorough exami-
nation of whether the OT Day of Atonement (Lev 16)
or the atoning death of Jewish martyrs (4 Macc
17:21f) provides the history-of-religions background for Paul, see P. Stuhlmacher, "Roemer
3,24-26." I find Barrett's view very sound:
"'Propitiation' is not adequate, for this means
that the offender does something to appease the
person he has offended, whereas Paul says that God
himself put forward Christ. Propitiation is truly
there, however, for, through the sacrifice of
Christ, God's wrath is turned away; but behind the
propitiation lies the fact that God actually wiped
out (expiated) our sin, and made us right with
himself" (Reading Through Romans, 16).

18. Romans, 99: "1:18-3:20 sets the past under the
     theme of the revelation of wrath not of the clem-
     ency which practices patience."

19. W. Schrage ("Rom 3:21-26," 74) represents a host
     of scholars when he comments on the righteousness
     of God in our text: "Righteousness in the OT is
     not the respecting of an ideal ethical or legal
     norm or a moral quality, but in a strict sense it
     is a behavior determined by a relationship . . .
     that means God's righteousness is his salvation-
     creating, rescuing intervention on behalf of his
     covenant partner."

20. The translation comes from A. Dupont-Sommer, The
     Essene Writings from Qumran, 102f.

21. The translation is from R.H. Charles, Pseudepi-
     grapha.

22. "Die Rechtfertigungslehre des Paulus: Theologie
     oder Anthropologie?" Similarly Bultmann, Theology,
     I, 46.

23. C.E.B. Cranfield, Romans, I, 97: "While it is of
     course true that the righteousness language of the
     OT and of late Judaism is the background against
     which Paul's expression δικαιοσύνη θεοῦ must be
     understood, there is no reason to assume that he
     must have used the language he took over just pre-
     cisely as it had been used. We must allow for the

265

possibility of his having used what he took over
with freedom and originality."

24. In determining the Semitic influences on Paul's
thinking the OT itself must be regarded as primary.
We <u>know</u> that he lived with this book; what else he
knew firsthand is largely a matter of conjecture.
Yet there is little reason to doubt that Paul was
influenced by the Jewish thought of his own day.
Therefore it may be of some significance to point
out that a case could be made that the conception
of God's righteousness I have developed has left
traces in the apocalyptic literature which
Kaesemann sees as the background of Paul's conception. 1 QS 1:26 reflects a punitive divine righteousness which has to be correlated somehow with
the saving righteousness in 1 QS 10:11,12;
11:3,5,10,12-15. The key may lie in the parallel
between glory/majesty and righteousness (1 QS
11:6,7,15). When 4 Ezra says, "For this, O Lord,
shall thy <u>righteousness</u> be declared, if thou wilt
compassionate them that have no wealth of good
works," the next verses picture God <u>refusing</u> to do
all that Ezra asks: he will rejoice only over the
righteous (8:39). And who are they? "Them that
have always put their trust in thy <u>glory</u>" (8:30).
"Them who . . . search out the <u>glory</u>" (8:51). But
not those who "have themselves defiled the <u>Name</u> of
him that made them."

25. Schlier, <u>Roemerbrief</u>, <u>107</u>; Cranfield, <u>Romans</u>, I,
204; Kaesemann, <u>Romans</u>, 95. Cf Apocalypse of
Moses, 20; Greek Apocalypse of Baruch 4:16; Genesis
Rabbah 12:6 (on 2:4).

26. That this complex of ideas so closely echoes the
teaching of Anselm is not due to any vested
interest I have in defending him. It is due I
suppose to the fact that his insights are more
Biblical than many of his critics (who seldom show
specific errors) think. See Saint Anselm, <u>Basic
Writings</u>, 201-10.

27. Nigel Turner, <u>A Grammar of New Testament Greek</u>,
III, 263. C.F.D. Moule, <u>An Idiom-Book of New
Testament Greek</u>, 54.

28. He comments innocuously, "A final sense is preferable to the consecutive sense since the εἰς τὸ

εἶναι refers back to the motif of ἔνδειξις"
(Romans, 100). But in what sense are the εἰς τὸ
εἶναι and the ἔνδειξις related? How are they
different, if they are? He does not say.

29. It should be noted that when I speak of God's
being righteous I am not referring to metaphysical
substances but to conditions of will. God's being
righteous is properly described in terms of faithfulness, allegiance, commitment, devotion, loyalty,
etc. He is righteous in that his inclination or
will is inexorably committed always to preserve
and display his glory. This eternal and unswerving
inclination precedes and grounds all his acts of
demonstration.

30. This "yet" must not be construed to mean that the
mercy of justification is contrary or adverse to
the righteousness of God. What the adversative
signifies is the apparent conflict between letting
sins go unpunished and God's commitment always to
preserve and display his glory. The putting Christ
forth as a propitiation reveals how in fact there
is no conflict: God is just and (with no tension
at all) justifier of the one who trusts Jesus.

267

NOTES FOR CHAPTER NINE

Notes from pp 132-135

1. Victor Pfitzner (Agon Motif, 135) argues against
    this: "The negative character of Paul's words
    also suggests as highly improbable a reference to the
    use of ץור/τρέχειν in such passages as Ps 58(59):4;
    118(119):32; Prov 1:16; Is 59:7. The image of the
    runner in these passages is intended to illustrate
    not effort, but the intentions on a course of
    behavior, whether according to or against God's
    commandments." Pfitzner does not address the
    kinds of arguments Noack and Maier present. His
    one argument here is weak for two reasons. 1) He
    is assuming in advance that Paul means effort when
    he writes τρέχοντος, whereas perhaps Paul wants to
    say that not even "intentness on a course of behav-
    ior" is the cause of God's mercy, but absolutely
    and only God himself. 2) On the other hand Paul
    may allude to "running the way of the commandments"
    not as the psalmist originally used it but as
    Paul's contemporary legalistic opponents practiced
    it.

2. The two closest analogies Bauernfeind (TDNT, VIII,
    232) claims to be able to find are Zech 4:6 ("Not
    by might, nor by power, but by my Spirit, says the
    Lord of hosts"), and Ass Mos 12:4,7, where Moses
    says to Joshua: "Nothing has been neglected by him
    even to the least thing, but all things he has
    foreseen and caused all to come forth . . . For not
    for any virtue or strength of mine but of his good
    pleasure have his compassion and long-suffering
    fallen to my lot." Since Ass Mos is generally
    held to be Essene in character (Rost, Einleitung,
    111) this coheres with Maier's argument.

3. Sanday and Headlam (Romans, 254) are right on
    target when they cite Jn 1:12f as an analogy to
    Rom 9:6: "He has given them the right to become
    children of God . . . who are begotten not from
    blood nor from the will of the flesh nor from the
    will of a man, but from God." Cf also the ἐξ
    αὐτοῦ of 1 Cor 1:30.

4. There is no point in quibbling over the precise
    name of the genitives in Rom 9:16. The genitive is a
    very flexible case and must derive its nuance of mean-
    ing from the immediate context. That God's bestowal

of mercy is not "of one who wills" must mean that the willing of that one is not the ultimately determining factor in whether he receives such a bestowal.

5. Zahn, Roemer, 449; Forster and Marston, God's Strategy, 66f: "First, we must remember that although individuals are involved, no one's eternal destiny is in question. Moses was 'converted' years before this episode, and any attempt to strain Paul's text to make it mean that Moses was eternally predestined to heaven and Pharaoh to hell is totally unwarranted. The question is not the eternal destiny of anyone, but the history of Israel and their significance as the chosen nation."

6. Hodge, Romans, 313; Stoeckhardt, Roemer, 434; Lagrange, Romains, 233; Kuss, Roemerbrief, III, 722; Munck, Christ and Israel, 45 note 53.

7. Beyschlag, Theodicee, 47; Meyer, Romans, II, 133; Alford, II, 409; Sanday and Headlam, Romans, 255; Schlatter, Gerechtigkeit, 301: "The one whom God hardens makes the fact evident that he gives his mercy to whomever he wills to give it."

8. In reality הפך in Ex 14:5 belongs here but since it is never translated in the LXX by σκληρύνειν, I do not include it in the table. The text reads: "And the heart of Pharaoh and his servants was turned (וַיֵּהָפֵךְ) toward (against) the people and they said, 'What is this we have done!'" The meaning is substantially the same as hardening. Cf note 23.

9. The "c" designates a converted imperfect.

10. Childs, Exodus, 171: "A rather clear picture of distribution among the sources also emerges. The Yahwist always uses kābēd. The Priestly writer normally chooses hāzaq, but once hiqšāh. The E source choice is parallel to P. There are several redactional passages whose usage varies from these patterns."

11. Against this see THAT, I, 540.

12. No doubt Moses does not mean a moral evil but evil in the sense of calamity. Cf Lam 3:38, "Is it not from the mouth of the Most High that good and evil come?" Amos 3:6, "Does evil befall a city unless the Lord has done it?" Is 45:6,7, "I am Yahweh and there is no other, forming light and creating darkness, making peace and creating evil; I Yahweh do all these things."

13. Ex R 13 (75^C): The Minim (possibly Christians) are alleged to have argued from Ex 10:1 that the repentance of Pharaoh did not depend ultimately on him. But the rabbinic response is, "After God had sent to [Pharaoh] five times, since he did not concern himself with these words, God said to him: 'You have made your neck hard and hardened your heart; behold, I will add uncleanness to uncleanness.' That is what the words, 'I hardened his heart' mean" (cited in Strack-Billerbeck, III, 259).

14. God's Strategy, 72: "The first instance of any act of God on Pharaoh's heart does not come until Ex 9:12, after Pharaoh himself has repeatedly rejected God's request."

15. Stoeckhardt, Roemer, 438; see others cited in Lagrange, Romains, 235.

16. Schmidt, "Verstockung," 17; Nygren, Romans, 367: "When a man hardens his heart against God, it is God who hardens him . . ."

17. Paul uses ἐξεγείρω only one other time: in 1 Cor 6:14 to refer to the resurrection. So his own usage is not much help.

18. Stoeckhardt, Roemer, 435: "the historical appearance and position of Pharaoh"; Hodge, Romans, 314: "his appearance and position in the history of the world"; Alford, II, 409: "called into action in his office"; Murray, Romans, II, 27: "the position Pharaoh occupied by the providence of God on the scene of history"; Meyer, Romans, II, 139: "the whole historical appearance has been brought about by me"; Michel, Roemer, 239: "to awaken, to cause to appear on the scene of history"; Beyschlag, Theodicee, 48: "I have raised you up, and caused you to make an appearance in history."

Notes from pp 147-151

19. Some (e.g. Bush, <u>Notes</u>, I, 116) argue that Paul
    meant that God raised Pharaoh from sickness
    (i.e. the boils, Ex 9:11) in the sense of Jam 5:15.
    But against this is the more common usage of ἐξεγείρω
    in the LXX (see above p 147). But decisive is the
    probability that if Paul had followed the LXX
    interpretation of הֶעֱמַדְתִּיךָ, he would not have
    bothered to choose a different word at all. Sanday and
    Headlam, <u>Romans</u>, 255, follow Meyer's interpretation.

20. The hithpael of עלל is used six other times in the
    OT. In Num 22:29, Balaam accuses his ass of
    making sport of him because three times he would
    not move as Balaam demanded. In Jud 19:25
    it refers to the extended sexual abuse of a woman.
    In 1 Sam 31:4 (= 1 Chr 10:4) and Jer 38:19 Saul
    and Zedekiah fear to be handed over to their
    enemies lest they abusively make sport of them.
    In 1 Sam 6:6 the reference is back to the Egyptians
    who hardened their hearts and of whom God made
    sport. The picture we get then is that God is
    drawing out his plagues upon Egypt and deriding
    the Egyptians in their pride (9:17; 10:3) and thus
    demonstrating in a startling way his absolute
    control.

21. I find Childs' (<u>Exodus</u>, 162) observation very mis-
    leading when he says Paul's "argument does not
    rest on an exegesis of the Exodus passage." On
    the contrary, not only does the relation between
    Rom 9:17 and 18 reveal exegetical reflection on
    the Exodus passage but the whole of Rom 9:17-23
    appears to be the distillation of much theological
    reflection on the whole OT context. Lagrange
    (<u>Romains</u>, 234) is right: "Again Paul has all the
    texts under his eye and he presupposes that they
    are known, as the σκληρύνει in verse 18 proves."
    See also Meyer, <u>Romans</u>, II, 139.

22. In Exodus the word מוֹפֵת occurs only in 11:9,10 and
    4:21; 7:3,9, so that the summary of the miracle-
    working in 11:9,10 is linked to the initial pre-
    dictions that God would harden Pharaoh in order to
    multiply his miracles (4:21; 7:3).

23. There is a similar usage of הָפַךְ in Ps 105:25 that
    shows how the psalmist saw the hardening work of
    God going all the way back to the early days of the
    Egypt sojourn. Israel comes into Egypt, increases

272

in number more than the Egyptians, and "[Yahweh]
turns (הֶפֵךְ) their heart to hate his people, to
deal craftily with his servants."

24. Similarly, Meyer, <u>Romans</u>, II, 139: "Verse 18, ὃν
δὲ θέλει σκληρύνει is not inferred from the <u>verbal
sense</u> of ἐξήγειρά σε but from the relation of the
ὅπως κ.τ.λ. to the ἐξήγειρά σε (εἰς αὐτὸ τοῦτο
evinces this),--a relation which would presuppose a
hardening of Pharaoh on the part of God and for
the reader who is familiar with the history (Ex
4:21; 7:3; 11:10; 14:4 et al) actually presupposes
it." Cf also Kuehl, <u>Theodicee</u>, 20. There is some
slight evidence that Paul's juxtaposition of hardening and mercy along with a reference to God's
self-glorifying purpose may reflect a later Jewish
tradition: Sirach 16:15,16 (omitted in the Hebrew
and some Greek manuscripts) says, "The Lord <u>har-
dened</u> (ἐσκλήρυνε) Pharaoh so that he would not
know him, in order that his works might be made
known (ὅπως ἂν γνωσθῇ ἐνεργήματα αὐτοῦ). To all
the creation under heaven his <u>mercy</u> (ἔλεος) is
manifest. And he divided his light and darkness
with a plumb line." Maier (<u>Mensch und freier
Wille</u>, 371f) maintains that Sir 16:15f is a dual-
istic gloss with a meaning related to Qumran and
in the spirit of Sir 33. "We may assume that Paul
knew Sir 16:15f." If this is the case it confirms
the earlier suggestion (Chapter Three, p 53f) that
Paul stands within the tradition of predestination
expressed in Qumran.

25. Meyer, <u>Romans</u>, II, 142 note 1: "In the second
clause [18b] this emphatic ὃν θέλει is then repeated,
on which occasion δέ ('again, on the other hand')
brings out the <u>corresponding symmetry of the relative definition on both sides</u>" (my emphasis).

26. I think this interpretation does not really cohere
with Murray's own insightful treatment of Rom
9:6-13 (cf Chapter Three, p 47). He senses the
inconsistency when he says, "It might appear that
the judicial character of hardening interferes
with the sovereign will of God upon which the
accent falls in this text." Murray denies this
interference, but then gets into deeper inconsistency when he says, "But . . . the sin and ill-
desert presupposed in hardening is also presupposed in the exercise of mercy. Both parts of

Notes from p 155

this verse [18] rest upon the premise of ill-desert."
Perhaps there is some technical ambiguity here in
the words "presuppose" and "premise," but if the
mercy referred to is the mercy of election in
9:11f, then its "premise" cannot be ill-desert,
since Jacob "had done nothing good or evil."

27. Meyer, Romans, II, 138. See p 146 for a comparison
of Paul's text with the Hebrew and LXX of Ex 9:16.

28. There is a difference between the way Paul infers
the freedom of God from the example of Jacob/Esau
and the way he does from Pharaoh. In the former
case they were not yet born and had not done any
good or evil when God chose one and rejected the
other. In the latter case Pharaoh had done much
evil when God declared to Moses that he was going
to harden him. So the argument from Pharaoh's
case is not built on the time when God revealed
his decision to harden Pharaoh, but the way that
he revealed it, namely by repeatedly grounding it
in his own purposes to glorify himself and never
in Pharaoh's sin. It is theologically possible
that from another angle God's act of hardening (as
opposed to his initial choice of whom to harden)
could be described as a judicial abandonment of
Pharaoh to his own sinful blindness, and thus a
punitive measure in response to Pharaoh's sin (so
Hodge, Romans, 316; Murray, Romans, II, 29). This
would not necessarily contradict Paul's angle of
view here. But it is virtually certain that this
is not the point Paul wants to make here, since it
is foreign to his emphasis on God's doing whatever
he will apart from being determined by human
willing or running.

29. Similarly, Michel, Roemer, 241: "There is no
reprobation by God without human accountability.
Nevertheless Paul contradicts the Jewish tradition
insofar as it views the disobedience of Pharaoh as
a presupposition of reprobation by God." Meyer,
Romans, II, 142: "The hardening here appears by no
means, as has lately been read between the lines,
'as a consequence of preceding conceited self-
righteousness' (Tholuck), or 'such as the man himself has willed it' (Th. Schott), or conditioned
by the divine standard of holiness confronting
human sin (Weiss), or with an obvious presupposition of human self-determination (Beyschlag).

Elsewhere the hardening may be adjudged as a
punishment by God (Is 6:9ff) but not so here."

30. Luz, Geschichtsverstaendnis, 77 note 208: "E.V.
     Dobschuetz, Praedestination, 12f, rightly points
     out that on account of 'apōleia' and 'orgē' the
     hardening of Pharaoh is to be thought of
     eschatologically."

31. This does not imply that the condition sometimes
     called hardness of heart (Eph 4:18) or mind (2 Cor
     3:14) cannot be altered by the merciful revivifying
     act of God (Eph 2:1-4). But it does imply that
     God is the one who sovereignly decides who will be
     shown such mercy and who will be decisively and
     finally hardened. It is hardening in this decisive
     sense that meets the demands of the argument in
     Rom 9:1-18.

32. For a comparison of Paul's quotation with the
     Hebrew and LXX texts see p 146. There are only
     two divergences from the LXX: ἵνα becomes ὅπως in
     the first purpose clause and ἰσχύν is changed to
     δύναμιν. Kuss (Roemerbrief, III, 723) may be right
     that both changes are "insignificant." But it is
     also possible that Alford (II, 409) is correct in
     suggesting that δύναμιν is "chosen . . . as more
     general, ἰσχύς applying rather to those deeds of
     miraculous power of which Egypt was then witness."

33. Schlier, Roemerbrief, 297, is right on target when
     he says, "If according to God's will, Israel are
     only Isaac's and not Ishmael's descendants, and if
     God loved Jacob and hated Esau, must one not say
     God is unjust? No! Because (according to Scrip-
     ture) God is only laying claim to his deity
     (Gottsein). God reveals his deity as freedom in
     pitying or hardening action. If God did not hold
     fast to this sovereign freedom, which to be sure
     appears to men as arbitrary; if he did not set his
     'righteousness' in and with this freedom; if he
     let it be dependent on something other than his
     freedom; and if it were measured by something
     other than his θέλειν (and thus by his ἐλεεῖν and
     σκληρύνειν) then he would surrender his deity.
     And with that he would also surrender his
     δικαιοσύνη."

Note from p 162

34. I have not discussed as yet the question of whether
    "mercy" and "hardening" are equally ultimate goals
    in God's plan or whether "σκληρύνειν serves ἐλεεῖν
    as a backdrop" (Weber, Problem der Heilsgeschichte,
    58). The latter may be implicit in the purpose
    clauses of 9:17, but the issue is addressed more
    directly in 9:22f. So we will take it up in the
    next chapter and draw in 9:17 at that point.

NOTES FOR CHAPTER TEN

1. Dodd, Romans, 159f; Forster and Marston, Strategy,
   86; Kaesemann, Romans, 272; Beyschlag, Theodicee,
   68. Those who would end the paragraph after 9:24
   include Kuss, Roemerbrief, III, 730; Gifford, Romans,
   175; Munck, Christ and Israel, 69; Murray, Romans,
   II, 37. Michel (Roemer, 244 note 1) cannot
   decide: "It is difficult in the case of an
   anacoluthon to make an accurate decision."

2. Munck, Christ and Israel, 69: "But here for the
   first time in our passage, the Gentiles are introduced into Heilsgeschichte." But not all agree.
   See Dinkler, "Praedestination," 88 note 19, for a
   strong argument that the second "Israel" in 9:6b
   ("not all those from Israel are Israel") refers to
   "all who belong to the eschatological people
   regardless of any ethnic origin." In other words,
   for him, Paul had Gentiles and Jews in view from
   9:6 onwards.

3. Lagrange (Romains, 236), Sanday and Headlam
   (Romans, 259) and Cranfield (Romans, II, 490) argue
   that the objection is not "No one can resist," but
   rather "No one has in fact ever resisted" (since
   even ostensible resistance achieves God's will).
   But surely this difference is of no great consequence. If no one has ever resisted, it is precisely because no one can. So Schlier (Roemerbrief, 298) is right: "Naturally, what is meant
   by verse 19b is: No one can resist God's will."

4. Luz, Geschichtsverstaendnis, 237: "In his answer
   Paul confirms the opponent's statement, but turns
   against the way the statement is brought forth."

5. They are referring to Lk 7:30 (a pillar text in
   their view): After Jesus' praise for John the
   Baptist we read, "When they heard this, all the
   people and the tax collectors justified God, having
   been baptized with the baptism of John; but the
   Pharisees and the lawyers rejected the purpose
   of God for themselves, not having been baptized by
   him." This text falls far short of proving that
   an individual can frustrate God's purposes for him.
   Forster and Marston assume that "for themselves"
   modifies "the purpose of God" (as indeed the RSV

277

might suggest) but the Greek word order makes it
more probable that it modifies "rejected" (so I.H.
Marshall, Luke, 299). Thus Luke is saying that
the plan of salvation preached by John the Baptist
was accepted by some and rejected by others. The
text cannot prove one way or the other whether God
ordains some individuals irresistibly to eternal
life. For Luke's view on this see Acts 13:48.

6. Romans, 209: "If this objection had been false,
   Paul would not have omitted to refute it."

7. Even Forster and Marston would have to admit this
   in some cases because they think that after the
   fifth plague God gave Pharaoh "supernatural
   strength to continue with his evil path of rebellion" (God's Strategy, 73). In other words it was
   in some sense God's will that for four more plagues
   Pharaoh not let the people of Israel go. Nevertheless, even after God had willed not to let
   Israel go, "The Lord said to Moses: 'Go to
   Pharaoh and say to him, "Thus says the Lord, Let
   my people go!"'" (Ex 8:1). So even in their
   scheme, Forster and Marston have to distinguish
   between God's "will of command" and his "will of
   decree."

8. For example, Gifford, Romans, 182: "Man does
   resist the will of God (θέλημα), that primary will,
   which leads him to repentance, but the event
   always corresponds to the Divine purpose
   (βούλημα)." I doubt that Gifford is right, however, in suggesting that these two wills can be
   assigned respectively to θέλημα and βούλημα. Cf
   θέλει in Rom 9:18 and τὴν βουλὴν τοῦ θελήματος
   αὐτοῦ in Eph 1:11. Also see Murray, Romans, II, 31,
   who says Paul and the objector have in view "not
   the will of precept but the will of determinate
   purpose . . ."

9. Calvin, Institutes, I, 18,3 (where he quotes
   Augustine); III, 20,43; III, 24,16. Jonathan
   Edwards (Works, II, 528): "His will of decree is
   not his will in the same sense as his will of command is. Therefore it is no difficulty at all to
   suppose that the one may be otherwise than the
   other: His will in both senses is his inclination.
   But when we say he wills virtue, or loves virtue
   or the happiness of his creature; thereby is

278

intended that virtue or the creature's happiness,
absolutely and simply considered, is agreeable to
the inclination of his nature. His will of decree
is his inclination to a thing not as to that thing
absolutely and simply, but with reference to the
universality of things. So God though he hates a
thing as it is simply may incline to it with
reference to the universality of things."

10. Mt 1:19 suggests a difference in the θελ- and βουλ-
word groups: "desiring (θέλων) not to make a
public display of her, Joseph planned (ἐβουλήθη)
to put her away." Thus according to Sanday and
Headlam (Romans, 25a) "βουλήματι . . . seems to be
substituted for the ordinary word θέλημα as
implying more definitely the deliberate purpose of
God." Similarly Schrenk, TDNT, I, 636. βούλημα
occurs in the NT only at Acts 27:43; Rom 9:19;
1 Pt 4:3.

11. Cf the conjunction of these words in Eph 1:11.

12. The question, "Who has resisted his will?" has
parallels in Job 9:12; Wis 11:21; 12:12. But "a
sure judgment in the question of literary dependence is in my opinion not possible," Luz,
Geschichtsverstaendnis, 237 note 37.

13. Mensch und freier Wille, 373: "The questioner can
be more closely characterized by comparing Ps Sol
9:4f: he belongs to the Jewish majority which
follows the teaching of the Pharisees. There we
find the conjunction of free will and recompense
that appears in the question in Rom 9:19; and
there God's just recompense is made dependent upon
human performance of righteousness or unrighteousness. Our supposition that Paul formulated Rom 9
in conscious opposition to Ps Sol 9:4f is strengthened therefore also by Rom 9:19 . . . But from
Ps Sol 9:4f, the history of the tradition leads
back to Sir 15:11-20 and from there forward again
to the Sadducees. Therefore, the questioner could
just as easily belong to the circle of the
Sadducees."

14. O. Michel, Roemer, 242: "Among the Rabbis and in
Hellenistic Judaism this imagery is well known and
loved, so that Paul not so much quotes as absorbs
and alludes."

15. C. Mueller, Gottes Gerechtigkeit, 27: "The potter and his activity is, in the OT and in later Judaism, a common figure for the Creator. The question in verse 20 (= Is 29:16) underlines, as does the explanatory verse 21, . . . the unconditional sovereignty of the Creator over his creation." So also Luz, Geschichtsverstaendnis, 239; Schlier, Roemerbrief, 299; Michel, Roemer, 242.

16. Romains, 240. He rejects the idea that "vessels of wrath prepared for destruction" refers back as an explanation to "vessel unto dishonor" for that would turn the parable into an allegory: "It is a matter of simple reminiscence; the terms employed in that comparison suggest others which this time are symbolic, without parabolic argumentation."

17. Christ and Israel, 67: "It may be questioned whether σκεῦη [in verses 22f] has the same significance as in verse 21."

18. Holding this same view are Alford (II, 411), Sanday and Headlam (Romans, 261), Murray (Romans, II, 33 note 41), Luz (Geschichtsverstaendnis, 242), Maier (Mensch und freier Wille, 378).

19. It is used in Mt 7:13; 26:8 = Mk 14:4; Jn 17:12; Acts 8:20; Phil 1:28; 3:19; 2 Thess 2:3; 1 Tim 6:9; Heb 10:39; 2 Pt 2:1,3; 3:7,16; Rev 17:8,11; and probably only Mt 26:8par lacks the eschatological sense. Sanday and Headlam, Romans, 266: "We cannot . . . minimize the force of the words by limiting them to a purely earthly destination . . . The use of the words εἰς δόξαν, εἰς ἀπώλειαν prove conclusively that he is looking as much as he ever does to the final end and destination of man." So also Schlier, Roemerbrief, 301, and Oepke, TDNT, I, 396.

20. Even Cranfield, who says (Romans, II, 495 note 4) that the vessels of 9:22f "are not to be taken as interpreting the vessels" of 9:21, still admits that the δέ at the beginning of 9:22 "makes the connexion between Paul's similitude [9:21] and what is, in effect, his application of it [9:22f]."

21. Meyer, Romans, II, 146: "In the application of the simile, the same lump denotes human nature in and

by itself, as it is alike in all with its opposite
moral capabilities and dispositions, but not yet
conceived of in its definite individual moral
stamp. Out of this, like the potter out of the
clay-dough which is susceptible of various molding,
God--who does not merely 'allow to come into
being' the different moral quality of individuals,
in order then to fulfill on them the ἐλεεῖν or
σκληρύνειν which he will (Hoffmann), but effec-
tively produces it--makes partly such as are destined to stand in honor (namely as partakers of
the Messianic glory), partly such as are to stand
in dishonor (namely, through the eternal
ἀπώλεια)."

22. Meyer, **Romans**, II, 147: "Wilt thou still be able
to venture the ἀνταποκρίνεσθαι τῷ θεῷ of ver 20?
Must thou not utterly become dumb with thy
replies?" Gifford, **Romans**, 173: "What further
objection can you make against his justice?"
Lagrange, **Romains**, 239: "What will there be to
say? All will be in order." Cranfield, **Romans**, II,
493: "What wilt thou say?" Munck, **Christ and
Israel**, 60: "Then no one would have the right to
protest against God's all powerful dealings."

23. One might object that the proximity of the main
verb ἤνεγκεν demands that ἵνα be dependent on that
verb instead of on the distant θέλων (Schlatter,
Gottes Gerechtigkeit, 305). I agree that this is
possible and that we cannot be dogmatic in our
reconstructions of the grammar here. But this is
not too troublesome because I cannot see much
difference in meaning between "God endured because
he desired to make known his glory" and "God
endured in order to make known his glory."

24. For those who, unlike Murray, view the ἵνα of 9:23
as grammatically dependent on the verb "endured"
in 9:22, the καί before ἵνα still signifies that
the purpose expressed in the ἵνα is coordinate
with some other previously stated purpose. On the
one hand, the commentators who construe the θέλων
of 9:22 as concessive (Sanday and Headlam, **Romans**,
261; Morison, **Exposition**, 155) cannot coordinate
the ἵνα-clause of 9:23 with θέλων or its infinitives because a concessive idea is not logically
coordinate with a purpose idea. Therefore, they
generally argue that "the καί couples ἵνα γνωρίσῃ

281

in thought with ἐν πολλῇ μακροθυμίᾳ" in 9:22
(Sanday and Headlam, Romans, 262): "God endures
in much long-suffering . . . and in order to make
known his glory . . ." On the other hand, the
commentators who construe θέλων causally recognize
that the καί before ἵνα in 9:23 probably is
reaching back to the purposive ideas expressed in
the infinitives of 9:22 (cf Cranfield, Romans, II,
494; Barrett, Romans, 190). Therefore, while not
viewing the ἵνα of 9:23 as dependent on the θέλων
of 9:22 (as I do) these commentators nevertheless
end up with an interpretation not substantially
different from my own.

25. Besides those already mentioned, cf Bornkamm,
"Anakoluthe," 91; Gifford, Romans, 174; Lagrange,
Romains, 239; Zahn, Roemer, 457; Michel, Roemer,
243 note 4; Kaesemann, Romans, 271; Kuss, Roemerbrief, III, 732.

26. The meaning "sustain and tolerate" for φέρω
(ἤνεγκεν in 9:22) is suggested by Weiss in TDNT, IX,
59, on the basis of Heb 1:3 (Christ "sustains" the
universe) and Heb 13:13 ("enduring" abuse; cf
Josephus Ant xii 342).

27. Beyschlag, Theodicee, 62: "The patience of God
refers to his leaving room and time for repentance
(4:24), but how could God wait for a repentance
from those from whom he has withdrawn the possibility
of repentance? So in the Calvinistic conception
the noble expression of love, which we call
patience, becomes a heartless preservation for
judgment for the sake of others."

28. J. Horst, TDNT, IV, 382f: "While τὸ χρηστὸν τοῦ
θεοῦ in Rom 2:4 leads to μετάνοια . . . it has
also to be recalled that the capital of wrath
(θησαυρίζεις) increases with the μακροθυμία shown,
and this side is emphasized even more clearly in
Rom 9:22. Here the reason for μακροθυμία is not
so much to allow time for repentance. The delay
is simply to bring out more clearly what God
already wills (θέλων) and knows, but allows to come
to plain fulfilment in man." H.A.W. Meyer, Romans,
II, 150: μακροθυμία in Rom 9:22 "is not that which
waits for the self-decision of human freedom . . .,
especially for amendment . . ., but that which
delays the penal judgment (cf Lk 18:7), the

prolongatio irae, Jer 15:15 et al. The passage
Rom 2:4f is no protest against this view, since
the apostle does not there, as in the present
passage, place himself at the standpoint of the
absolute divine will." Cf also Lietzmann, Roemer,
93, and Kuss, Roemerbrief, III, 732.

29. Michel, Roemer, 244: both the passive "fitted"
and the active "he prepared before" "point back to
the pretemporal-prehistorical action of God." So
also Kaesemann, Romans, 271; Kuss, Roemerbrief, III,
732 f; Luz, Geschichtsverstaendnis, 245; Maier,
Mensch und freier Wille, 381; Calvin, Romans, 212.

30. K. Mueller, Zuvorersehung, 16: "Certainly
κατηρτισμένα cannot mean that they fit themselves
for destruction; nor can it be given merely an
adjectival meaning. The lost have to be fit for
destruction--by whom? That remains a mystery,
exactly as in 1 Cor 1:18; 2 Cor 2:15."

31. Cf Michel, Roemer, 244; Kaesemann, Romans, 272;
Luz, Geschichtsverstaendnis, 244; Maier, Mensch
und freier Wille, 381.

32. Gifford, Romans, 174: the ἵνα clause "is a direct
and primary purpose . . ."; Zahn, Roemer, 459;
Calvin, Romans, 212: "God's chief praise consists
in acts of kindness"; Kaesemann, Romans, 271: "Salvation and perdition are not counterbalanced, as might
at first appear. Chapter 11 will show explicitly
that perdition serves salvation." Luz
(Geschichtsverstaendnis, 242 note 57) uses most of
the same arguments as Cranfield. On the other
side see Lagrange, Romains, 241.

33. This is an excerpt from his as yet unpublished
typescript, The Unity of the Bible (Pasadena:
Fuller Theological Seminary, 1973), pp xx,4,5.

34. Cf F. Davidson, Predestination, 13: "Mercy apparently cannot be conceived apart from its pure
negation, σκληρύνει. Hence even the merciful disposition of God cannot be rightly apprehended,
except through the conception of the absence of
mercy . . ." Similarly, Jonathan Edwards (Works,
II, 528) argued as follows: "It is proper that
the shining forth of God's glory be complete; that
is, that all parts of his glory should shine forth,

that every beauty should be proportionably effulgent, that the beholder may have a proper notion
of God. It is not proper that one glory should be
exceedingly manifested, and another not at all;
for then the effulgence would not answer the
reality. For the same reason it is not proper
that one should be manifested exceedingly, and
another but very little. It is highly proper that
the effulgent glory of God should answer his real
excellency; that the splendor should be answerable
to the real and essential glory, for the same
reason that it is proper and excellent for God to
glorify himself at all. Thus it is necessary that
God's awful majesty, his authority and dreadful
greatness, justice and holiness, should be manifested. But this could not be unless sin and punishment had been decreed; so that the shining
forth of God's glory would be very imperfect, both
because these parts of divine glory would not
shine forth as the others do, and also the glory
of his goodness, love, and holiness would be
faint without them; nay, they could scarcely shine
forth at all. If it were not right that God
should decree and permit and punish sin, there
could be no manifestation of God's holiness in
hatred of sin, or in showing any preference, in
his providence, of godliness before it. There
would be no manifestation of God's grace or true
goodness, if there was no sin to be pardoned, no
misery to be saved from. How much happiness
soever be bestowed, his goodness would not be so
much prized and admired, and the sense of it not
so great . . ."

35. Fuller appends a note at this point which may be
found helpful in reflecting on the problem of
human accountability (Unity of the Bible, xx, 6):
"It should be pointed out that in 9:19-24 Paul is
not answering the question how men are responsible
for their actions, but the question of how the
sovereign God is righteous to inflict punishment
on evil. It is Romans 1:18-20 which answers the
question why men who are slaves of sin are themselves without excuse so that their punishment is
just. Here the basis of men's accountability lies
in their having access to the knowledge that God
should be worshipped as God. The fact that they
do not want to worship God, and in their rebellion
hold down the truth that God should be worshipped,

does not excuse them at all from being responsible
to worship God. We should note how our own con-
sciences work exactly on this principle. Our con-
sciences condemn us for failure to do right when
the reason for that failure is, simply, that we
wanted to do something else. But if the failure
is . . . [caused by some force to which our strongest motive and volition is opposed (e.g. the
unavailability of knowledge or some bodily incapac-
ity)] then conscience lies quiet. Why conscience
should do this when motives are ultimately a given
is, in my opinion, simply a reflection of the fact
that God is sovereign (so motives are given) and
yet glorious (so conscience accuses for failure to
do right brought about simply by motives). If God
is God, it could not be otherwise."

NOTE FOR CHAPTER ELEVEN

Note from p 205

1. On the way true Christian hope necessarily leads to
    a life of loving service, see my article "Hope as
    the Motivation of Love: 1 Peter 3:9-12."

BIBLIOGRAPHY

Alford, H., The Greek Testament, vol 2, Chicago 1968.
Althaus, P., Der Brief an die Roemer, NTD 6, Goettingen 1966.
Anselm, St., Basic Writings, trans S.N. Deane, Lasalle, Illinois 1962.
Baldensperger, W., Die Messianisch-Apokalyptischen Hoffnungen des Judentums, Strassburg 1903.
Barrett, C.K., The Epistle to the Romans, HNTC, New York 1957.
Barrett, C.K., Reading Through Romans, Philadelphia 1977.
Barth, K., Church Dogmatics, 2/2, Edinburgh ET, 1957.
Bauer, W., A Greek-English Lexicon of the New Testament, Cambridge ET, 1957.
Beasley-Murray, G.R., "The Righteousness of God in the History of Israel and the Nations: Romans 9-11," RevExp 73, 1976, pp 437-50.
Becker, J., Das Heil Gottes, Goettingen 1964.
Beer, G., Exodus, HAT 3, Tuebingen 1939.
Bengel, J.A., Gnomon, Band II, trans C.F. Werner, Stuttgart 1970.
Benoit, P., "La question juive selon Rom IX-XI d'après K.L. Schmidt," RB 55, 1948, pp 310-12.
Betz, O., "Die heilsgeschichtliche Rolle Israels bei Paulus," TheolBeit 9, 1978, pp 1-21.
Beyerlin, W., Herkunft und Geschichte der aeltesten Sinaitradition, Tuebingen 1961.
Beyschlag, W., Die paulinische Theodicee, Roemer IX-XI: Ein Beitrag zur biblischen Theologie, Halle 1868.
Blackman, C., "Divine Sovereignty and Missionary Strategy in Romans 9-11," CJT XI, 1965, pp 124-34.
Blackman, C., "Romans 3:26b: A Question of Translation," JBL 87, 1968, pp 203f.
Blass, F., and A. Debrunner, Grammatik des neutl. Griechisch, 13th ed, Goettingen 1970.
Bornkamm, G., "Der Lobpreis Gottes (Roemer 11:33-36)" in: Das Ende des Gesetzes, Munich 1952, pp 70-75.
Bornkamm, G., "Die Frage nach der Gerechtigkeit Gottes (Theodizee und Rechtfertigung)" in: Das Ende des Gesetzes, Munich 1952, pp 196-210.
Bornkamm, G., "Die oekumenische Bedeutung der historisch-kritischen Bibelwissenschaft" in: Geschichte und Glaube, Munich 1971, pp 11-20.
Bornkamm, G., "Paulinische Anakoluthe in Roemerbrief" in: Das Ende des Gesetzes, Munich 1952, pp 76-92.
Bornkamm, G., "Theologie als Teufelskunst, Roemer 3:1-9" in: Geschichte und Glaube, Zweiter Teil, Munich 1971, pp 140-48.

Bousset, W., Die Religion des Judentums in neutestament-
lichen Zeitalter, Berlin 1903.
Bowker, J., Jesus and the Pharisees, Cambridge 1973.
Brauch, M.T., "Perspectives on 'God's righteousness' in
recent German discussion" in: E.P. Sanders, Paul and
Palestinian Judaism, Philadelphia 1977, pp 523-42.
Bultmann, R., "ΔΙΚΑΙΟΣΎΝΗ ΘΕΟΫ," JBL 83, 1964, pp 12-16.
Bultmann, R., "Geschichte und Eschatologie im NT" in:
Glauben und Verstehen. Gesammelte Aufsaetze III,
Tuebingen 1960, pp 91-106.
Bultmann, R., Theology of the New Testament, vols 1 & 2,
New York 1951, 1955.
Bush, G., Notes, Critical and Practical, on the Book of
Exodus, 2 vols, Chicago 1881.
Caird, G.B., "Predestination - Romans 9-11," ET 68, 1957,
pp 324-27.
Calvin, J., The Epistles of Paul the Apostle to the
Romans and to the Thessalonians, trans Ross Mackenzie,
Grand Rapids 1973.
Cambier, J., "La doctrine paulinienne de la justice de
Dieu, principe d'unité dans l'Eglise et source de
paix dans le monde" in: Verborum Veritas, eds O.
Boecher, K. Haacker, Wuppertal 1970, pp 159-70.
Cambier, J., L'évangile de Dieu selon L'épître aux
Romains, Tome 1, Studia Neotestamentica 3, Paris
1967.
Cerfaux, L., The Church in the Theology of St. Paul,
New York 1959.
Cerfaux, L., "Le privilège d'Israel selon saint Paul"
in: Recueil Lucien Cerfaux, vol 2, Gembloux 1954,
pp 337-64.
Charles, R.H., The Apocrypha and Pseudepigrapha of the
Old Testament, 2 vols, Oxford 1913.
Childs, B.S., The Book of Exodus, A Critical Theological
Commentary, Philadelphia 1974.
Childs, B.S., "The Canonical Shape of the Prophetic
Literature," Interp XXXII, 1978, pp 46-55.
Cohen, A., Everyman's Talmud, New York 1949.
Conzelmann, H., An Outline of the Theology of the New
Testament, New York ET, 1969.
Conzelmann, H., "Die Rechtfertingungslehre des Paulus:
Theologie oder Anthropologie?" in: Theologie als
Schriftauslegung, Munich 1974, pp 191-206.
Corley, B., "The Jews, the Future and God (Romans
9-11)," Southwestern Journal of Theology 19, 1976, pp
42-56.
Corley, B., The Significance of Romans 9-11: A Study
in Pauline Theology, Diss. Southwestern Baptist
Theological Seminary, 1975.
Cosgrove, C., "The Mosaic Law Preaches Faith: A Study
in Galatians 3," WJT 41, 1978, pp 146-64.

Cranfield, C.E.B., A Critical and Exegetical Commentary on the Epistle to the Romans, 2 vols, Edinburgh 1975 and 1979.
Cranfield, C.E.B., "Some Notes on Romans 9:30-33" in: Jesus und Paulus, eds W.G. Kuemmel, E.E. Ellis, Goettingen 1975, pp 35-43.
Cremer, H., Die paulinische Rechtfertigungslehre, Guetersloh 1899.
Cruesemann, F., "Jahwes Gerechtigkeit," EvTh 36, 1976, pp 427-50.
Cullmann, O., The Christology of the New Testament, Philadelphia ET, 1963.
Dahl, N.A., Das Volk Gottes, Eine Untersuchung zum Kirchenbewusstsein des Urchristentums, Darmstadt 1963.
Dalmer, J., Die Erwaehlung Israels nach der Heilsverkuendigung des Apostels Paulus, Guetersloh 1894.
Danby, H., The Mishnah, Oxford 1933.
Dantine, W., "Rechtfertigung und Gottesgerechtigkeit," Verkuendigung und Forschung 11, 1966, pp 68-100.
Davidson, F., Pauline Predestination, London 1945.
Davies, G.H., Exodus: Introduction and Commentary, London 1967.
Davies, W.D., Paul and Rabbinic Judaism, New York 1948.
Delling, G., Der Kreuzestod Jesu in der urchristlichen Verkuendigung, Goettingen 1972.
Denney, J., Commentary on Romans in: The Expositor's Greek Testament, II, London 1900.
Dibelius, M., Paulus, Berlin 1970.
Dietzfelbinger, C., Heilsgeschichte bei Paulus, Munich 1965.
Dillmann, A., Die Buecher Exodus und Leviticus, EHAT 12, Leipzig 1897.
Dinkler, E., "The Idea of History in Earliest Christianity" in: Signum Crucis, Tuebingen 1967, pp 313-50.
Dinkler, E., "Praedestination bei Paulus: Exegetische Bemerkungen zum Roemerbrief" in: Festschrift fuer Gunther Dehn, ed W. Schneemelcher, Neukirchen 1957, pp 81-102.
Dion, H.M., "La prédestination chez saint Paul," Recherches de Science Religieuse 53, 1965, pp 5-43.
Dion, H.M., "Predestination in Saint Paul," Theological Digest 15, 1967, pp 144-49.
Dobschuetz, E. von, "Praedestination," Theologische Studien und Kritiken 106, 1934.
Dodd, C.H., The Bible and the Greeks, London 1935.
Dodd, C.H., The Epistle of Paul to the Romans, MNTC, New York 1932.
Dodd, C.H., "ΙΛΑΣΚΕΣΘΑΙ, Its Cognates, Derivatives and Synonyms in the Septuagint," JTS 32, 1931, pp 352-60.
Doeve, J.W., "Some Notes with Reference to ta logia tou theou in Romans 3:2" in: Studia Paulina in Honorem Johannis de Zwann, Haarlem 1953, pp 111-23.

Donfried, K.P., The Romans Debate, Minneapolis 1977.
Driver, S.R., The Book of Exodus, Cambridge 1929.
Dupont-Sommer, A., The Essene Writings from Qumran, Oxford 1961.
Edwards, J., The Works of Jonathan Edwards, 2 vols, Edinburgh 1974.
Eichholz, G., Die Theologie des Paulus in Umriss, Neukirchen-Vluyn 1972.
Eichrodt, W., Theologie des Alten Testaments, Teil 1, Berlin 1948.
Eichrodt, W., Theology of the Old Testament, 2 vols, Philadelphia 1961.
Ellicott, C.J., A Critical and Grammatical Commentary on the Pastoral Epistles, Minneapolis 1978 reprint, original, 1861.
Ellingworth, P., "Translation and Exegesis: A Case Study (Rom 9:22ff)," Biblica 59, 1978, pp 396-402.
Ellis, E.E., Paul's Use of the Old Testament, Edinburgh 1957.
Ellison, H.L., The Mystery of Israel, Grand Rapids 1966.
Epstein, I., ed, The Babylonian Talmud, London 1935.
Erasmus, D., On the Freedom of the Will in: Luther and Erasmus: Free Will and Salvation, eds E.G. Rupp and P.S. Watson, Philadelphia 1969, pp 35-100.
Ernst, J., Schriftauslegung, Beitraege zur Hermeneutik des N.T. und im N.T., Munich 1972.
Fahlgren, K.Hj., "Die Gegensaetze von ṣedākā im AT" (1932) in: Um das Prinzip der Vergeltung in Religion und Recht des AT, Darmstadt 1972, pp 87-129.
Fahy, T., "A Note on Romans 9:1-18," Irish Theological Quarterly, 1966, pp 261f.
Feuillet, A., "Le plan salvifique de Dieu," RB 57, 1950, pp 336-87.
Fichtner, J., "Zum Problem Glaube und Geschichte in der israelitisch-juedischen Weisheitsliteratur," TLZ, 1951, pp 145-50.
Fitzer, G., "Der Ort der Versoehnung nach Paulus," ThZ 22, 1966, pp 161-83.
Flueckiger, F., "Christus, des Gesetzes telos," ThZ 11, 1955, pp 153-57.
Forster, R.T., and V.P. Marston, God's Strategy in Human History, Wheaton 1973.
Fridrichsen, A., "Nochmals Roemer 3,7-8," ZNW 34, 1935, 306-08.
Fuller, D.P., Gospel and Law: Contrast or Continuum?, Grand Rapids 1980.
Fuller, D.P., "Paul and the Works of the Law," WJT 38, 1975, pp 28-42.
Fuller, D.P., Unity of the Bible, Pasadena 1973.

292

Furnish, V.P., "The Historical Criticism of the New
  Testament: A Survey of Origins," BJRL 56, 1974, pp
  336-70.
Giblin, C.H., In Hope of God's Glory. Pauline Theologi-
  cal Perspectives, New York 1970.
Gifford, E.H., Epistle of St. Paul to the Romans,
  London 1886.
Glueck, N., Das Wort hesed im alttestamentlichen Sprach-
  gebrauche, Berlin 1961.
Gnilka, J., Die Verstockung Israels: Isaias 6,9-10 in
  der Theologie der Synoptiker, Munich 1961.
Godet, F., Commentary on St. Paul's Epistle to the
  Romans, New York ET, 1883.
Goppelt, L., Christentum und Judentum im ersten und
  zweiten Jahrhundert, Guetersloh 1954.
Goppelt, L., "Israel und die Kirche, heute und bei
  Paulus" in: Christologie und Ethik, Goettingen 1968,
  pp 165-89.
Goppelt, L., Theologie des Neuen Testaments, Teil 2,
  Vielfalt und Einheit des apostolischen Christuszeug-
  nisses, Goettingen 1976.
Goppelt, L., "Tradition nach Paulus," Kerygma and Dogma
  4, 1958, pp 213-33.
Gore, C., "The Argument of Rom. IX-XI" in Studia
  Biblica et Ecclesiastica 3, Oxford 1891, pp 37-45.
Graham, H.H., "Continuity and Discontinuity in the
  Thought of Paul," ATR 38, 1956, pp 137-46.
Guettgemanns, E., "'Gottesgerechtigkeit' und stukturale
  Semantik. Linguistische Analyse zu dikaiosunē theou"
  in: Studia Linguistica Neotestamentica, Munich 1971,
  pp 59-98.
Guettgemanns, E., "Heilsgeschichte bei Paulus oder
  Dynamik des Evangeliums? Zur strukturellen Relevanz
  von Roemer 9-11 fuer die Theologie des Roemerbriefs"
  (1970) in: Studia Linguistica Neotestamentica,
  Munich 1971, pp 34-58.
Gyllenberg, R., Rechtfertigung und Altes Testament bei
  Paulus, Stuttgart 1973.
Hall, J., A Critical and Exegetical Commentary on the
  Book of Exodus, New York 1881.
Harrison, E.F., "Romans" in: The Expositor's Bible
  Commentary 10, ed Frank E. Gaebelein, Grand Rapids
  1976, pp 1-172.
Hatch, E., and H. Redpath, A Concordance to the Sep-
  tuagint, 2 vols, Graz 1975.
Helfgott, B.W., The Doctrine of Election in Tannaitic
  Literature, New York 1954.
Hesse, F., Das Verstockungsproblem im Alten Testament,
  Berlin 1955.
Hill, D., Greek Words and Hebrew Meanings: Studies in
  the Semantics of Soteriological Terms, SNTS Monograph
  Series 5, Cambridge 1967.

Hodge, C., A Commentary on the Epistle to the Romans, Philadelphia 1870.

Hoppe, T., Die Idee der Heilsgeschichte bei Paulus, Guetersloh 1926.

Huby, J., Saint Paul Épître aux Romains, Verbum Salutis X, Paris 1957.

Huebner, H., "Existentiale Interpretation der paulinischen Gerechtigkeit Gottes: Zur Kontroverse Rudolf Bultmann - Ernst Kaesemann," NTS 21, 1975, pp 462-88.

Hunter, A.M., Introducing the New Testament, Philadelphia 1975.

Huonder, V., Israel Sohn Gottes, Orbis Biblicus et Orientalis 6, Goettingen 1975.

Hyatt, J.P., Commentary on Exodus, New Century Bible, London 1971.

Jenni, E., ed, Theologisches Handwoerterbuch zum Alten Testament, 2 vols, Munich 1971.

Jervell, J., "The Letter to Jerusalem" in: The Romans Debate, ed K.P. Donfried, Minneapolis 1977, pp 61-74.

Kaesemann, E., An die Roemer, HNT 8a, 2nd ed, Tuebingen 1974.

Kaesemann, E., Commentary on Romans, Grand Rapids ET, 1980.

Kaesemann, E., "Justice for the Unjust," Colloquium 1, 1978, pp 10-16.

Kaesemann, E., "On the Subject of Primitive Christian Apocalyptic" in: New Testament Questions of Today, Philadelphia 1969, pp 108-27.

Kaesemann, E., "Rechtfertigung und Heilsgeschichte in Roemerbrief" in: Paulinischen Perspectiven, Tuebingen 1969, pp 108-39.

Kaesemann, E., "The Righteousness of God in Paul" in: New Testament Questions Today, Philadelphia 1969, pp 168-82.

Kaesemann, E., "Zum Verstaendnis von Roemer 3,24-26" in: Exegetische Versuche und Besinnungen, I, Goettingen 1960, pp 96-100.

Kaiser, O., Der Prophet Jesaja, Kapitel 1-12, ATD 17, Goettingen 1970.

Kautzsch, E., Die Derivate des Stammes צדק im alttestamentlichen Sprachgebrauch, Tuebingen 1881.

Kautzsch, E., ed, Gesenius' Hebrew Grammar, Oxford 1910.

Keil, C.F., and F. Delitzsch, Biblical Commentary on the Old Testament, Isaiah, vol 1, Grand Rapids 1969.

Keil, C.F., and F. Delitzsch, Biblical Commentary on the Old Testament, The Books of Ezra, Nehemiah and Esther, Grand Rapids 1969.

Keil, C.F., and F. Delitzsch, Biblical Commentary on the Old Testament, The Minor Prophets, vol 2, Grand Rapids 1971.

Keil, C.F., and F. Delitzsch, Biblical Commentary on the Old Testament, The Pentateuch, 2 vols, Grand Rapids 1968.

Kertelge, K., 'Rechtfertigung' bei Paulus, Muenster 1967.

Kidner, D., Psalms 73-150, TOTC, Downers Grove 1975.

Klein, G., "Bibel und Heilsgeschichte. Die Fragwuerdigkeit einer Idee," ZNW 62, 1971, pp 1-47.

Klein, G., "Gottes Gerechtigkeit als Thema der neuesten Paulus-Forschung" in: Rekonstruktion und Interpretation, Munich 1969, pp 225-36.

Klein, G., "Roemer 4 und die Idee der Heilsgeschichte" in: Rekonstruktion und Interpretation, Munich 1969, pp 145-69.

Kotansky, R.D., "A Note on Romans 9:6: ho logos tou theou as the Proclamation of the Gospel," SBT VII, April, 1977, pp 24-30.

Kramer, W., Christos Kyrios Gottessohn, Zurich 1963.

Kuehl, E., Der Brief des Paulus an die Roemer, Leipzig 1913.

Kuehl, E., Zur paulinischen Theodicee, Goettingen 1897.

Kuemmel, W.G., "Die Probleme von Roemer 9-11 in der gegenwaertigen Forschungslage" in: Die Israel Frage nach Roemer 9-11, ed L. DeLorenzi, Rome 1977, pp 14-33.

Kuemmel, W.G., "πάρεσις und ἔνδειξις," ZThK 49, 1952, pp 154-67.

Kuhl, C., The Prophets of Israel, Richmond 1960.

Kuss, O., Der Roemerbrief. Dritte Lieferung (Roemer 8,19-11,36), Regensburg 1978.

Kuss, O., Der Roemerbrief. Erste Lieferung (Roemer 1,1-6,11), Regensburg 1957.

Kuss, O., "Ueber die Klarheit der Schrift: Historische und hermeneutische Ueberlegungen zu der Kontroverse des Erasmus und des Luther ueber den freien oder versklavten Willen" in: Schriftauslegung, ed Josef Ernst, Munich 1972, pp 89-149.

Kuss, O., "Zur Geschichtstheologie der paulinischen Hauptbriefe," Theologie und Glaube 46, 1956, pp 241-60.

Kuyper, L.J., "The Hardness of Heart according to Biblical Perspective," SJT 27, 1974, pp 459-74.

Ladd, G.E., "Righteousness in Romans," Southwestern Journal of Theology 1976, pp 6-17.

Ladd, G.E., A Theology of the New Testament, Grand Rapids 1974.

Lagrange, M.J., Saint Paul Épître aux Romains, Paris 1950.

Lange, J.P., Exodus or the Second Book of Moses, New York 1876.

Leenhardt, F.J., The Epistle to the Romans, A Commentary, London ET, 1961.
Lekkerkerker, A.F.N., Roemer 7 und Roemer 9 bei Augustine, Amsterdam 1942.
Liechtenhan, R., Die goettliche Vorherbestimmung bei Paulus und in der posidonianischen Philosophie, FRLANT 35, Goettingen 1922.
Lietzmann, H., Roemer, HNT 8, Tuebingen 1971.
Ljungvik, H., "Zum Roemerbrief 3,7-8," ZNW 32, 1933, pp 207-10.
Lohse, E., "Die Gerechtigkeit Gottes in der paulinischen Theologie" in: Die Einheit des NT, Goettingen 1973, pp 209-28.
Lohse, E., ed, Die Texte aus Qumran, Darmstadt 1971.
Lohse, E., Martyrer und Gottesknecht, Goettingen 1955.
Luck, U., "Gerechtigkeit in der Welt - Gerechtigkeit Gottes," Wort und Dienst 12, 1973, pp 71-89.
Luehrmann, D., "Der Verweis auf die Erfahrung und die Frage nach der Gerechtigkeit" in: Jesus Christus in Historie und Theologie, ed Georg Strecker, Tuebingen 1975, pp 185-96.
Luehrmann, D., "Rechtfertigung und Versoehnung. Zur Geschichte der paulinischen Tradition," ZThK 67, 1970, pp 437-52.
Luther, M., Lectures on Romans, Library of Christian Classics XV, Philadelphia 1961.
Luther, M., On the Bondage of the Will in: Luther and Erasmus: Free Will and Salvation, eds E.G. Rupp and P.S. Watson, Philadelphia 1969, pp 101-334.
Luz, U., Das Geschichtsverstaendnis des Paulus, Munich 1968.
Lyonnet, S., "De doctrina praedestinationis et reprobationis in Rom 9," Verbum Domini 34, 1956, pp 193-201, 257-71.
Mach, R., Der Zaddik in Talmud und Midrasch, Leiden 1957.
Maier, G., Mensch und freier Wille nach den juedischen Religionsparteien zwischen Ben Sira und Paulus, WUNT 12, Tuebingen 1971.
Maier, W., "Paul's Concept of Justification, and Some Recent Interpretation of Romans 3:21-31," Springfielder 37, 1974, pp 248-64.
Marquardt, F.W., Die Juden im Roemerbrief, Theologische Studien 107, Zurich 1971.
Marshall, I.H., Commentary on Luke, NIGTC, Grand Rapids 1978.
Martin, R., New Testament Foundations, 2 vols, Grand Rapids 1975.
Martyr, J., Writings of Saint Justin Martyr, trans Thomas B. Falls, in: The Fathers of the Church, ed Ludwig Schapp, New York 1948.

Metzger, B., A Textual Commentary on the Greek New Testament, London 1971.
Meyer, H.A.W., Critical and Exegetical Handbook to the Epistle to the Romans, 2nd ed, vol 2, Edinburgh ET, 1876.
Michel, O., Der Brief an die Roemer, MK, Goettingen 1966.
Michel, O., "Opferbereitschaft fuer Israel" in: In Memoriam Ernst Lohmeyer, ed Werner Schmauch, Stuttgart 1951, pp 94-100.
Mihaly, E., "A Rabbinic Defense on the Election of Israel," Hebrew Union College Annual 25, 1964, pp 103-35.
Minear, P.S., The Obedience of Faith: The Purposes of Paul in the Epistle to the Romans, Naperville 1971.
Montefiore, C.G., Judaism and St. Paul, New York 1915.
Montefiore, C.G., and H. Loewe, A Rabbinic Anthology, New York 1974.
Moore, G.F., Judaism in the First Centuries of the Christian Era, 3 vols, Cambridge 1927.
Moore, G.M., Judaism, vols 1 & 2, Cambridge 1955.
Morison, J., Exposition of the Ninth Chapter of the Epistle to the Romans, London 1888.
Morris, L., The Apostolic Preaching of the Cross, Grand Rapids 1965.
Morris, L., "The Meaning of Hilastērion in Romans 3:25," NTS 2, 1955, pp 33-43.
Moule, C.F.D., An Idiom-Book of New Testament Greek, 2nd ed, Cambridge 1959.
Moulton, J.H., and N. Turner, A Grammar of New Testament Greek, vol 3, Edinburgh 1963.
Mueller, C., Gottes Gerechtigkeit und Gottesvolk. Eine Untersuchung zu Roemer 9-11, Goettingen 1964.
Mueller, K., Die goettliche Zuvorersehung und Erwaehlung in ihrer Bedeutung fuer den Heilsstand des einzelnen Glaeubigen nach dem Evangelium des Paulus, Halle 1892.
Munck, J., Christ and Israel: An Interpretation of Romans 9-11, Philadelphia 1967.
Murphy, R.E., "Psalms" in: Jerome Biblical Commentary, ed R.E. Brown, Englewood Cliffs, New Jersey 1968.
Murray, J., The Epistle to the Romans, vols 1 & 2, NIC, Grand Rapids 1968.
Nicole, R., "C.H. Dodd and the Doctrine of Propitiation," WJT 17, 1955, pp 117-57.
Nicole, R., "Hilaskesthai Revisited," EQ 49, 1977, pp 173-77.
Nissen, A., Gott und der Naechste im antiken Judentum, WUNT 15, Tuebingen 1974.
Noack, B., "Celui qui court. Rom. IX, 16," StTh 24, 1970, pp 113-16.
Noth, M., Exodus: A Commentary, Philadelphia 1962.
Nygren, A., Commentary on Romans, Philadelphia 1949.

Oepke, A., "Dikaiosunē theou bei Paulus in neuer
Beleuchtung," TLZ 78, 1953, pp 257-64.
Oesterreicher, J.M., "Israel's Misstep and Her Rise.
The Dialectic of God's Saving Design in Rom. 9-11,"
Analectica Biblica 17-18, 1963, pp 317-27.
Oesterreicher, J.M., The Israel of God, Englewood Cliffs
1963.
Olivieri, O., "Quid ergo amplius Iudaeo est? Rom
3:1-8," Biblica 10, 1929, pp 31-52.
Olley, J.W., 'Righteousness' in the Septuagint of
Isaiah: A Contextual Study, Missoula 1978.
Pedersen, F.N., "Roemer 9. Eine Studie ueber paul-
inische Praedestinations-verkuendigung," Dansk
Teologisk Tiddskrift XVII, 1954, pp 138-72.
Pfitzner, V.C., Paul and the Agon Motif, Leiden 1967.
Piper, J., "Hope as the Motivation for Love: I Peter
3:9-12," NTS 26, 1979, pp 212-31.
Plag, C., Israels Weg zum Heil, Stuttgart 1969.
Plummer, W.S., Commentary on Romans, Grand Rapids 1971.
Pluta, A., Gottes Bundestreue. Ein Schluesselbegriff
in Roemer 3:25a, Stuttgart 1969.
Plutta-Messerschmidt, E., Gerechtigkeit Gottes bei
Paulus, Eine Studie zu Luthers Auslegung von Roemer
3:5, Tuebingen 1973.
Pohlenz, M., Vom Zorn Gottes, FRLANT 12, Goettingen
1909.
Price, J.L., "God's Righteousness Shall Prevail,"
Interp 28, 1974, pp 259-80.
Quispel, G., "Zeit und Geschichte im antiken Christen-
tum," Eranos-Jahrbuch, 1951.
Räisänen, H., The Idea of Divine Hardening. A Com-
parative Study of the Notion of Divine Hardening,
Leading Astray and Inciting to Evil in the Bible and
Qur'an, Publications of the Finnish Exegetical
Society 25, Helsinki 1972.
Reichrath, H., "Roemer 9-11: Ein Stiefkind christlicher
Theologie und Verkuendigung," Judaica 23, 1967,
pp 160-81.
Rese, M., "Die Vorzuege Israels in Roem 9,4-5 und Eph
2,12," ThZ 31, 1975, pp 211-22.
Richardson, P., Israel in the Apostolic Church, SNTS
10, Cambridge 1969.
Ridderbos, H., Paul, An Outline of His Theology, Grand
Rapids 1975.
Roetzel, C., "Diathēkai in Romans 9:4," Biblica 51,
1970, pp 377-90.
Rost, L., Einleitung in die alttestamentlichen Apokryphen
und Pseudepigraphen, Heidelberg 1971.
Rowley, H.H., The Biblical Doctrine of Election, London
1950.
Rupp, E.G., and P.S. Watson, eds, Luther and Erasmus:
Free Will and Salvation, Philadelphia 1969.

Russel, D.S., The Jews from Alexander to Herod, London 1967.

Russel, D.S., The Method and Message of Jewish Apocalyptic, Philadelphia 1964.

Sanday, W., and A.C. Headlam, The Epistle to the Romans, ICC, Edinburgh 1902.

Sanders, E.P., Paul and Palestinian Judaism, Philadelphia 1977.

Sandmel, S., The Several Israels, New York 1971.

Schechter, S., Aspects of Rabbinic Theology, New York 1909.

Schelkle, K.H., "Erwaehlung und Freiheit im Roemerbrief nach der Auslegung der Vaeter," ThQ 131, 1951, pp 189-207.

Schelkle, K.H., Paulus Lehrer der Vaeter, Die altkirchliche Auslegung von Roemer 1-11, Duesseldorf 1956.

Schlatter, A., Erlaeuterungen zum Neuen Testament, 10 vols, Stuttgart 1964.

Schlatter, A., Gottes Gerechtigkeit. Ein Kommentar zum Roemerbrief, Stuttgart 1964.

Schlier, H., "Das Mysterium Israels" in: Die Zeit der Kirche. Exegetische Aufsaetze und Vortraege, Freiburg 1956, pp 232-43.

Schlier, H., Der Roemerbrief. Kommentar, HThK 6, Freiburg 1977.

Schmid, H.H., Gerechtigkeit als Weltordnung, Tuebingen 1968.

Schmidt, K.L., Die Judenfrage im Lichte der Kapitel 9-11 des Roemerbriefs, Theologische Studien 13, Zurich 1942.

Schmidt, K.L., "Die Verstockung des Menschen durch Gott," ThZ 1, 1945, pp 1-17.

Schoeps, H.J., Paul, Philadelphia 1961.

Schopp, L., The Writings of St. Justin Martyr, New York 1948.

Schrage, W., "Roemer 3:21-26 und die Bedeutung des Todes Jesu Christi bei Paulus" in: Das Kreuz Jesu, ed Paul Rieger, Goettingen 1969, pp 65-88.

Schrenk, G., Der goettliche Sinn in Israels Geschick, Zurich 1943.

Schrenk, G., Die Weissagung ueber Israel im Neuen Testament, Zurich 1951.

Schrey, H.H., H.H. Walz, and W.A. Whitehouse, The Biblical Doctrine of Justice and Law, Ecumenical Biblical Studies 3, London 1955.

Snaith, N.H., The Distinctive Ideas of the Old Testament, London 1944.

Stendahl, K., "The Called and the Chosen" in: The Root and the Vine, ed A. Fridrichsen, Philadelphia 1953.

Stewart, R.A., Rabbinic Theology, Edinburgh 1961.

Stoeckhardt, G., Kommentar ueber den Brief Pauli an die
Roemer, St. Louis 1907.
Strack, H., and P. Billerbeck, Kommentar zum Neuen Tes-
tament aus Talmud und Midrasch, 6 vols, Munich 1969.
Strauss, J.D., "God's Promise and Universal History:
The Theology of Romans 9" in: Grace Unlimited, ed
Clark Pinnock, Minneapolis 1975, pp 190-208.
Stuhlmacher, P., Gerechtigkeit Gottes bei Paulus,
FRLANT 87, Goettingen 1966.
Stuhlmacher, P., "Zur Interpretation von Roemer
11,25-32" in: Problema Biblischer Theologie,
ed H.W. Wolf, Munich 1971, pp 555-70.
Stuhlmacher, P., "Zur neueren Exegese von Roemer
3,24-26" in: Jesus und Paulus, ed E.E. Ellis,
Goettingen 1975, pp 315-33.
Talbert, C.H., "A Non-Pauline Fragment at Romans
3:24-26?" JBL 85, 1966, pp 287-96.
Thyen, H., Studien zur Suendenvergebung, FRLANT 96,
Goettingen 1970.
Turner, N., A Grammar of New Testament Greek (J.H.
Moulton), vol 3, Syntax, Edinburgh 1963.
Vischer, W., "Das Geheimnis Israels, Eine Erklaerung
der Kapitel 9-11 des Roemerbriefs," Judaica 6, 1950,
pp 81-132.
von Rad, G., Old Testament Theology, 2 vols, New York
1962.
Vos, G., Biblical Theology. Old and New Testaments.
Grand Rapids 1948.
Vriezen, Th.C., An Outline of Old Testament Theology,
Wageningen, Holland 1960.
Watson, N.M., "Simplifying the Righteousness of God: A
Critique of J.C. O'Neill's Romans," Scottish Journal
of Theology 30, 1977.
Weber, E., Das Problem der Heilsgeschichte nach Roemer
9-11: Ein Beitrag zur historisch-theologischen
Wuerdigung der paulinischen Theodizee, Leipzig 1911.
Weber, V., Kritische Geschichte der Exegese des 9.
Kapitels, resp. der Verse 14-23, des Roemerbriefs bis
auf Chrisostomus und Augustinus einschliessliche,
Wuerzburg, 1889.
Weiser, A., Das Buch der zwoelf kleinen Propheten, II,
ATD 24, Goettingen 1967.
Wengst, K., Christologische Formeln und Lieder des
Urchristentums, Guetersloh 1972.
Whaling, T., "Adoption," Princeton Theological Review
21, 1923.
Wrede, W., Paulus in: Das Paulusbild in der neueren
deutschen Forschung, ed K.H. Rengstorf, Darmstadt
1969, pp 1-97.
Wright, G.E., God Who Acts, London 1952.
Zaenker, O., "Dikaiosunē theou bei Paulus," ZST 9, 1932,
pp 398-420.

Zahn, T., _Der Brief des Paulus an die Roemer_, Leipzig 1910.
Zeller, D., _Juden und Heiden in der Mission des Paulus._
Studien zur Roemerbrief, Stuttgart 1972.
Zeller, D., "Suehne und Langmut. Zur Traditions-
geschichte von Roemer 3,24-26," _Theologie und_
Philosophie 43, 1968, pp 51-75.
Zenger, E., _Die Sinaitheophanie. Untersuchung zum_
jawistischen und elohistischen Geschichtswerk,
Forschung zu Bibel 3, Wuerzburg 1971.
Zerwick, M., "Drama populi Israel secundum Rom 9-11,"
Verbum Domini 46, 1968, pp 321-38.
Ziesler, J.A., _The Meaning of Righteousness in Paul_,
Cambridge 1972.
Zimmerli, W., "Biblische Grundlinien zur Judenfrage,"
Judaica I, 1945, pp 93-117.

INDEX OF PASSAGES CITED

I. The Old Testament

INDEX OF AUTHORS

INDEX OF SUBJECTS